IV

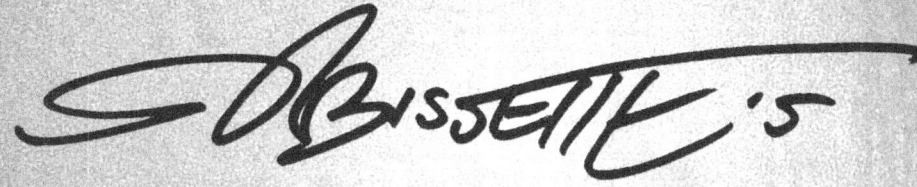 CRYPTID CINEMA:
Meditations on BIGFOOT, BAYOU BEASTS & BACKWOODS BOGEYMEN *of the Movies*

SpiderBaby Grafix & Publications

CRYPTID CINEMA™
Cryptid Cinema™ is a trademark of Stephen R. Bissette

Copyright © 2017 Stephen R. Bissette, with the exception of:

All interior illustrations are © their respective owners;
Introduction ©2017 David Coleman, original to this book;
"The First Four-Color Swamp Thing" ©2017 Lou Mougin, original to this book;
Arthur C. Pierce interview excerpt and photograph portrait ©2017 Kevin R. Danzey, reprinted with permission;
Virgil W. Vogel interview excerpt ©2017 Tom Weaver, reprinted with permission;
Front cover and interior illustration artwork © 2017 Stephen R. Bissette;
Back cover ZAAT portrait ©2017 Robert Hack, used with permission.

The moral rights of the author and contributors has been asserted.
All rights reserved.

Cover & Book Design and Digital Production by Tim Paxton
Image Wrangling & Restoration, Editorial Oversight: Tim Paxton and Steve Fenton
Packaged and published by SpiderBaby Grafix & Publications, October 2017

9 8 7 6 5 4 3 2 1

The views and opinions expressed in this book are those of the respective authors. This book contains copyrighted material, the use of which has not always been specifically authorized by the copyright owner. We are making such material available in our efforts to advance understanding of cultural issues pertaining to academic research. We believe this constitutes a 'fair use' of any such copyrighted material as provided for in section 107 of the US Copyright Law. In accordance with Title 17 U.S.C. Section 107, this book is sold to those who have expressed a prior interest in receiving the included information for research and educational purposes.

All rights reserved. Except for review purposes, no part of this book may be reproduced or transmitted in any form or by any means, electronic or mechanical, including photocopying, recording or by any information storage and retrieval system, nor be circulated in any form other than which it is published, without permission in writing from the publisher. The stories and characters depicted in this book are entirely fictional. Printed in the United States of America.

SpiderBaby Grafix & Publications
PO Box 157, Windsor VT 05089
srbissette.com

ISBN-13: 978-1975938130
ISBN-10: 1975938135

Printed and bound by Createspace/Amazon

This book is dedicated to the late, great Bernie Wrightson

—

For Daniel

Table of Contents

A Note from the Author	xiii
Introduction by David Coleman	xv
BIGFOOT on My Mind	1
Sleepy LaBeef's Swamp Thing	14
The First Four-Color Swamp Thing by Lou Mougin	18
Bigfoots Before BIGFOOT: One Step Beyond	23
IVANPAH aka TEENAGERS BATTLE THE THING	26
BIGFOOT: AMERICA'S ABOMINABLE SNOWMAN	29
Yes, Yeti!	35
A Note on NOT YETI...	43
NOT YETI: Revisiting RYMDINVASION I LAPPLAND	45
Arthur C. Pierce interview excerpt by Kevin R. Danzey	47
Virgil Vogel interview excerpt by Tom Weaver	48
A Note on Cryptid Casefiles	58
Cryptid Files: THE KILLER SHREWS	60
A Note on "I Sing the Body Prohaska"	65
"I Sing the Body Prohaska"	67
"Why Don't You Give the Bear a Cookie?"	75
THE LAST BROADCAST: A Foreword	77
Jersey Devils: Notes on THE LAST BROADCAST	78
A Note on Lovecraftian Cryptid Cinema	82
Dean's Dueling DUNWICH HORRORS	87
Music of the Devil God Cult	95
EQUINOX: Occult Barrier Between Good & Evil!	98
CREATURE, Sans Comforts	107
Mad Doctors & Bogeymen	119
What's ZAAT?	119
Swamp Shit	144
Cracking THE GLASSHEAD	154
"Why Don't You Ask Him If He's Going to Stay?"	193
"I Am the Walrus"	198
The Stranger Things Study & Viewing Guide	201
Adrift in the Upside Down: An Episode Guide	204
Drawing Sasquatch: A Preview	217
The Cryptid Cinema Poll	221
Author's Choice	236
Contributor Biographies	237
Bigfoot's Bibliography	239
Author's Biography	245

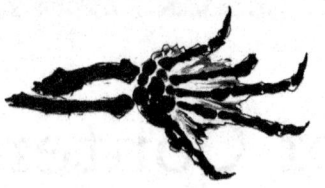

Acknowledgements

The photo on p.x is from Bernard Heuvelmans' *Sur la piste des bêtes ignorées* (two volumes, Librarie Plon, France, 1955), published in English as the single-volume *On the Track of Unknown Animals* (1958).

The front cover artwork for *Cryptid Cinema* originally appeared on the signed and limited hardcover edition of *The Mountain King* by Rick Hautala (Cemetery Dance/CD Publications, 1996).

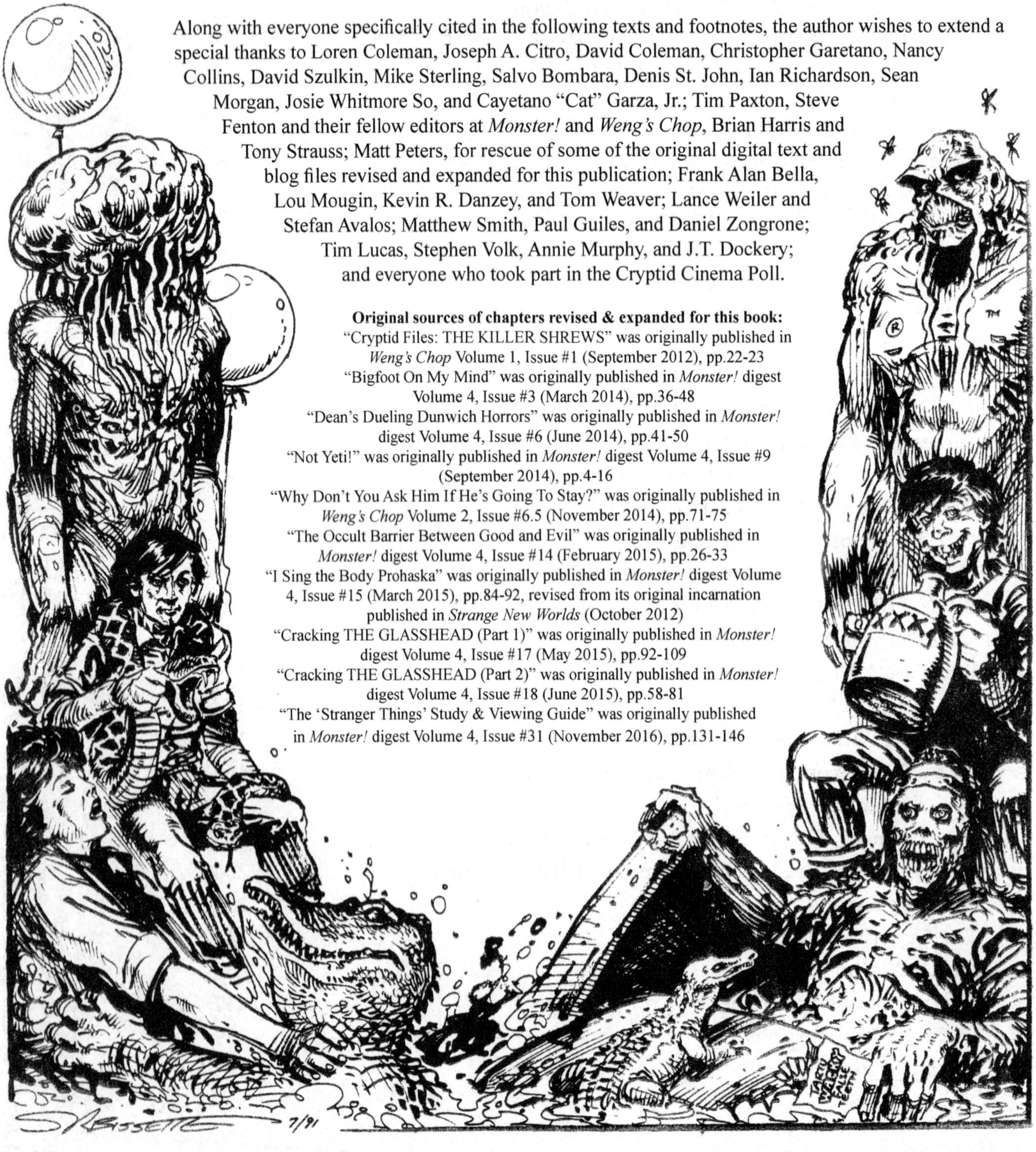

Along with everyone specifically cited in the following texts and footnotes, the author wishes to extend a special thanks to Loren Coleman, Joseph A. Citro, David Coleman, Christopher Garetano, Nancy Collins, David Szulkin, Mike Sterling, Salvo Bombara, Denis St. John, Ian Richardson, Sean Morgan, Josie Whitmore So, and Cayetano "Cat" Garza, Jr.; Tim Paxton, Steve Fenton and their fellow editors at *Monster!* and *Weng's Chop*, Brian Harris and Tony Strauss; Matt Peters, for rescue of some of the original digital text and blog files revised and expanded for this publication; Frank Alan Bella, Lou Mougin, Kevin R. Danzey, and Tom Weaver; Lance Weiler and Stefan Avalos; Matthew Smith, Paul Guiles, and Daniel Zongrone; Tim Lucas, Stephen Volk, Annie Murphy, and J.T. Dockery; and everyone who took part in the Cryptid Cinema Poll.

Original sources of chapters revised & expanded for this book:
"Cryptid Files: THE KILLER SHREWS" was originally published in *Weng's Chop* Volume 1, Issue #1 (September 2012), pp.22-23
"Bigfoot On My Mind" was originally published in *Monster!* digest Volume 4, Issue #3 (March 2014), pp.36-48
"Dean's Dueling Dunwich Horrors" was originally published in *Monster!* digest Volume 4, Issue #6 (June 2014), pp.41-50
"Not Yeti!" was originally published in *Monster!* digest Volume 4, Issue #9 (September 2014), pp.4-16
"Why Don't You Ask Him If He's Going To Stay?" was originally published in *Weng's Chop* Volume 2, Issue #6.5 (November 2014), pp.71-75
"The Occult Barrier Between Good and Evil" was originally published in *Monster!* digest Volume 4, Issue #14 (February 2015), pp.26-33
"I Sing the Body Prohaska" was originally published in *Monster!* digest Volume 4, Issue #15 (March 2015), pp.84-92, revised from its original incarnation published in *Strange New Worlds* (October 2012)
"Cracking THE GLASSHEAD (Part 1)" was originally published in *Monster!* digest Volume 4, Issue #17 (May 2015), pp.92-109
"Cracking THE GLASSHEAD (Part 2)" was originally published in *Monster!* digest Volume 4, Issue #18 (June 2015), pp.58-81
"The 'Stranger Things' Study & Viewing Guide" was originally published in *Monster!* digest Volume 4, Issue #31 (November 2016), pp.131-146

A Note from the Author

The title *Cryptid Cinema* is pretty all-encompassing. After all, any and all unexplained and as-yet undiscovered/unverified-by-science lifeforms fit the bill, which means Neodinosaurs (surviving prehistoric lifeforms), Lake Monsters, Sea Serpents, and the creatures I'm saving for the *Paleo Pop*™ book series *should* have been represented here in some way, shape, or form, but haven't been.

I've also stretched the *Cryptid Cinema* term to fit films and TV series that feature imaginary lifeforms spawned by mad science or occult magic. Thus, sharing pages here with the Yeti, Sasquatch, Bigfoot, the Jersey Devil and other official cryptids, I'm spicing the cryptid-zoo with Swamp Thing and various other swamp things, including the much-reviled (but a personal favorite of recent years) **CREATURE** from 2011, and everything from 1954's **CREATURE FROM THE BLACK LAGOON** to the fish-man of **THE SHAPE OF WATER** (2017). Certain rural legends—included wholly invented ones (i.e., **THE GLASSHEAD** [1998])—fit the bill, too, which may rub some cryptid devotees the wrong way, but to me they're all fair game.

If a screen monster strut from or malingered in the backwoods or brackish backwaters of America, I consider them eligible: H.P. Lovecraft's products of miscegenation between human and non-human beings, the magic-book-born beasts of **EQUINOX** (1967/1970), serum-transformed Walking Catfish-Men and surgically-created "Glassheads' and Walrus-Men, genetically-bred **KILLER SHREWS** (1959), and the dimensional invader of *Stranger Things* (2016-)—all resonate for me as cinematic cryptids.

As you'll see by the informal *Cryptid Cinema* Poll that closes this book, I'm not alone in casting such a wide net.

Whether I make an adequate case for their inclusion here or not is up to the individual reader, but I did wish to cover a lot of ground in this first volume dedicated to *Cryptid Cinema*, if only to lay a strong foundation for future explorations of the subgenre.

Finally, according to cryptozoologist Loren Coleman,

> The International Cryptozoology Museum, the International Cryptozoology Society, and in my own personal writings, all follow the style established by the International Society of Cryptozoology and their Journal's editor, Richard Greenwell. This is to capitalize all cryptids, thus Sasquatch, Bigfoot, and Yeti, versus discovered former cryptids that are now known zoological species with lower case spellings (such as okapi, giant panda, and giant squid).[1]

This is the style I have followed in this book, and will in all future *Cryptid Cinema* texts.

---

[1] Loren Coleman, email to the author, August 10th, 2017, quoted with permission.

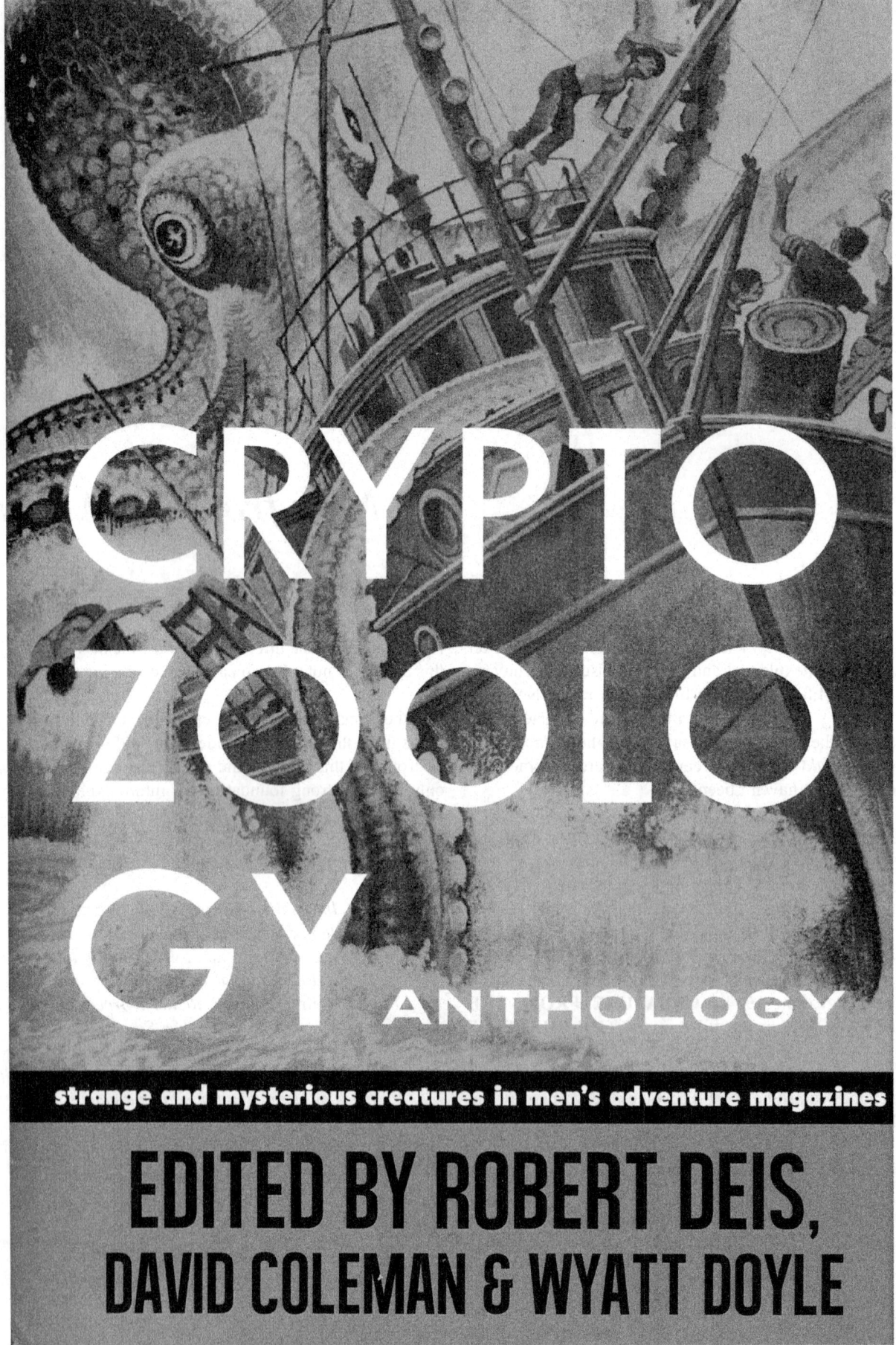

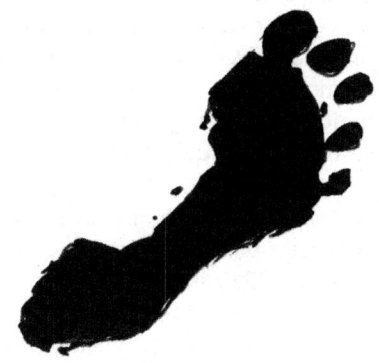

Introduction by David Coleman

What is it about cinematic cryptids that fascinate its typically obsessive fans so? Ever since my youth in the piney woods of rural Mississippi, growing up on the proverbial diet of monster magazines, comic books and B-movies, and now well into my "graybeard" era of quieter contemplation, I have pondered this question. Pondered, and even written extensively, about the phenomena of cryptids in films and print, in a well-intended but hapless task of exorcising my spellbound imagination from their Fortean grip. And all to no avail.

Like author and illustrator Stephen Bissette will entail in the following delightfully idiosyncratic pages, Cryptid Cinema fixation is not a necessarily *rational* obsession. Nor an easy one necessarily to openly—even spiritedly—support. There is, of course, the condescending tone many otherwise tolerant movie lovers exhibit towards the cryptid genre (or is it a *sub*genre?) itself. Even otherwise respectful fans of the worst of non-subtitled, VHS-smeary Turkish superhero films find it acceptable to dismiss Cryptid Cinema as beneath consideration. Short of verifiable snuff films, Cryptid Cinema seems to occupy the proverbial bottom of the cult movie film vault, even if only a few have dared to previously explore the subterranean passages in search of passable examples worthy of respect and critical admiration.

First things first. What *are* cryptids? Most folks think of Bigfoot, Sasquatch and Yeti when they first read or hear this term. This hirsute trio and their various cousins, such as the Skunk Ape, Yowie, the Alma, the Grassman, and so many more, are considered hominids in cryptozoology (the study of unknown-but-suspected animals). Or, more precisely, crypto hominids (or even relict hominids), because "hominids" refers scientifically to extinct or extant species of *Homo* which have been physically recovered (as opposed to crypto hominids, which—and some would disagree, based on footprints, hair samples, filmed evidence, etc.—have not been classified via any physical remains). Mind you, this doesn't include relict or extant cryptids, such as the Loch Ness Monster, Thunderbirds, Lizard Men, Jersey Devils, Chupacabras and related cryptozoological phenomena, either,

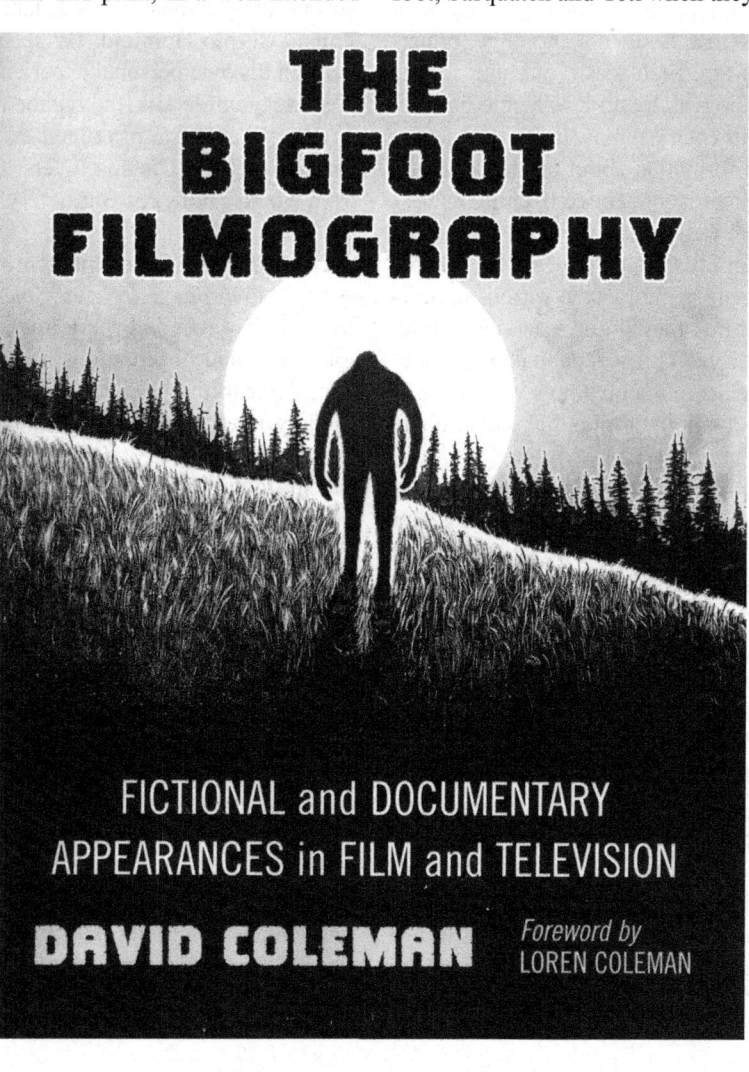

THE BIGFOOT FILMOGRAPHY

FICTIONAL and DOCUMENTARY APPEARANCES in FILM and TELEVISION

DAVID COLEMAN Foreword by LOREN COLEMAN

which further widens the field. Cryptid Cinema, it readily becomes apparent, is a *many*-varied subject.

I tried to expunge my peculiar love of it via writing extensively about it. Lord knows, I tried! I wrote countless fanzine and then later film magazine articles about Cryptid Cinema. But still I was left meticulously stalking every mention of Bigfoot in movies, TV and print. I collected every VHS, DVD, magazine and book about crypto hominids I could find. When such endeavors didn't satiate my Sasquatch movie fanaticism, I spent years researching and writing *The Bigfoot Filmography: Fictional and Documentary Appearances in Film and Television* (McFarland, 2012). To say I was obsessively complete is like saying Stanley Kubrick preferred multiple takes on rare occasions. In the massive tome's 344 pages, I literally attempted to review every movie, TV, rock video and even commercial appearance by any known crypto hominid my research could uncover. I knew when holding its final, bulky form (which resembled a New York telephone directory in large size and small font) that even if *The Bigfoot Filmography* was never a compleatist's holy grail, it would still make an excellent emergency flotation device during, say, a catastrophic flood. One could always bob atop it until rescued, I reasoned, if it served no other earthly purpose (or until it eventually waterlogged and sank like a very heavy stone!).

I was thrilled, then, by the unexpected enthusiasm the book brought forth. It turned out that I was not the only formerly-closeted Cryptid Cinema fan. Enthusiasm ran high for the book. Real-world cryptozoologists found it valuable because of the catalog of rare documentary movie listings, many of which contained research information about the elders in the field. *Fortean Times* magazine recommended it, citing its "exhaustively researched" depth (and yes, I was very exhausted the day I completed it, no doubt). Cryptid Cinema fans shared with me how many pleasurable memories the various reviews of often obscure, regional films they'd not seen since childhood brought back to them. Even classical debunkers, such as *Skeptical Inquirer* magazine, gave it a rave review because of the plethora of cultural information, despite their doubt about the validity of the subject matter itself.

But one reviewer of the lot proved particularly fortuitous. For none other than the author of the book you now hold in your hands, lucky reader, also liked it. I still recall signing onto my Facebook page one frosty morning in 2012 and finding several private messages from friends alerting me that *the* Stephen Bissette had given *The Bigfoot Filmography* a proverbial 'thumbs-up!' on his timeline. As I was a fan of his creative work (but had never had the pleasure of interacting with him prior), I immediately befriended and thanked him for his generosity. As a benefit, I was rewarded with expanding my own knowledge re: Cryptid Cinema in the coming years (as well as having a truly talented new comrade in hairy arms). Stephen's timeline always seemed fresh with the latest news and reviews about the genre (and yes, I'm calling it a genre, because few call the Zombie film a subgenre, nor a Vampire film a subgenre, but nearly always the Zombie genre or the Vampire genre;

why should Bigfoot take a backseat to those creatures of the night when he's arguably the most American monster of them all? Strike another winning blow for Yankee cultural imperialism! Besides of which? *Merriam-Webster* defines genre as "a category of artistic, musical, or literary composition characterized by a particular style, form, or content," and surely, Cryptid Cinema is that by very definition; no more, no less).

In short, reading Stephen's loving tributes to all-things-cryptid online has been a genuine pleasure. I encourage all enthusiastic readers of this book to likewise seek him out via Facebook and add him to appreciate his almost daily mix of expert musings and critiques on comics, films and other topics. You won't be disappointed.

As an exhaustive (there's *that* word again!) as my book was, it was an overview. Not only were certain films inevitably not mentioned (though I tried my damnedest), but likewise, it was meant as a precursor. A hopeful "first strike" towards what would later become a more thoroughly-examined, even newfound genre: Cryptid Cinema. In this regard, *Cryptid Cinema: Meditations on Bigfoot, Bayou Beasts & Backwoods Bogeymen of the Movies* is the next huge leap forward in examining said filmic field. By offering his own unique, minutely-researched thoughts and analyses of Cryptid Cinema, Stephen Bissette expands and elucidates the genre in a way that is both mesmerizing to read and substantial in its contribution to All Things Crypto Hominid. By specifically tailoring his essays through his own personal experiences and wedding it with rarified research details, the author gives his ensuing text a truly Bon Vivant taste of refined excellence. Drink and eat of it heartily, Cryptid Cinema lovers, for you are unlikely to feast from a better buffet of Bigfootery any time soon.

Each reader and fan of the genre will inevitably have his or her own favorites in *Cryptid Cinema*. But I can't help but cite some of my own and share my enthusiasm. I'll try to slip in some personal observations here and there, but for the most part, defer to the wit and wisdom of the author. Oh, and one friendly note: If you are a believer in "Spoiler Alerts!" as a reading methodology, I advise you to skip forward from here and straight into Mr. Bissette's first entry.

"Bigfoot On My Mind" is a rich treasure trove of Cryptid Cinema lore, trivia and fact. I well recall the Ormonds as filmmakers from my own childhood until now. In fact, I was lucky enough to have seen the referenced Christian "scare film" the Ormonds made called **THE BURNING HELL** (1974) in a Baptist tent revival one 1970s summer in my teen years. Most of the cinematic opus is a snoozing bore, replete with sinners who gleefully fail to heed the warning sirens of their impending doom. It plays as a kind of Jack Chick comic brought to hellish life. But the shocking ending is truly a repulsive nightmare even a similar, bigger-budgeted attempt in **THE DEVIL'S RAIN** (1975) could not top in terms of visceral horror. The already sweltering tent revival in which I witnessed the sinners' fiery apocalypse seemed to raise ten degrees hotter as the terrified teenaged audience gasped with disbelief. I even managed not to take the Lord's name in vain or think of premarital sex for almost a full week after its deadly impact on my psyche. It was a much more innocent era, obviously.

Much later in 1998, as the creator of Bijou Café nee BijouFlix Releasing (an early video-streaming site dedicated to cult, B-movies and indie filmmakers), I had discussions with Tim Ormond, the Ormonds' adult son, who had acted in several of their films as a child, about the possibility of releasing **THE EXOTIC ONES** (a.k.a. **MONSTER AND THE STRIPPER**, 1968) and several other of his parents' movies on DVD and streaming formats. Alas, Tim seemed to lose interest in the concept, and nothing ever came from it save his sending me a library of VHS tapes of many rare titles made by the Ormonds during their pre-Christian period that I adore to this day.

(A fascinating side-note: the Ormonds, as Stephen catalogs, made many regional B-movies with lurid themes to insure drive-in and grindhouse release until they almost died in a plane crash. After narrowly surviving the wreck, Ron and June Ormond attributed their fate to divine intervention and as a sign from God that they should alter their sinful ways. They plunged into Christian-themed filmmaking with the same gusto as they had their earlier sleaze oeuvre, hence the first film I ever saw of theirs being **THE BURNING HELL**. It all comes around!)

In writing about **TERROR IN THE MIDNIGHT SUN** (1959), the author cites how influential the plethora of Fortean-themed paperbacks as well as cryptid comic books published in the same era were on cryptozoology and Cryptid Cinema. These invaluable efforts were truly a complete experience unto themselves, as Loren Coleman (no relation) relates from first-hand experience. I would only add that interested readers who wish to experience another seminal marker on later Cryptid Cinema should explore *Cryptozoology Anthology: Strange and Mysterious Creatures in Men's Adventure Magazines* (New Texture, 2015), which I co-edited with Robert Deis and Wyatt Doyle. This heavily-illustrated book traces how men's adventure magazines such as *Argosy*, *True*, *Man's Illustrated* and other pulp-inspired magazines mixed lurid hominid fiction and cryptozoological fact-based reports from prominent researches in the crypto field to popularize Bigfoot, Thunderbirds, Nessie, and a host of related cryptid monsters.

One other thought about the beloved/detested cryptid creature in **TERROR IN THE MIDNIGHT SUN**. In my book *The Bigfoot Filmography*, I posit this as the first of a long series of what I dubbed "Space Cryptids". Throughout Cryptid Cinema (and TV) history, there have been recurrent appearances by such stellar hominids—in essence, Bigfoot from the stars. Just a few citations to whet the appetite for more to come about these outer space cryptids cited by the author include: the blue-colored Yetis in **SNOW DEVILS** (*La morte viene dal pianeta Aytin*, 1966, Italy), the ape-like anthropoids who attack Spock and crew in the "Galileo Seven" (1967) episode of *Star Trek*; and then the white-furred, Yeti-like cryptid the Mugato in "A Private Little War" (1968) of the same series; the robotic Yetis (of earthly origin, but who serve an alien mind called the Great Intelligence) in the original *Doctor Who* series (circa 1967-68); the bionic Bigfoot from *The Six Million Dollar Man* (1976) who is built by hostile aliens; Chewbacca in **STAR WARS** (1977); the Wampa which attacks Luke Skywalker on the ice world Hoth in **THE EMPIRE STRIKES BACK** (1980); and on and on…

There is so much to amplify and call attention to throughout these pages. The overdue tribute to master costumer Janos Prohaska; the Jersey Devil's cinematic debut in the sadly neglected but influential indie cryptid film **THE LAST BROADCAST** (1998); the Lovecraftian influence on portrayals in much of Cryptid Cinema; the regionally-birthed indie monsters, such as the nutria-derived swamp creatures from **TERROR IN THE SWAMP** (1985) and the goofy but entrancing underwater aqua cryptid in **ZAAT** (1971); a feature by the author/illustrator teaching one how to draw Bigfoot (how I would have *killed* for this instructional piece of nirvana as a child, endlessly sketching my own cryptid monsters!); the obscure status (undeservedly so) of **GLASSHEAD** (1998); and the proverbial—but actual, in this case—"so much more."

But alas, no amount of introductory text can possibly prepare you for the enthralling hours of dedicated delight that now await you. And so, dear reader, the time has come to turn the reins over to a talent who by now needs no further introduction. A multi-talented force who is only challenged by the fictional Sherlock Holmes as a dedicated, encyclopedic sleuth and the late David Foster Wallace in a mind-boggling use of subtextual footnotes (a subgenre all to themselves in both men's skillful hands).

A final thought to carry with you: There is a Fortean, interconnected aspect to all cryptid cinema research, I have discovered. Notice as you leaf through these pages how earlier sections are rhymed and echoed in later pages. Alert readers will see how interlayered so much of the observations that follow are as you proceed through the larger text. How one fact unearthed leads inevitably to several more, and so on, seemingly ad infinitum. This is the latent thrill of Cryptid Cinema. Unlike Film Noir, Westerns, SF and so many others that have been sincerely but sometimes overly-explored? Cryptid Cinema is still an unknown, albeit nascently explored, genre of filmmaking. It is fascinating because, like its subject matter, it is truly terra (or is that *terror*?) incognita. Thus, you are along as a virtual explorer, unearthing connections as they are being first-time discovered by the author.

As such, it deserves not only your serious attention, but thoughtful acknowledgment. Pioneers such as Stephen Bissette are mapping a heretofore-neglected body of work. All film lovers should not only be grateful for their dedication, but enchanted by their insights. I am confident you will feel both grateful and enchanted throughout the pages that follow.

—David Coleman, August 2017

The famed *Argosy* February 1968 issue publishing photos of the Bigfoot from the Roger Patterson/Bob Gimlin film footage, and images from *Cryptozoology Anthology* edited by Robert Deis, David Coleman, and Wyatt Doyle.

BIGFOOT ON MY MIND

There's Good Bigfoots in this world, and there's Bad Bigfoots in this world, and in **BIGFOOT** (1970), Nick Raymond played two roles, appearing as "Slim" and seen here in full makeup as "Evil Creature."

We have to start somewhere in discussing Cryptid Cinema: to that end, Bigfoot is on my mind.

Bigfoot *movies*, that is. If you grew up during the 1970s, you *know* what I'm talking about. So, wondering as I do about such things, I ask myself:

What was "the first" Bigfoot movie; the first narrative, non-documentary Bigfoot movie? That would be Ron Ormond's **THE EXOTIC ONES** (a.k.a. **THE MONSTER AND THE STRIPPER**, 1968), which I believe was the first-ever fictional American Bigfoot/Sasquatch movie ever made (see sidebar, "Sleepy LaBeef's Swamp Thing").

This all takes some qualifying, mind you. For the purposes of this first *Cryptid Cinema* book, I'm not counting the 1950s Abominable Snowman/Yeti movies (see sidebar, "Yes, Yeti!"), one of which (i.e., W. Lee Wilder's **THE SNOW CREATURE** [1954]) turned its tall-actor-wrapped-in-yak-fur-and-parka-with-fuzzy-mitts-and-tootsies Yeti loose in urban Los Angeles. The Yeti movies don't count, and *he* sure don't count, though a case could be maybe made for Wilder's Yeti providing breeding stock for the Bigfoot to follow. Though Billy Wilder's less-talented sibling W. Lee did show his Yeti moving (*interminably!*) in-and-out of dark places (apparently repeating the same footage over-and-over, both forward and reversed) during the tall shaggy one's jaunt, that didn't and doesn't sufficiently suggest "the old in/out," so it's highly unlikely he seeded the Sasquatch that followed in the 'Seventies.

The first reports of American Bigfoot/Sasquatch began hitting newspapers and magazines like *Argosy* and *True* in the late 1950s, and both terms drifted into popular lore in the 1960s during my formative years (a drift I experienced as an avid UFO/monster/weird shit-obsessed kid). This chapter (and its sidebars) covers how Bigfoot movies came about, and the marvels, mysteries, mini-moguls, and morons behind 'em. This family tree of Cryptid Cinema arguably branched out on its own with **BIGFOOT**(1969/1970)—with some qualifications.

Coming on the heels of **THE EXOTIC ONES**, and with a copyright on its onscreen title of 1969 (though it apparently didn't score an actual screening until 1970), there were actually *two* "**BIGFOOT**" titles that kissed the screen in 1969-1970. If we count Bigfoot documentaries, the first **BIGFOOT** movie actually in-production (there is a contract in existence dated May 26th, 1967)—if not yet in the can—was Roger Patterson's **BIGFOOT: AMERICA'S ABOMINABLE SNOWMAN**.

Roger Patterson is the man who "produced" the first-ever "true-life" Sasquatch film footage. That instant-classic bit of cryptozoological cinema was and remains the Zapruder footage of Sasquatchology: Roger Patterson and Robert Gimlin reported that, on October 20th, 1967, they filmed a purported Sasquatch with a 16mm camera at Bluff Creek, California. This monster footage became known as "the Patterson-Gimlin film." *Peculiar*, isn't it? These guys set out to make a travelogue/documentary about Bigfoot—the first. They borrow money

and rent a camera to do it. Then they "somehow" subsequently capture a live Sasquatch on film while shooting their low-budget feature. Patterson and Gimli did get their film made (see sidebar, "Bigfoots Before **BIGFOOT** – **BIGFOOT: AMERICA'S ABOMINABLE SNOWMAN**") and it *did* play Northwest regional theatrical venues in 1969 and 1970.

Decades later, one Mr. Bob Heironimus (who claimed to be an acquaintance of Patterson's) went public saying that he had worn "an ape costume" to play the Sasquatch seen in the Patterson-Gimlin footage.

I *didn't* buy Heironimus' claims then, and I *don't* now. The footage was and is more convincing than anything any low-budget (or, for that matter, well-heeled big-budget) makeup effects or special effects creators were capable of concocting in 1967. At that time, Janos Prohaska and his family (who died in a 1974 plane crash while playing prehistoric men in their own makeup creations for the David Wolper TV series *Primal Man*; see the "I Sing the Body Prohaska" chapter) and John Chambers (creator of **PLANET OF THE APES**' Oscar-winning makeups, circa 1967) were the best in the business, and they never concocted anything like it in their lifetimes. Chambers denied his speculated involvement in the Patterson-Gimlin footage to his dying day (see *Popular Paranoia: A Steamshovel Press Anthology* [Adventures Unlimited Press, 2002, p. 169]; Chambers died on August 25th of 2001).

Anyway, the first entirely fictional—as opposed to potentially fictitious/fabricated—Bigfoot movie ever to exploit the moniker Bigfoot was the other 1969/1970 Bigfoot feature film, the completely-made-up, no-bones-about-it fictional narrative feature **BIGFOOT** (1969/1970). Former Marilyn Monroe Romeo/spouse (a dubious claim letter discredited) Robert F. Slatzer co-scripted and directed it, with just one previous feature to his name (the biker flick **THE HELLCATS** [1967]). However meager his means and budget, Slatzer was working with a dream cast.

Now, I must admit from the outset that I like all 1970s Bigfoot movies. Yes, critically speaking, **BIGFOOT** *does* suck (many do, truthfully, much as I love most of them), but I find it endlessly and enormously entertaining. Incredibly, **BIGFOOT** remains a family-friendly movie while proposing that its Bigfoot is interbreeding with kidnapped human females… which is an *unusual* feat in and of itself.

Despite its paucity of pacing and budget, **BIGFOOT** mightily delivers as a monster movie. It features a character who is a human/Bigfoot hybrid—not the first of the Cryptid Cinema genre to do so, mind you (Jerry Warren's 1956 Yeti adventure **MAN BEAST** takes that honor)—and it has fully *six* Bigfoots in it. **BIGFOOT** also features Bigfoot Sex (off-screen, but implied), and *that's* a whole lot of Bigfoot bang (pun intended) for your Bigfoot buck, particularly in '69. Without cheating, **BIGFOOT** boasts babes, bikers and Bigfoots.

This, my fellow Cryptid Cinéastes, is *true love*!

Above: Jerry Crew, master-plaster-caster of Patterson-Gimlin's alleged Bigfootprint, poses with a (17-inch-long!) supposed cast of one of the beast's tracks; which has since been exposed—at least by some—as a hoax.
Top: Pressbook for the US release of one of Jerry Warren's most-bearable movies.

How do we love thee, **BIGFOOT**? Let me count the ways:

I.

Let's be honest. **BIGFOOT** is most definitely a precursor to later classics of Bigfoot erotica—the first masterpiece of that genre being, without a doubt, Robert Crumb's marvelous *"Whiteman Meets Bigfoot"* in *Homegrown Funnies* (Kitchen Sink Press, 1971).

Denis Kitchen once told me this was the all-time best-selling underground comic he ever published (it enjoyed multiple printings for almost two decades), and I'd argue it's Crumb's second full graphic novel (after *The Yum-Yum Book*) and his first *great* singular narrative work. It's an expansive (other than three pages of an Angelfoot McSpade/Snoid story, *"Whiteman Meets Bigfoot"* comprises the entire issue of *Homegrown*), surprisingly upbeat Crumb masterwork, in which uptight urban everyman Whiteman is kidnapped by a female Bigfoot, only to find true love, back-to-nature peace and tranquility, and…well, go read it. It's fucking brilliant.

Of course, Crumb's *"Whiteman Meets Bigfoot"* is, arguably, the *only* masterpiece of Bigfoot erotica to date—and no, I am not making up that genre. Bigfoot erotica is a subgenre that includes drive-in movies like the Uschi Digard vehicle **THE BEAST AND THE VIXENS** (a.k.a. **BEAUTIES AND THE BEAST**, 1974; the pressbook boasted, *"The Unbelievable Erotic Adventure!"*) and XXX porn like **THE GEEK** (1981) to mysterious tomes like *The Creature: Personal Experiences with Bigfoot* (Allegheny Press, 1976) by "John Klement".

(Curious? So am I; I'll leave it to cryptozoologist Loren Colemen, who knows more about Sasquatch lore than I'll ever shake a stick at, to face death threats trying to get to the bottom of this rare book's bizarre legacy—*"Was Klement an earth sciences professor? A biology professor? A high school science teacher? Is he still alive? Did he ever exist? Did he see what he says he saw happening between a cow and a Bigfoot?"*—and the mystery of "John Klement" and his *true* identity, at the venerable CryptoMundo 'blog/site, at *http://cryptomundo.com/cryptozoo-news/klement/* and *http://cryptomundo.com/Bigfoot-report/klement-2/*).

If it's raunchy, risible Sasquatch sexual antics you seek, I recommend the 1977 gem *Nights With Sasquatch* by John Cotter and Judith Frankle (*"An Explosive Ordeal of Rape and Revenge Beyond Any Woman's Experience!"*), or John Boston's *Naked Came the Sasquatch*. Though its European origins exclude it from true Bigfoot erotica as a genre (an American genre), Walerian Borowczyk's **LA BÊTE/THE BEAST** (1975) is the best of the 1970s cinematic bunch, and the most sexually explicit.

Barring that, there's always back issues of the *World Weekly News*!

OK, back to **BIGFOOT**, the seminal movie:

I must stress, too, that I'm not simply *guessing* there was some hanky-panky implicit in Slatzer's **BIGFOOT**'s family movie scenario. While no Bigfoot sex was shown, much less Bigfoot/human sex, **BIGFOOT** went beyond simply implying such couplings had happened and would happen again; it was more explicit than that, spelling it right out while remaining tastefully family-friendly.

At one point, when the two female leads, Joi Landis (Joi Lansing) and biker babe Chris (Judy Jordan), talked while lashed to saplings (on an obvious interior stage set) as captives of the Sasquatch clan, all was revealed. Joi explained to an incredulous Chris what's in store for them: *they are breeding stock for the Sasquatch!*

Joi actually *says* the Sasquatch are breeding with humans, and nodding to the li'l fuzzy half-breed (Jerry Maren), refers to "it" as a "hybrid"! Dialogue references to women disappearing in the mountains for years further cinches this plot point.

In any case, I believe I'm correct to cite the 1969/1970 **BIGFOOT** movie as the wellspring of this fertile Sasquatch sexual frontier.

II.

BIGFOOT introduced the Bigfoot extended family, too.

This lends profound sociological significance to *Bigfoot* that can no longer be ignored.

Like I said right from the start, there are *six* Bigfoot family members shown in **BIGFOOT**. The acute observational insights offered in the film are worthy of anthropologists and behavioral experts like Margaret Mead or Miss Jane Goodall: we *see* them interact as a unit, shunning their hybrid sibling (clearly, bottom of the pecking order here), and fearing the almighty patriarch of their clan. Oh, it's a stunning work of speculative anthropological fiction, almost as moving as the major studio production **SKULLDUGGERY** (1970) and its invented throwback race, the Tropis.

(*QUICK ASIDE:* That film, too, was a pioneering work, hinging its narrative on human/Tropi love, sex, and miscegenation; but I am here to praise **BIGFOOT**, not dig **SKULLDUGGERY**. Maybe some future book will accommodate my writing about the forgotten Universal Pictures oddity **SKULLDUGGERY** with Pat Suzuki as the female tropi Topazia of New Guinea; she ends up mating with sleazy Otto Kreps (Roger C. Carmel, "Mudd" of the *Star Trek* episode

Robert Crumb's classic *"Whiteman Meets Bigfoot"* (1971) has inspired various Robert Crumb original sketches in the decades since (all artwork ©year of origin, 2017 Robert Crumb)

THE PROVINCE, Mon., Oct. 6, 1958

New 'Sasquatch' found
—it's called Bigfoot

JERRY CREW ... something's afoot

EUREKA, Calif. (AP) — Jerry Crew, a hard-eyed catskinner who bulldozes logging roads for a living, came to town this weekend with a plaster cast of a footprint.

The footprint looks human, but it is 16 inches long, seven inches wide, and the great weight of the creature that made it sank the print two inches into the dirt.

Crew says an ordinary foot will penetrate that dirt only half an inch.

"I'VE SEEN hundreds of these footprints in the past few weeks," said Crew.

He added he made the cast of a print in dirt he had bulldozed Friday in a logging operation in the forests above Weitchpeg, 50 miles north and a bit east of here in the Klamath River country of northwestern California.

Crew said he and his fellow workmen never have seen the creature, but often have had a sense of being watched as they worked in the tall timber

BIGFOOT, as the Bluff Creek people call the creature, apparently travels only at night

Crew said he seems fascinated by logging operations, particularly the earth moving that Crew does with his bulldozer in hacking out new logging trails.

"Every morning we find his footprints in the fresh earth we've moved the day before," Crew said.

CREW SAID Robert Titmus, a taxidermist from Redding, studied the tracks and said they were not made by any known animals.

"And they can't be made by a bear, as there are no claw marks."

"The foot has five stubby toes and the stride averages about 50 inches when he's walking and goes up to 10 feet when he's running."

TWO YEARS AGO reports from this area told of logging camp equipment tumbled about, including full 50-gallon drums of gasoline scattered by some unknown agency.

Is this the first newspaper use of the term "Bigfoot," circa 1958? This rare clipping is from John Green's two-volume *On the Track of Sasquatch, Book One* and *Book Two* (1980, Cheam Publishing Ltd.).

indigenous cultures) Toho Studios/Inoshiro Honda/Eiji Tsuburaya gem **HALF HUMAN** (獣人雪男 / *Jū jin yuki otoko*, 1955/1958), which involved the tragic plight of parent/child Yeti relations at the cruel hands of exploitative capitalists. Still, **BIGFOOT** took it further, making **BIGFOOT** the first and best Bigfoot-movie-featuring-a-Bigfoot clan ever made (and yes, I *am* counting **HARRY AND THE HENDERSONS**; sorry, that was just a climactic sight gag, lacking any intensive analysis of Bigfoot clan relations, much less the existence of sasquatch/human hybrids).

This is significant, folks. No less an authority than the *World Weekly News* later reported, *"A secret Department of the Interior report reveals that Bigfoot has been mating with campers for the past 20 years—resulting in a population explosion of Bigfoot-human hybrids in the Pacific Northwest…"* (*World Weekly News*, August 28, 2001).

III.

BIGFOOT was, is, and will forever remain the critical missing link between **KING KONG** (1933) and **THE LEGEND OF BOGGY CREEK** (1972).

Now, this is self-evident, and I'm frankly shocked I even have to type out that sentence.

Sasquatch may have well been an American species and cinematic phenomenon, but the world knew and knows **KING KONG**. Whether you consider **BIGFOOT** a Sasquatch movie or a Sasquatch sex film

"Mudd's Women"), which becomes evidence the Tropis are human in the trial that ends the film. Of course, Kreps could have also buggered sheep, but that's not the point.)

One can cite the precursor, the long-suppressed (by the studio, due to objections from Japanese tribal representatives objecting to the film's portrayal of

THE ABOMINABLE SNOWMAN

Above: Yeti and Sasquatch on postage stamps; sadly ones that were not issued in the USA. A Canadian "Sasquatch" stamp *[top]* and one from Bhutan featuring "The Abominable Snowman".

The so-called "Japanese Bigfoot," commonly referred to as the *Hibagon* (ヒバゴン), is said to lurk in the forestlands and surrounding wilderness of its namesake Mt. Hiba in Northern Hiroshima.

Top left: Tropi (Pat Suzuki) in **SKULLDUGGERY** (1970); Yeti (Fuminori Ôhashi) and Chika (Akemi Negishi) from **HALF HUMAN** (1955/1958). Above: from an unidentified *manga*; the human is afraid until the *jujin* (雪男 - Yeti) says his *onigiri* (rice balls) look delicious and the guy says "Go ahead!" (translated by Jolyon Yates).

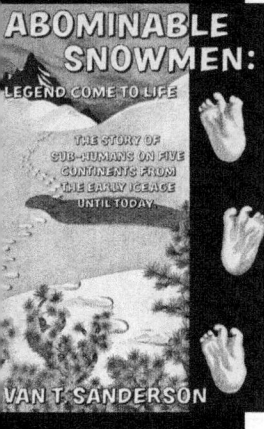

Ivan T. Sanderson, *Abominable Snowmen: Legend Come to Life* (1961, Chilton Books)

"In recent years, this image has been misidentified as an Almas or Almasty, merely because it was found recopied in an 18th century Mongolian manuscript. But Ivan T. Sanderson refers it to the Gin-Sung of Szechwan, south central China, originally from the 14th century, via Prof. Vlec. Sanderson does mix up his Gin-Sung with his Dzu-Teh, the giant Yeti, the form that may be a bear, so something is amiss. This is not a bear; intriguingly, it has four toes on one foot and the other foot almost hides a toe, like with the True Giants" (Loren Coleman, 2017, quoted with permission).

BIGFOOT (1970): Sasquatch (James Stellar or Nick Raymond), Joi Lansing, John Carradine.

(and nobody knew sex films in 1969-1970 like the Swedes), there's no denying that while Americans slumbered, the rest of the world recognized **BIGFOOT** as the "missing link" between **KING KONG** and what was to come. This wasn't psychic abilities at work, or precognition: it was *obvious* to everyone outside America!

I offer you as further self-evident proof the Swedish one-sheet poster for **BIGFOOT**'s Sweden release (pictured on p. 8; thanks to Loren Coleman and Jacob Jarvela for bringing this to my attention). *King Kong's Son*, indeed! Hear, hear!

Bigfoot indeed emulated **KING KONG** in its bold narrative structure, with specific characters, and with its stirring final dialogue between Joi Lansing and John Carradine. In case you miss these subtleties, allow me to be a bit more specific:

1. The credit for the actor playing the "real" Bigfoot makes explicit the link between *King Kong, "The Eighth Wonder of the World"*, and *Bigfoot, "The Eighth Wonder of the World"*. This is so understated that it is admittedly easy to miss, unless you're paying close attention to the movie.

2. John Carradine's character, Jasper B. Hawks, is clearly patterned after Carl Denham (Robert Armstrong), and aspires to bring Bigfoot back to civilization for the same selfless reasons as Denham.

3. The biker hero, Rick (Christopher Mitchum), is patterned after John Driscoll (Bruce Cabot) in **KING KONG**, except for the fact he is completely ineffectual.

4. Can it be sheer coincidence that Joi Lansing, heroine of **BIGFOOT**, was blonde? I think not! In fact, the female Sasquatch tie Joi up between two trees, offering her as a sacrifice to the <u>BIG</u> Bigfoot (James Stellar), their patriarchal "god" that lives atop the Skull Mountain-like bare-rock summit of the nearest, largest mountain. This, too, is easy to miss if you're not paying strict attention to the proceedings.

5. The escape/capture/escape final act betwixt Joi and Bigfoot is thrillingly patterned directly upon the escape/capture/escape structure of **KING KONG**.

6. In the concluding minutes, Hawks (Carradine) says damn near the same things Carl Denham said in **KING KONG**. I mean, it's almost deliberate. Uncanny, actually. I'm surprised nobody ever pointed this out before.

In Sweden, they knew this: the film was released there as **KING KONGS** [sic] **SON BIG FOOT** (*"Den största monster filmien sen 'King Kong'!"*). That Swedish retitling was absolutely justifiable. This is, in many ways, the ideal remake of **KING KONG**.

There are other **KING KONG** connotations I must illuminate, to further prove my point. Forgive me, here, gentle reader, for we now *must* get down and dirty for a few paragraphs.

While we may never know (or, more likely, be able to ask; he'd no doubt smash in the skull of anyone who dares to ask with a baguette) whether Robert Crumb

7

Naughty Bigfoot

Evil Bigfoot

stumbled, stoned, into a nabe or drive-in showing of **BIGFOOT** before concocting *"Whiteman Meets Bigfoot"*, we *certainly* will *never* be able to ask the mysterious unknown author behind the nom-de-plume "Jan Klement" if *he* saw **BIGFOOT**, the movie. But I have my suspicions.

Cryptozoologist Benjamin Radford raised my suspicions back in July of 2008, when he wrote the following online at "The Radford Files" (archived at *http://alibi.com/news/24123/Bigfoot-Sex.html*):

> *"Jan Klement describes in his book* The Creature: Personal Experiences with Bigfoot *his encounters with a Bigfoot he named Kong."*

Got that? *KONG?* Could Klement have been of Swedish lineage, and actually seen **BIGFOOT** under its title **KING KONGS SON BIGFOOT**? I mean, really! What other *possible* explanation could there be for a man, in 1976, to refer to a Sasquatch as *"Kong"*? I breathlessly await confirmation of this likely fact.

But wait, there's more. Continuing:

> *"Set in the early '70s at a rural Pennsylvania cabin, Klement writes that during one of his visits, he noticed that 'Kong had arrived at the cabin with this massive erection. Usually his penis hung limp and after a time it ceased to exist ... Limp, it seemed to be about an inch in diameter and about six inches long. It looked very human with a red head that occasionally poked out from the foreskin. His testicles were not overly large but they hung to about the same length as the penis.'*

> *"Just when you're thinking that Klement is perhaps sharing a little too much, he describes another event: 'There was a commotion among the cows ... Kong was mounted on a large Holstein cow and was shoving away. The cow would start to walk away and Kong would lift his legs and hang on with his hands cupped against the side of the cow until it would stop and then he would begin working his buttocks rapidly again'. (Klement does not report any foreplay, nor is there a record of whether or not Kong called the next day.)*

> *"Bigfoot's bent for bovine buggery isn't all. A Canadian lumberjack named Albert Ostman claimed that in 1924 he had been kidnapped by a family of Bigfoot while camping in a British Columbia forest. He said he was abducted while in a sleeping bag and held captive for about a week. He said he was taken as a suitor for the young female Bigfoot of the family, whom he described as shy and flat-chested. That coupling apparently didn't happen, though he did pay attention to the penis on the father, which he reported was about two inches long".*

Whoa. I'm glad I left it to Benjamin Radford to elucidate those fine points, allowing me to simply quote him extensively, with credit and a link, to prove that

"Apemen scary in appearance but really quite gentle alarms workers": Cover art (by Rino Ferrari) for a 1960s issue of the French magazine *Radar*, which featured hominid cryptids on its covers more than once.

Left: The Swedish poster art for **BIGFOOT** slightly customized the American ad art, but like German market Godzilla retitlings that exploited (nonexistent) associations with Frankenstein, the Swedish title played-up the thematic cryptid hominid links to **KING KONG** (1933).

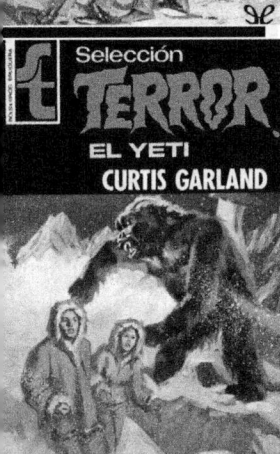

The Yeti was featured in the popular Spanish pulp novel series *Selección Terror* (1973 to May 1985, 617 issues) in stories by Clark Carrados (#45, *Bajo la ventisca* / Under the Blizzard," 1974) and Curtis Garland (#117, *"El Yeti* / The Yeti," 1975); the series also offered *"Terror en la Antartida* / Terror in Antarctica" by Joseph Berna (#541, 1983).

Right: Full scan from the SpiderBaby Archives of the VHS cover art for World Video Pictures, Inc.'s early 1980s release of **BIGFOOT** (WV 1013); the back cover shows Joi Lansing, John Carradine, and Nick Raymond (as "Evil Bigfoot"). The film was later released on VHS again by Goodtimes Home Video (1990, #05-09399).

I *don't* think about Bigfoot dongs for more than the brushstroke or two required to create the illusion of a penis dangling twixt sasquatch legs when I'm dragging—I mean, uh, *drawing* 'em.

IV.

BIGFOOT is, as I've stated, a family movie. And that means *families* made it. Families are in it. It's a family movie, the familiest family Bigfoot movie ever!

Robert Mitchum's brother John Mitchum co-starred as bearded huckster Elmer Briggs; his nephew, Robert's son Christopher Mitchum, played the nominal biker hero, "Rick," and was one of the second unit assistant directors. Bing Crosby's son Lindsay Crosby appears as one of Rick's biker buddies, "Wheels," and Lindsay's first wife Susan (here "Suzy") Marlin Crosby is his main squeeze biker babe "Suzy". Brothers Earl and Rick Phillips were the property masters on the movie. The movie's producer Anthony ("Tony") Cardoza (best known for **BEAST OF YUCCA FLATS**, and producer of Slatzer's earlier **THE HELLCATS**) is in it (as "fisherman"), as is Kim Cardoza (as "Kim").

And that's not all! Family ties aside, you've got Del "Sonny" West of the Hell's Angels in here, as biker "Mike" (FYI, the bikers in this movie rode Yamahas, with the dealership duly thanked in the final credits). It's hog heaven for low-budget movie fans: model/movie and TV performer Joi Lansing (the blonde who hears the "ticking" of the car bomb in the opener of Orson Welles's **TOUCH OF EVIL**, 1958) in her final film role, with vets John Carradine, James Craig, Ken Maynard, Doodles Weaver, Noble "Kid" Chissell—what a cast! **FASTER, PUSSYCAT, KILL, KILL!**'s Haji was in it (as a biker babe), and *Hee-Haw*'s Jennifer (here "Jenifer") Bishop was in it, too!

Noble "Kid" Chissell appeared in the film as Hardrock, a character seeking revenge for the creature having torn off his arm years before. Chissell was a vet character actor who started in crime films in the mid-1930s and became a fixture of 1940s-1950s B Westerns (and was a.k.a. Noble LaPorte Chisman, Kid Chissel, Kid Chissell, and N. "Kid" Chissell). Lois Red Elk also appeared in **BIGFOOT** as "Falling Star," a Native American character; Lois Red Elk started on network TV (*The Virginian, Ironsides, Cannon*, etc.) and later appeared in **JOE PANTHER** (1976), the TV movie **LAKOTA WOMAN: SIEGE AT WOUNDED KNEE** (1994) and **SKINS** (2002).

V.

Oh, and let's talk about the Bigfoot family in the movie, too. The main Bigfoot was played by James Stellar. There was also the "evil" Bigfoot (Nick Raymond), and the female Sasquatch members of Bigfoot, plus offspring. The women Sasquatch were played by Gloria Hill, Nancy Hunter, and A'leisha Brevard (a.k.a. A'leisha Lea), and Jerry Maren lent his talents to the profoundly moving role of the human/sasquatch hybrid "Baby Creature".

The crazed-looking Bigfoot grave guard referenced in the credits as *"Evil Creature"* resembled one of the makeups for the mutant Neanderthals in **VALLEY OF THE DRAGONS** (1961). As I noted, the "Evil Creature" was played by Nick Raymond, who also

9

appeared in **BIGFOOT** sans monster makeup late in the movie as an eager monster hunter named "Slim." Raymond had a brief but curious career in low-budget films, debuting as a crime syndicate flunkie associated with the "smut ring" in Ed Wood's **THE SINISTER URGE** (1960). Raymond subsequently appeared in three features produced by Anthony Cardoza: Coleman Francis's **NIGHT TRAIN TO MUNDO FINE** (1966) and Robert F. Slatzer's two narrative films, **THE HELLCATS** (1967) and **BIGFOOT** (Slatzer also helmed the Right-wing Vietnam War documentary **NO SUBSTITUTE FOR VICTORY**, 1970). Nick Raymond subsequently appeared in Dwayne Avery's vet-kills-hippies actioner **BOOBY TRAP** (1973) and John Hayes' prison zombie opus **GARDEN OF THE DEAD** (1974)—and nothing more that I can find. He died in Los Angeles in October, 1995.

VI.

But the weirdest celebrity family connection, and greatest mystery, of **BIGFOOT** is the fact that 1970s and early '80s teen stars Kristy and Jimmy McNichol said in interviews back in 1981 that *their mom was in a Bigfoot movie*—and, despite all evidence to the contrary, this *has* to be the Bigfoot movie she was in. James (a.k.a. Jimmy) McNichol referenced his mother appearing *"in a Bigfoot movie"* when he was publicizing his starring role in William Asher's sleeper **NIGHT WARNING** (a.k.a. **BUTCHER, BAK-ER, NIGHTMARE MAKER**, 1983) in various teen magazines.

But—who is she? What role could she have possibly played? It's a mystery, and I welcome any information that would clear it up.

According to the American Film Institute, it's true: Kristy and Jimmy McNichol's mother, Carolyn McNichol, appeared in two movies: **WINNING** (1969) and **BIGFOOT** (1970).

However, *no such name appears on the actual on-screen film credits*; the cast credits for **BIGFOOT** listed in the IMDb accurately reflects the film's onscreen list of players (I've checked). *"Carolyn McNichol"* does appear in the credits for **WINNING** (as *"Party Girl [uncredited]"*), and when you track that actress name only *one* other credit—as executive producer for **MY OLD MAN** (a 1979 TV movie)—is cited. Well, it's not the first time IMDb has been suspect, right?

With nothing else to go on in the film's actual credits, with the help of a couple folks on Facebook I find an online check of Kristy McNichol's family records (at *http://www.countyhistorian.com/cecilweb/index.php/ Kristy_McNichol*). I turned up the following:

Kristy and Jimmy's mother Carolyn was born *"Carolyn D. Zakoor... born about 1941/2, the daughter of Donald Zakoor by his wife Leona M Jones. She married first to James V McNichol Jr. They had three children and then divorced in 1966. She later married to Siegfrie[d] K Lacas in 1981".*

Would she have used a different name on a movie like **BIGFOOT**? **WINNING**, after all, was a major studio credit (even if she was uncredited): James Goldstone directed, Paul Newman starred.

Carolyn would have been 26-27 years old when **BIGFOOT** was made; what name might she have used? "Carolyn Gilbert"? There is a "Carolyn Gilbert" of the correct age playing the fleeting "Mrs. Cummings" role (the woman whose face is never fully seen who is shopping at Mr. Bennett's store, with Mr. Bennett played by former B-Western star Ken Maynard).

The thing is—another family association in **BIGFOOT**—Carolyn Gilbert is seen in that scene with her own child, Denise Gilbert, listed as *"child in store"* in the credits (Denise also played "the little girl" in Bill Brame's Bruce Dern biker opus **THE CYCLE SAVAGES**, 1969).

IMDb lists "Carolyn Gilbert" as having appeared in four low-budget movies: **SWAMP COUNTRY** (1966), **BIGFOOT**, as a nurse in **THE INCREDIBLE 2-HEADED TRANSPLANT** (1971), and in an unnamed role in writer/director/star Sean MacGregor's **NIGHTMARE COUNTY** (1977).

Sex-with-Sasquatch accounts predate John Cotter and Judith Frankle's "sensational shock-a-page novel" *Nights With Sasquatch* (1977, Berkley Medallion), which claimed to be adapted from a "technical report of the encounter" in a 1976 issue of *Journal of Mammalogy* and a "forthcoming treatise" for *New Scientist*, but it sure reads like a '70s sexploitation novel ("I screamed when he entered me, erupting in a new fury of pain, outrage, and humiliation, coughing and gagging through my sobs…").

With 1993's *Naked Came the Sasquatch*, RPG Dungeons & Dragons pioneer publisher TSR Inc. joined the Sasquatch sexploitation genre with the debut novel from "ranch hand, television news director, high school basketball coach, newspaper and magazine editor, youth counselor, advertising director, and seeker of the Abominable Snowman" author John Boston, who handily folded lycanthropy (including a pregnant werewolf) into the mix.

Far Right:
Original cover art for Roger Patterson's 1966 book (self-published).

So, not to be weird or anything, but according to the *www.countyhistorian.com* records and citations, Kristy (born "Christin") and Jimmy *didn't have* a sister named Denise, so "Carolyn Gilbert" most likely couldn't and can't be "Carolyn McNichol":

> *California Marriage Index, 1960-1985 showing : "James V McNichol, 21, Carolyn D Zakoor, 18; 16 Jul 1960 Los Angeles" California Birth Index, 1905-95 showing : "James V McNichol, born 2 Jul 1961, Los Angeles County, mother's maiden name Zakoor" California Birth Index, 1905-95 showing : "Christin A McNichol, born 11 Sep 1962, Los Angeles County, mother's maiden name Zakoor" California Birth Index, 1905-95 showing : "Thomas R McNichol, born 4 Jul 1964, Los Angeles County, mother's maiden name Zakoor" California Divorce Index, 1966-1984 showing : "James V McNichol, Carolyn D Zakoor, Los Angeles, Jan 1966"*

So, if Carolyn McNichol wasn't in *this* Bigfoot movie, **BIGFOOT**, which Bigfoot movie *could* she have appeared in prior to 1980?

Oh, **BIGFOOT**! Will you *ever* yield up all your secrets?

VII.

BIGFOOT enjoyed a single video release in the early 1980s from World Video Pictures, Inc. of Los Angeles. It has never been legally rereleased, to my knowledge, in any format, though there are bootleg DVDs on eBay and Amazon from time to time. All that I've sampled end up being transfers from the World Video video.

The World Video video release is how I first saw **BIGFOOT**, and I love these old "big box" cassettes. Note that World Video didn't reuse the original **BIGFOOT** one-sheet poster art; they paid someone to trace or recreate that ad art (and it's far superior to some of the packaging art other World Video titles sported).

World Video was one of the exploitation labels that briefly flooded the new videocassette market with oddball titles, including Mick Jackson's harrowing BBC nuclear cautionary drama **THREADS** (1984), Veronica Lake's ignoble final film **FLESH FEAST** (1970), Andy Milligan's **THE BODY BENEATH** (1970), Ted V. Mikels' **THE CORPSE GRINDERS** (1971), Herb Robins and Mikels' **THE WORM EATERS** (1977), Harry Essex's **THE CREMATORS** (1972), the Texan drive-in sleeper **SMOKEY AND THE HOTWIRE GANG** (1979), the direct-to-video **SLEDGEHAMMER** (1983), the Priscilla Alden cannibal creeper **CRIMINALLY INSANE** (1975), softcore sexploitation like **SWINGING WIVES** (1971), **SECRETS OF SWEET SIXTEEN** (1973) and many more!

World Video Pictures was one of the big-box labels I used to ferret out for rental and, later, in blowout sales bins. I've held on to every one of their titles I lucked into. FYI, my personal favorite World Video Pictures release was, and remains, the made-in-Connecticut **ATTACK OF THE BEAST CREATURES** (1985; retitled from its original moniker, **HELL ISLAND**).

They really, really don't make 'em like that anymore.

Well, that's all we've got time and space for…

Keep your feet big, and your heart bigger.

Bibliography:

- The most fun write-up of **BIGFOOT** online remains the one posted at *Monster Movie Music*'s blog; it's at http://monstermoviemusic.blogspot.com/2011/06/Bigfoot-richard-podolor-give-me-Bigfoot.html

-Check out cryptozoologist Loren Coleman's past posts on Craig Woolheater's *Cryptomundo.com* site, including his brief but tasty post about Robert F. Slatzer's **BIGFOOT** at *http://cryptomundo.com/cryptozoo-news/slatzer-Bigfoot/*. I owe a further nod to Loren and *Cryptomundo* for bringing the **KING KONGS SON BIGFOOT** one-sheet to my attention.

- Among the other invaluable online resources I consulted was *http://forums.randi.org/showthread.php?t=174311* from the *JREF Forum*—the James

11

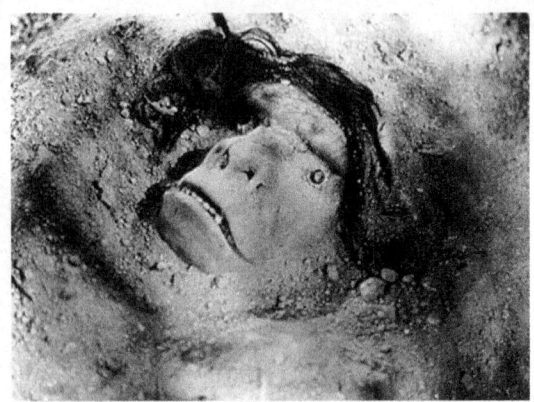

BIGFOOT (1970): The bikers discover a Sasquatch grave site [left] and uncover the buried body of one of the Bigfoot—a further indication of the tribal life and rituals of the hominids.

Randi Educational Foundation forum, *"a place to discuss skepticism, critical thinking, the paranormal and science in a friendly and lively way"*, dedicated to analysis of the Patterson-Gimlin Bigfoot film. If you want a one-stop shopping overview (with plentiful eye candy) of that famed October 1967 footage, this is the place.

Being a book and hard-copy researcher, though, I must also direct you to the best books I've found on the subject, all highly recommended:

- If you can find a copy at all, first editions of Roger Patterson's self-published hardcover book *Do Abominable Snowmen of America Really Exist?* (Franklin Press, 1966) are awfully dear.

I've only ever seen one in my lifetime, in a locked cabinet in a Seattle bookshop back in the 1990s, with a $230 price tag (and that, I was assured, was a bargain). I sure couldn't afford it, and my patience was recently rewarded with the publication of a reprint edition, *The Bigfoot Film Controversy: The Original Roger Patterson Book Do Abominable Snowmen of America Really Exist?* by Roger Patterson with all-new framing material by Chris Murphy (Hancock House Pub Ltd, Blaine, Washington, U.S.A., 2005).

This "updated edition" is comprised of Patterson's original 1996 book and Murphy's "Update Supplement" (*"The Filming and its Aftermath; the Film Questions"*), and for obvious reasons it's the Ground Zero for any sasquatch film research.

- Sasquatch scholars and skeptics will also require the companion volume, *The Making of Bigfoot: The Inside Story* by Gregory Long (foreword by Kal K. Korff; Prometheus Books, 2004), an *ad hominum* autopsy which tears into Roger Patterson's obsession with Bigfoot. Long, a native of Washington state, offers a heavily documented account (including interviews with those who knew Patterson, and a definitive accounting of Patterson's filmmaking efforts) of Patterson as a *"part-time rodeo rider, chronically unemployed and dying of cancer"* who, according to Long, *"propelled himself into short-lived fame and fortune by exploiting his obsession with the Bigfoot subject and leveraging his expertise in manipulating and conning people to pull off one of the world's great hoaxes"*. Long offers quite a paper trail to support his account, including court documents, contracts, newspaper articles, and more. If nothing else, Long offers a must-have book for Bigfoot film devotees, nailing Patterson as *the* pioneer of that 1970s subgenre.

- There are both hardcover and paperback editions of the seminal Sasquatch tome *Manlike Monsters on Trial: Early Records and Modern Evidence* edited by Marjorie Halpin and Michael Ames (hardcover first edition from University of British Columbia Press, Vancouver & London, 1980; paperback from Western Publishers, Calgary, Alberta, Canada, 1984). This book publishes papers by "experts, amateurs, and scholars" presented at a groundbreaking conference on *"Sasquatch and Similar Phenomena"* hosted in May, 1978, by the Museum of Anthropology at the University of British Columbia. The book is a fascinating document of that conference, offering a multitude of conflicting, even acrimonious (even caustic) scholarship from the Bigfoot decade.

- Dead-serious Sasquatch scholars will also want to track down *The Sasquatch and Other Unknown Hominoids (The Research on Unknown Hominoids 1)*, edited by Vladimir Markotic and Grover Krantz (Western Publishers, Calgary, Alberta, Canada, 1984), a rarity which gathers the papers from the 1978 Canadian conference that were *excluded* from the "official" publication of papers in *Manlike Monsters on Trial*. It is sizeable (335 pages with Illustrations, glossary, references, bibliography, etc.), and thus, if you will, the "Lost Books of the Sasquatch Bible" to some Bigfoot academics.

You can't keep a sensual Sasquatch down! With cover copy evoking the bond 'twixt Fay Wray and King Kong and the saucy Sasquatch sexploitation of the 1970s and '80s, *Monster* by John Tigges (1995, Leisure Books) offers bon mots like "She had cried after the explosion of the Sasquatch's ejaculation, more out of surprise and frustration than from being held against her will." Well, wouldn't everyone?

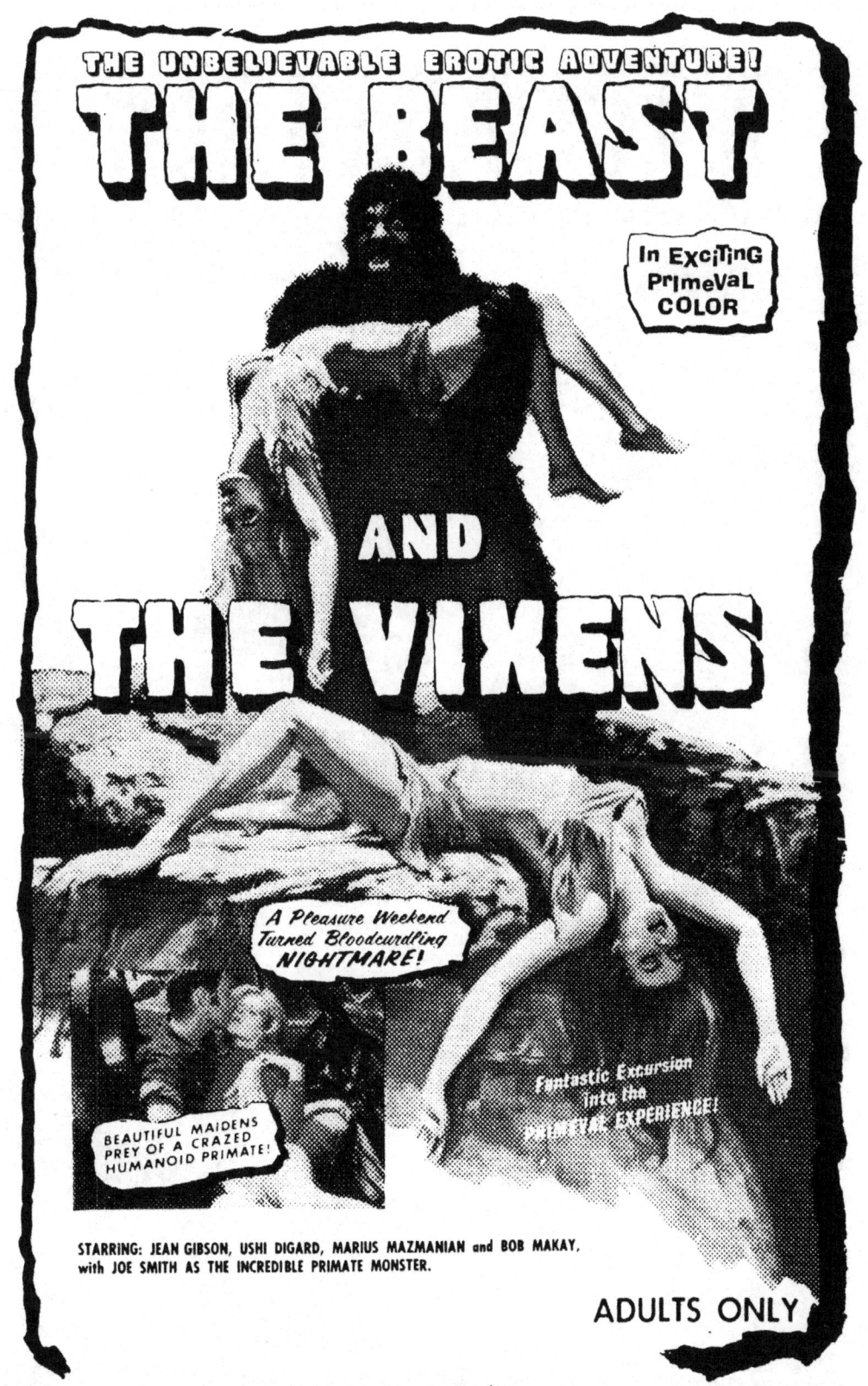

The original pressbook ad-art for **THE BEAST AND THE VIXENS** (1974); this adult film enjoyed a videocassette afterlife as **BEAUTIES AND THE BEAST**, but the best of the breed(ing) remains Walerian Borowczyk's **LA BÊTE** (a.k.a. **THE BEAST**, 1975, France).

This chapter is revised and expanded from the original serialized *S.R. Bissette's Myrant* article "Summer Sasquatch Film Fest"#1: Bigfoot!" (June 20–23, 2011), archived online at *http://srbissette.com/summer-sasquatch-film-fest-1/* , *http://srbissette.com/summer-sasquatch-film-fest-1-part-2/* , and *http://srbissette.com/summer-sasquatch-film-fest-1-addendum/*

REGURGITATING HORRORS
The Night Shrieks with the Shredding of Soft Flesh !!!
NEW ORLEANS TIMES
EXTRA EXTRA EXTRA
MONSTER MANGLES NITE CLUB STRIPPER.
IN COLOR
SHOCKING
MUTILATED
BRUTALITY
VIVID-REALISM
SEE The MONSTER Beat A Man To Death With His Own Arm!
BOURBON STREET
WARNING!!
So SHOCKING unless you can stand VIVID REALISM . . . IT MIGHT SNAP YOUR MIND!
JUNE & RON ORMOND PRESENT
THE EXOTIC ONES
Distributed by ORMOND ORGANIZATION

SIDEBAR #1: SLEEPY LaBEEF'S SWAMP THING: THE EXOTIC ONES AKA MONSTER AND THE STRIPPER (1968)

The truth must be told: the infamous Ormond clan spawned Swamp Thing!

That is to say, before DC Comics' *Swamp Thing*, co-created by writer Len Wein and the late great artist Bernie Wrightson, there was Sleepy LaBeef's "Swamp Thing".

I could go on and on about Ron and June Ormond. Take my word for it, the Ormonds were amazing.

Ron Ormond's 1950s writings alone—on flying saucers, meditation, Eastern religious belief systems and increasingly bizarre fusions of Christian and Eastern faiths, etc.—should have earned him some status as one of his generation's most adventurous and prolific eccentrics. I've a number of the Ormond books and chapbooks in my own collection, and they're fascinating artifacts. But add to that the Ormonds' cinematic legacy, and you've got a bedrock American visionary clan whose antics (and films) outstrip even the Ed Wood legend and *oeuvre*.

The Ormonds produced almost forty singularly cheapjack and outré oddities over three decades, and those that I've managed to track down and screen were transcendentally atrocious. These aren't by any stretch of the imagination 'good' films, but they are unique, memorable and unlike any I've ever seen before. Ron Ormond himself directed over half of them, beginning with **KING OF THE BULLWHIP** (1950) and ending with the Christian fundamentalist cult classic **39 STRIPES** (1979), dramatizing the life of Ed Martin, the former chain gang convict who found Christ while in prison in the '40s, and was the founder of the HopeAglow Prison Ministries.

Between those two titles, the Ormonds ground-out all manner of impoverished exploitation, from the almost indescribable **MESA OF LOST WOMEN** (1953)—their best-known and most widely-seen curio by far—and the gorilla-bride jungle opus **UNTAMED MISTRESS** (1956) to sexploitation (**PLEASE DON'T TOUCH ME** [1963]), hillbilly (**FORTY ACRE FEUD** [1965]) and moonshiner melodramas (**WHITE LIGHTNIN' ROAD** [1967]), and finally Bible-belt hellfire-and-brimstone roadshowers like **IF FOOTMEN TIRE YOU, WHAT WILL HORSES DO?** (1971).

While driving with my family (first wife Marlene, our 6-month-old daughter Maia Rose, and my parents) across the Florida panhandle in 1984, during my collaborative tenure on DC Comics' revival title *Saga of the Swamp Thing*, we followed a capped pickup truck adorned with outrageous hand-painted promotional art for the Ormond Christian horror flick **THE BURNING HELL** (1974). *"See Souls Burn in Hell!"* was emblazoned atop a crude depiction of screaming souls reaching up from a sea of flames. I was driving at the time, and ached to see more. The best way to do so was to pass the vehicle; as we made our way around the truck in the passing lane, more lurid depictions of the agonies of hell decorated the side of the wooden pickup bed cap, and the driver was as straight-laced looking as you can imagine. His white shirt looked starched, his hair was slicked back, and he was intent on his driving, never once looking over to our vehicle. "Must be driving to his next church showing," my Dad said offhand, and I'm sure he was.

Had we seen a member of the Ormond clan roadshowing their indie Christian epics en route from one southern venue to another? Who can say, but I like to *think* we did!

Among the many claims to fame the Ormonds deserve is the fact that they beat Len Wein, Berni (later Bernie) Wrightson and DC Comics to the creation of *Swamp Thing* by at least a couple of years (though Charlton Comics also beat DC to the punch: see Sidebar #2). The self-distributed, self-"X"-rated (in the newspaper ads that appeared after the emergence of the MPAA ratings) **THE EXOTIC ONES** starred Smackover, Arkansas-born rockabilly star Thomas Paulsley LaBeff a.k.a. "Sleepy LaBeef" (1935-) in his only feature film role as Swamp Thing, a towering (i.e., 6½-foot) bayou Bigfoot hauled out of the Louisiana swamplands to mainline as the new sensation at a seedy New Orleans stripclub.

Sleepy's skanky Swamp Thing is sort of a much-more-downscale Cajun "**KING KONG**", if you will, but the lineage of the Sasquatch and the Skunk Ape is much more applicable. Needless to say, Sleepy's Swamp Thing doesn't sit still for the stripclub shenanigans and abuse he's subjected to, and bloody mayhem follows (*"See the Monster Beat a Man to Death With His Own Arm!"*).

Kicking-off with a tacky procession of strippers (many of whom were inadvertently hilarious!), **THE**

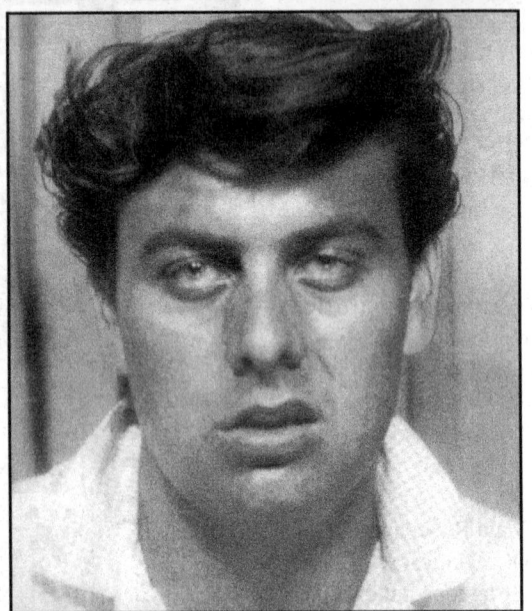
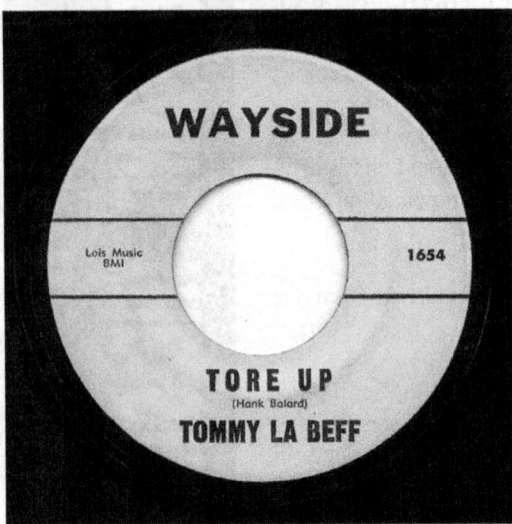

From Top to Bottom: Lurid newspaper headline from **THE EXOTIC ONES**; Tommy LaBeff a.k.a. "Sleepy LaBeef" strikes a badass pose in his hepcat heyday; before LaBeff/LaBeef was tearing-off arms, his original 45 rpm release of "Tore Up" was an early rockabilly hit for the Texas label Wayside (b/w "Lonely" [#1653/1654], Tommy LaBeff and His Versatiles, 1962–63); give it a listen at *https://www.youtube.com/watch?v=x29lcLwBi_c)*

EXOTIC ONES boasts all the characteristics of the Ormond 1960s films: hideous color, stereotypical characters, stilted performances, nonsensical scripting, et cetera. But that hardly matters: like the Ormond paranormal/exotic/religious books and chapbooks, it's quite an artifact. **THE EXOTIC ONES** was shot in-part on authentic Bourbon Street locations in the venerable French Quarter of New Orleans, pre-Hurricane-Katrina, and that makes this an American archival regional treasure. It also featured a great LaBeef monster, and is probably the first-ever American big-screen Bigfoot movie, predating 1969's **BIGFOOT: AMERICA'S ABOMINABLE SNOWMAN** (see Sidebar #3) and the 1970s flood that began in earnest with the 1970 **BIGFOOT** (not counting the 1950s *Yeti* movies, natch, which weren't homegrown monsters).

If you want to see it today (*recommended!*), its video title was **THE MONSTER AND THE STRIPPER**. The Ormonds supervised the release of their core 1960s films to videocassette in the late 1990s under the "Midnite Mania Drive-In" masthead, and these are well worth seeking out while you still can; they've never received any official DVD release, though bootleg editions do pop up on eBay and elsewhere from time to time.

I actually met June Ormond at one of the VSDA (Video Software Dealer Association) trade shows when I co-managed and was the buyer at First Run Video (of Brattleboro, VT). It *didn't* go well. She was tired, surly and unhappy with the reception they'd received on the trade floor show; in the context of the market, the trade shows were on the decline (as the major studios cut bait and abandoned the VSDA shows, beginning their move to taking over the San Diego Comicon), average retailers weren't getting much traction out of anything but new-release contemporary titles, and DVD was already the new kid on the block. This meant the Ormond titles had three strikes agin 'em before they were even on the trade show floor, and it's possible I was one of the precious few retailers attending who even knew who the Ormonds were. I felt bad for June, but at least I got to meet her and wished her well in the launch. We carried their entire line at First Run, and I bought a set for myself, natch.

THE EXOTIC ONES also sported one of the most lurid one-sheets of the entire Ormond legacy, and that's sure saying something. It earns its place of dishonor in the "Ugliest Movie Ad Art" pantheon for its tacky graphics, akimbo combo of bad line drawings and cut-and-paste gore photos, "Regurgitating Horrors" ballyhoo and vomitous color scheme. It truly is one *ugly* exploitation poster—what a GEM!

Was **THE EXOTIC ONES** the first Bigfoot movie of the 1960s? Possibly.

But the fact also remains that the Ormond clan created the—well, okay, *a*—first humanoid cryptid named "Swamp Thing".

You can take that to the bank.

Revised and expanded from *S.R. Bissette's Myrant*, "Swamp Monsters: Ugliest Movie Ad Art Reveals First-Ever Swamp Thing!!!," November 18th, 2009, archived at *http://srbissette.com/swamp-monsters-ugliest-movie-ad-art-reveals-rst-ever-swamp-thing/*

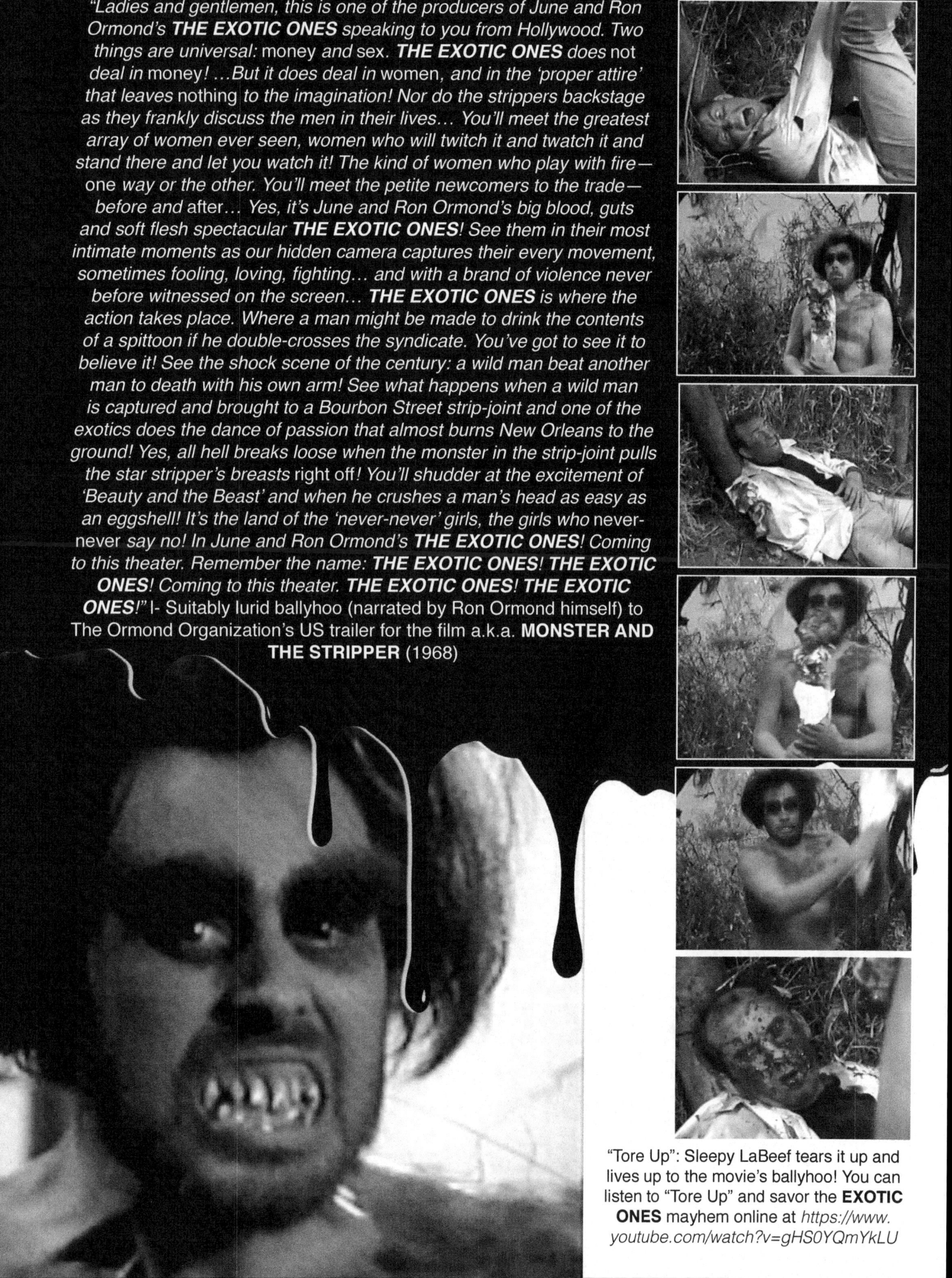

"Ladies and gentlemen, this is one of the producers of June and Ron Ormond's **THE EXOTIC ONES** speaking to you from Hollywood. Two things are universal: money *and* sex. **THE EXOTIC ONES** does not deal in money! ...But it does deal in women, *and in the 'proper attire'* that leaves nothing *to the imagination!* Nor do the strippers backstage as they frankly discuss the men in their lives... You'll meet the greatest array of women ever seen, women who will twitch it and twatch it and stand there and let you watch it! The kind of women who play with fire— one way or the other. You'll meet the petite newcomers to the trade— before *and* after... Yes, it's June and Ron Ormond's big blood, guts and soft flesh spectacular **THE EXOTIC ONES**! See them in their most intimate moments as our hidden camera captures their every movement, sometimes fooling, loving, fighting... and with a brand of violence never before witnessed on the screen... **THE EXOTIC ONES** is where the action takes place. Where a man might be made to drink the contents of a spittoon if he double-crosses the syndicate. You've got to see it to believe it! See the shock scene of the century: a wild man beat another man to death with his own arm! See what happens when a wild man is captured and brought to a Bourbon Street strip-joint and one of the exotics does the dance of passion that almost burns New Orleans to the ground! Yes, all hell breaks loose when the monster in the strip-joint pulls the star stripper's breasts *right off!* You'll shudder at the excitement of 'Beauty and the Beast' and when he crushes a man's head as easy as an eggshell! It's the land of the 'never-never' girls, the girls who never- never *say no!* In June and Ron Ormond's **THE EXOTIC ONES**! Coming to this theater. Remember the name: **THE EXOTIC ONES**! **THE EXOTIC ONES**! Coming to this theater. **THE EXOTIC ONES**! **THE EXOTIC ONES**!" I- Suitably lurid ballyhoo (narrated by Ron Ormond himself) to The Ormond Organization's US trailer for the film a.k.a. **MONSTER AND THE STRIPPER** (1968)

"Tore Up": Sleepy LaBeef tears it up and lives up to the movie's ballyhoo! You can listen to "Tore Up" and savor the **EXOTIC ONES** mayhem online at *https://www.youtube.com/watch?v=gHS0YQmYkLU*

It's well-known in comics and graphic novel circles that The Heap was the first popular four-color comicbook swamp monster 'hero,' appearing as the ongoing backup strip in the Hillman title *Airboy Comics* (debuting in *Air Fighters Comics* #3, December 1942; the regular backup feature began with the Heap's fourth appearance in the retitled *Airboy Comics* Vol. 3, No. 5, October 1946, through to *Airboy*'s final issue, Vol. 10, #4, May 1953). The term "Swamp Thing" was also used in a single panel of Harvey Kurtzman and Bill Elder's Heap satire "Outer Sanctum!" in *Mad* #5 (June 1953), in which a mad doctor creates his own Heap to rob banks, until the Heap goes off to (successfully) find a mate. Both the Hillman and Kurtzman/Elder Heaps were prominent among a procession of Pre-Code swamp monsters that appeared in various horror anthology titles, none (to my knowledge) named "swamp thing" per se.

The first continuous comicbook Swamp Thing appeared in the pages of Charlton Comics' teen humor title *Go-Go* (9 issues, June 1966-October 1967[1]), in the serialized *Peyton Place* parody "Return to Peculiar Place." Peculiar Place's Swamp Thing was spotlit (with dialogue references only) on the cover of *Go-Go* #7 (January 1967). Since comics writer, scholar, and historian Lou Mougin brought *Go-Go* to my attention, it only seems fair to let Lou share his insights on the series – **SRB**

SWAMP THING A-GO-GO

by Lou Mougin

The first Swamp Thing in comics, as most good scholars will tell you, was in *House of Secrets* #92 (1971), right? *Right?*

Wrong!

In the fairly obscure Charlton comic, *Go-Go* #7, a satirical serial called "Return To Peculiar Place" combined elements of then-current TV soaps, *Peyton Place* and *Dark Shadows*, in a mashup drawn by Mo Marcus and Rocco Mastroserio. (It was written by D.J. Arneson, a.k.a. Norm DiPluhm; his "Great Scot!" is a tell.) Mostly the strip concerned wicked old geezer P.F. Peculiar, who pretty much owned Peculiar Place, and his nemesis, good-guy ghoul Walter Warlock. There was also the Cranberry Swamp, in which lies the mysterious factory of the Warlocks which produced...well...*something*. We never seemed to find out what.

And on the cover of that issue, dated June 1967, we saw the floating heads of five Peculiar Place cast members speaking the following dialogue:

> *"Good Lord! (Choke!)"*
> *"Yechh! What is it?"*
> *"It's too horrible for words! (Gasp!)"*
> *"It...it's the SWAMP THING!"*
> *"Yeah! (Sigh!) Isn't it beautiful?"*

Whatever this Swamp Thing was, it wasn't shown on the cover. But in the story proper, after 3 pages that caught us up with the doings of the cast, we got a panel of a prep-school-dressed kid, Micky Peculiar, drawn à *la* Jack Davis and running for his life. He ran all the way from Cranberry Swamp into town, terrified, and was examined by a doctor who shone a flashlight through one ear and watched the beam come out the other. Micky had been aching to try out his brand-new grenade launcher on the Warlock Works factory, but... *"The Warlock Works moved!"*

"Great Scot!" said the doctor. "The Swamp Thing...it's back!"

Meanwhile, Micky's uncle P.F. And a host of townspeople had come to the swamp and were bent on destroying the Warlock Works—him out of spite, with a bazooka, them out of fear, with torches. But when P.F. Peculiar's launched grenade went awry, the land under the Warlock Works factory...well...

...the land lifted up the factory resting on it and took itself on the lam. "Come back here!" howled P.F. "That's my factory you've got, you...you...*thing*!"

---
1 For a peek at the complete run of *Go-Go*, see https://www.mycomicshop.com/search?TID=191261

The Swamp Thing, which was nothing more nor less than a couple acres of land, went and sat itself down on turf owned by Walter Warlock, thus putting the factory back into Walter's hands again. This disturbed P.F. to no end and, after a few more character bits (in which we learned that Dr. Rizzo was cleared of charges of operating with a coat hanger!!), Theodore Beau, the editor of the Peculiar Place newspaper did an outro: "The best thing that could happen to this town is that the Swamp Thing should sit on it..."

And that was the end of the story.

It was also the end of the Swamp Thing Mark I. *Go-Go* only lasted two more issues, and the sentient piece of real estate does not seem to have appeared in either of them.

Still, if Alec Holland had ever found his way into the Cranberry Swamp...well...*who knows* what crossovers might have happened...?

[©2017 Lou Mougin, published with permission and written especially for this book; thanks, Lou!]

Yep, that's "Swamp Thing" (!?) in the panels above from the *Go-Go* #7 (January 1967, Charlton Comics) story "Return To Peculiar Place"; script by D.J. Arneson a.k.a. "Norm DiPluhm," art by Mo Marcus and Rocco Mastroserio.

With Charlton's *Go-Go* doing it's utmost to tap the Archie comics teen vibe, no surprise to find Archie had its share of cryptid references—such as this gag from *Archie's Joke Book* #123 (April 1963), a throwaway 'yawn' for Betty Cooper and Veronica Lodge in the one-pager "Slope Hope." The Gillman himself (or a carbon copy) also appeared on the covers of *Jughead* #79 (December 1961) and *Laugh* #130 (January 1962). Uncle Scrooge, Donald Duck, and Huey, Dewey and Louie met Gu, the Abominable Snowman, in the Carl Barks 19-page classic "The Lost Crown of Genghis Kahn!" in *Uncle Scrooge* #14 (June-August, 1956, Dell Comics), reprinted as the cover story of *Uncle Scrooge* #84 (December 1969, Western Publishing/Gold Key, cover art by Larry Mayer); ©1956, 1969, 2017 Walt Disney Productions, Inc./The Walt Disney Company. The Yeti also made appearances in Gold Key's *Daffy Duck* #98 (December 1975), as well as *The Adventures of Big Boy* #71 (May 1962), *Jerry Lewis* #116 (January 1970, DC Comics), Jack Kirby's *Black Panther* #5 (September 1977, Marvel Comics), and many more; Bigfoot was in the cover story for *Super Richie* #9 (May 1977, Harvey Comics), among others.

21

Long before Bernie Wrightson and Len Wein co-created Swamp Thing in *House of Secrets* #92 (June-July, 1971), Wrightson completed one of his earliest art duties in the late 1960s from an uncredited script for a 10-page story entitled "Things Old… Things Forgotten," concluding with this page that clearly anticipates Swamp Thing. Much to Wrightson's chagrin, the story malingered in DC's flat files (job #Z84), seeing print for the first time in *House of Mystery* #195 (October 1971), looking painfully crude compared to Wrightson's current work at the time (including his stunning "Bat Out of Hell!" cover for the same issue). This scan is from the original art, which is part of the author's collection (SpiderBaby Archives).

THE EXOTIC ONES may be the first unofficial "Bigfoot" movie of the 1960s, but I've little doubt at this point that **BIGFOOT: AMERICA'S ABOMINABLE SNOWMAN** (1969, USA) is the first "official" Bigfoot/Sasquatch documentary and feature film of that decade.

Before **THE EXOTIC ONES** there was the weird independent horror opus **TEENAGERS BATTLE THE THING** (1958 or 1959/1963)—a.k.a. **IVANPAH**, or whatever the original title was (?). **IVANPAH** is the title indicated on the 1997 Monument Entertainment/Program Power Entertainment VHS release of this curio (which I stumbled onto and snapped-up in one of the now-long-defunct Media Play chain stores back in '97). **IVANPAH / TEENAGERS BATTLE THE THING** was produced by Etiwanda Productions, scripted by J.T. Fields (actually James T. Flocker), and directed by Don Fields (the *nom de plume* of Dave Flocker), and it is arguably the first Bigfoot feature film, though I have strong reservations about that (read on!). There remains considerable online confusion about what roles the brothers John and Dave Flocker played creatively, both behind the camera and onscreen.

I'd count the episode of the ABC-TV series *One Step Beyond* entitled "Night of the Kill" (aired October 20th, 1959) as *the* first-ever Bigfoot in mainstream American visual media to reach a nationwide audience; I'm happy to be corrected if something else turns up!

Given both "Night of the Kill" and the filming of **IVANPAH / TEENAGERS BATTLE THE THING**, 1958-1959 is the year we moved from the 1950s' Yeti movies to American Sasquatch/Bigfoot antics.

Let's take a look at all three of these productions…

One Step Beyond: "Night of the Kill":

The program's host and director John Newland was a genre pioneer in American television. Running three seasons and clocking 96 episodes, Newland's paranormal anthology series *One Step Beyond* (January 20th, 1959 to July 4th, 1961) remains Newland's most-syndicated-and-seen effort, though his later TV movie **DON'T BE AFRAID OF THE DARK** (October 10th, 1973) may eventually claim that honor in its place.[2] Merwin Gerard created the series, which was produced by Collier Young, but Newland was its 'face' and guiding vision, culminating in the extraordinary "The Sacred Mushroom" (January 24th, 1961), which documented the mind-altering effects—and cults—of psychedelic mushrooms. While the bulk of the series was dedicated to covering paranormal phenomena, including psychic visions, premonitions, telepathy, telekinesis, ghosts, spontaneous human combustion, and other such phenomena, only a couple of episodes could actually be classified as 'monster' stories: prominent among them being the story about the deformed son hidden away in the attic in "Ordeal on Locust Street" (September 22nd, 1959) and the Merwin Gerard-scripted "Night of the Kill" (October 20th, 1959).

In rural California, the parents (Fred Beir, Ann McCrea) of seven-year-old David Morris (Dennis Holmes) are understandably distraught when their son gets lost for four days in the nearby forest. When Davey is found—safe and well-fed—on a rocky slope by a search party, his folks become even more alarmed at their son's account of being sheltered by an oversized, hairy "friend." In the face of parental and adult skepticism, Davey clings to his story, which nobody believes until he disappears again from his own bedroom. The creature's outsized footprints are discovered outside the house, along with evidence of Davey's "friend" devouring meat stored in the family's smokehouse (at Davey's invitation). When the creature returns to check on Davey, it is met with violence. A vigilante mob quickly forms to track down and deal with the creature, fomenting the titular "Night of the Kill" as the creature's woodland home is set ablaze. *Talk about ingratitude!*

The episode initially unfolds as an essentially silent visual narrative with the failure of the search party, ramping-up its action upon the discovery of Davey safely high-and-dry atop the cliff and the gradual awakening to the mystery of who—or *what*—Davey's enigmatic rescuer

---

2 For more on *One Step Beyond* and John Newland, see John Kenneth Muir's definitive *An Analytical Guide to Television's* One Step Beyond: *1959-1961* (2001, McFarland & Company Inc.).

BEYOND STEP ONE

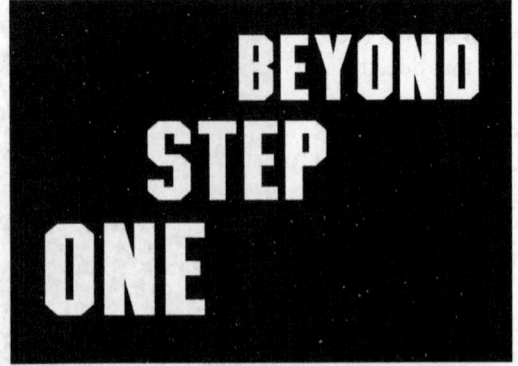

and protector might be. The locale and story makes this a seminal Sasquatch drama, though the Bigfoot remains unnamed as such and is coyly kept firmly offscreen for the entirety of the episode.

In many ways, "Night of the Kill" established the template for low-budget Bigfoot productions to come, initiating the role of a credulous narrator (series regular John Newland, who in his closing narration refers to "that huge creature reported to be seen so often in Oregon's lumber country") to assert the authenticity of the events being dramatized. Bigfoot's paternal, protective predisposition toward innocent juvenile human characters is also introduced herein; as in later a-boy-and-his-Bigfoot movies, the creature's kindness is reciprocated by Davey, who repeatedly risks his own life to save his monstrous "friend" once he realizes what the adults are up to. "Night of the Kill" also keeps its creature affordably and atmospherically out-of-sight: only its footprints and its strong odor evidence its presence. Davey's story of the creature lifting him out of his second-story bedroom window indicate its uncanny height, as does the high ledge Davey is found perched upon, a perch that is impossible for Davey to have reached on his own. In other ways, "Night of the Kill" amplifies the suggested size and anatomy of the creature well beyond that of later Sasquatch films: with three toes in front and one behind, its essentially saurian footprints are quite unlike actual Bigfoot prints, as is its size (estimated at one point as being 16-feet-high, or, as Davey puts it, "almost as tall as the house").

Given hindsight, the most famous cast member of "Night of the Kill" is John Marley (1907-1984) as the voice of reason Dr. Frazier, who changes his tune once he sees the creature and lethally escalates the mob violence leveled against the benevolent mysterious "friend" in the forest ("Don't you worry about him," Frazier tells Davey after they rescue the lad, "we'll take care of him"). Marley cut his teeth in character roles for feature films and television beginning in the 1940s, including early roles on *The Big Story* (1949-50), *The Philco-Goodyear Television Playhouse* (1949-50), *Armstrong Circle Theatre* (1950), *Believe It or Not* (1950), *Danger* (1950), *The Web* (1951), *The Adventures of Ellery Queen* (1952), *Suspense* (1952), *Omnibus* (1953), and "The Hermit" episode of the horror/suspense series *Inner Sanctum* (January 23rd, 1954), among many others. Marley later appeared on genre anthology programs like *Thriller* (the crime tale "The Guilty Men," October 18th, 1960), *The Outer Limits* ("The Man With the Power," October 7th, 1963), *The Twilight Zone* (1962-63), *The Alfred Hitchcock Hour* (1963-64), and *Kraft Suspense Theatre* (1964) even as his big screen career gained momentum (i.e., **CAT BALLOU** and **NIGHTMARE IN THE SUN** [both 1965]; John Cassavetes' **FACES** [1968]; **LOVE STORY** [1970] *et al*). The same year Marley unforgettably played **THE GODFATHER**'s Jack Woltz—who found his prize race horse's severed head in his satin-sheeted bed—he also appeared in Armando Crispino's *giallo* **THE DEAD ARE ALIVE** (*L'etrusco uccide ancora* [1972]), followed by playing key roles in Bob Clark's and Alan Ormsby's chilling shocker **DEAD OF NIGHT** (a.k.a. **DEATHDREAM** [1974]), **THE CAR** (1977), as well as Larry Cohen's **THE PRIVATE FILES OF J. EDGAR HOOVER** (1977) and **IT LIVES AGAIN** (1978).

Encino, California-born Dennis Holmes was nine years old when the episode was broadcast (eight years old when it was filmed), and his dialogue, devotion, and performance lends the never-shown Sasquatch whatever modicum of personality it's afforded. Holmes was a busy child and teen actor in 1950s and early 1960s television, playing Tiny Tim for *General Electric Theater*'s western spin on the Charles Dickens tale in "The Trail to Christmas" (December 15th, 1957), and appearing on shows like *Leave It to Beaver* (1958), *Father Knows Best* (1958), *Bonanza* (1960), *Bachelor Father* (1960), *The Andy*

Griffith Show (1960), *The Adventures of Ozzie and Harriet* (1961), *Laramie* (1963), *Wagon Train* (various episodes, 1958-64), et cetera, as well as feature films like **HOUND-DOG MAN** (1959), **KEY WITNESS** (1960), **THE MIRACLE OF THE WHITE REINDEER** (1960), and **THE FIERCEST HEART** (1961). Like all-too-many child performers, Holmes' screen career essentially ended after his voice broke.

The actors playing his parents, Ann McCrea (1931-) and Fred Beir (1927-1980), were even more familiar to TV audiences. Future two-time spaghetti/paella western star Beir was a staple character actor on television, with guest appearances (I'll spare you the specifics on the years of his frequent appearances) on *Bonanza, Perry Mason, Maverick, The Andy Griffith Show, Wagon Train, The Twilight Zone, Ben Casey, The Outer Limits, The Munsters, The Time Tunnel, Gomer Pyle, U.S.M.C., Honey West, Mission: Impossible, Hawaii Five-O, The FBI, The Odd Couple, Kung Fu, The Six Million Dollar Man, The Rockford Files, Barnaby Jones, Dallas,* and *Lou Grant*. McCrea's career (1952-71) included movie roles (**WILL SUCCESS SPOIL ROCK HUNTER?, THE SAD SACK** [both 1957], **CHINA DOLL** [1958], etc.) and frequent TV roles on anthology programs and shows like *Bachelor Father* (1959-60), *Surfside 6* (1961-62), *Wendy and Me* (1964-65), and *My Three Sons* (1966-68), though she was most famous for playing "Midge Kelsey" on *The Donna Reed Show* (in 70 episodes, 1963-66).

"Night of the Kill" also paved the way for the eventual Sasquatch/Bigfoot TV stardom of the 1970s, with America's favorite hominid cryptid stomping into almost every niche of network broadcasting. Bigfoot 'guest-starred' in primetime documentaries (Robert Guenette's trendsetting special *Monsters! Mysteries or Myth?* [November 25th, 1974], which was snapped up by Sunn Classic Pictures and expanded with new narration—supplanting Rod Serling's original narrator for Peter Graves—into the surprise hit theatrical feature **THE MYSTERIOUS MONSTERS** [1976]), popular SF/action series like *The Six Million Dollar Man* (debuting—played by late 7' 4"-tall pro wrestler André the Giant—in the two-parter "The Secret of Bigfoot," February 1st-4th, 1976, and returning next season played by 6' 9" actor Ted Cassidy) and a series crossover with *The Bionic Woman* ("The Return of Bigfoot, Part 2 [September 22nd, 1976], again with Cassidy as Bigfoot), and eventually landing a co-starring lead in Saturday morning children's programming (the live-action *Bigfoot and Wildboy* on *The Krofft Supershow* [Season 2, September 10th, 1977-78], moving to its own series [June 2nd to August 18th, 1979]).

It could be said that this was the most prescient accomplishment one could chalk up to *One Step Beyond*.

—

Bigfoot stayed off-screen in the *One Step Beyond* episode "Night of the Kill" (October 20th, 1959). **Facing Page:** series host John Newland *[p.24, 2nd image]* directed this episode, in which rescued rural Californian 7-year-old Davey Morris (Dennis Holmes) tells his parents (Fred Beir, Ann McCrea) *[left, center photo]* of a giant "friend" in the forest; *[left, 4th photo]* his father, Dr. Frazier (John Marley, in white shirt), and local citizens track the "friend" to a woodland cavern *[bottom left]* and torch the area… **This Page, Above:** …leaving host John Newland *[right]* to deliver the eulogy ("Not so much as even a charred bone was ever found in these ashes…perhaps the creature, or whatever it was, escaped—or are you thinking, perhaps, that it never really existed at all…"); kicking-off the procession of enigmatic TV cryptid accounts to follow.

IVANPAH
a.k.a. TEENAGERS BATTLE THE THING:

The late professional wrestler André The Giant as Bigfoot co-starring with Lee Majors as Steve Austin and, *The Six Million Dollar Man*, in that series's two-part adventure "The Secret of Bigfoot" (February 1st-4th, 1976), scripted by Kenneth Johnson (who later developed and produced *The Incredible Hulk*, 1977–1982, and the miniseries and spinoffs *V*, 1983–85+), directed by Alan Crosland, Jr., make-up by Scott H. Eddo.

The **IVANPAH** title refers to the Mojave National Preserve in San Bernardino County, California, where the world's largest solar energy plant (the Ivanpah Solar Electric Generating System, or ISEGS) now operates. Ivanpah lacks a village even today; it lies at the crossroad of Ivanpah Road and the Union Pacific Railroad, on the Ivanpah Valley bajada (= fan-shaped geological deposits) on the northeast edge of the New York Mountains; the Ivanpah Mountains are to the northwest. Bordering Arizona, these locations have befuddled future viewers of the 1978 expanded version: is the film set in California? Arizona? The Pacific Northwest? In its original form, the title **IVANPAH** clearly establishes the location.

Notable for being the first cryptid opus ever to be filmed in color, **IVANPAH** was shot in 1958 and released either later that same year or in 1963 (read on!). Chronologically, then, this is the first America-set "Bigfoot" movie (the cryptid stalking Los Angeles in W. Lee Wilder's and Myles Wilder's California-filmed **SNOW CREATURE** [1954], was a Yeti shipped-in from the Himalayas, and hence is disqualified; it does, however, remain the first Yeti movie ever made).

Then again, **IVANPAH**'s monster is a reanimated bestial mummy, not a Sasquatch *per se*, and is more akin to the resurrected Spanish Conquistador of Richard E. Cunha's **GIANT FROM THE UNKNOWN** or the reanimated volcanically-ossified Pompeiian 'mummy' of Edward L. Cahn's **CURSE OF THE FACELESS MAN** (both 1958) than any subsequent cinematic Sasquatch. What the hell *is* it? In both **IVANPAH / TEENAGERS BATTLE THE THING** and **CURSE OF BIGFOOT** (1976), the prologue clearly presents the titular "thing" (played by screenwriter James T. Flocker[3])—a pop-eyed, fang-toothed

TV series tie-in novels were a going merchandizing cottage industry in the 1970s, and ABC-TV's popular *The Six Million Dollar Man* Bigfoot episodes left footprints there, too! The October 1976 Mike Jahn novel—"adapted from episodes written by Kenneth Johnson"—was a hit, enjoying multiple printings (the SpiderBaby Archives copy is a fifth print edition).

---
3 At age 70, Flocker was arrested and sentenced "to seven years in

monster, with curious goat-like pupils in those orbs, or sort of like the horizontal pupils Universal's Gillman sported—as a prehistoric pre-human, and one that occasionally attacked and killed early man in as economical a bit of primitive man splatter as was ever filmed. In **IVANPAH / TEENAGERS BATTLE THE THING**, once we're in modern times (circa 1959/1963) the story proper begins at the Lincoln County Museum with an archeological dig composed of high school students checking out petroglyphs and exploring a cave, stumbling upon a mummified subhuman primordial humanoid "hundreds of thousands of years old" encased in ossified mud. The students haul the 'mummy' out of the cave, whereafter the creature comes to life in the final 23 minutes, causing a ruckus (claiming the life of only one victim: a woman alone in her bedroom, played by Mary Brownless) before going up in flames in a gas-fueled pyrotechnical stunt that still looks pretty hazardous onscreen to this day.

I'd love to know more about the backstory of this production. There's an interview online conducted by "The Movie Vigilante" with Jan Hart, the actress who played Sharon in the film, and Jan pegs the production and initial California premiere as having gone down in 1959.[4] The copyright year on the credits (in the original screen credit font, mind you) is 1963, which may well be when the film was retitled **TEENAGERS BATTLE THE THING**. Jan recalls, "This was filmed during the summer of 1958 in the orange groves and nearby interesting places around Upland and Alta Loma, California. It took us about 6 weeks to film it and then it played one night at the Grove Theater in Upland..."[5] That Grove Theater exhibition (in 1958, or 1963, or—?) was most likely the film's only theatrical showing in its original form, but it does mean that **IVANPAH** a.k.a. **TEENAGERS BATTLE THE THING** is arguably the first big-screen 'Bigfoot' feature film, if one considers its resurrected hominid as a cryptid.

Jan also says her brother saw it on TV at some point, indicating either a regional (CA) or national TV movie package included this title in their lineup. Jan clarifies some matters, deepening the mystery behind this oddity in other ways. The film runs just under 60 minutes; Hugh Thomas' "supervising producer" credit is in a different font from the rest of the credits; curious, that, leading to more questions…

IVANPAH / TEENAGERS BATTLE THE THING was later revised and expanded into 1978's **CURSE OF BIGFOOT**; according to Phil Catalli, one of the actors in the additional scenes, this new footage was shot in 1976.[6] The 1958/1959/1963 version was eventually released on VHS in 1997, in black-and-white (its transfer possibly mastered from an old TV print?); **CURSE OF BIGFOOT**, including all the **IVANPAH / TEENAGERS BATTLE THE THING** footage, had already debuted

---

prison to be followed by 10 years of supervised release for trading child pornography"; see *https://archives.fbi.gov/archives/sacramento/press-releases/2010/sc090810.htm*

4 See The Movie Vigilante, "TEENAGERS BATTLE THE THING," February 2nd, 2015, archived online (@ *http://movievigilante.blogspot.com/2015/02/teenagers-battle-thing.html*).

5 *Ibid.*
6 *Ibid.*

Among the many wonders of the VHS era was how essentially "lost" films would inexplicably surface, sometimes enjoying their only known release, as in the case of the 1958/1959/1963 version of **TEENAGERS BATTLE THE THING**—popping up in 1997 in a crisp black-and-white transfer (though the film was made in color, as seen in the revised **THE CURSE OF BIGFOOT**) from Monument Entertainment, Inc. and Program Power Entertainment, Inc. (#2078).

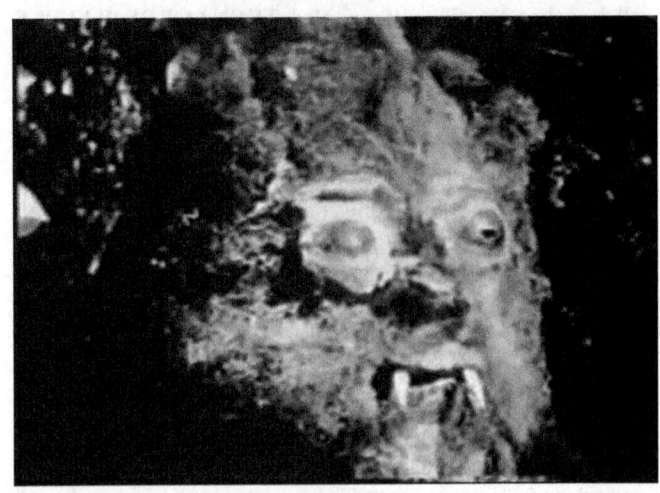

Is it a resurrected prehistoric hominid, a resurrected mummy, or the first big-screen North American Bigfoot? The fried-egg-eyed "Thing" (played by screenwriter James T. Flocker) that pesters a professor and his college student assistants in **IVANPAH** a.k.a. **TEENAGERS BATTLE THE THING** (1958/1963) is *all three* of those 'things'!

in color in or about 1978. It was *not* colorized (a costly process that only started in the late 1970s at the earliest; the improved process was patented in 1991); so obviously, **IVANPAH / TEENAGERS** was originally filmed in color.

CURSE OF BIGFOOT retains the original **IVANPAH / TEENAGERS** credits and presents the latter's original footage as an extended flashback, as told by the now-visibly-advanced-in-age Roger Mason (this time played by Dave Flocker, *not* original cast member Bob Clymire, as some online sources claim, including the IMDb[7]), the older, wiser, and decidedly *haunted* high school science teacher who had led the original **IVANPAH** expedition. The hair/dress styles of the '70s students in this all-new classroom footage (particularly the long locks seen on the teenage boys, as well as on one of the loggers) 'dates' the film and pads out its running time to a much-lengthier 88 minutes. Included in the new footage is a zombie sequence—unreeling in the opening nine minutes *sans* explanation until it is revealed as a 16mm film being screened in the classroom, as "the classic example of the Hollywood monster"—along with extensive short clips from travelogues and extensive footage from an educational film about the logging industry intercut with a staged Bigfoot attack on a two-man logging crew. *This* creature remains offscreen, save for glimpses of hairy torso and extremities and plentiful point-of-view shots from behind vegetation, accompanied by heavy breathing. Sasquatch sightings by, and even reported attacks upon, logging camps and/or crews had long been central to the real-world accounts of Sasquatch encounters; if nothing else, the added attack on the pair of loggers pushes the film firmly into the 1970s Bigfoot monster movie pantheon—but only *just*.

The rest of the film is a verbatim presentation of **IVANPAH / TEENAGERS BATTLE THE THING**; we do not return to the classroom after the abrupt finale and "End" title (which was always followed by a final shot of the burning monster's body, to fadeout).

Alas, the Flocker Brothers were arguably too slow to jump aboard the 1970s exploitation movie "Bigfoot Express", relegating **CURSE OF BIGFOOT** to a limbo almost as remote as that which **IVANPAH / TEENAGERS BATTLE THE THING** had been consigned to. **CURSE OF BIGFOOT**'s quick sale to TV movie syndication and various 1980s videocassette releases ensured its longevity, becoming a public domain staple into the DVD era of the 21st Century and a 'must-see' artifact for self-professed "bad movie" aficionados.

While the original self-published edition of Roger Patterson's 1966 book *Do Abominable Snowmen of America Really Exist?* (see p. 11) is long out-of-print, the complete contents have been legally reprinted as part of *The Bigfoot Film Controversy* (2005, Hancock House Publishers), with extensive additional material by Christopher Murphy; it is the perfect companion (and antidote) to Greg Long's *The Making of Bigfoot: The Inside Story* (2004, Prometheus Books). Read 'em both, watch the Patterson/Gimlin film yourself over and over, make up your own mind.

---

[7] Jan Swihart is quite certain about the fact that "Bob Clymire played my boyfriend. I'm sure of that," while the Movie Vigilante identifies Dave Flocker as the director of the film who also played Roger Mason in both **IVANPAH / TEENAGERS BATTLE THE THING** and **CURSE OF BIGFOOT**. Phil Catalli—who plays Danny, "the Griffin dude" (who answers his teacher's question identifying an illustration of the mythical creature the Griffin)—asserts, "The teacher who was in the first part of the movie was Dave Flocker... he's not a professional actor but a teacher at the school where we filmed this scene in 1976... Alta Loma High School... Dave was the brother of Jim Flocker aka ...'Jim Fields', the writer and director of the original 1958 version of **TEENAGERS BATTLE THE THING**... Dave actually is in that movie as well... The movie was not long enough when a distributor wanted to buy rights to the movie, so Jim added the extra *[half-hour]* scene in the beginning... He didn't even change the credits!.... Very low budget as you can see... I worked for Jim at the time and was an aspiring actor at the time so he wrote *[me]* in as Danny. [...] Jim Flocker was a great mentor in my life at the time even tho *[sic]* he made a lot of low budget late night type TV movies..." *[all ellipses save the bracketed one are in the original text]*. Jan responded, "My memory that it was Don Flocker or Fields who directed the movie and his brother, J.T. Fields is who is shown in the photo you showed Phil Catalli. J.T. also played in the film as the teacher.... I still don't recall anyone named Dave Fields or Flocker. Don is what I remember." To this, the Movie Vigilante author/editor responded, "...it's possible that Dave Flocker not only used his pseudonym Don Fields on screen but also on the film set which would explain Jan remembering him as Don." Jan, Phil, and the *Movie Vigilante* are quoted from *Ibid*.

BIGFOOT: AMERICA'S ABOMINABLE SNOWMAN:

The 1967 Roger Patterson/Bob Gimlin filmed-in-Humboldt County, California footage of a Sasquatch (apparently a female) walking away from the filmmakers has enjoyed a half-century of fame and infamy. Running less than a minute in length, it's no exaggeration at this point to say that this 16mm Patterson/Gimlin footage has been examined almost as intently as the Zapruder 8mm footage of the November 22nd, 1963 President John F. Kennedy assassination in Dallas, Texas.

According to multiple online sources, including Wikipedia,[8] the Patterson/Gimlin footage "debuted" in Robert Guenette's TV special *Monsters! Mysteries or Myth?* (November 25th, 1974), which Guenette expanded into the Sunn Classic Pictures surprise boxoffice theatrical hit **THE MYSTERIOUS MONSTERS** (1976). That simply isn't true. The fact is that Roger Patterson and another business partner, Al DeAtley, had already roadshowed their footage to rural theaters as the documentary feature **BIGFOOT: AMERICA'S ABOMINABLE SNOWMAN** over five years before Guenette's Thanksgiving TV special was broadcast.

A brief overview of the celebrated and reviled Patterson/Gimlin film is in order. According to journalist Jack Moore, "Scientists and reporters Thursday viewed the world premiere of a 20-second film *[actually 53–59 seconds, depending on the correct frames-per-second (FPS) projection speed]* of a large, hairy animal" on October 26th, 1967:

"The film, said to have been shot in northern California late last week, showed a creature nearly seven feet tall walking away from the camera and disappearing into brightly-colored autumn woods. Another short film showed 14-inch tracks left by the creature after it ran away from the photographer."[9]

Essentially lost to time, however, is the feature film Roger Patterson constructed around that 1967 footage, **BIGFOOT: AMERICA'S ABOMINABLE SNOWMAN**. Completed in the winter of 1968, this first-ever official Bigfoot feature film apparently opened at the Memorial Coliseum in Portland, Oregon on Friday, March 14th, 1969, with Roger Patterson making a personal appearance. This debut was immediately followed by showings in Portland, Oregon high school auditoriums—Madison High, Wilson High, and Franklin High, four showings per day per location, Saturday and Sunday, March 15th

---

8 "**THE MYSTERIOUS MONSTERS** was the first movie to feature the home movie taken by Roger Patterson in 1967 reported to show a Bigfoot." Quoted from *https://en.wikipedia.org/wiki/The_Mysterious_Monsters* as it appears online on August 10, 2017

9 Jack Moore, "Sasquatch animal? Film doesn't convince," October 27th, 1967; newspaper source uncited, but the original clipping is archived (@ *http://www.pattersonfilm.com/styled-9/styled-10/index.html*); Moore's article was published simultaneously as "Many Not Convinced By Film of Sasquatch," *Walla Walla* [Washington] *Union-Bulletin*, Friday, October 27th, 1967, archived online (@ *http://www.pattersonfilm.com/styled-9/index.html*)

Paddy Sherman, editor of the morning Province, said after the press viewing:

"I've been a devout sceptic for many years. Why on earth didn't they shoot the thing?"

Newark (O.) Advocate Fri., Jan. 12, 1968

Editor Buys Film Clip Of Sasquatch

VANCOUVER, B.C. (AP) — John Green, a weekly newspaper editor, and Rene Dahinden, a lead salvager, said Thursday they have bought the Canadian rights of a 30-second film clip said to show an abominable snow woman, or sasquatch.

They said they bought the film, which Roger Patterson of Yakima, Wash., said he made in Northern California last fall, for $1,500.

The pair said they intended to use the film in a one-hour movie they are making in hopes of proving sasquatches do exist on the West Coast.

Abominable Snowman *1968*

A man who claims he saw an "abominable snowman" will describe his sighting of the strange creature, in a presentation at Central Washington State College Monday.

Roger Patterson will present a documentary film which includes scenes of his quest for the "abominable snowman." The film showing will be followed by a question-answer session.

Patterson, a native of Yakima, has travelled the mountains of Washington, Oregon, California, Idaho and British Columbia in search of the fabled "big foot."

The "abominable snowman" movie and discussion will be in McConnell Auditorium, Monday at 7 p.m. There is no admission charged.

News wire services around the world were buzzing over the Roger Patterson/Bob Gimlin Sasquatch film footage throughout 1967 and 1968, making the frame stills of the walking Woodperson an instant 1960s icon, accompanied by endless speculation—including outrage over the shaky footage not being as conclusive evidence as a body (*The Province* had been reporting on Sasquatch/Bigfoot sightings for well over a decade)—and the earliest coverage of the first Bigfoot documentaries to incorporate the footage into well-padded features.

and 16th—and eventually rolled-out to regional motion picture theaters into the spring of 1970.[10]

"Patterson, an ex-cowboy from Yakima, Wash., is the man who made the movie film of a strange hair-covered female giant in the Mt. Shasta area of California last fall. His film has become the basis for a documentary made by the British Broadcasting Co.... The BBC film and additional footage of expeditions into Western wilderness will be shown at Portland's Memorial Coliseum March 13 and 14."[11]

Northwest Research Assn. a.k.a. Northwest Films self-distributed the feature to a clutch of Northwestern US theaters, ballyhooing the BBC footage Patterson constructed his film around as a pedigree: "Filmed in Part by the British Broadcasting C." and "Listen to renowned scientists discuss the BIGFOOT discoveries, filmed in part by the British Broadcasting Corp. in FULL COLOR and SOUND," newspaper ads boasted.[12] The 1968 BBC documentary Patterson "creatively appropriated" should not be confused with the Sasquatch episode of the later BBC Chris Packham series *The X Creatures*, "Shooting the Bigfoot" (September 16th, 1998).[13] According to Guy Edwards, "The *[1968]* BBC documentary was never made whole and a lot of BBC footage was given back to Patterson. Some of the footage can be seen in the BBC series, *X Creatures: Shooting Bigfoot*...."[14]

Loren Coleman's *Bigfoot! The True Story of Apes in America* (Paraview Pocket Books, 2003) remains the best single volume on the subject, but **BIGFOOT: AMERICA'S ABOMINABLE SNOWMAN**'s case history requires deeper readings. The original Roger Patterson/Bob Gimlin film footage has been autopsied ad infinitum, both in print and online, and a swelling cottage industry of books debunking the famous/infamous 1967 footage has entrenched itself at *amazon.com*; it's tough to sort the wheat from the chaff. As a compendium of articles predating the Patterson/Gimlin footage, I highly recommend *The Bigfoot Film Controversy* by Roger Patterson and Christopher Murphy (Hancock House Publishers Ltd., 2005), which also reprints the complete text of Patterson's 1966 *Do Abominable Snowmen of America Really Exist?* I recommend the book only as the ideal compilation of articles and Patterson's rare book content. The fullest account in print of the making and tanking of **BIGFOOT: AMERICA'S ABOMINABLE SNOWMAN** remains that offered in *Bigfoot: The Life and Times of a Legend* by a very skeptical but thorough Joshua Blu Buhs (University of Chicago Press, 2009). Along with essential source material first published in Greg Long's *The Making of Bigfoot: The Inside Story* (2004, Prometheus Books)—the most exhaustive and detailed account of **BIGFOOT: AMERICA'S ABOMINABLE SNOWMAN**'s making and exhibition in existence—Buhs' research reveals that in 1967 and 1968 Patterson and Gimlin worked with lawyer Walter Hurst to incorporate Bigfoot Enterprises and pitched a feature film to various Hollywood producers, without success, and that author/naturalist/cryptozoologist Ivan T. Sanderson handled foreign film rights for the original Patterson/Gimlin footage, handling the footage's appearance in the BBC documentary. Meanwhile, for the sum of $1,500 (US), Patterson sold Canadian exhibition rights for the 1967 footage only to Canadian weekly newspaper editor John Green and Rene Dahinden, footage with which Green toured the provinces in the summer of 1969. According to the Associated Press article on the purchase, "The pair said they intended to use the

---

10 See the vintage newspaper ads compiled and archived at *Patterson Film.com: An Analytical Look at the 1967 Patterson Gimli Bigfoot Incident*, archived online (@ http://www.pattersonfilm.com/styled-9/index.html and http://www.pattersonfilm.com/styled-9/styled-10/index.html)

11 Marge Davenport, "Evidence Mounting That 'Bigfoot' Inhabits Wilderness in Northwest," newspaper unknown, March 11, 1969; article clipping courtesy of Jerry Riedel, archived online (@ http://www.pattersonfilm.com/styled-9/index.html).

12 **BIGFOOT** ads in *Walla Walla Union-Bulletin,* Friday, March 14th, 1969, and *Fond du Lac Commonwealth Reporter,* Friday, March 13th, 1970, archived online (@ http://www.pattersonfilm.com/styled-9/index.html).

13 For more on this series, see S. Parkash, "Shooting the Bigfoot: A BBC Investigation into Bigfoot," bigfoot-lives.com, archived online (@ http://www.bigfoot-lives.com/html/shooting_the_bigfoot.html).

14 Guy Edwards, "Today in Bigfoot History / 1968 / Roger Patterson Tours his Documentary with BBC Footage," *Cryptomundo*, March 13th, 2013, archived online (@ http://cryptomundo.com/bigfoot-report/roger-patterson-bbc/) and at Bigfoot Lunch Club, March 13th, 2013, archived online (@ http://www.bigfootlunchclub.com/2013/03/today-in-bigfoot-history-mar-13-1968.html).

film in a one-hour movie they are making in hopes of proving sasquatches do exist on the West Coast."[15] To the best of my knowledge, that "one-hour movie" is a 'lost' film, as well... *if it ever existed at all*.

Greg Long and Joshua Blu Buhs provide the backstory to the Portland, Oregon March 1969 world premiere of **BIGFOOT: AMERICA'S ABOMINABLE SNOWMAN**. Long interviewed Patterson's business partner Al DeAtley at length; DeAtley's account, taken at face value, remains the only extant version of events by a living participant.[16] Shortly after completing his final edit in the winter of 1968, Patterson and Al DeAtley "met Ron Olson, an Oregon man two years returned from the military and working for his father's film company, American International Enterprises":

"Olson had seen [Ivan T.] Sanderson's article in Argosy *and thought a movie about Bigfoot would be of interest to his audience... Hollywood had rejected Patterson and his film; Olson provided another way to get Sasquatch onto the big screen and the cultural firmament...*

Along with a cadre of competing independents, American National Enterprises was... pioneering a new way of marketing and distributing movies... focused on rural areas, renting entire theaters—all four walls, as it were, giving them their nickname, "four-wallers"—to show their movies. (In smaller towns without theaters, they rented high school gymnasiums or Elk's clubs.) The films usually played in the winter, when there was abundant free time and few competing entertainments... But the four-wallers also relied on techniques associated with mass culture. They did intensive market research, surveying rural communities and using computers to discern patterns in the responses. American National Enterprises spent three times more on surveys and marketing than on production, an absurd ratio that was unheard-of in Hollywood at that time... With their audience's desires carefully measured and films made to match those desires, four-wallers then saturated local television markets with advertisements for their movies... deploying what they had found in their surveys to create a demand for the movie. Crowds came out in droves; the four-wallers took the ticket money, the theater owner received the rent and what was made from concessions—and then the film was gone, in a few days, maybe a week... The four-wallers had to open and close quickly to beat word of mouth. And then it was on to the next town, the next market, sinking the profits into another huge advertising buy... When American National Enterprises went public in 1970, it grossed $5,000,000 in nine months, netted $605,000, and earned 39¢ per share.

---

15 Greg Long, *The Making of Bigfoot: The Inside Story* (Prometheus Books, 2004), pp.167, 260-261, and Joshua Blu Buhs, *Bigfoot: The Life and Times of a Legend* (University of Chicago Press, 2009), pp.142-144; AP article (tagged "Vancouver, B.C.") quoted from "Editor Buys Film Clip of Sasquatch," *Newark* [Oregon] *Advocate*, Friday, January 12th, 1968, clipping archived online (@ http://www.pattersonfilm.com/styled-9/styled-10/index.html). I have retained the non-capitalization of "sasquatches" as in the original text.

16 Long, *Ibid.*, pp.260–276.

Olson was persuasive enough to convince DeAtley and Patterson to experiment with four-walling. They rented a high school auditorium in Lakeview, Oregon, to showcase their Bigfoot film. It was a success. After the movie, DeAtley, Patterson, and others working with them retired to their motel room with a trashcan full of money. "'We were throwing it on each other on the bed and stuff!' DeAtley remembered... "Bullshit on these guys," DeAtley later remembered when thinking about American National Enterprises. 'We'll just do it ourselves. They'd given me the whole recipe.' Patterson's movie was replicated again and again and again until there were thirty-eight prints to show at different venues. Through the early months of 1969, DeAtley, Patterson, and a troupe of employees that DeAtley hired crisscrossed the Pacific Northwest and Midwest, blitzing an area with advertising, showing the film, and leaving with pockets full of cash."[17]

BIGFOOT: AMERICA'S ABOMINABLE SNOWMAN played throughout Oregon before moving on to venues in Idaho, Utah, Colorado, Nebraska, North and South Dakota, Wisconsin, and Minnesota. By 1970, audience interest ebbed along with the business partners' enthusiasm for four-walling, and Patterson was succumbing to the Hodgkin's disease that eventually claimed his life on January 15th, 1972. Patterson and DeAtley cut their losses and reportedly cleared $100,000 or so for their efforts. Before Patterson's death, DeAtley signed-off on Patterson selling the film to American National Enterprises,

Continued on page 35

---

17 Buhs, *Ibid.*, pp.154-156.

Sunn Classics Pictures thrived in the 1970s with its inventive exploitation innovations with documentaries targeting family audiences, including use of regional distribution rollouts and saturation local TV ad spots, 'four-walling' theatrical distribution tactics, etc. Among their successful acquisitions was their pick-up and revision of Robert Guenette's TV special *Monsters! Mysteries or Myth?* (November 25th, 1974) into the surprise boxoffice theatrical hit **THE MYSTERIOUS MONSTERS** (1976).

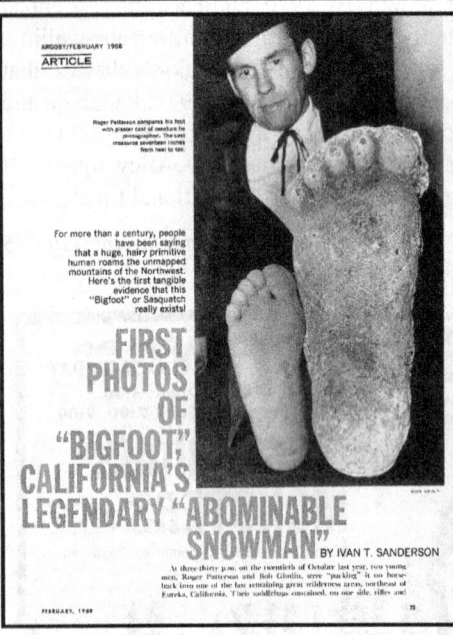

Top Left: Lawrence Crowley's **BIGFOOT: MAN OR BEAST** (1972) was reedited with additional footage to become **IN SEARCH OF BIGFOOT** (1976), restored and released to DVD *[top center]* by Vinegar Syndrome paired with Philip Yordan's and Jay Schlossberg-Cohen's **CRY WILDERNESS** (1987), which has become an instant 2017 season *Mystery Science Theater 3000* favorite. **Top Right:** Charles B. Pierce's **THE LEGEND OF BOGGY CREEK** (1972) was the breakthrough Bigfoot movie sensation, a regionally-produced independent documentary that truly launched the genre. **Middle Row, Left & Center:** Ivan T. Sanderson's many illustrated articles for *Argosy* made cryptids a 1960s newsstand staple, and many of these were collected by the publisher into the one-shot special *Monsters* (1975). **Center Right:** Thanks in part to **THE LEGEND OF BOGGY CREEK**, Fouke, Arkansas is still a destination spot for avid and amateur monster-hunters. **Bottom Left:** the cover story 'splash'-page from *Tales to Astonish* #24 (October 1961, art by Jack Kirby and Dick Ayers).

Tom Yamarone photo

Only five prints are known to survive of the original 1968 **BIGFOOT: AMERICA'S ABOMINABLE SNOWMAN** documentary. One resides in the collection of the International Cryptozoology Museum, Portland, Maine (above, right), another in the Willow Creek-China Flat Museum, Willow Creek, California (shown here, left, in the photo with the additional display materials). For a variety of reasons—all having to do with legal entanglements—it's likely this historic documentary will forever remain unreleased on any home viewing format, and the surviving elements are fragile, requiring special storage and preservation (which Loren Coleman, founder/curator of the International Cryptozoology Museum, assures the author has been seen to). [Photos: ©2016, 2017 Loren Coleman, Tom Yamarone.]

Right: Almost a year after the Portland, Oregon premiere of **BIGFOOT: AMERICA'S ABOMINABLE SNOWMAN** the film continued to play, sparking Bigfoot hunting parties which were reported in Northwest newspapers.

Walla Walla Union-Bulletin
Sunday, February 1, 1970

New Sasquatch Hunt Launched

COLVILLE, Wash. (AP) — An estimated 50 men were combing the rugged country of northeastern Washington Saturday for signs of a shaggy, cream-colored, man-like beast known as a sasquatch or "bigfoot."

This latest of a number of searches for the legendary sasquatch was touched off Tuesday when prospector Joe Metlow of Valley, Wash., reported he had seen one of the creatures feeding near his mining claim in northern Stevens County, near the Washington-British Columbia border.

Metlow said the beast was about nine feet tall and weighed an estimated 1,000 pounds. The prospector claims the hairy beast, standing erect like an ape, was scraping snow away from ferns with its front "hands" and eating the plant roots.

The report was picked up by a large number of dedicated sasquatch, or "bigfoot" hunters in this northeastern Washington community and relayed to others who have pursued sighting of giant tracks, supposedly belonging to the animal, for years.

Two professional sasquatch hunting groups were spearheading the latest search. One group is the Northwest Research Assn., headed by Roger Patterson of Yakima, Wash., and a Canadian group headed by Rene Dahinden of British Columbia. Another of the searchers is an unidentified Washington State Game Dept. inspector.

The search was not started until late in the week because Metlow refused to divulge exactly where he saw the live sasquatch until someone pays him what he considers a proper price for the information. One report is that he has rejected a $55,000 offer.

But on Friday, groups of hunters left Colville by plane, helicopter, in various vehicles and on showshoes in an attempt to find the beast on their own.

Fond du Lac Commonwealth Reporter
Friday, March 13, 1970

FIRST HISTORIC FILMS of LIVE CREATURE — A FACT!

Actual cast of creature's footprint. Roger Patterson in "Bigfoot country."

BIGFOOT
"America's Abominable Snowman!"

Northwest Films brings you the first films ever taken of this creature, over 7 feet tall. Thrill to the excitement of the discovery of the tracks. Listen to renowned scientists discuss the BIGFOOT discoveries, filmed in part by the British Broadcasting Corp. In FULL COLOR and SOUND.

Life "...film is clear view of this creature"
Reader's Digest "...one of world's most intriguing mysteries"
National Wildlife "...150 year legend comes to life in this film"

TAKE THE FAMILY! — LIMITED SHOWINGS

Now Showing at the **CAPITOL Theatre**
5 More DAYS! OPEN 4:45 682-7044
Showings: 5:00 - 7:00 - 8:30
SORRY, NO PASSES FOR THIS ATTRACTION

Walla Walla Union-Bulletin
Walla Walla, Wash. 99362, Friday, March 14, 1969

NORTHWEST PICTURES ASSN. Presents BIGFOOT
FILMED IN PART BY THE BRITISH BROADCASTING CO.

IN FULL COLOR & SOUND

The First Actual Motion Pictures of BIGFOOT - AMERICA'S ABOMINABLE SNOWMAN

SEE Roger Patterson come face to face with a female creature that stood over 7 feet tall. He is the first person ever to film BIGFOOT.

LISTEN to renowned scientists discuss these creatures, as in LIFE, READER'S DIGEST and NATIONAL WILDLIFE.

FEEL the excitement as the expedition finds tracks of these sub-human creatures.

Walla Walla—Lacy Auditorium
Friday March 14 at 7:00 and 8:30 P.M.

Elgin, Oregon—Stella Mayfield Auditorium
Thursday March 13 at 7:00 and 8:30 P.M.

Enterprise, Oregon—Vista Theatre
Thursday March 13 at 7:00 and 8:30 P.M.

Milton-Freewater, Oregon
McLoughlin High School
Friday March 14 at 7:00 and 8:30 P.M.

ADMISSION: Adults $1.50—Under 12, 75¢
Tickets at Box Office

Do Monsters Exist in America?

By WARREN SMITH

Family Weekly, July 21, 1968

SINCE THE dawn of time, convincing stories have been told about real or mythical monsters. Today many people claim there are mysterious monsters lurking in the U.S. wilderness.

While few persons give credence to these fanciful tales, scientists admit certain strange species of life could have survived in isolated areas.

There are definite patterns to the stream of "monster" reports over the past two decades. These include:

Sasquash or Big Foot: This creature is described as a two-footed mammal that walks upright and is believed to be a species between man and ape. Seven to ten feet in height, the creature weighs between 400 and 900 pounds. Except for the feet, hands, and nose, the monster is covered by one-inch-long reddish black hair. It has been sighted on more than 600 occasions in California, Washington, Idaho, Oregon, Canada, and Alaska.

At 3:30 p.m. on Oct. 20, 1967, "monster hunters" Roger Patterson and Bob Gimlim were searching the great forest northwest of Eureka, Calif., when suddenly they sighted a strange, fur-covered beast walking upright through the timber. Patterson grabbed his movie camera and zoomed in on the beast as it scurried away. The result is a highly controversial strip of 16 mm. color film.

Scientist Ivan T. Sanderson, author of "Snowman—Legend Come to Life," arranged for several distinguished scientists to view the film in Washington, D.C. A biologist from the Smithsonian Institution "observed nothing to point directly to a hoax." Another scientist speculated that hairy, humanlike creatures possibly could have migrated from Asia to America, thus giving rise to the speculation that the Sasquash is a relative of the "Yeti" ("Abominable Snowman")

Roger Patterson took this 1967 photo of a creature believed to be the elusive "Sasquash."

Florida's Abominable Sandman: Residents of Holopaw, Fla., locked their doors and oiled their guns last year when a midget version of the Sasquash invaded the state. Something described as "five-feet tall, covered with hair, and twice as broad as a man" raided garbage cans, plundered homes, and frightened dogs and livestock. When the community settled down, no one was ever sure whether it was a bear or a real monster.

In 1946 a similar apelike creature killed livestock and destroyed property around Coatesville and Lebanon, Pa. Terrified farmers hired a professional hunter to track the beast which "screamed like a baby." Elusive as ever, the creature disappeared into obscurity.

Lake Monsters: Since 1933, Scotland's Loch Ness monster has been a topic of conversation among monster lovers. Less publicized are similar creatures sighted in North American waters.

A Lyons Falls, N.Y., fisherman was astonished a few years ago to see a "15-foot something" rise out of the Black River. The dark brown monster had a round, tapered body and "eyes that stood out like silver dollars!"

Flathead Lake, Mont., and Payette Lake, Idaho, contain long-necked "Loch Ness" monsters. Local newspapers frequently report sightings by dozens of witnesses. The long-neckers "have a cow-like head on a long, slender neck. There are humps on their backs, and they travel with an up and down motion."

Oscar, the friendly monster in Big Pine Lake, Minn., has surfaced to stare quietly at boaters on the lake. Few fishermen have tried to lure him, though.

Scientists pay little attention to the sightings, but eyewitnesses strongly believe "there is *something* in our lakes."

The Mammoth Mothman: "I am a hard guy to scare, but I was for getting out of there," Roger Scarberry told police in Point Pleasant, W. Va. He said his car was chased by a flying monster on the night of Nov. 16, 1966.

Scarberry, his wife, and Mr. and Mrs. Steve Mallette all said "the bird was about six-feet tall, gray-colored, with two-inch eyes that glowed in the dark." The "thing" chased their speeding car for several miles. It was named the "Mammoth Mothman."

What can we believe about monsters? Repeated sightings indicate there may be "something" out in the boondocks. Until someone hauls a monster into a news conference, however, we can only maintain an open—but skeptical—mind. ✦

THE LETHBRIDGE HERALD
Saturday, December 2, 1967

Hairy Beast Photographer Faces Charge

YAKIMA, Wash. (AP) — Roger Patterson, 34, the man who said he photographed an abominable snowwoman in the mountains of northern California this fall, has been charged with grand larceny involving a 16 MM movie camera.

Patterson pleaded not guilty to the charge in Yakima County Superior Court and was released on his personal recognizance.

Harold Mattson, general manager of a Yakima Camera shop, said Patterson rented the camera May 13 and was to return it two days later.

Patterson showed a 20-second film of a large, hairy animal to a group of scientists and reporters in Vancouver, Oct. 26. He said it showed a Sasquatch he had seen about 100 miles northeast of Eureka, Calif.

The viewers remained largely unconvinced.

Thanks to Jerry Riedel for this story.
11 MAR 69

Evidence Mounting That 'Bigfoot' Inhabits Wilderness In Northwest

By MARGE DAVENPORT
Journal Staff Writer

When and if Roger Patterson encounters another "Bigfoot," he intends to shoot it with a tranquilizing gun and capture it.

Patterson, an ex-cowboy from Yakima, Wash., is the man who made the movie film of a strange hair-covered female giant in the Mt. Shasta area of California last fall.

His film has become the basis for a documentary made by the British Broadcasting Co. and subsequent articles in Life, the Reader's Digest, Argosy and National Wilderness magazines. The BBC film and additional footage of expeditions into Western wilderness will be shown at Portland's Memorial Coliseum March 13 and 14.

EARLY NEXT week Patterson and three companions intend to go into the Cascades east of Portland on the first of a series of three "ape-hunting trips" he is planning this year.

Reports of sightings and footprints in this area from an Estacada logger, who claims to have seen the giant creatures on three different occasions, prompted the Oregon expedition. Both Patterson and Rene Dahinden of British Columbia, who has spent the last 16 years hunting the sasquatch (Canadian name for the creatures), are convinced the logger is telling the truth. Dahinden visited the area a week ago and inspected piles of rocks supposedly piled up by the mystery creatures as they looked for hibernating rodents.

AFTER the Oregon expeditions Patterson and the Northwest Research Association, which he heads, plan trips to the Mt. St. Helens area in Washington and the Mt. Shasta country in California.

In Portland this week, Patterson said he felt the search for "Bigfoot" is drawing to a close.

"We know enough about Bigfoot's habits and habitats that we should be able soon to lure one into a position where we can capture it," Patterson declared.

HE SAID footprints and sightings indicate the creatures frequent certain areas, or pass through areas at specific times of the year. The expedition intends to use "animal distress calls" and scents to try to arouse "Bigfoot's curiosity." Patterson believe that most animals in the forest respond to a distress call even though it is from an entirely different species.

Although the question of whether "Bigfoot" really exists remains unsettled in the minds of most persons Patterson says more and more scientists are impressed with the growing amount of evidence about the creature.

PLASTER CASTS of giant footprints found in Northwest and Canadian wilderness are shown by Roger Patterson who is out to capture one of legendary giants. His movie film of "Mrs. Bigfoot," taken last year in California, and British Broadcasting Co. documentary on creatures filmed in Northwest will be shown at Coliseum Thursday and Friday.

Walla Walla Union-Bulletin
Sunday, February 1, 1970

New Sasquatch Hunt Launched

COLVILLE, Wash. (AP) — An estimated 50 men were combing the rugged country of northeastern Washington Saturday for signs of a shaggy, cream-colored, man-like beast known as a sasquatch or "bigfoot."

This latest of a number of searches for the legendary sasquatch was touched off Tuesday when prospector Joe Metlow of Valley, Wash., reported he had seen one of the creatures feeding near his mining claim in northern Stevens County, near the Washington-British Columbia border.

Metlow said the beast was about nine feet tall and weighed an estimated 1,000 pounds. The prospector claims the hairy beast, standing erect like an ape, was scraping snow away from ferns with its front "hands" and eating the plant roots.

The report was picked up by a large number of dedicated sasquatch, or "bigfoot" hunters in this northeastern Washington community and relayed to others who have pursued sighting of giant tracks, supposedly belonging to the animal, for years.

Two professional sasquatch hunting groups were spearheading the latest search. One group is the Northwest Research Assn., headed by Roger Patterson of Yakima, Wash., and a Canadian group headed by Rene Dahinden of British Columbia. Another of the searchers is an unidentified Washington State Game Dept. inspector.

The search was not started until late in the week because Metlow refused to divulge exactly where he saw the live sasquatch until someone pays him what he considers a proper price for the information. One report is that he has rejected a $55,000 offer.

But on Friday, groups of hunters left Colville by plane, helicopter, in various vehicles and on showshoes in an attempt to find the beast on their own.

All manner of 1967–1970 newspaper reports followed the Roger Patterson/Bob Gimlin Bigfoot encounter and filming whose board of director's reluctance scotched any chance of the kind of wider release of the feature as Patterson and DeAtley had exhibited it occurring, or whatever success American National Enterprises would have nurtured; compare, for instance, the enormous success Charles B. Pierce enjoyed with his Texarkana/Arkansas regional "true life" monster movie, **THE LEGEND OF BOGGY CREEK** (1972), in the hands of distributor Howco International, reaping an estimated $20 million during the film's healthy nationwide run.

As already noted, Patterson's 'lost' feature film—one of five surviving known prints resides in the collection of the International Cryptozoological Museum in Portland, Maine—was cobbled-together by adding new footage to a print of a 1968 BBC documentary that was never broadcast in the US. Whether the BBC provided Patterson with a print of their documentary under contractual terms negotiated by Sanderson—permitting the BBC to use his 1967 footage in their production in exchange for payment *and* Patterson legally exhibiting his own revamp of the BBC documentary with their permission—is unknown. Existing verbal accounts posit that the BBC had granted Patterson permission to use the BBC footage in his own theatrical film, as long as it was not on or for television,[18] but no surviving paperwork licensing the BBC footage for theatrical exhibition seems to exist; it's likely that American National Enterprises would have cleaned-up such glaring legal loose ends had Patterson and DeAtley initially contracted the film to Olson, but their decision to four-wall the film themselves terminated that possibility. After the fact, American National Enterprises waffled; ANE did use the 1967 footage to create a documentary short which they paired with Bill Mason's **CRY OF THE WILD** (1973), and Buhs writes that the company "distributed another mockumentary on Bigfoot, this one about the exploits of Sasquatch hunter Robert Morgan,"[19] which would be either Lawrence Crowley's **BIGFOOT: MAN OR BEAST** (1972) or the reedited variant **IN SEARCH OF BIGFOOT** ([1976] recently restored and released to DVD by Vinegar Syndrome paired with Philip Yordan's and Jay Schlossberg-Cohen's **CRY WILDERNESS** [1987]). Coupled with the tangled legal wake of Patterson's dealing and misdealings, and subsequent to Patteron's death Bob Gimlin's legal claims to proceeds from the 1967 footage and all documentaries and/or derivative works incorporating the footage,[20] this leaves **BIGFOOT: AMERICA'S ABOMINABLE SNOWMAN** caught in a legal limbo that will probably forever prevent the film from being released in any manner for the foreseeable future.

[Special thanks to Loren Coleman for fact-checking this sidebar; thanks, Loren!]

---

18 Long, Ibid., p.261.
19 Buhs, *Ibid.*, p.157.
20 Long, pp.318–327, and prepare thyself, for it's a *tangled* web indeed! Note in particular pp.325–326 and the details about Patterson's agreements with American National Enterprises.

YES, YETI!

The first cryptids of popular cinema may have been the ogres of the earliest fantasy and fairy tale films—if that isn't stretching the definition of cryptid too far into folklore and the realm of the faeries.

Prominent among the first feature-length films to boast cryptids is **THE LOST WORLD** (1925), with its glorious Willis O'Brien-animated stop-motion Neodinosaurs; but the actor (and makeup) appearing onscreen as the Troglodyte, one Bull Montana, had played a surgically-created 'gorilla man' five years earlier in the comedy-thriller **GO AND GET IT** (1920). While silent and early sound movies were populated by plenty of men-in-suit simians and primates, I'd nominate Bull Montana in **GO AND GET IT** as the first cinematic half-man / half-ape creature evocative of the Yeti, Sasquatch, and Bigfoot to come.

With the notable exception of the Swedish *sort-of*-Yeti from **TERROR IN THE MIDNIGHT SUN** (*Rymdinvasion i Lappland*, a.k.a. **INVASION OF THE ANIMAL**

Above: Author's sketch of Bumble from *Rudolph the Red-Nosed Reindeer* (December 6th, 1964).

films and TV series covered in this volume. This regretfully had me abstaining from articles on the first wave of non-Neodinosaur cryptid films, the Abominable Snowman movies of the 1950s.

This means I had to leave out the most popular Yeti in American pop culture, the Abominable Snowman of the North a.k.a. "Bumble" from the beloved Rankin/Bass Productions stop-motion animated TV special *Rudolph, The Red-Nosed Reindeer* (December 6th, 1964 on NBC; and yes, I saw it that very night it was first broadcast!). *Rudolph* has been telecast every single year since—it's the longest-rerun-Christmas special in broadcast history—making Bumble the A-Number-1 star of the Yeti subgenre. Bumble even scored his own U.S. Post Office postage stamp (2014)!

You won't be finding plush dolls in toy stores anytime past, present, or likely future of W. Lee Wilder's and Myles Wilder's **THE SNOW CREATURE** (1954), Ishirō Honda's **JŪJIN YUKI OTOKO** (獣人雪男, a.k.a. **HALF HUMAN**, 1955, Japan), Nigel Kneale's and Rudolph Cartier's *BBC Sunday-Night Theatre* teleplay *The Creature* (January 30th, 1955), Jerry Warren's **MAN BEAST** (1956), or the Hammer Films adaptation of Kneale's *The Creature*, **THE ABOMINABLE SNOWMAN OF THE HIMALAYAS** (1957).

The family life of the Yeti figured in most of the 1950s cycle: **THE SNOW CREATURE** was shown to have a wife and offspring (killed when the titular male Yeti deliberately causes a cave-in to protect them from the human interlopers, only to accidentally kill his own kin); the enigmatic guide of **MAN BEAST**, named Varga (George Skaff), revealed himself to be a Yeti hybrid *passing* as human, intent on wiping out the expedition save for his unsavory plans for the film's heroine (Asa Maynor, credited as Virginia Maynor). Nigel Kneale's Yeti prove to be sophisticated social beings, intent on saving their own from the ruthless game-hunter head of the expedition, and eventually demonstrating extraordinary powers to ensure their survival.

Nigel Kneale's script and Val Guest's direction ensures that **THE ABOMINABLE SNOWMAN OF THE HIMALAYAS** is without a doubt the best of the cycle—and will be the subject of an in-depth analysis in my next *Cryptid Cinema* tome—but my favorite is the original, uncut version of the aforementioned Ishirō Honda gem **JŪJIN YUKI OTOKO** (獣人雪男, 1955, Japan), which was extensively cut with additional American-filmed footage (starring John Carradine, Morris Ankrum, and Toho/Tsuburaya's original 'baby Yeti' suit lying on a table, representing the dead infant's corpse) and released stateside as **HALF HUMAN** (1958). **HALF HUMAN** actually had a legal VHS release, but the original cut Japanese **JŪJIN YUKI OTOKO** was pulled from release due to subsequent concerns over the film's caricature of the *burakumin* people.

Too long out of circulation, the film is a 'missing link' in and of itself, in many ways: the first Toho Studios expedition/monster adventure movie, with a monster-god worshipping tribe; it's also very much Toho's in-house special effects master Eiji Tsuburaya's "**KING KONG**", including a cliffside rope-pull scene and a fleeting bit of stop-motion animation (as the yeti climbs a cavern wall with the heroine in his arms). It's a *good* monster movie, in every way, for its era. Too bad this essential, formative Toho *daikaiju-eiga* has been so lost for so long—banned, in effect, and withdrawn from circulation since the 1950s by Toho—save for diehard viewers/collectors and the bootleg market. In one way, I can see why Toho pulled it (the *burakumin* people[1] are depicted essentially as birthmark-riddled,

Continued on page 39

---

1 Some sources claim the tribal culture represented are the *Auni*, but that is erroneous; see Steve Ryfle and Ed Godziszewski, *Ishiro Honda: A Life in Film, From Godzilla to Kurosawa* (2017, Wesleyan University Press), pp. 116–117.

Page 36, top to bottom: Bull Montana in makeup as the surgically created gorilla man of **GO AND GET IT** (1920), a role essentially recreated (makeup by Cecil Holland) for Montana's role as the troglodyte *(bottom photo)* in First National's adaptation of Sir Arthur Conan Doyle's **THE LOST WORLD** (1925); Willis O'Brien and his stop-motion animation team also ensured **THE LOST WORLD** had the most believably 'alive' neodinosaurs of the silent era, paving the way for O'Brien's masterpiece **KING KONG** (1933). **This page: top, left, and above:** 20th Century Fox ad art for their release of Hammer Films/Nigel Kneale/Val Guest's **THE ABOMINABLE SNOWMAN OF THE HIMALAYAS** (1957) inexplicably cribbed its clothed monster from ad art for Warner Bros.'s 3D Poe pic **PHANTOM OF THE RUE MORGUE** (1954), while Fox's companion campaign *(center)* played up nonsensical "secret camera" and cautionary "Warning!" ballyhoo. **Top, center:** newspaper ad for DCA's 1957 double-bill of the giant-wasps-in-Africa opus **MONSTER FROM GREEN HELL** and **HALF HUMAN**, Kenneth G. Crane's cut-and-padded (with new footage featuring John Carradine) release of Ishiro Honda's 獣人雪男 / **JŪJIN YUKI OTOKO** (1955).

Right, top to bottom: Key ad art, pressbook synopsis, cast and credits for producer/director Jerry Warren's **MAN BEAST** (1956), filmed on mountainous wintery locations in Bishop, CA, in Bronson Caves in Griffith Park in Los Angeles, and at Hollywood's Keywest Studios. **Page 38:** Author's sketches of the most beloved Yeti in American pop culture *Rudolph the Red-Nosed Reindeer*'s Bumble; Nate Rainey's cover art for Ross Kearney and Rainey's *Be My Friend? A Yeti Tale* (2016). **Page 39:** Key ad art, synopsis, cast and credits for W. Lee Wilder and Myles Wilder's **SNOW CREATURE** (1954).

Synopsis

When Connie Hayward (Virginia Maynor) and Trevor Hudson (Lloyd Cameron) arrive at a Tibetan outpost at the foot of the Himalayas, they find they are too late. They have come to find Connie's brother, Dr. James Hayward, because his doctor has declared that the high altitude will be fatal to him. Jim left two days earlier to set up camps in the mountains for Dr. Erickson (George Wells Lewis). Connie and Hud learn this from Steve Cameron (Tom Maruzzi). Since it is imperative to Connie that she reach her brother, and Dr. Erickson has only one day's head start on them, Steve, a guide, consents to lead them up. Steve explains to Connie and Hud that Jim and Dr. Erickson have formed an expedition to search for the Abominable Snowman, monster of the high snows. These creatures are known as Yeti to the natives. As they tackle the perilous and taxing ascent, Hud weakens and openly declares to Connie that he is sorry that he volunteered to help her. Finally they catch up with Dr. Erickson, Kheon, and Lon Raynon, and explain their mission. The doctor is enthusiastic about the prospect of encountering the Yeti,—he has a theory that they are human, prehistoric humans. His views only frighten Hud more. Soon they reach the camp where they expect to find Jim and his guide Varga (George Skaff) . . . Instead they find the camp mysteriously torn apart. They set up the camp and go out in search of the missing men. When they return Varga is in the camp. He reports that Jim is missing and he has no idea where he could be. The party resolves to continue their search for him. The following day the group intensifies its search. Hud gets separated from the others and when they rejoin him they learn of his exciting discovery. He found tracks. He followed them to an ice cave. Dr. Erickson, convinced that Hud saw Yeti tracks insists on returning to the cave. Inside the cave havoc breaks loose. Monsters appear from every crevice. They would attack if it were not for a silent signal from Varga not to. One Yeti menacing Hud forces him to back off the edge of a cliff. Varga sees that Steve is poised to shoot at one of the Yeti and throws a club at him. The gun goes off and Steve is unconscious. Hud is killed by one of the monsters. The next day Steve and Connie try to get the Doctor to leave but he won't consider it. They strongly suspect Varga of something but cannot be sure of what. Varga asks Dr. Erickson if he'd like to return to the cave. Of course he is delighted. Steve says he'll go too, but he goes to protect the doctor. Connie arranges to meet Steve at a designated spot later. On route to the cave Varga instructs the Yeti to start an avalanche to kill Steve. It is not successful in killing him but it does prevent his going to the cave. Inside the cave Varga reveals to the doctor that he is part Yeti. He is fifth generation. They kidnap women to breed our the Yeti strain and Connie is to be their next victim. Varga then shoots Dr. Erickson, and starts after Connie. He tells her that Steve is dead and the doctor wounded and needs to see her. Steve has managed to free himself from the fallen snow and arrives on the scene in time to aid Connie by attacking Varga. At their first chance they start down the mountain. Varga quickly revives and continues his pursuit. He throws his rope over a cliff and prepares to slide down it. Connie and Steve below watch. Halfway down, the peg holding the rope snaps and Varga falls screaming to a horrible death.

Cast and Credits

CAST

LON RAYNON	ROCK MADISON
CONNIE HAYWARD	VIRGINIA MAYNOR
STEVE CAMERON	TOM MARUZZI
TREVOR HUDSON	LLOYD NELSON
DR. ERICKSON	GEORGE WELLS LEWIS
VARGA	GEORGE SKAFF
KHEON	JACK HAFFNER
TRADER	WONG SING

CREDITS

A Jerry Warren Production. Produced and Directed by Jerry Warren; Screenplay by B. Arthur Cassidy; Photographed by Victor Fisher; Film Editor, James R.Sweeney; Associate Producer, Ralph Brooke; Music Direction, Josef Zimanich; Editing by Ashcroft Film Service.

If you love *Rudolph the Red-Nosed Reindeer*'s Bumble, you'll love Maine-based author Ross Kearney and artist Nate Rainey's illustrated children's book *Be My Friend? A Yeti Tale* (2016), which provides an excellent entry-level intro to cryptid culture. It's available via mail-order from https://coastcitycomics.com/collections/books/products/be-my-friend-a-yetis-tale-by-ross-kearney-and-nate-rainey and from amazon (*https://www.amazon.com/Be-My-Friend-Yetis-Tale/dp/1519475144/ref=sr_1_1?s=books&ie=UTF8&qid=1507408265&sr=1-1*) and on Kindle (via https://www.amazon.com/Be-My-Friend-Ross-Kearney-ebook/dp/B01BFW3A0S/ref=sr_1_2?s=digital-text&ie=UTF8&qid=15074082 14&sr-1-2).

The Story
(not for publication)

An expedition of ten Sherpa natives, a Tibetan guide Subra, a photographer, Peter Wells and their leader Dr. Frank Parrish, set out from the Tibetan village of Shekar to explore the flora of the Himalaya Mountains. One night Subra's wife Talla whom he left at home is abducted by the Snow Creature within sight of Leva, Subra's brother. Leva catches up to the expedition and tells Subra what has happened. Subra asks Dr. Parrish to help him look for the Snow Creature. Parrish scoffs at the story of a Snow Creature and refuses. Subra becomes angry and conspires to rob Parrish and Wells of their ammunition. Subra takes the men and searches the mountains. Parrish and Wells are forced to go along. They find enormous footprints and follow them to a cave. In the cave they find the Snow Creature and rescue Talla. Subra tries to kill the Snow Creature but is prevented from doing so by Dr. Parrish, who is anxious to bring him back alive to the United States. This he succeeds in doing. A great deal of red tape ensues with the Immigration authorities as to whether the Snow Creature should be admitted to the country. While this discussion is going on, the Snow Creature escapes, commits two murders and terrifies the frightened city. The police search everywhere for him but he manages to elude them. Suddenly Dr. Parrish realizes that the Snow Creature must be in need of cool air and probably is hiding in the sewers of the city. That is where the police find him and attempt to capture him alive. They are about to succeed when the Snow Creature manages to get a death grip on Parrish and the police are forced to kill him.

RUNNING TIME: 70 MINUTES

Official Billing
"SNOW CREATURE"
starring
**Paul Langton, Leslie Denison,
Teru Shimada and Rollin Moriyama**

Produced and Directed by W. Lee Wilder
Story and Screenplay by Myles Wilder
Released by United Artists

The Cast

Frank Parrish	Paul Langton
Peter Wells	Leslie Denison
Subra	Teru Shimada
Leva	Rollin Moriyama
Inspector Karma	Robert Kino
Airline Manager	Robert Hinton
Joyce Parrish	Darlene Fields
Corey, Jr.	George Douglas
Fleet	Robert Bice
Dr. Dupont	Rudolph Anders
Lieutenant Dunbar	Bill Phipps
Edwards	Jack Daly
Guard in Warehouse	Rusty Westcott

The Staff

Director of Photography	Floyd D. Crosby, A.S.C.
Production Supervision	Mack V. Wright
Film Editor	Jodie Copelan, A.C.E.
Special Effects	Lee Zavitz
Art Director	Frank Sylos
Music composed and conducted by	Manuel Compinsky

Continued from page 36

crippled, semi-deformed primitives); on the other hand, it would be like burying every western that misrepresented Native Americans (bye-bye, John Ford's **STAGECOACH** [1939]!).[2] Given all the tribes (mis)represented and caricatured in *daikaiju-eiga*, it's tragic that this keeps the then-innovative, still-remarkable film in the vaults forever. It's much like the situation with Walt Disney's **SONG OF THE SOUTH** (1946) here in the US.

The family angle is prominent (though, despite the publicity photo Toho circulated and which appears in various monster magazines and *daikaiju-eiga* histories, the baby yeti *doesn't* ride a bear!), and the murder of the infant Yeti is central to the narrative, suggesting an urgent reason for the Yeti's kidnapping of the expedition's female member. There's confusion whether Fuminori Ohashi or Harou Nakajima plays the adult Yeti; August Ragone confirms it was Ohashi in the role, without a doubt. The shots of the yeti moving through the night forest, eyes glowering, after the death of its child are truly haunting.

The Yeti of **JŪJIN YUKI OTOKO** is emotionally and physiologically the closest Tsuburaya ever came to his beloved Willis O'Brien prototype, King Kong. The stunning moment of stop-motion animation in the climax (cut from the US version, alas), while crude, makes it clear how near and dear this project was to Tsuburaya. In many ways, **JŪJIN YUKI OTOKO** is also the precursor to **MOTHRA** (モスラ / *Mosura*, 1961): the template is all there, including two female "sacrifices".

2 My friend and fellow monster-loving artist Bob Eggleton noted back on July 11th, 2011, during our Facebook conversation about **HALF HUMAN**, "For a time, the film **THE PROPHECIES OF NOSTRODAMUS** [ノストラダムスの大予言 / *Nosutorademusu no daiyogen*, 1974] was also banned due to *one* scene showing these post-nuclear deformed humans. It's seen in the US version **THE LAST DAYS OF PLANET EARTH**, which was hacked down to 90 mins from three hours!! This one scene comes out of the blue and, it's frightening and highly effective on a rather large 'blasted earth' set. The makeups are similar to **THE ELEPHANT MAN**, though not as elaborate but still, grisly. The p/s, edited US LD and VHS became prized items in Japan in the '90s because it left intact this one scene."

Above: Posed 'construct' still from Toho Studios for 獣人雪男 / **JŪJIN YUKI OTOKO** (1955) used to promote the 1957 US edit **HALF HUMAN**, showing proud poppa (Fuminori Ohashi) and son (Takashi Itô) in a scene absent from all versions of the film. Fuminori Ohashi (born Yukitoshi Ôhashi, a.k.a. "Ryûnosuke Kabayama") played the Yeti parent under the screen name "Sanshirô Sagara." Jolyon Yates references the article by Peter Hayes Brothers in *G-Fan* #69 (2004), and a photo of Ohashi revealing himself in the Yeti suit with head/mask removed; *daikaiju-eiga* expert August Ragone confirms Ohashi's role herein.

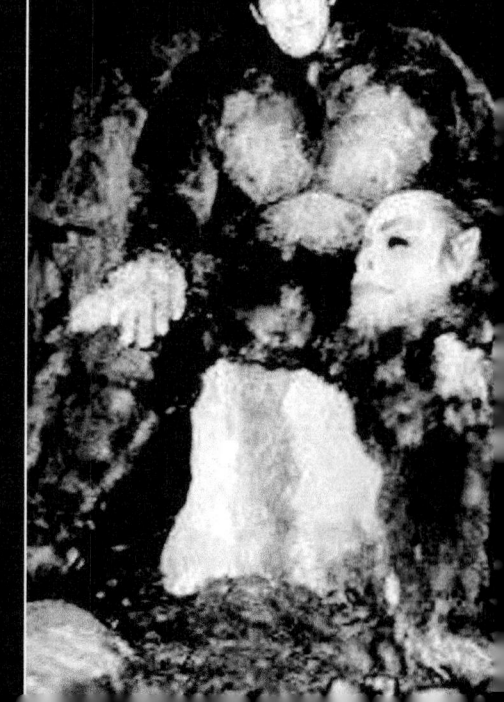

***"INVASION OF THE ANIMAL PEOPLE**... Out of the sky comes science fiction's most startling adventure of all time! Beyond description is the secret mission perpetrated by these strange creatures from another world! **INVASION OF THE ANIMAL PEOPLE** bursts forth a tide of violence as never witnessed upon the face of the Earth! Animal People, with a brain advanced by a million years of evolution! **INVASION OF THE ANIMAL PEOPLE** surpasses reason! Challenges your own sanity! If ever a motion picture will be remembered above all others, the terrifying **INVASION OF THE ANIMAL PEOPLE** will stand as a pillar of granite as it rips forth its eerie shocks, its strange and pulsating story! Don't miss... **INVASION OF THE ANIMAL PEOPLE!**"*

– Overemphatic voiceover from Jerry Warren's US release trailer for the altered, retitled version of
TERROR IN THE MIDNIGHT SUN

Two New Thrillers Screen Currently

Invasion of the Animal People together with Terror of the Bloodhunters make up twin shocker show now playing at the .... theater.

Thrills and high adventure beginning at the freezing arctic and ultimately reaching the dark Amazon jungle are to be seen as the two new pictures make their mark in chilling tradition.

Invasion of the Animal People deals with the landing of alien creatures from another world and the great havoc and destruction these monsters cause to Lapland villages and everything that blocks their path. As a scientific expedition finds itself powerless against the thrust of gigantic forces possessed by the aliens its plight is doubled by terrifying exposure to the perilous arctic elements including explosive avalanches of tremendous proportions.

Loaded with thrills and chills from the frozen glaciers of one of the remote stretches of the planet upon which we live Invasion of the Animal People explodes with unexpected events caused by the monster men from another world as they land upon earth and create terror in the hearts of all in their path. Seeming to possess only a bestial nature but having at their control powerful forces of advanced scientific design the animal people prove that humanity is a weak match by comparison. The picture is endowed with great excitement and suspense together with a surge of added peril, this the strange elements of the arctic circle.

New Science Fiction Film

Invasion of the Animal People, a new science fiction thriller is currently playing at the .... theater. The picture deals with alien monsters from another world and their treacherous attack upon the earth.

(ADVANCE)

One of the most startling adventures of science fiction opens.................at the......................theater and unfolds its unusual story of beings from another part of the universe who land on our own planet earth.

What with today's peering into deep space and all it engulfs with endless possibilities of life on many of the worlds in our solar system as well as thousands of others it becomes apparent that a visit from alien planets could soon be an actuality. In invasion of the animal people John Carradine takes the audience to a remote part of our world where such a landing by space people causes thrills of magnitude together with dramatic impact throughout the entire picture. Scenes beautifully photographed in the vast arctic circle are authentic and bring to the screen a scope of splendor along with the erie suspense and action.

Well photographed and directed, Invasion of the Animal People features together with Carradine, Barbara Wilson and Robert Burton who enact the unique story in convincing fashion. The animal people themselves due to effective makeup are viewed with a feeling of reality and bring forth a frightening series of thrills as they move with authority amid the well planned special effects.

The picture is designed for all age groups and will please the sophisticated audience as well as others. Other half of the double feature program is the shocker Terror of the Bloodhunters.

New Dimension Of Thrills in 'Animal People'

(CURRENT)

John Carradine, one of Hollywood's veteran showmen takes the audience to the far away arctic circle for science fiction adventure in Invasion of the Animal People now playing at the............................theater.

The picture is showing with another shocker Terror of the Bloodhunters.

41

For thousands of years it has stalked the earth, feasting on the flesh of humans

SNOW MAN

Norman Bogner

David McAllister, cover artist for the 1979 UK edition of Norman Bogner's *Snow Man* ("First published in Great Britain in 1978 by New English Library / First NEL paperback edition December 1979"), painted a *Famous Monsters of Filmland*-worthy portrait of the alien "Not Yeti" from **RYMDINVASION I LAPPLAND / TERROR IN THE MIDNIGHT SUN** a.k.a. **INVASION OF THE ANIMAL PEOPLE** (1959/1962)

A NOTE ON NOT YETI...

In the strict context of Cryptid Cinema—apart from all other aspects of genre cinema history, which will be duly considered in the following essay—the Swedish SF opus **TERROR IN THE MIDNIGHT SUN** (*Rymdinvasion i Lappland*, a.k.a. **INVASION OF THE ANIMAL PEOPLE**, 1959/1962) is a curious specimen. If nothing else, **RYMDINVASION I LAPPLAND** (literal translation: "Space Invasion of Lapland") was the first theatrical feature film from any nation to mix UFOs with outsized hairy hominids. In the pop-cultural vocabulary of the time, "Yeti" or "The Abominable Snowman" would have been the handy reference point, and that's certainly what the giant 'Snowman' of **RYMDINVASION** resembles in terms of the 1950s SF cinema it emerged from.

Pulp science-fiction literature and SF comicbooks were quite another story—hairy bipedal humanoid aliens of all colors, shapes, and sizes had been populating stories for quite some time prior to 1959—but '59 was a banner year for a resurgence of such imagery and themes. If we count only the Comics Code Authority-approved monster SF comics from Atlas/Timely (soon to become better-known as Marvel Comics) from editor/writer Stan Lee and writer/artists Jack Kirby, Steve Ditko, Don Heck, and others, variations on the species were frequent four-color visitors to the comicbook spinner racks. The first of all the Atlas/Timely/Marvel giant monsters was sort-of a big hairy biped (the Heap-like horror of "The Ghoul Strikes!" in *Marvel Tales* #93, 1949), but that pre-Code creature's successors exploded in the publisher's monthly titles from 1959 until Marvel's new breed of superheroes took over in 1962 and '63.

Just before cheapjack hackmeister Jerry Warren cut-and-dubbed **RYMDINVASION I LAPPLAND** into **INVASION OF THE ANIMAL PEOPLE** and unleashed his abomination onto American drive-ins and nabes, comic books like *Strange Tales, Tales of Suspense, Journey Into Mystery*, and johnny-come-lately *Amazing Adventures* (launched in spring 1961) were fertile breeding grounds for Jack Kirby/Stan Lee hairy giant monster/alien invasion tales. Let's just look at the winter of 1961-62, which cover-featured "I Found the Abominable Snowman" (*Tales to Astonish* #24, October 1961), in which a filmmaking crew's actor-in-a-Yeti-costume is snatched by a *real* giant Yeti and taken to its fellow alien invaders, who are actually giant bipedal humanoid *reptiles* who merely disguise themselves as Yeti "…whenever *[we]* go to the surface world, to protect *[themselves]* against the cold!" That very same month, Kirby's and Lee's "Beware of Bruttu" (*Tales of Suspense* #22, October 1961) was also for sale. Bruttu was the result of a sad-sack scientist making a wish in the proximi-

43

ty of "a new type of atomic machine" after envying the size and strength of a monster named Bruttu featured in "a fantasy magazine on display" at his local newsstand; lo and behold, he turns into Bruttu and goes on a rampage. A month later, a big hairy alien warrior kidnapped the protagonist of Kirby/Lee's "I Was Captured by the Creature from Krogarr!" (*Tales to Astonish*, November 1961); this giant hairy alien stepped out of a rewired TV set. Big-and-hairy "Lo-Karr, Bringer of Doom!" (*Journey Into Mystery* #75, December 1961) appeared to be an alien threatening planet Earth, but he was really a robot constructed by a human being to terrorize mankind into ending war and peacefully cooperating to prepare to meet alien invaders. One month later, Kirby and Lee's "The Death of Monstrollo!" (*Tales of Suspense* #25, January 1962) had another big-hairy-bipedal-monster scare-off an invading alien fleet, saving Earth despite the fact Monstrollo was really a giant robot monster constructed for a low-budget monster movie—a plot device so ingenious that Kirby/Lee had another big-and-hairy robot monster (this one with insect-like pincers over its maw) scare-off another pack of cowardly aliens in "Follow the Leader" (*Journey Into Mystery* #76, January 1962). And that was just the *first half* of that winter's output!

Science-fiction movies began to conflate Yeti-and-alien imagery and concepts in the coming decade. Among the colorful trio of Italian-American "Gamma-One" SF features directed by "Anthony M. Dawson"/Antonio Margheriti in the mid-1960s, comicbook *Batman* co-creator and writer Bill Finger had a hand in co-scripting **SNOW DEVILS** (*La morte viene dal pianeta Aytin*, 1967), in which global climate-change and the melting of the polar ice caps results in the discovery of giant hairy aliens up in the Himalayas—the *real* guise of the so-called Yeti—who call themselves the Aytia and plan on creating a new Ice Age to match their home-world's climate so they can escape their dying planet and colonize a frozen Earth.

If this all seems very, very far afield from the subgenre of Cryptid Cinema, consider how **RYMDINVASION I LAPPLAND** curiously anticipates a development in the cataloguing and speculative texts concerning what ufologist Jerome Clark referred to as "Hairy Biped" sightings. Attention to such reports gained momentum a decade or more after the Swedish invader-from-space oddity was released. In his Foreword to *Bigfoot Casebook Updated: Sightings and Encounters from 1818-2004* by Janet & Colin Bord (revising and expanding their classic 1982 text), Loren Coleman writes about the 1970s fusion of UFO studies, Sasquatch/Bigfoot studies, and the often-wild extrapolations that resulted:

"...It was an era in which the mixing of several threads of the inexplicable overlapped, danced about together, and merged. Bigfoot met Forteana, whether it was globes, cattle mutilations, electromagnetic effects, or other bizarre imports from the world of the so-called paranormal... During the 1970s, individuals like California researcher Peter Guttilla began discussing what he saw as the overlapping nature of Bigfoot and UFO reports. Mostly unaccredited talks between Guttilla, Barbara Ann Slate, and Alan Berry would lead to writings by Slate and Berry highlighting the UFO link to Bigfoot sightings.

"In Pennsylvania, UFO researcher Stan Gordon was promoting attention for the strange hairy creature reports that were coming his way. He was especially intrigued by a rash of reports beginning in 1973 that seemed to link sightings of Bigfoot and UFOs... Other ufologists were getting into the Bigfoot business too. Coral Lorenzen, Leonard Stringfield, Andrew Collins, Dr. Leo Sprinkle, John S. Derr, R. Martin Wolf, and Steven Mayne began looking into hairy creature sightings during the 1970s. These individuals' ufological philosophies caused them to think in terms of their frame of references and their literature now contains clear-cut Bigfoot accounts, which were collected by ufologists. There is no doubt a body of work that has Bigfoot-like creatures directly connected to UFO sightings [which] *has been deduced and chronicled by ufologists (not Forteans, not cryptozoologists) as worthy of their time. Other authors, such as Brad Steiger, Warren Smith, and their humorously combined single author, known under the pseudonym 'Eric Norman,' were also producing paperback books full of new stories of UFOs and apemen."*[1]

For many, Keel's *Strange Creatures from Time & Space* (Gold Medal Books, 1970) was the seminal text to emerge from this period. Coleman's own early collaborative efforts co-authored with Jerome Clark, *The Unidentified: Notes Towards Solving the UFO Mystery* (Warner Books, 1975) and *Creatures of the Outer Edge* (Warner Books, 1978; reprinted together in one volume by Anomalist Books in 2006), were aligned with the writings of Jacques Vallee and John Keel on such matters: rationalist probing of the blurred boundaries between sightings of inexplicable objects or creatures, and the possible paranormal implications of their elusive natures. Self-published chapbooks like Dennis Pilichis' *Night Siege: The Northern Ohio UFO-Creature Invasion* (1982)—eccentric by any measure—posited ever-more-convoluted evidence and "explanations" for associative links between Bigfoot/Sasquatch, UFOs, and unknown agencies.

As Coleman notes in his introduction to the Bords' invaluable book, "The impact of those times still influences the stories gathered, and the books produced today." Undigested regurgitation of such conflations continue unabated online today.[2] The same goes for genre films and television, making **RYMDINVASION I LAPPLAND** a curious landmark of sorts, despite its obscurity.

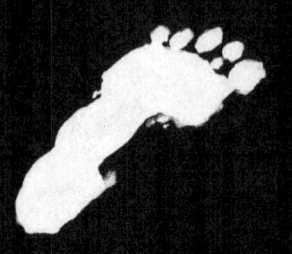

---

1 Loren Coleman, Foreword to *Bigfoot Casebook Updated: Sightings and Encounters from 1818-2004* by Janet and Colin Bord (2005, Pine Woods Press); Loren's complete Foreword is online at http://pinewindspress.com/coleman_foreword.htm

2 For instance, see http://www.huffingtonpost.com/dr-franklin-ruehl-phd/is-bigfoot-possibly-an-alien_b_1578844.html

NOT YETI!

Revisiting
Rymdinvasion i Lappland
a.k.a. *Invasion of the Animal People*
(1959/62)

I love wintery horror movies. I especially love winter-set monster movies.

Maybe it's growing up in Vermont that determined that, but it doesn't matter. I love 'em.

Along with Jalmari Helander's **RARE EXPORTS** *(2010) and Erik Blomberg's shapeshifter gem* **THE WHITE REINDEER** *(Valkoinen peura, 1952)—both from Finland—my personal favorite of all winter weirdo movies remains the utterly bizarre Swedish SF opus* **RYMDINVASION I LAPPLAND** *(a.k.a.* **INVASION OF THE ANIMAL PEOPLE***, 1959 [US release: 1962]). Besides the two I just mentioned, there are much, much better winter monster movies—particularly from 2010, the year of the Dutch Dick Maas'* **SAINT NICK** *(Sint) and André Øvredal's* **TROLLHUNTER** *(Trolljegeren) from Norway, as well as the aforementioned* **RARE EXPORTS**—*but give me the Swedish not-yeti of* **RYMDINVASION I LAPPLAND***, please.*

It's difficult to articulate the reasons why, really, save for the one outstanding element in the movie: its monster.

What's as baffling as the film itself is its curious legacy. This movie had and has quite a pedigree: it was directed by none other than Virgil W. Vogel, from a story and script by Arthur C. Pierce and an uncredited Robert M. Fresco. One is tempted to give Fresco considerable due, despite the lack of screen credit, since he had monsters in his blood. A few years earlier, Fresco scripted the teleplay for "No Food for Thought" on *Science Fiction Theater* (1955, USA) and parlayed that in record time into scripting its big-screen expansion into Universal-International's giant spider hit **TARANTULA** (1955). Fresco also scripted the imaginative crystals-from-space sf gem **THE MONOLITH MONSTERS** (1957) for the same Universal stable, and had an uncredited role in the writing of **THE 27th DAY** (1957) and **THE ALLIGATOR PEOPLE** (1959) for other studios.

The Universal connection is stronger still: Vogel had been a contract editor at Universal (and its 1950s incarnation, Universal-International) until his directorial debut with **THE MOLE PEOPLE** (1956, USA). Vogel helmed **RYMDINVASION I LAPPLAND** after completing **THE KETTLES ON OLD MACDONALD'S FARM** and **THE LAND UNKNOWN** (both 1957) for Universal, and *before* his plunge into directing for television (in 1959 alone, Vogel directed episodes of *Shotgun Slade, Mike Hammer, M Squad*, and *Laramie*), where he labored for decades. Vogel directed only one other theatrical feature film, a rather anachronistic fantasy for Universal, **THE SWORD OF ALI BABA** (1965). By then, Arthur C. Pierce had a hand in no less than *seven* science-fiction films either in theaters or in production—**THE HUMAN DUPLICATORS, MUTINY IN OUTER SPACE** (both 1965, USA), **WOMEN OF THE PREHISTORIC PLANET, DESTINATION INNER SPACE, THE NAVY VS. THE NIGHT MONSTERS, DIMENSION 5**, and **CYBORG 2087** (all 1966, USA)—with the SF/spy adventure **THE DESTRUCTORS** (1968, USA) soon to follow. Genre scholar/

Two more of Arthur C. Pierce's 1960s sf scripts made it to the big screen during Pierce's busiest year: the man-fish tale **DESTINATION INNER SPACE** and the carnivorous sentient plant thriller **THE NAVY VS. THE NIGHT MONSTERS** (both 1966).

Lars Åhrén as the monster: Åhrén also appeared in the film as a military man (the officer in the white parka who interrupts our hero's dance with the heroine to corral everyone for a midnight jaunt on a snowcat) and as the tall alien which appears to the heroine (and points to the monster footprint in the snow).

author/interviewer Tom Weaver has discussed this Swedish diversion in print with Vogel and Pierce, but given what's actually on the screen, there's little in **RYMDINVASION I LAPPLAND** and even less in **INVASION OF THE ANIMAL PEOPLE** traceable to either Vogel or Pierce. It's such a singular, strange, and suffocating SF film: one cannot help but wonder, *who dunnit?* True, the film, such as it was and is, was contemporary to a flurry of activity from Pierce, who wrote and scripted **THE COSMIC MAN** (1959, USA) and **BEYOND THE TIME BARRIER** (1960, USA), and there arguably are elusive, primarily *atmospheric* bonds with those two curios, though that's a stretch.

Still, how did it all congeal in Sweden—and who to primarily credit or blame? Follow the money. Producer Bertil Jernberg had only two features to his name (including Bengt Blomgren's **LINJE SEX**, 1958), and his brother appeared in this film (as a telegraph operator and as one of the aliens). Jernberg was the shaker-and-mover behind the scenes. However, it was co-producer Gustaf Unger who sold the movie to Jerry Warren.[1] Unger had been a screen actor since the late 1930s, and worked his way up to become associate producer of Albert Band's borderline-horror Stephen Crane adaptation **FACE OF FIRE** (1959, USA) and producer of the ill-fated unsold TV series *13 Demon Street* (also 1959). Three of the five unsold episodes of *13 Demon Street*[2] were edited into **THE DEVIL'S MESSENGER** (1961, USA); Unger likely washed his hands of **RYMDINVASION I LAPPLAND** in desperation, given all the labor surrounding *13 Demon Street*'s ambitions and failure. Whatever the case, Unger couldn't have cherry-picked a worse American distributor. Unless it was a marketplace orphan, one can only wonder how Jerry Warren ended up with **RYMDINVASION I LAPPLAND**, which was completely laundered of its Swedish heritage once Warren was done with it. We should perhaps credit the extraterrestrial yeti-like monster design to special effects man Odert von Schoultz—his sole screen credit, as far as I can see—and the

Jack Kirby/Dick Ayers cover art, *Tales to Astonish* #18 (April 1961)

Jack Kirby/Dick Ayers splash page art, *Journey Into Mystery* #75 (December 1961)

---

[1] There is considerable confusion at IMDb and affiliated on-line sources (including Swedish sites) over who Unger is, his relationship with Jernberg. Bertil Jernberg's commentary track on the 2001 Something Weird DVD has been grossly misinterpreted, confusing Unger for Jernberg's brother; they were not one and the same person. Unger's brother was actor Bertil Unger (see http://www.imdb.com/name/nm0881129/?ref_=nmbio_trv_1), not Bertil Jernberg. Co-producer Gustaf Unger has a cameo in the film—at the 8m 10s point in **TERROR IN THE MIDNIGHT SUN**, Unger is the man with the moustache wearing dark glasses on the plane seated behind the heroes—at which point in the commentary track Jernberg points Unger out, and indicates it was Unger who sold the US rights to Jerry Warren and kept the money for himself ("...it was a tragedy...he treated a lot of film companies [badly]...we had no idea what happened [until afterwards]..." cited from 8m 10s through 9m 33s). The subsequent conflating of Unger with Jernberg's "brother" is in complete error—Jernberg clearly (and quite happily) points out his brother as another player altogether in two different cameos. He doesn't sound pleased when pointing out Unger, whom Jernberg never refers to as "my brother." A subject for further research and long overdue correction; for more on Bertil S. Jernberg, see http://smdb.kb.se/catalog/id/000151464#.

[2] The complete *13 Demon Street*—all thirteen episodes!—is still available from Something Weird Video on DVD-R at http://www.somethingweird.com/product_info.php?products_id=21502

Top: original Swedish poster art.
Above: the monster is shot in the face after delivering evidence of the heroine's plight (the wound is visible on the right side of its snout); former journalist and co-owner of AB Iris-Film (Stockholm-based distributor of the film) Lars Åhrén donned the monster suit.

47

the **INVASION OF THE ANIMAL PEOPLE** theatrical release would attract any sentient being anywhere near a movie theater.

Furthermore, it's difficult to believe that *any* movie could be as dreadful as the advertising artwork created for the American 1962 double-bill. **INVASION OF THE ANIMAL PEOPLE** truly sported, hands-down, the *worst-ever* SF ad art for *any* American theatrical rollout.[3] I'll happily stand corrected if someone knows of worse promotional artwork for a theatrical release—and yes, I know, there's some mighty stiff competition—but cheapjack independent producer/director Jerry Warren sank lower than ever before (or after) with this ad campaign.

But there's truth in advertising here: the Jerry Warren version of the movie really *is* as disorienting and dreadful as the ad campaign.

—

Cheapjack indy producer/director Jerry Warren picked up this Swedish science-fiction oddity, mucked about with it for possibly two years (rendering it truly incomprehensible in the bargain), and dumped it on American markets with a film entitled **TERROR OF THE BLOODHUNTERS** (1962, USA), a Jerry Warren original. **BLOODHUNTERS** was and remains anachronistic and grueling, but its painfully talky 60 minutes of escaping-from-Devil's-Island-to-faux-Brazil jungle movie antics were (and remain) the more coherent of the two movies—**BLOODHUNTERS** actually makes *linear sense*, which is more than anyone ever could have said about **INVASION OF THE ANIMAL PEOPLE.**

This does not mean **INVASION OF THE ANIMAL PEOPLE** is *worse*. It only means it makes no sense, and that, in a winter-set monster movie, could be a good thing.

At the tender age of seven, I was far too young to convince any sane adult with a driver's license to take me to the local drive-in to see **INVASION OF THE ANIMAL PEOPLE**, so I had to wait until it surfaced on broadcast television, after midnight, on some regional equivalent of *The Late Show.*

I caught it, appropriately enough, in the dead of winter, when the living room windows were

imagery to Stockholm-born Ingmar Bergman cinematographer Hilding Bladh, but these crazy-quilt credentials only deepens the mysterious allure of this most peculiar monster movie.

While I am a great advocate for viewing movies in the context of their original era and theatrical release, I have strong reservations about doing so with this film. For one thing, the movie is oddly timeless, as in it doesn't seem to harken from any specific time in cinema history, nor does it seem to unreel in anything remotely resembling real time. For another thing, it's hard to fathom how anyone thought the wretched ad campaign cooked up for

John Carradine appeared in Jerry Warren's **THE INCREDIBLE PETRIFIED WORLD** (1957) and **FRANKENSTEIN ISLAND** (1981), and insert footage for Warren's imports.

Far Left: The painfully crude ad and promotional art for Jerry Warren's US release version incorporated cut-and-paste elements from Warren's **MAN BEAST** (1956).

Jerry Warren: *"**ANIMAL PEOPLE** was really not an import; that was an American production that was shot in Northern Sweden and the Arctic Circle. Virgil Vogel directed the stuff over there, I directed extra scenes here. I did my scenes for **ANIMAL PEOPLE** in color, and I don't remember why. It was released in black-and-white. That was all done in English language."*

(Warren, interviewed by and © 1988, 2006, 2017 Tom Weaver, quoted with permission, from *Interviews with B Science Fiction and Horror Movie Makers: Writers, Producers, Directors, Actors, Moguls, and Makeup* by Tom Weaver, John and Michael Brunas (1988, McFarland; reprinted 2006).

---

[3] Also see the British quad poster for the UK release of the same film under the title **TERROR IN THE MIDNIGHT SUN**—it's not *much* better than the Jerry Warren ad art, but it at least does some measure of justice to the mighty Yak-Yeti monster. The British artist rendered the beast as a curly-furred koala bear-kinda monster with "Wacky Teeth" inserts, firing rays from its eyes. It's better than the Jerry Warren US release art, and it isn't *ugly* ad art—just stupid movie ad art.

TERROR IN THE MIDNIGHT SUN is the title that some English-speaking theatrical markets used, as evidenced by this generic Australian daybill poster that revealed nothing of the film's SF premise or nature.

A closeup of Lars Åhrén in the monster mask and suit, affording a closer look at how the mask fit and the makeup artist's attention to the facial wound the beast suffers.

blurred with frost. I had to keep the sound *really low* so as not to wake my parents; I could barely hear the damned thing. For that matter, I could barely *see* it, either! Obscured by static and poor reception (in the days of antennae-only TV reception), unable to hear much of anything, and fearing I was somehow dropping off to sleep between commercials (surely, the movie had to make *some* sense, right? I must have been missing something vital!), **INVASION OF THE ANIMAL PEOPLE** was among the most impenetrable movies I'd ever endured in the wee hours on TV. Maybe **MONSTER A-GO-GO** (1965, USA) was more incomprehensible—I know I stayed awake for every agonizing second of that atrocity—but it was a tough call.

Years later, I caught up with **INVASION OF THE ANIMAL PEOPLE** again as a teenager. I stayed awake this time; I made certain of that. *I hadn't slept through a nanosecond.* So it was true: **INVASION OF THE ANIMAL PEOPLE** *made absolutely no sense!*

Jerry Warren had hacked the original film down, rendering it utterly incoherent, *then* tried to remedy the crude lobotomy with his usual ploy: adding interminable insert footage of John Carradine prattling gibberish, but sounding as authoritative as hell.

Adding to the mush, Warren *also* stuck *another* lengthy expositional sequence into **ANIMAL PEOPLE** that seemed to have been concocted for some hellish classroom educational film. A "scientist" in a bare-walled set talked about hearing (a lengthy passage I recall actually putting my ear against the TV console speaker in hopes of hearing this dope yap about hearing). He manhandled a prop skull to demonstrate, oh, I don't know what, and droned on *and on and on* until I was ready to rupture my eardrum with an icepick just to *shut him up*.

No wonder I was in a haze as a mere lad, trying to fathom the unfathomable!

Alas, this was a typical Jerry Warren tactic, one I later endured via late-night broadcasts of

RYMDINVASION I LAPPLAND's downed spaceship emulated Ray Bradbury/Jack Arnold's **IT CAME FROM OUTER SPACE** (1953)'s UFO.

continued on page 53

It would seem that **RYMDIN-VASION I LAPPLAND** was doomed to have horrible theatrical art no matter what country released it outside of its native Sweden. **Left, top to bottom:** The afro-sporting monster from a Spanish poster, The "as drawn by a five-year-old" creation for its UK release, and the fuzzy wuzzy featured on a Mexican lobby card that thankfully included an actual photo of the monster from the movie!

Below: The only legit release on DVD of the film was from Mike Vraney's Something Weird Video. It features both versions of the film, the original and Jerry Warren's butchered and bastardized edition. The DVD is full of extra bonus material which includes audio commentary from producer Bertil Jenberg, assorted shorts subjects, and an episode of the ultra-rare Swedish TV show *13 Demon Street* which was produced by **RYMDINVASION I LAPPLAND**'s Gustaf Unger. As of this writing the DVD is still in print and available from various online sources

Jack Kirby/Dick Ayers cover art, *Tales to Astonish* #12 (October 1960)

Excitement, Thrills in Invasion of the Animal People

(REVIEW)

Invasion of the Animal People is an unusual film drama even for good science fiction. It yesterday thrilled a receptive audience at the .... theater. It is a story placed in the icy territory of the artic circle where survival is quite difficult even without the added menace of the huge creatures that land in their space craft after a long journey from another planet. A scientific expedition led by Dr. Frederic Wilson, an eminent geologist find the giant space ship between the walls of a glacier and flee to tell the world of their discovery. The scientists find they are actually prisoners in the wilderness of snow as their airplane was demolished by one of the space creatures who are twenty feet tall with tremendous power. The tension and suspense begins to mount as actual contact is made with the terrifying monsters. The action races to a most effective climax amid the fury of thousands of frightened natives of the arctic country in their bid to free themselves of the invading monsters.

The picture was well directed, and has many outstanding angles that photograph the impact with startling effects. Performances by John Carradine, Barbara Wilson and Robert Burton are crisp interpretations of the interesting story.

Two New Thrillers Screen Currently

Invasion of the Animal People together with Terror of the Bloodhunters make up twin shocker show now playing at the .... theater.

Thrills and high adventure beginning at the freezing arctic and ultimately reaching the dark Amazon jungle are to be seen as the two new pictures make their mark in chilling tradition.

Invasion of the Animal People deals with the landing of alien creatures from another world and the great havoc and destruction these monsters cause to Lapland villages and everything that blocks their path. As a scientific expedition finds itself powerless against the thrust of gigantic forces possessed by the aliens its plight is doubled by terrifying exposure to the perilous arctic elements including explosive avalanches of tremendous proportions.

Loaded with thrills and chills from the frozen glaciers of one of the remote stretches of the planet upon which we live Invasion of the Animal People explodes with unexpected events caused by the monster men from another world as they land upon earth and create terror in the hearts of all in their path. Seeming to possess only a bestial nature but having at their control powerful forces of advanced scientific design the animal people prove that humanity is a weak match by comparison. The picture is endowed with great excitement and suspense together with a surge of added peril, this the strange elements of the arctic circle.

New Science Fiction Film

Invasion of the Animal People, a new science fiction thriller is currently playing at the .... theater. The picture deals with alien monsters from another world and their treacherous attack upon the earth.

This Page & Next: Jerry Warren's pressbook material to promote **INVASION OF THE ANIMAL PEOPLE** and its lackluster jungle movie co-feature **TERROR OF THE BLOODHUNTERS**; note the elements from Warren's **MAN BEAST** (1956) *[bottom right on p.52]* ad-art integrated into the **ANIMAL PEOPLE** ad-slick's graphics.

(ADVANCE)

One of the most startling adventures of science fiction opens....................at the....................theater and unfolds its unusual story of beings from another part of the universe who land on our own planet earth.

What with today's peering into deep space and all it engulfs with endless possibilities of life on many of the worlds in our solar system as well as thousands of others it becomes apparent that a visit from alien planets could soon be an actuality. In invasion of the animal people John Carradine takes the audience to a remote part of our world where such a landing by space people causes thrills of magnitude together with dramatic impact throughout the entire picture. Scenes beautifully photographed in the vast arctic circle are authentic and bring to the screen a scope of splendor along with the erie suspense and action.

Well photographed and directed, Invasion of the Animal People features together with Carradine, Barbara Wilson and Robert Burton who enact the unique story in convincing fashion. The animal people themselves due to effective makeup are viewed with a feeling of reality and bring forth a frightening series of thrills as they move with authority amid the well planned special effects.

The picture is designed for all age groups and will please the sophisticated audience as well as others. Other half of the double feature program is the shocker Terror of the Bloodhunters.

New Dimension Of Thrills In 'Animal People'

(CURRENT)

John Carradine, one of Hollywood's veteran showmen takes the audience to the far away arctic circle for science fiction adventure in Invasion of the Animal People now playing at the....................theater.

The picture is showing with another shocker Terror of the Bloodhunters.

INVASION OF THE ANIMAL PEOPLE
SYNOPSIS

A young girl, Diane Wilson is awakened during the night by a strange pulsating sound that seems to come from above. As she jumps from her bed she feels the strange sensation of some kind of magnetism which draws at her. The high pitched sound continues and she becomes panicky trying to maintain her senses. Diane runs from the house and out to the street trying to escape the force that engulfs her. A police patrol car sees the pajama clad girl in the streets and upon finding her in shock takes her to the hospital. Specialists examine Diane and outside of reports of a mystery object seen in the sky can find no theory for her seizure. Diane recovers fully in a few days and apparently has no ill effects. She leaves for Switzerland and a needed vacation. Being a ski enthusiast Diane enjoys the beautiful snow covered slopes of Switzerland and a reunion with her uncle, Dr. Frederick Wilson, a geologist. Her quietude is undisturbed until Dr. Wilson receives a call from the science institute stating he is to leave at once to investigate a strange phenomena, that of a giant meteor that has fallen in the snow covered mountains. Diane, full of adventure and intrigue by her uncle's young assistant Eric Engstrom, wents to join the expedition. Dr. Wilson turns thumbs down on the request and tells her to wait for them to return.

Diane devilishly decides to stow away on her uncles plane and join the expedition anyway. She is discovered by Eric just before the plane lands in the icy plains of the arctic circle. The group of scientists take Diane with them as they push through the snow to the sight of the giant meteor. Upon reaching it they find it is certainly no meteor but instead a space craft of alien origin. They leave quickly to radio the information from the plane but upon reaching it find only shambles of what once was the machine that flew them there . . . Leading away from the wrecked plane they see giant footprints made by a monster. Dr. Wilson sends Eric and Diane on skis to try to reach help at a village in the hope a rescue party can be dispatched before they freeze to death.

Eric and Diane start off but never reach the village. The entire arctic circle is ravished by the monsters from another world who seem bent upon destroying everything in their path. They crush their way through village after village leaving shambles everywhere. Diane is captured by a huge creature and taken to the space craft for observation. Eric, Dr. Wilson and hundreds of native Laplanders attack the monster in the attempt to save Diane. They start snow and ice tumbling from the mountains in a gigantic avalanche. Diane is rescued as the space ship takes off in fear of being covered by the tons of ice and snow.

ATTACK OF THE MAYAN MUMMY (1964 Warren re-edit of the 1957 Mexican opus LA MOMIA AZTECA), in which it was Roger Corman regular Bruno VeSota's mad gibbering that made me want to rip off my own face.

Okay, back to my childhood first-exposure to ANIMAL PEOPLE. It was slow going. I was tired. I had school the next day. The sound was muffled, the picture fizzing in and out of static. I feared I was falling asleep. I couldn't figure out what the hell was going on.

Still, I stuck with it. Those photos Forry Ackerman had published in *Spacemen* and *Famous Monsters of Filmland* had promised me a big, furry, fanged monster, and by the Jesus, *I was going to stay awake long enough to see it!*

Eventually, things happen; it's outdoors, it's fucking cold, snow is everywhere, people are skiing around, there's a crashed UFO, and then—*oh-thank-God!*—the hunky Yeti-kinda-guy galumphs into the proceedings.

—

I'll get back to the movie in a moment—first, I want to trace my adult attempts to wrestle and re-engage with this curio.

Mind you, it wasn't the *movie* that stuck with me, it was the *monster*, and the stubborn enigma of the damned movie surrounding it. What was this cockamamie creature concoction? I couldn't shake my obsession with it! Complicating my memories were the incredible photos of the monster that would pop up in Denis Gifford books and the occasional magazine, which made its allure stronger.

Eager to see the monster anew, I caught it again on late-night TV as a teenager. ANIMAL PEOPLE seemed to vanish from the airwaves in the 1970s, but in the 1980s I bought it on VHS when it was first available via Sinister Cinema. Damn—that didn't help at all. It was *still* impenetrable.

Thankfully, the late great Mike Vraney also had a soft spot in his skull for this movie. Under Vraney's helm, Something Weird Video & Image co-packaged Warren's aborted fetus of a movie *with* the original unedited Virgil Vogel Swedish feature RYMDINVASION I LAPPLAND on DVD in the summer of 2001, allowing us to at last see the real McCoy.[4]

The British Panther Book paperback cover art for the classic 1953 'contactee' account by Desmond Leslie and George Adamski, which was translated in multiple languages and became a bestseller. The controversial Adamski also wrote *Inside the Spaceships* (1955, a.k.a. *Inside the Flying Saucers*), *Telepathy: The Cosmic or Universal Language* (three volumes, 1958), *Flying Saucers Farewell* (1961, a.k.a. *Behind the Flying Saucer Mystery*), and *Cosmic Philosophy* (1961) before his death on April 3rd, 1965 at age 74.

The film's oddball aliens, that sort of resemble "Nordic" humanoid extraterrestrials of old school 1950s contactee days

And, well, to be honest, clocking in at a mere 69 minutes, the original Swedish movie is still a slight confection. There's still precious little of either Vogel's, Arthur Pierce's, or Robert Fresco's imprimatur evident, though it does sport a theme song—"Terror in the Midnight Sun"—sung by the Golden Gate Quartet, anticipating Otto Brandenburg's singing of "Journey to the 7th Planet" in 1962 for that Danish Sidney Pink extravaganza.

Let me put it this way: Denmark has REPTILICUS, and Sweden has RYMDINVASION I LAPPLAND, and all is right with the world of giant monster movies that they each have only the one.

But RYMDINVASION I LAPPLAND *is* atmospheric and weird, and—damn it all—I *love* it for the mongrel dog it is; and, per usual, Mike's crew added special bonus features, including footage from a genuine celebratory Lapland reindeer festival that boasts women gelding reindeer with their teeth.

I kid you not. This, of course, makes for essential viewing.

Thanks to that Something Weird DVD release, which as I mentioned includes the original Swedish version, I now grok *some* of what happens.

Let's see: American skater Barbara Wilson is in love with a young scientist, or he's in love with her (it seems reciprocal); a meteor-thingie crashes into the snow, but it *isn't* a meteor, it's a spacecraft of some kind. Something is alive inside—we get occasional glimpses of the big-headed alien

---

[4] At the time of this writing, you can still pick up the Something Weird/Image DVD release for bargain prices online, and at Amazon (http://www.amazon.com/Terror-Midnight-Invasion-Animal-Special/dp/B00005KH2Q/ref=sr_1_1?ie=UTF8&s=dvd&qid=1258832768&sr=8-1). There was also a Swedish DVD release of RYMDINVASION I LAPPLAND released by Klubb Super 8 in 2005; it looks like the contents are identical to the Something Weird/Image DVD, and it was still in print as of this writing (via http://klubbsuper8.com at their web shop: http://shop.textalk.se/se/article.php?id=7769&art=1303958)

53

The snowman demolishes a Lapland lavvu, or kota (we call 'em tipis); it's not as spectacular as Godzilla leveling Tokyo, but it's all relative.

humanoids, sometimes vague, sometimes sharp and clear—and whatever-they-are materializes or manifests, somehow, the big fuzzy Yeti-kind-of-thingie that stomps around in the snow and puts the bricks to a Lapp village.

This destruction (pretty low on the "monster on the loose" yardstick, mind you, but cool nonetheless) naturally pisses off the Lapp villagers, who mobilize into a torch-wielding mob and torch Yeti-guy. Bye-bye, Yeti-guy. All this overt hostility prompts the hasty retreat of the meteor (via the crash footage being rerun backwards). Invasion averted!

As a kid, I loved the big hairy Yeti-like monster; it was all worth the wait once he showed up. Yeti-guy seemed to be servant to the barely-seen alien invaders. Did they carry him in their ship? Did they make him? Did they crash-thaw Yeti-guy out of an icy prison? It's not clear, but whatever the case, he seems to be their servant.[5]

He reminded me of my favorite giant bugaboos in the Jack Kirby/Stan Lee (pre-Marvel) Atlas giant monster comics. I doodled portraits (*"poor-traits"*) of the fanged yak yeti in my school notebooks (and on the edge of the pages of my science textbook, which got me some lumps from my teacher). I even drew a couple of my own crude comics stories with the yak-yeti-thingie-

---

[5] In the 2001 Something Weird Video DVD commentary track, producer Bertil Jernberg explained, "...the monster was like a search dog they sent out to look... and he was a kind monster—but we didn't know that, because he was tall." You know, he always seemed like a benevolent monster, to me, though his origins remain sketchy—and it was impossible to see the gunshot wound on his muzzle in the TV broadcasts of the fuzzy Jerry Warren prints.

guy, spinning wilder yarns than the film offered. In the movie, the monster didn't really do much of anything, it seemed.

Watching it as an adult, I see I was right. Yak-yeti-dude *didn't* do much: he killed some reindeer (off-screen), stomped and trashed some *tipis* (actually, *lavvu* or *kota* in Lapland) and cabins, smashed an airplane (maybe two), then he did the **KING KONG** routine, carrying a dummy of the heroine around in his furry talons until those torch-wielding skiers turned up the heat, setting yak-yeti-dude on fire. He plunged off a cliff to his apparent death, a demise so murkily conveyed that I'm not sure I really understood that was what had happened to him when I was watching the movie as a kid (by then, it must have been almost 1 AM; maybe I had fallen asleep, but I don't think so). Again, I chalk my confusion up to the crappy Jerry Warren prints and fuzzy TV signals: it's obvious in the original version of the film that the torched monster is completely immolated.

Just like in the Lee/Kirby monster comics, the humans taking out the big ugly sent its alien masters packing (reverse-motion handily tidying up any lingering snow skidmarks as they lifted off).

Though I can't really recommend the movie, I still love it. It seems like I always have. It boasts an uncanny atmosphere, some haunting imagery, and I'm drawn to it every couple of years for a revisit.

It's slow as slogging through six-foot snowdrifts with snap-up boots on your feet, and the imagery is often so dimmed (by alternating brightness, murk, and darkness) that I often wonder if I'm still snowblind from that time at age eight I was outside for too long in a blazing January sun trekking over the wintery Duxbury VT landscapes we used to freeze our fingers and feet playing on. But that's part and parcel of its enduring charm.

So, like much in life: lame frame, cool monster.

©2006, 2010, and 2014 Stephen R. Bissette, revised and expanded from *Myrant* November 21, 2006 (http://srbissette.com/?p=7067) and December 23, 2010 (http://srbissette.com/?p=10589)

The following Arthur C. Pierce interview excerpt is from the cover-feature interview originally published in Raymond F. Young's excellent fanzine Magick Theatre #8 (1987); cover reprinted with permission. [Scan courtesy of The Fentonian Institution.]

ARTHUR C. PIERCE
(1923–1987)

To further illuminate the backstory behind **TERROR IN THE MIDNIGHT SUN** (*Rymdinvasion i Lappland*, a.k.a. **INVASION OF THE ANIMAL PEOPLE**, 1959/1962, USA/Sweden), Kevin R. Danzey's "Arthur C. Pierce" cover interview from the NYC-based fanzine *Magick Theatre* #8 (1987) offers the screenwriter's account of the film's making. The following excerpt (and accompanying photo of Pierce) appears in print here with Kevin's very kind permission; deepest thanks, Kevin!

As with imaginative author/filmmakers like Ib Melchior, Pierce (September 8th, 1923 to November 17th, 1987) was involved in a number of inventive low-budget science-fiction films from the 1950s and 1970s that are too-often dismissed or laughed at as artifacts worthy only of derision. I've great affection for Pierce's creative screen efforts, which began with his work in industrial films leading into scripting the short *The Adventures of Sam Space* (1955), the unsold pilot for the proposed series *The Silent Service* ("The Cravelle's Mine Plant," 1958), **THE COSMIC MAN** (1959), **TERROR IN THE MIDNIGHT SUN**, and **BEYOND THE TIME BARRIER** ([1960] the latter directed by Edgar G. Ulmer, in which Pierce is briefly seen onscreen in an uncredited role as one of the renegade mutants). Working with Hugo Grimaldi, Pierce subsequently wrote and co-directed (sans screen credit) the one-two punch of **MUTINY IN OUTER SPACE** and **THE HUMAN DUPLICATORS** (both 1965), which he also co-produced without credit; the former was essentially remade just four years later, without acknowledgement, as **THE GREEN SLIME** (ガンマー第3号 宇宙大作戦 / *Ganmā daisan gō: uchū daisakusen*, 1968, USA/Japan). 1966 was the banner year for Pierce, having scripted (both with and without credit) the double-bill of **THE NAVY VS. THE NIGHT MONSTERS** and **WOMEN OF THE PREHISTORIC PLANET** (which he also directed, with credit), the peculiar 'fish-man' SF movie **DESTINATION INNER SPACE**, and both **DIMENSION 5** and **CYBORG 2087**; the latter especially holds up as an entertainingly original, at times prescient, precursor to much-more-successful later SF productions like **THE TERMINATOR** (1984). Pierce also scripted **THE DESTRUCTORS** (1968), three episodes of the short-lived TV series *The Next Step Beyond* (1978) and the feature **THE ASTRAL FACTOR** (1978), plus two segments of the popular teleseries *Fantasy Island* (1982, 1983). Kevin Danzey's *Magick Theatre* interview with Pierce remains Pierce's definitive account of his filmmaking career.

Interviewer Kevin R. Danzey's favorite photo of the late great Arthur C. Pierce (photo ©1987, 2017 Kevin R. Danzey, used with permission).

Author's Note: *The interview from which the following is an excerpt originally appeared in Raymond F. Young's excellent New York-based fanzine* **Magick Theatre** *(#8, 1987). ©1987, 2017 Kevin Robert Danzey; excerpted with Kevin's kind permission.]*

KRD: So THE COSMIC MAN [*1959, USA*] was completed, and you had your first screenwriting credit...

ACP: Well, it was a marvelous experience, but I couldn't really use it too well because I wasn't a member of the guild. I had to have another credit, so it was called—*originally* called—**TERROR IN THE MIDNIGHT SUN** [*TERROR I MIDNATTSOLEN*].

KRD: Which was retitled INVASION OF THE ANIMAL PEOPLE!! I know you don't like to talk about that one.

ACP: It's just *awful* what they can do to you. And yet the picture made money! It still plays once in a while on TV. A lot of people think it's a good science fiction picture.

KRD: I like it. There are some parts in it that are really good.

ACP: Well, the monster is totally ridiculous.

KRD: You're talking about the big woolly thing.

ACP: It was totally wrong! I mean, the concept was not that hideous-looking of a thing. They had flashing lights in his teeth, and he was too huge and hairy. It made no sense. Why would they bring such a creature here? It wasn't supposed to be *that* gigantic. And then they added scenes.

KRD: With John Carradine lecturing for several minutes...

ACP: They shot those here (the bulk of the film was shot in Sweden), and they had *nothing* to do with it. To me, it screwed it all up.

KRD: What a lot of people like are the very atmospheric scenes of the aliens and the girl.

ACP: They were neat. I liked them. Virgil Vogel directed that picture, and I'm glad he did.

KRD: But there's a directing co-credit for Jerry Warren.

ACP: Well, that's because of the stuff with Carradine. But Virgil *really* liked that script, and wanted to make something of it, and he did as best he could.

KRD: So what happened?

ACP: They had trouble getting a release, so they added scenes and got Carradine's name in, and that helped them.

[End of excerpt]

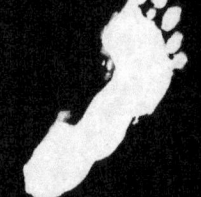

VIRGIL W. VOGEL on TERROR IN THE MIDNIGHT SUN
(a.k.a. INVASION OF THE ANIMAL PEOPLE)

Here is an excerpt from Tom Weaver's interview with director Virgil W. Vogel (1919-1996), reprinted with the kind permission of Tom Weaver. The full interview was originally published in Fangoria *magazine (#73, May 1988) under the heading "Terror on the Low-Budget Express". Both Vogel and Weaver referred to the film by its alternate release title* **TERROR IN THE MIDNIGHT SUN** *during the interview, so it shall remain. [Any editorial additions are inserted in italics within square brackets.]*

TW: How did you become involved on TERROR IN THE MIDNIGHT SUN?

VWV: Gustaf Unger [*1920-1995*], a Swedish newspaper columnist here in LA who had been connected with the film business for years, decided to make a science-fiction picture in Sweden. He contacted a fellow in the Universal [*Pictures*] publicity department and asked him who was a good director. I had been very heavily connected with all the Universal sci-fi things, so he recommended me... Universal had just gone broke, and just as they were closing up, this publicity fellow told me to call Unger, who was looking for a director. So I did, and I went. We stayed in Riksgränsen in Northern Sweden, above the rail center at Abisko. It's a very interesting place up there, but colder than shit! We were up there in the wintertime, and it was 60 degrees below zero. I was very young then, but I don't think I've ever been so cold... Gustaf and his co-producer brother Bertil [*Unger*] are identical twins, and to this day they dress alike and wear monocles. One wears the monocle in the right eye; one wears it in the left eye. They are real characters.

TW: What kind of money went into this film?

VWV: The American investment in that film was something like $20,000—that was supposed to have been *half* of it—and the Swedes put up the other $20,000. But, of course, working above the Arctic Circle slowed things down to a halt at times, and everything took longer than we'd anticipated. We went out one day and we did some aerial photography. Really, we got some beautiful footage that day. When the picture ran out of money, they ran this footage for the lab, and the lab came up with some money for us because they thought it looked so good! ...I could not ski, and there was no other method of transportation up there. If you didn't go on skis, you went by helicopter. One morning they put the cameraman and myself and two Arriflexes with tripods, batteries and film in the helicopter to fly us down to

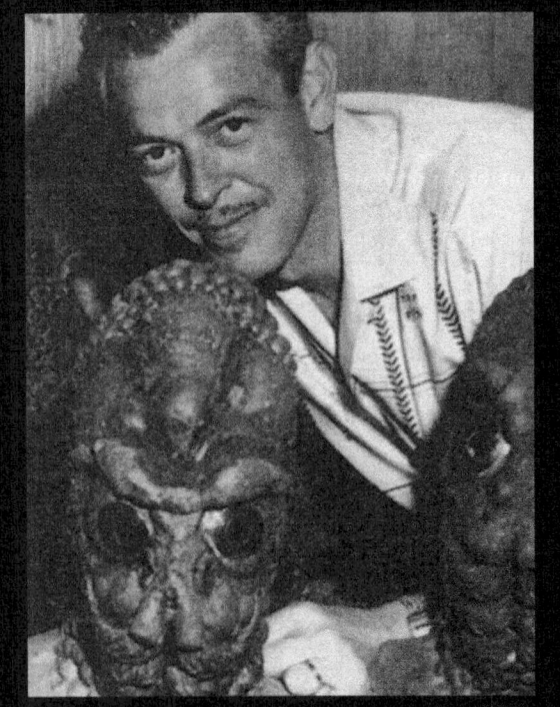

Virgil W. Vogel with masks from Universal's 1956 classic **THE MOLE PEOPLE**, *which was his first directorial job*

the location. As we were flying down, we flew over the site of an accident: There had been an avalanche which had descended on an ore train, and it scattered the cars like matchboxes all over the white snow. The engines were all smoking, making lots of steam, and a few guys were running around. We flew over there and looked at it, and the cameraman pointed out to me how it happened and so on. Then we went down to Abisko and shot our scene. I later realized how *dumb* that was—here I was, doing this story about a monster attacking the Northland. All we'd have to do was put the helicopter down and we could have made a whole sequence out of it. But instead we looked at it like tourists, then went on about our business!

TW: There's a lot wrong with TERROR IN THE MIDNIGHT SUN, but many fans like its strange, arty atmosphere.

VWV: I had just worked with Orson Welles as film editor on **TOUCH OF EVIL** [*1958, USA*], and my heart was full of Orson [*laughs*], so I did all I could. But then, of course, Jerry Warren, who released the picture in the US, took as much of that *out* of the picture as he could. You should have seen it before he got ahold of it. It was a great piece of artistic work.

TW: What do you remember about the man who played the monster?

VWV: He was a newspaperman [*named Lars Åhrén, according to the IMDb and producer Bertil Jernberg's commentary track on the Something Weird DVD*], and he came in and did it as a lark. He also put some of the Swedish money into it. He just had the ball of his life.

TW: Were you pleased with other members of your Swedish cast?

VWV: The acting in **TERROR IN THE MIDNIGHT SUN** was horrendous, but that's because we were dealing with Swedish actors, most of whom couldn't speak English, and I couldn't speak Swedish. We had this great Swedish comedian Bengt Blomgren [*1923-2013*], who did this one major role, and he had his English-language lines written phonetically in Swedish on *everything*. He had 'em hidden every place he was going to work. He would have a piece of paper with the phonetic lines wrapped around the barrel of his pipe! It was really tough on everyone… I hid the performance with production values. There was some really great, beautiful stuff I shot. We brought it home and I got my agent to look at the film, and he said, "The story's not worth shit, the performances aren't good, but visually it's a beautiful film. You've got a lot to be proud of here". It was released in Europe and did quite well,

so Gustaf and the guys in Sweden got their money out of it right away.

TW: But there was a delay before it was released over here.

VWV: There was a delay, yes. Why? I don't know. It was not my job to sell it. Many people who saw it thought it was a very, very artistic piece of work. As I mentioned before, some of the Swedish people who were speaking English were not the best performers because most times they didn't comprehend what they were saying, but the effects were very good and the scenery was gorgeous. It had all the values; maybe part of the delay was the fact that it had no recognizable names in it except Robert Burton, and he was not what you'd call a major star by any manner or means… Finally, Jerry Warren [*1925–1988*] gave them $20,000 for the rights in the US. He took the film and put John Carradine [*1906-1988*] in it. Carradine sat around and just *talked* for half the show, and Warren cut out all this great stuff I had shot, great skiing stuff and really fabulous scenery. He cut that all out and had people *sit* and *talk*! He also changed the title to **INVASION OF THE ANIMAL PEOPLE**. The original version was a hell of a lot better.

Original interview and excerpt ©1988, 1991, 2000, 2006, and 2017 by Tom Weaver, excerpted with permission. This was originally published in *Fangoria* #73 (May 1988) and subsequently reprinted in *Science Fiction Stars and Horror Heroes: Interviews with Actors, Directors, Producers, and Writers of the 1940s Through 1960s* by Tom Weaver and Michael Brunas (1991, 2006, McFarland) and *Return of the B Science Fiction and Horror Heroes: The Mutant Melding of Two Volumes of Classic Interviews* by Tom Weaver and Michael Brunas (2000, McFarland). Our thanks, Tom!

A Note on the Cryptid Casefiles…
Making the Case for a Cryptid 'Nature Guide'

A case could be made for many of the terrestrial monster movies of the past being, essentially, cryptid films. For the purposes of this book, however, it was necessary to narrow that focus down to only movie monsters which recognizably fit within the 'real-world' cryptozoological boundaries.

But, think about it: *how did/do most monster movies typically begin…?*

(1) Someone gets a fleeting glimpse of some unusual, unidentifiable creature in an environment in which it shouldn't exist and survives the encounter to report the sighting to incredulous authorities (see: **THE BEAST FROM 20,000 FATHOMS** [1953, USA], **RODAN** [空の大怪獣 ラドン / *Sora no daikaiju Radon*, 1957, Japan], **THE GIANT CLAW** [1957, USA], etc).

(2) A mysterious disappearance, cataclysmic event, or crime scene is discovered with evidence of its victims (whether human, bovine, equine, or whatever) indicating they have been attacked by some unidentified inhuman or nonhuman creature (see: **THEM!** [1954, USA], **GODZILLA, KING OF THE MONSTERS** (ゴジラ / *Gojira*, 1954, Japan], **THE BEAST OF HOLLOW MOUNTAIN** [*El monstruo de la montaña hueca*, USA/Mexico, 1954/1956], **IT CAME FROM BENEATH THE SEA** [1955], **THE BLACK SCORPION** [1957], **THE MONSTER THAT CHALLENGED THE WORLD** [1957], **EARTH VS. THE SPIDER** [1958, all USA], etc).

(3) Reports or evidence (e.g., fossils, footprints, etc.) of an unusual, unidentified or 'impossible' lifeform discovered in an exotic location initiates an expedition to the remote locale to determine whether such creatures exist—and if they do, to return with proof of their existence (see: Sir Arthur Conan Doyle's *The Lost World* [1912, UK], **THE LOST WORLD** [1925], **KING KONG** and **SON OF KONG** [both 1933], **THE JUNGLE** [1952] **CREATURE FROM THE BLACK LAGOON** [1953], **THE SNOW CREATURE** [1954, all USA], **THE ABOMINABLE SNOWMAN OF THE HIMALAYAS** [1957 UK], etc).

(4) Characters (e.g., explorers, treasure hunters, hapless travelers, etc.) stranded in a remote environment discover a previously-unknown species and try to capture it or fall prey to it, initiating a battle for survival (**UNKNOWN ISLAND** [1948], **LOST CONTINENT** [1951], **PORT SINISTER** [1953], **ATTACK OF THE CRAB MONSTERS** [1957], **THE KILLER SHREWS** [1959, all USA], etc).

It's not much of a stretch to fantasize that if such lifeforms had ever existed, popular science texts describing such creatures would exist, too. As much fun as it might be to concoct a sort of 'Golden Books/Herbert S. Zim nature guide' to these critters, I'd like to propose a more in-depth naturalist approach, including specifics of the life cycles and behavioral characteristics of such cryptids, along the lines of the seminal hominid cryptid studies which Ivan T. Sanderson and Loren Coleman have published…

How large could island-dwelling "killer shrews" grow? This 1894 engraving of the Cuban hutia (aka Desmarest's hutia, aka the hutia-conga, aka "banana rats") *Capromys pilorides* offers a formidable real-life candidate that grows up to three feet in length, weighing up to twenty pounds. It is the largest true hutia extant, but is much smaller than the now-extinct giant hutias which colonized the Caribbean islands from their South American origins, reaching the Greater Antilles over 20 million years ago.

all that was left after...

THE KILLER SHREWS

Cryptid Files: THE KILLER SHREWS

Kingdom: Animalia
Phylum: Chordata
Subphylum: Vertebrata
Class: Mammalia
Order: Soricomorpha
Family: Soricidae
Subfamily: Soricinae
Species: Blarina rex

Though scientists have long known of the Giant Mexican Shrew (Genus Megasorex) and the Giant Elephant Shrew (Rhynchocyon petersi), the so-called 'Killer Shrew' (Blarina rex) seems to be an anamoly particular to only two known island habitats off the coast of Texas. The existing populations were apparently the result of dramatic mutation caused by agents unknown; no records exist of any authorized experimentation that might have been a catalyst for such extreme mutation. Both island populations apparently succumbed to species cannibalism.

As with the common North American shrew species found in nearly all terrestrial habitats, it appeared the Killer Shrew populations favored damp brushy woodlands, bushy bogs and marshes, and weedy and bushy borders of fields. Evidence indicates they sought shelter in standing barns, cellars and sheds on both islands during inclimate weather, surviving at least four hurricanes. Investigation of the islands indicated the shrews had constructed elaborate subterranean runways between man-made shelters, and nests were found in tunnels and under larger logs and rocks.

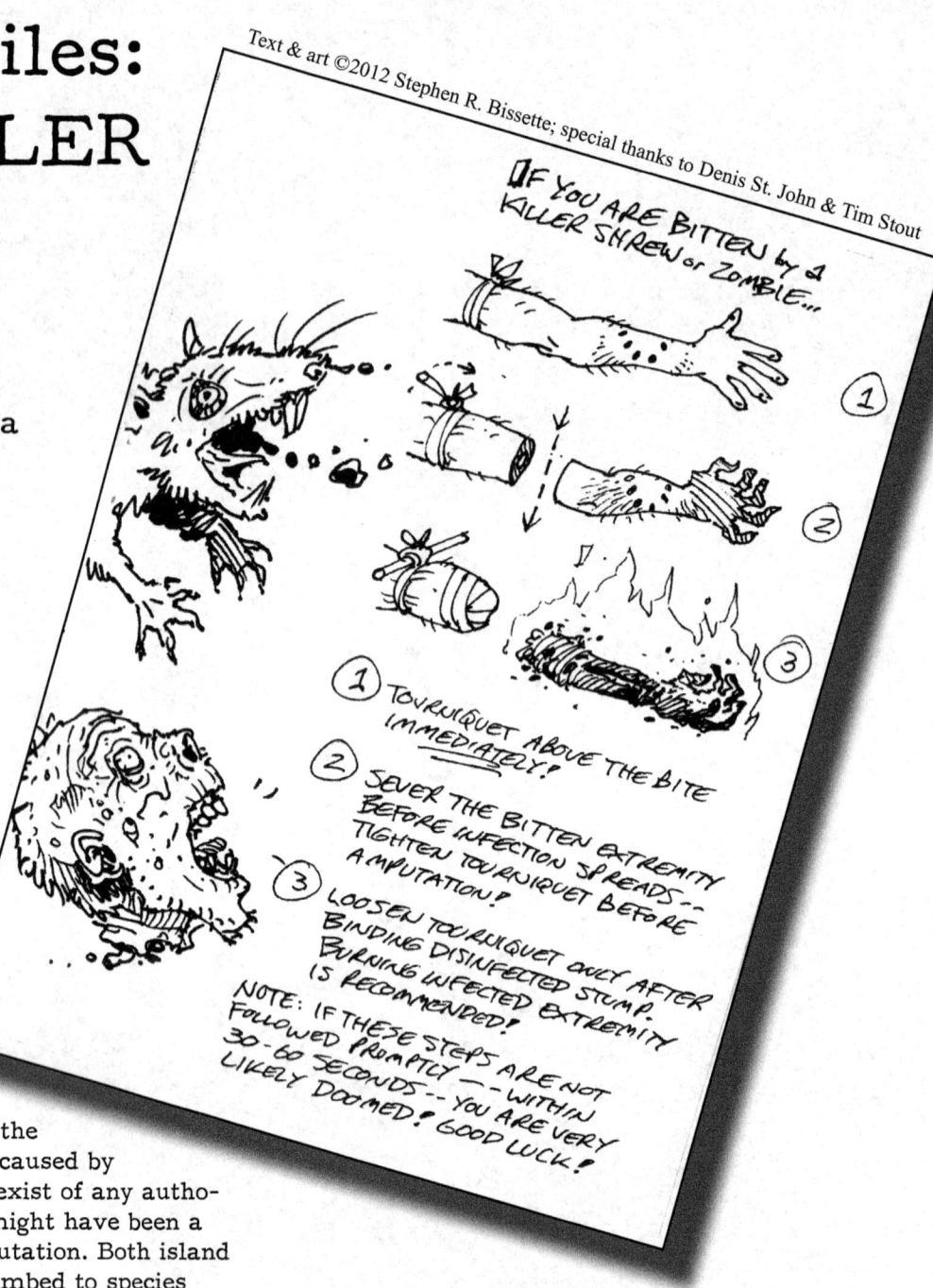

Blarina rex carcasses and remains indicate the species reached a total body length, from tip of the nose to tip of the tail, from 1000 to 1500 mm in males, and 870 to 1370 mm in females. Tail length ranges between 600 to 825 mm. Males weighed from 30 to 80 kg, with an average of 55 kg, females from 23 to 55 kg, with an average of 45 kg. Height (measured from base of paws to shoulder) generally ranged from 60 to 90 cm.. Males were slightly larger than females, especially in the skulls. The fur was velvety and soft, and the color almost uniformly brown-gray, with the underparts being only slightly paler. For the duration of their existence, Blarina rex were robust, the snout longer and heavier than that of other shrews, the tail long, the eyes small, and the ears almost completely hidden by the fur.

Some key physical features:
endothermic ; bilateral symmetry .

Sexual dimorphism: male larger.

Reproduction:

Breeding interval
Female 'Killer Shrews' may have had multiple litters throughout the warm months of the year, depending on food availability.

Breeding season
The breeding season lasted from March through September.

Number of offspring
3 to 10; avg. 6

Gestation period
22 days (high)

Time to weaning
20 days (low)

Age at sexual or reproductive maturity (female and male)
65 days (average)

Elaborate mating nests were found on both islands, built out of shredded grass or leaves and placed in deep tunnels or under logs and rocks. The breeding season extended from early spring to early fall (March-September), although some scattered reproductive activity seemed to occur throughout the entire year. Females may have up to 3 litters per year, although 2 is more usual. Gestation was 21-22 days and litter size was 3-10, although 5-7 pups is most common. The young left the nest when 18-20 days old and were weaned several days later. Females reached sexual maturity at 6 weeks, while males matured at 12 weeks. The life span may have been as long as 6 years, had they not devoured one another in less than 3.

Note: No remnants of other animal or human victims were found, though previous census figures indicate one of the two islands was inhabited prior to the Blarina rex infestation. The information provided here is in part speculative in nature, in part based on reports found sealed on the previously-uninhabited island that detailed the life cycle of the species. Portions of these documents were water-damaged; only those detailing the life cycle and habits of Blarina rex survived. The others -- which preliminary restoration indicates may have once contained information about the origin of this peculiar and unique species -- are beyond repair.

EXTRA
The Daily Tribune
EXTRA
GIANT KILLER SHREWS
IMPERIL MANKIND!
SCIENCE LOSES CONTROL
PANIC SWEEPS ENTIRE NATION
HORRIBLE DEATH WITNESSED
THE KILLER SHREWS
INGRID GOUDE ★ JAMES BEST
KEN CURTIS
GORDON McLENDON ★ BARUCH LUMET
KEN CURTIS, Producer
RAY KELLOGG, Director
A McLENDON RADIO PICTURES RELEASE

HOW TO DO A TON OF BUSINESS WITH "THE SHREWS" AND "THE MONSTER"

Dear Mr. Exhibitor:

Highly successful test markets show that the basic campaign on this double feature is radio. Television spots are excellent, either as supplementary to radio or as primary when radio is impractical.

When you use radio, we suggest as an ideal the following, realizing its impossibility in certain markets:

One 55-second spot per hour--plus one i.d. tagged onto station's call letters, or, better, one of our recorded 20-second spots--from 7 a.m. through 8 p.m. (13 daily spots) 72 hours preceding opening day and continuing same schedule for 4 days following opening. For succeeding days, suggest 1 55-second announcement every other hour in same periods. We prefer an independent, pop music and news station--or combination of such stations--with a total of approximately 40% share of audience locally in a recognized coincidental telephone survey -- Hooper, Trendex or your own pilot survey. A list of suggested radio i.d.'s is enclosed.

Although radio campaigns are available on both "The Killer Shrews" and "The Giant Gila Monster", when the pictures are played as a double feature all emphasis should be directed to the radio campaign on "The Killer Shrews"-- 7 55-second announcements and several 20-second announcements.

A good teaser i.d. for your local radio station is: "This is Station WKKK, and we urge you to report to your local authorities at once any sighting of a giant Killer Shrew." Obviously, these teasers should precede any regular advertising campaign. Incidentally, don't fail to order the teaser theatre trailer on "The Killer Shrews"--it causes tremendous comment. Naturally, it precedes the regular trailer. An excellent t.v. teaser trailer is also available to precede regular t.v. trailers.

Another teaser i.d. for radio is "This is Station WKKK, where the Killer Shrews are coming."

Remember, these two pictures, properly promoted, set all-time house records in their initial engagements.

The July, 1959, issue of TRUE MAGAZINE spotlighted a feature article on the Killer Shrews. Our 20-second radio spots are built around this article. A blowup of the TRUE article was used in front of the theatre on the opening engagement with tremendous effect.

Fess Parker's Cascade Records has issued a catchy rock and roll number -- "The Gila Monster" -- which is already on Top 40 charts throughout the country. Make every effort to get your local radio stations to saturate with this record well in advance of your opening.

We think our newspaper ads on these pictures are excellent but, wherever possible, we recommend basic radio and supplementary television -- with other promotional material noted in this letter and in the press book -- for maximum boxoffice dollars.

Cordially,
Mitchell J. Lewis
National Director of Promotion and Publicity

SYNOPSIS
(Not for Publication)

When charter boat captain Thorne Sherman (JAMES BEST) and his negro side-kick Rook (JUDGE DUPREE) arrive to deliver supplies to a scientist's isolated and remote island, they find the small group of inhabitants choked with terror and mystery.

The director of research, Dr. Craigis, (BARUCH LUMET) is anxious for the captain to depart immediately with his beauteous daughter, Ann (INGRID GOUDE), even in the face of an imminent hurricane.

Two co-scientists (KEN CURTIS and GORDON McLENDON) throw little light on the cause of their obvious fright and concern for their lives.

The reason finally is divulged when the Captain tries to return to his cruiser at nightfall and learns from Ann at gun point their cause for alarm.

Through chemical experiments and injections, tiny Blarina shrews — deadly poisonous and vicious — have grown to the size of giant grey wolves and escaped from the laboratory. By necessity, they must eat three times their body weight every 24 hours or starve. As they exhausted the natural supply on the island their cravings were directed toward the only remaining source — Man, their scientific creator.

Rook is devoured by the ravenous beasts as he innocently seeks refuge from the storm. Three others are to die immediate and violent deaths when the carniverous shrews burrow through the rain-soaked adobe walls in quest of the terrorized remaining survivors.

Only when Captain Sherman ingeniously devises a human tank made from makeshift storage barrels and threads his way through the dense underbrush with Dr. Craigis and his daughter to the water's edge are the remaining three at last safe from the blood-thirsty, man-created beasts.

CAST

Thorne Sherman	James Best
Ann Craigis	Ingrid Goude
Dr. Craigis	Baruch Lumet
Jerry Lacer	Ken Curtis
Radford Baines	Gordon McLendon
Mario	Alfredo DeSoto
Rook	J. H. "Judge" Dupree

FRONT & LOBBY DISPLAY ART

A great many traffic-stopping effects have been obtained through inexpensively creating eye-catching lobby and front spectaculars. For instance, TRUE MAGAZINE'S (July, '59) issue carries a feature article on the savage shrews ("Half-Ounce Hellers"). One theater made maximum advantage of the article by "blowing it up" (through photostating), thereby lending sidewalk strollers further encouragement to attend the feature and see shrews in giant form. Reprints can be obtained from Fawcett Publications, New York, New York or, in most cases, directly from your local library files.

The long range gains to be derived from these specially produced advance teasers cannot be too highly stressed. TV and movie teasers, voiced by McLendon, simply warn the viewers of an epidemic of shrews and ask that any sightings be reported to local health officers. A variation, worked with local radio stations, is for disc jockeys to interject, frequently through the day, the following short, one sentence announcement:
"Any residents sighting giant killer shrews, please call local authorities at once." No more, no less! You'll be amazed at the response such an advance "steamroller" campaign can have when the pictures open at your theater.

ADVANCE RADIO TV & MOVIE TEASERS

EARN $ AT THE BOX OFFICE

The Gorn from the *Star Trek* episode "Arena" (January 19, 1967); designed by Wah Chang, played by Bobby Clark, Gary Combs, and Bill Blackburn, vocal by Ted Cassidy. Janos Prohaska could have done it all!

A NOTE ON "I SING THE BODY PROHASKA"

Can it be true that Roger Patterson and Bob Gimlin paid somebody to manufacture a man-in-suit Sasquatch to fake their 1967 footage? I've read all there is in print in the English language I can lay hands on, and for me the short answer is: *NO*, they didn't. I don't believe they *could* have.

At this point, there been numerous exposés written by folks who knew or claimed to know Patterson *et al*—and frankly, the 'explanations' I've read (one of them book-length) are more incredible than us just accepting that the Patterson-Gimlin footage might actually have been something they stumbled upon and filmed—but hey, that's just me.

I have a partial-library-shelf now of 'I was the guy in the suit' bullshit chapbooks, books, articles—it's damn near a *cottage industry*, and has long been at the hysteric level of the 'I was King Kong' and the 'I did Popeye's voice for the cartoons' string of liars. The evidence demonstrates that Patterson could barely even afford the 16mm camera they'd rented. Patterson in fact stiffed on that rental due, among other fiscal matters; so, no, the more I've read (especially the attacks on Patterson's personal character, intended to 'prove' him a fraud), the more I can't believe he could have *afforded* anything as convincing as what was filmed that fateful day.

The basic claim—that a Sasquatch suit like that could have been manufactured, paid for, used, and kept absolutely secret, given the dire financial straits of Patterson—is highly dubious, as is the fact that *nobody* in the makeup/effects world was doing work of such caliber in the mid-1960s. Even *with* high budgets, the results were rarely convincingly alive, and we were always aware of the performers within the suits and/or makeup (i.e., as in **PLANET OF THE APES**, which wasn't that high a budget, really; **2001: A SPACE ODYSSEY**, which embodied the cutting-edge of the available man-in-suit simian makeup technology, with its 'Moonwalker' protohumans).

And when you are versed (as we who were alive and watching everything we could of the kind in 1967 were) in what was then-state-of-the-art 'monkey men' suits and such of the period—George Barrows, Bob Burns, Janos Prohaska, etc.—and studio makeup/effects of the era, nothing comes close to the naturalism of *whatever-that-was* in the Patterson-Gimlin footage. Compare what was in movies and TV of the time (including, pre-1967, *The Outer Limits*, *Star Trek*, the Irwin Allen SF programming, etc.) and tell me that you could 'easily' find a convincing Sasquatch suit-maker in 1967, much less an 'affordable' and convincing one. And if such an artist *did* exist, that Sasquatch suit would have quickly been its creator's calling card to professional work and go on to become a familiar face-and-figure on genre television and movies.

I always found those scant 20-30 seconds of footage to be pretty believable and, given the fact that not *one* movie made with

when Roger met Patty
by William Munns

1 Minute of Film
47 Years of Controversy

The Patterson-Gimlin Film, the Hominid seen in it, the remarkably intense debate that it has provoked, and the solution to the mystery.

far more money than Patterson could ever have gotten together even managed to approximate anything else like it in its day... well, that Sasquatch in the Patterson-Gimlin footage still looks convincingly *alive* to me, and is quite unlike anything that was seen onscreen until Rick Baker revolutionized 'gorilla suit' technologies in the 1970s and '80s.

And the best of them all, prior to Rick Baker, was the great Janos Prohaska.

It's impossible for me to shift gears into this retrospective of one of the first truly great TV 'monkey-and-monster men' without mentioning that Prohaska himself was interviewed on-camera in Lawrence Crowley's American National Enterprises' documentary feature **BIG FOOT: MAN OR BEAST?** (1972). Prohaska's Hungarian accent was quite thick, but his English was quite good:

"The movement was the only thing that threw me a little, there, 'cause he moved more like a man than animal; because you could see all the muscles on the body, and the whole movement. It didn't move like a costume at all. And the size of it was

Frame grab of Janos Prohaska, interviewed on-camera while wearing one of his most familiar primate suits, in Lawrence Crowley's American National Enterprises' documentary feature **BIG FOOT: MAN OR BEAST?** (1972).

enormous, *big size; I don't know where they found a big man like that.*"

When asked if it would be possible to create such a costume, Prohaska replied,

"*That would be difficult. I don't think so, 'cause that costume— if it would be a costume—that would have taken such a long time to put the hair [on]. You should put the hair by glue, glue 'em on, that would take about ten hours, the whole makeup job. And it looked to me very, very real. I'm doing this thing since 1939, and if that was a costume, that was the best I have ever seen.*"[1]

Prohaska is cited in only one book in entire the cottage industry of books on the Patterson-Gimlin footage, and that is the one written by none other than the makeup man who created the original movie **SWAMP THING** makeup effects (for Wes Craven's 1982 adaptation). The same fellow also created makeup effects for **THE BEASTMASTER, SUPERSTITION** (both 1982), **THE RETURN OF THE LIVING DEAD** (1985), The ABC Weekend Special *The Adventures of Teddy Ruxpin* (1985), and my personal favorite of his creations, **THE BOOGENS** (1981). William Munns is his name, and to fans (like myself) it seemed that Munns disappeared after the 1980s (the fact is, he shifted gears into creating full-scale wildlife and prehistoric man models instead), only to resurface around 2009-2010 on series like *American Paranormal* and *Monsterquest*.

The latter appearance (on the episode "Critical Evidence" [July 8th, 2009]) was a precursor to Munns' self-published 508 page-extravaganza *When Roger Met Patty: 1 Minute of Film, 47 Years of Controversy* (CreateSpace Independent Publishing Platform, July 24th, 2014):

"*William 'Bill' Munns has been a makeup and special effects artist in Hollywood for many years, and a filmmaker in general as well, and he applies his unique perspective to the analysis of the famous 1967 Patterson-Gimlin Film. In the last seven years, Bill has assembled the finest image data archive on film and photographic material related to this classic 'Bigfoot' mystery, and analyzed this strange creature seen in the film with state-of-the-art analysis technology. His book,* When Roger Met Patty, *is the culmination of that seven year research program, and after 47 years, the Patterson-Gimlin Film mystery is finally solved.*"

Just bringing this volume to your attention, folks!

And now, without further ado, meet Janos Prohaska, whose work was indeed the state-of-the-art for television monster-making and performing before and after 1967…

Lucille Ball encounters an amorous albino Gorboona (Janos Prohaska)—a cross between a gorilla and a baboon—in the *Here's Lucy* episode "Lucy's Safari" (March 3, 1969). Prohaska first appeared with Lucille Ball in *The Lucy Show* episode "Lucy and the Monkey" (December 5, 1966), and appeared two other times on *Here's Lucy* playing bears; Prohaska's white gorilla costume first appeared in *Voyage to the Bottom of the Sea*, "Fatal Cargo" (November 5, 1967) and was customized into the Mugato (aka the Gumato) for *Star Trek* (see next page).

---

1 Janos Prohaska, **BIG FOOT: MAN OR BEAST?** (16 minutes, 5 seconds–17m 29s). Note that the onscreen title actually gives the main subject as "**BIG FOOT**," not "**BIGFOOT**".

I SING THE BODY PROHASKA

There was a time when it was not only hard to find out who was behind the monsters in movies and on TV—it was impossible. Movie credits weren't the marathon text-crawls they are today, ten-minute-long processions of every name associated with a big-screen production, and TV program credits were sparer still.[1]

Thus it was that the names of Jonas and Robert Prohaska—father-and-son "monkey men" and monster makers/players extraordinaire—were a slow revelation. I didn't catch their names on the cast lists of the TV programs they worked for and appeared in, if they were indeed there to be seen, though I came to connect-the-dots and know and recognize their work, their creatures, over time. I didn't see their names or faces in the pages of *Famous Monsters of Filmland* (among men-in-suit monster performers, only "gorilla man" Charles Gemora was repeatedly cited in *FM* over the years) or *Castle of Frankenstein*, either, though occasional photos of their creations graced the pages of monster magazines during their decade or so of active onscreen labor.

I mainly recognized the Prohaskas from their performances, their body movements and particular manner of pantomime. Gradually, the look and feel of these performances spoke volumes to me, though I still had no name to put to them.

The revelation as to who and what the Prohaskas were arrived in a rather unlikely home fixture. *TV Guide* (issue #826, for January 25-31, 1969; Vol. 17, No. 4) featured a three-page color-illustrated uncredited[2] article on Prohaska and son entitled

Behind-the-scenes photo from the set of the *Star Trek* second season Vietnam War-allegorical episode "A Private Little War" (February 2, 1968), a shot featuring Janos Prohaska as the Mugato (whose venomous bit figures in the story; see left)

"'Thank you, but we don't need no chimps today'" (pp.21-23). The article touted the "rather small (5-feet-5)… quite muscular" Prohaska as "the chief monster man in Hollywood…a mild-mannered Hungarian émigré… [who] started out in Europe performing in circuses and in the mid-Fifties made his way to the United States and Hollywood. Here he worked as a stunt man and became typecast as a chimpanzee", playing said primate on the TV series *Riverboat* (44 episodes, September 13, 1959-January 2, 1961; the *TV Guide* article reads like Prohaska was a series regular, but he in fact played the thieving "Koko the Ape" in only one

---

1 Of course, now TV and movie credits are essentially invisible on television—especially in reruns and cable broadcasts—reduced into tiny insert screens and scrolled by at super speeds, a contractual obligation barely observed. But I digress.

2 The author of the anonymous article is not cited anywhere in this issue of *TV Guide*, which I do possess; at the time, *TV Guide*'s Hollywood bureau was led by Dwight Whitney and comprised of Leslie Raddatz, Joseph Finnigan, Dick

Hobson, and photographer Laddie Marshack (who may have provided the photos accompanying the article). Any one of them may have interviewed Janos Prohaska and scribed the article. Along with the rest of my *TV Guide* collection, this issue will join the SpiderBaby Archives for researcher access sometime in the future, most likely in the Stephen R. Bissette Collection at HUIE Library, Henderson State University, Arkadelphia, Arkansas.

67

'Thank you, but we don't need no chimps today'

The plaintive observations of Janos Prohaska, who'd rather be a candy monster anyhow

Hungary and its environs—Transylvania and Moldavia—have been known lo, these many years for monsters. Werewolves, vampires and things that go bump in the night are rumored, via books and movies, to abound there. So it is not surprising that the chief monster man in Hollywood is a mild-mannered Hungarian émigré named Janos Prohaska. Prohaska (he's in the white gorilla suit above—his son, Robert, is clad in black) started out in Europe performing in circuses and in the mid-Fifties made his way to the United States and Hollywood. Here he worked as a stunt man and became typecast as a chimpanzee: "Actually I am a stunt man. First TV series I do is *Riverboat*. . it is about a traveling circus, and I played the chimp. But then I got type roled. People keep telling me, 'Thank you, we don't need →

21

We didn't learn about Janos and Robert Prohaska and their monsters in the pages of *Famous Monsters of Filmland*—we learned about them in *TV Guide* (issue #826, for January 25-31, 1969; Vol. 17, No. 4)! Here's the spread, uncredited photos most likely by staff photographer Laddie Marshack

episode, "Witness No Evil," November 1, 1959). That typecasting provided ongoing employment for Prohaska—playing chimps or gorillas for *The Red Skelton Hour* (starting in 1961), *Bourbon Street Beat* ("Wagon Show", June 13, 1960), *The Outer Limits* ("The Sixth Finger", October 14, 1963), the theatrical feature **BIKINI BEACH** (1964, USA), *Perry Mason* ("The Case of the Grinning Gorilla," April 29, 1965), *Honey West* ("Slay, Gypsy, Slay", February 25, 1966), *The Lucy Show* ("Lucy and the Monkey", December 5, 1966), etc. The uncredited *TV Guide* article incorporated quotes from a personal interview with Prohaska, who said, "Then Ivan Tors put me in *Man and the Challenge*…" [playing a human role in "Invisible Force", October 17, 1959], though it was still man-in-suit animal roles Prohaska built his career upon. "I played a gorilla, and I saw they needed a bear, so I make a bear. Then when monster shows start, I start to make monsters…" (cited *TV Guide* article, p.22).

And oh, what monsters!

———

I was a crewcut eleven-year-old in remote Duxbury, Vermont, and school had just started—my last year (6th grade) in the four-room red Duxbury Elementary schoolhouse just across the field from my home: the shortest walk to the classrooms imaginable, unless school were in my own house. Next year would be the major life-change that was junior high, entering the 7th grade at a

Janos Prohaska made his theatrical feature film debut in one of his primate suits in **BIKINI BEACH** (1964)

Janos Prohaska, working on a gorilla head in his studio.

continued

no chimps today.' Then Ivan Tors put me in *Man and the Challenge*. I played a gorilla, and I saw they needed a bear, so I make a bear. Then when monster shows start, I start to make monsters." Prohaska creates all of his creatures himself, working in his rather modest home in Santa Monica. "From the whole block the children in my neighborhood know when I have finished a monster and they all come around me, taking pictures of the new monster. I do not know how they know when I have finished a new one, but they know." What he'd really like to *do* is a children's show with thoroughly unscary monsters (that's something of a contradiction in terms). "Most of the time I do not want to be frightening. I did a show with Lucille Ball. That was amusing. I like that. I would like to be a candy monster I would like to do a children's series. I would like it to be about a little boy who has all these monsters in his room, but they are only toys. He dreams at

22

Prohaska in 'thing' outfit causing a bit of a stir on a Los Angeles street.

night that he can control all the monsters from a little black box or something, so he imagines they are big. But it is a child's fantasy, not as something frightening. I'd rather do something funny, not killing." If Prohaska aspires to be a kind and gentle monster it must be remembered that he seems capable of creating any sort of monster he desires. He is an extremely ingenious craftsman who constructs extremely clever devices. A good example is the thing (unnamed) at the bottom of these pages. Distinctly of the nonunfrightening genre, it is something of a tour de force of monsterdom. To move it about, Prohaska stands inside on stilts, holding crutches for the front "arms." The 10-foot-tall grotesquery has hoses running through its "arms" which connect to a vacuum cleaner strapped to Prohaska's back. With these it can pick things up, and spray steam, water or powder In addition, its eyes move, its ears waggle and stomach and head inflate. Of course you can't be a pantywaist and still make

Latex, cheese cloth and foam 'vegetable.'

things like these monsters work, and Prohaska is anything but a pantywaist. Rather small (5-feet-5), he is quite muscular and in the sort of physical shape that befits his background as a stunt man and acrobat. His splendid condition may not help to alleviate the discomfort of some of his roles, but at least it makes playing the roles possible. Naturally there are hazards involved in any stunt work, but Prohaska has managed to literally fashion a few new problems. In his outfits he frequently scares people. Women faint, others run, and once he was almost shot by a policeman. No wonder he'd like to work as an unscary monster contradiction or not.

brand new school, Harwood Union High School, as the first-ever class to endure the entirety of 7th-through-senior-graduation at Harwood. But, hey, that was a year away, and I was finally in the king-shit ruling class at Duxbury.

And if this rite of passage weren't daunting enough, I had a choice to make:

Do I just resign myself to seeing a brand-new show I was hankering to see on our little black-and-white TV, or do I talk my parents into letting me watch the new science-fiction TV show debuting Saturday night on the family *color* TV?

This brand-new show was something called *Star Trek*, on NBC—the color network, in those days, with the peacock logo—which we got pretty well on our TV antennae (this was pre-cable, folks: if it didn't come in on the antennae or via "rabbit ears" antennae on the TV set, you didn't and couldn't see it) via WPTZ-TV out of Plattsburgh, NY, just across Lake Champlain. The ads in the newspaper (an eye-catching painting by no less than James Bama, the man who did the Aurora monster model kit box art) and the *TV Guide* listing looked mighty tempting. It took some finagling, but I even managed to score watching that September 8, 1966 debut episode on our living-room color TV.

"Man Trap" was the name of it, and, man oh man, it was *soooooo* much better than *Lost in Space* and *Voyage to the Bottom of the Sea*! It was better than a lot of the science-fiction movies I eagerly caught on *The Early Show* afternoon movie and *The Late Show* after the 11 p.m. news (and, lucky us in northern VT., Canada's Channel 6 Monday night *Science-Fiction Theater*). It was damned near the coolest thing I'd ever seen on television up to that point in my life, actually. And it was *in color*.

I don't have to tell you more, do I? About the Enterprise, and Captain Kirk, and Mister Spock, and the crew, now, do I? Nah, I don't. You know all about them and the show. What the episode was, though, was a spin on **FORBIDDEN PLANET**—only this time, the stranded scientist was played by that guy (Alfred Ryder) who had made himself up as a hunchback copying a street bum in that episode of *Way Out* I saw when I was, like, six years old—man, *that scared the shit out of me!* That one gave me nightmares.[3] So, even though I'd seen this actor in tons of TV since (*Wagon Train, Dr. Kildare, Route 66, The Defenders, Combat!*)—even on an episode of *Outer Limits*—it was his *Way Out* thing that I remembered, so I was suspicious the minute he was onscreen

The 'salt vampire' was played by stunt woman Sandra Lee Gimpel (a.k.a. Sandy Gimpel), here seen with the Wah Chang mask removed.

Sandra Lee Gimpel (a.k.a. Sandy Gimpel) as monster-maker Wah Chang's "salt vampire" in *Star Trek*'s debut episode, "Man Trap" (September 8, 1966)

as Professor Crater. Then, he introduces his wife (supplanting Doctor Morbius's sexy daughter in Fred McLeod Wilcox's **FORBIDDEN PLANET**, [1956, USA])—*well,* anyhoot, the Enterprise rescues them, and then crew members start turning up dead, with red sucker marks on their faces, and Bones says they've been drained of salt (*salt!!!*), and…what the *hell* is going on?!

Man, I loved these characters. I loved this story. The clincher for me, though, was the climax.

Do I really have to worry about spoilers after, what, 46 years? I won't.

See, it's the old professor's wife—*she's not his wife,* she's a creature he "wed" in place of his dead wife. Once her true nature was revealed in all its glory, my stomach actually turned a little: rugose skin, a shock of long white hair, a teeth-ringed lamprey mouth, pitch-black sad eyes, and fingers tipped with octopus-like suckers, ready to sink into another victim's flesh. I'm sure it's a letdown in 2015, but it sure was a shock and a clincher in 1966, and I was *hooked*.

It wasn't just the appearance of the creature that was genuinely jarring, it was the queasy fusion of tangled emotions tied to this thing—dread, pity, her human "husband's" love (what *else* did they do together, alone on that planet all those years?), and the primal disgust roused by any and all parasites, like leeches, particularly big ones—that made it such a potent cocktail at the tender age of eleven.

This was mind-blowing monster stuff. She was scarier than the giant bloodsuckers feeding in their grotto in **ATTACK OF THE GIANT LEECHES** (1959, USA, D: Bernard L. Kowalski); she was

---

[3] And, as I later discovered in adult life, that *Way Out* episode—"False Face" (May 26, 1961)—was scripted by Larry Cohen, and that nightmare-inducing makeup was by Dick Smith!

Behind-the-scenes shot of the filming of the climax of "Man Trap," as the M-113 creature (Sandra Gimpel, in a monster design/suit by Wah Chang) begins feeding on Captain James T. Kirk (William Shatner). During production, the episode was entitled "The Unreal McCoy"

the grandmother of the liver-eating Tooms and the chemical-toilet-dwelling Fluke Man to come eons later on *The X-Files*.

She was, in two words, *scary shit*.

The very next week—the second show—gave us the heartbreaking teen Charlie X (Robert Walker, Jr.), who came on as if Billy Mumy in that wicked *Twilight Zone* episode "It's a Good Life" had been exiled to a distant planet and grew up. Once on the Enterprise, he made minds melt and faces disappear.

The very next week ("Where No Man Has Gone Before"), we got not one but *two* psions—a man and a woman, wielding telekinetic and telepathic tyranny over mere mortals—locked in mortal combat; a primer for David Cronenberg's **SCANNERS** (1981) and the superhero movies to come decades later.

So, there it is.

I never became a "Trekkie", once those existed and had been identified as a species, but I never missed an episode of *Star Trek* after that. I saw 'em all (sometimes on little black-and-white TVs at relative's houses, when we were traveling, much to my Dad's ire), and loved most of them, even "Spock's Brain". The frequent fun (and occasional queasy) factor of its menaces kept me watching, too: along with *The Outer Limits*, this was far, *far* more adult SF than anything else on primetime.

There were still aliens, thankfully, week after week, and smart stories (*Lost in Space* forever lost its lackluster allure after I saw "Man Trap"), and there were monsters—some of them were dumb, some of them were terrific, but they were constant enough to keep me addicted and happy. They also were more imaginatively embodied than the all-pervasive "gnarled forehead" Gene Roddenberry fallback-alien-design that eventually seemed to inexplicably dominate the galaxy (an inadvertently hilarious weakness of Roddenberry's that even infected his one-shot 1977 TV movie/pilot **SPECTRE**, wherein, once the demonic forces manifested themselves in the body of John Hurt, he—*had a crinkly forehead, like a Klingon!!! Yow! Scary!!!*). If only Gene had realized mandrill and baboon asses are way more terrifying than walnut-textured foreheads…

There were the barely-seen hairy troglodytes plaguing "The Galileo Seven"; the humanoid dinosaur Gorn pitted against Captain Kirk in a battle to the death in "Arena" (and yes, I was at the time already well-read enough in literary science-fiction to gleefully recognize this as an adaptation of the justifiably famed Fredric Brown [1906-1972] short story from 1944), the pathetic withering meat-things glimpsed at the end of the Halloween episode "Catspaw". My peculiar favorite, despite their laughable mode of animation, were the flying-dog-vomit pizza-slice-like brain parasites that flitted from under support beams and ledges to latch onto the nape of the neck or your head and drain your brain in "Operation – Annihilate!"

Surprisingly, those little flitting parasitic fuckers

The brutal Troglodytes who attacked "The Galileo Seven" (*Star Trek*, January 5th, 1967) were never shown in the final edit, but publicity stills of the monster (Robert "Big Buck" Maffei, a.k.a. Buck Maffei) were circulated, this one with Yeoman Mears (Phyllis Douglas).

News image of the March 1974 White Mountain Peak plane crash that took the lives of Janos and Robert Prohaska and 34 others; for more information, see https://www.gendisasters.com/california/4906/bishop%2C-ca-television-film-crew-dies-crash%2C-mar-1974

had a long shelf-life in the collective memory. A full decade later, when I was a mature, upstanding, forward-thinking, career-oriented college student at the Joe Kubert School of Cartoon and Graphic Art, Inc. in Dover, NJ, during one of the many pizza joint jaunts my classmates and I indulged we unexpectedly tapped our shared instant recall of "Operation – Annihilate!" Madman and skilled cartoonist Tom Ricotta—always willing to do almost anything for a laugh—seized a pizza slice off the plate, and, with the cry of *"Spock, look OUT!"* slammed it full force into his forehead. We exploded with laughter, and it took hours to stop giggling like little girls.

This brings me back to the man in the TV monster suits of my childhood, preteen, and teen years, the great Janos Prohaska—the Horta, the Mugato, the Yarnek, and more.

Before *Star Trek*, he was the go-to monkey guy on **BIKINI BEACH** and for TV shows: *Perry Mason, The Outer Limits* (he was the ape in the episode wherein David McCallum hyper-evolved into the big-brained man with "The Sixth Finger"), *Honey West, The Lucy Show, Gilligan's Island, Voyage to the Bottom of the Sea, Lost in Space*, and so on. After *Star Trek*, he was still a TV staple, and ironically played one of the "real" apes in 20th Century Fox and Arthur P. Jacobs' popular *Planet of the Apes* movies (an uncredited Prohaska played Heloise in **ESCAPE FROM THE PLANET OF THE APES**, 1971, USA, D: Don Taylor).

Janos was the Cookie Bear on *The Andy Williams Show,* Olga the Dancing Bear on *The Munsters*, Buster the Boxing Bear on *The Red Skelton Hour*, Hercules the Bear on *Dusty's Trail*, and lots of unnamed TV bears elsewhere.[4] He was the goofy man-sized Do-Do bird on *Bewitched*; he was the man in the monster-suit playing the scary-ass fake-Thetan Robert Culp was surgically turned into in the classic *Outer Limits* episode "Architects of Fear" (September 30, 1963), and that microscopic blob called the Mikie in the final episode of the last season of that same series ("The Probe", January 16, 1965).

Along with his son Robert, who played the titular "model" in *Night Gallery*'s memorable H.P. Lovecraft adaptation "Pickman's Model" (December 1, 1971), the Prohaskas were omnipresent, it seemed, on American television.

Posed shot of Janos Prohaska as the surgically-created faux-Thetan in the classic *Outer Limits* episode "Architects of Fear" (September 30, 1963).

They were not, alas, immortal…

A single day before my 19th birthday, on March 13, 1974, Janos and Robert Prohaska were killed in a fatal plane crash, en route to or from a remote California location. The plane inexplicably slammed into a ledge; I have never found or read an account offering any explanation for the accident. The Prohaskas were en route to or from location, acting (as prehistoric men) in a David Wolper prestige production entitled *Primal Man* (the show was retitled *Up from the Ape*, and eventually aired later that same year).[5]

---

[4] Prohaska co-starred in an unsold Soupy Sales pilot, *The Bear and I* (1972), playing a talking bear that everyone believed was just a man-in-a-suit; only kiddie-show host Sales knew otherwise, that it really *was* a talking bear. See http://www.imdb.com/name/nm0698512/

[5] David Wolper (1928-2010) was among the most prestigious of all TV producers, twice nominated for Academy Awards for his documentary feature films (**THE RACE FOR SPACE** [1959], and **THE HELLSTROM CHRONICLE**, which won Best Documentary for 1971), and producer of the beloved **WILLY WONKA & THE CHOCOLATE FACTORY** (1971), among other theatrical feature films. Based upon the controversial books and writings of anthropologist and behavioral theorist Robert Ardrey, co-directed by Walon Green and Mel Stuart, *The Primal Man* TV specials were broadcast between 1973-74. There is considerable confusion in multiple print and online sources about the series, variously listed under individual episode titles, *The Primal Man* (1973-74)*, The Animal Within* (1974), and (listed on *imdb.com* as) *Up from the Ape* (1975). That confusion is evident on the official David Wolper website filmography as well (see http://www.davidlwolper.com/shows/filmography.cfm); a subject for further research, and I would welcome any VHS or DVD

71

William Shatner faces the Horta (Janos Prohaska) in *Star Trek*'s "The Devil in the Dark" episode (March 9, 1967); the Horta was a variation on Prohaska's blob-like Mikie in *The Outer Limits* episode "The Probe" (January 16, 1965)

According to that January 1969 uncredited *TV Guide* interview/article, the Prohaskas did all their work from "a modest home in Santa Monica", California. Like Paul and Jackie Blaisdell before them, and their immediate contemporary (and surviving "gorilla man") Bob Burns, the Prohaskas worked their monster magic without the support of a major studio or studio makeup/effects department. "From the whole block the children in my neighborhood know when I have finished a monster", Janos Prohaska told the *TV Guide* interviewer, "and they all come around me, taking pictures of the new monster. I do not know how they know when I have finished a new one, but they know…" (previously cited *TV Guide* article, p.22).

copies of the specials themselves. Anyone?

Behind-the-scenes *Star Trek* shot of Prohaska as the silicon-based Horta of Janus VI, "The Devil in the Dark"

Who knows what the Prohaskas might have accomplished, had they lived into the transformative era of fellow artists like Dick Smith, Rick Baker, Rob Bottin, and others?

They might have been at the top of the game—pushed the entire field further, faster—again, who can say?

The fact is, according to that *TV Guide* article/interview, that the Prohaskas didn't want to fuel nightmares. Perhaps he'd have found himself most at home working with Jim Henson, had that fateful creative collaboration ever come to pass.

"Most of the time I do not want to be frightening," Janos told *TV Guide*. "I would like to be a candy monster. I would like to do a children's series. I would like it to be about a little boy who has all these monsters in his room, but they are only toys. He dreams at night that he can control all the monsters from a little black box or something, so he imagines they are big. But it is a child's fantasy, not as something frightening. I'd rather do something funny, not killing." (cited *TV Guide* article, pp.22-23).

It's easy to see why Prohaska found such fruitful collaboration earlier in the 1960s with Wah Chang/Gene Warren's Project Unlimited and *The Outer Limits*. Alas, for all his and Robert's broadcast television work and credits, Hollywood barely tapped what the Prohaskas were capable of. Their grassroots homemade monsters incorporated traditional man-in-suit techniques while pioneering animatronics were still in studio-helmed infancy. The *TV*

Janos Prohaska as an alien monster, Wally Cox as the nomadic Tiabo, and Bill Mumy as Will Robinson in *Lost in Space*, "Forbidden World" (October 5th, 1966).

Guide article included a photo of an original cyclopean Prohaska creation that never graced a TV or movie screen, "a tour de force of monsterdom. To move it about, Prohaska stands inside on stilts, holding crutches for the front 'arms'. The 10-foot-tall grotesquery has hoses running through its 'arm' which connect to a vacuum cleaner strapped to Prohaska's back. With these it can pick things up, and spray steam, water or powder. In addition, its eyes move, its ears waggle and stomach and head inflate." (*ibid.*, p.23) There's also a photo of an impressive makeup creation: a human/vegetable hybrid, a "green man", made of "latex, cheese cloth and foam" (according to the photo caption).

Oh, what might have been, had they lived longer—and had studio television producers been more open to the Prohaskas imaginative creations, rather than relegating them to occasional freelance gigs—but let's savor what they did in their lifetimes, and what we *have* from them.

Prohaska played some of my all-time favorite *Star Trek* critters: the Mugato in "A Private Little War", the silicon-based blob the Horta in "Devil in the Dark", the briefly-glimpsed bird-thingy and the humanoid pig-nosed ape-creature that Captain Pike (Jeffrey Hunter) sees while strangling one of the big-brained women in "The Menagerie" (actually footage from the *Star Trek* pilot "The Cage", which is one of my favorite 1960s SF movies, period, and the monster itself was an *Outer Limits* creation).

Prohaska was so seemingly *everywhere*, yet uncredited, in so much TV that I just assumed he was *every* monster on *Star Trek* when it was first broadcast (I was wrong).

Let me put it this way: if Janos had been the Gorn in "Arena", it would have been an even better episode (instead, the saurian-like Gorn was played by

Prohaska as the Mikie in *The Outer Limits*, "The Probe" (January 16, 1965)

four actors: Ted Cassidy voiced the Gorn, while Bobby Clark, Gary Combs, and Bill Blackburn rather clumsily inhabited the monster suit).

So, here's to salt-sucking lamprey women, ceiling-secreted brain parasites, narcotic plant spores, psions, and shapeshifters and little wispy Goth-addicted meat puppets, and all the *Star Trek* critters that so enhanced my youth.

But, above all, here's to Janos and Robert Prohaska, the monster men of my youth!

———

Article ©2012, 2015, *Star Trek* fan art ©2013, 2015 Stephen R. Bissette, all rights reserved. The art originally appeared in *Monster Pie #2* (2013); this article is considerably revised and expanded from an article published in the fine one-shot *Star Trek* zine *Strange New Worlds* (Denis St. John, October 2012); to read the complete *TV Guide* article from January 1969, go to *http://www.hollywoodgorilla-men.com/2012/03/rare-treat.html*

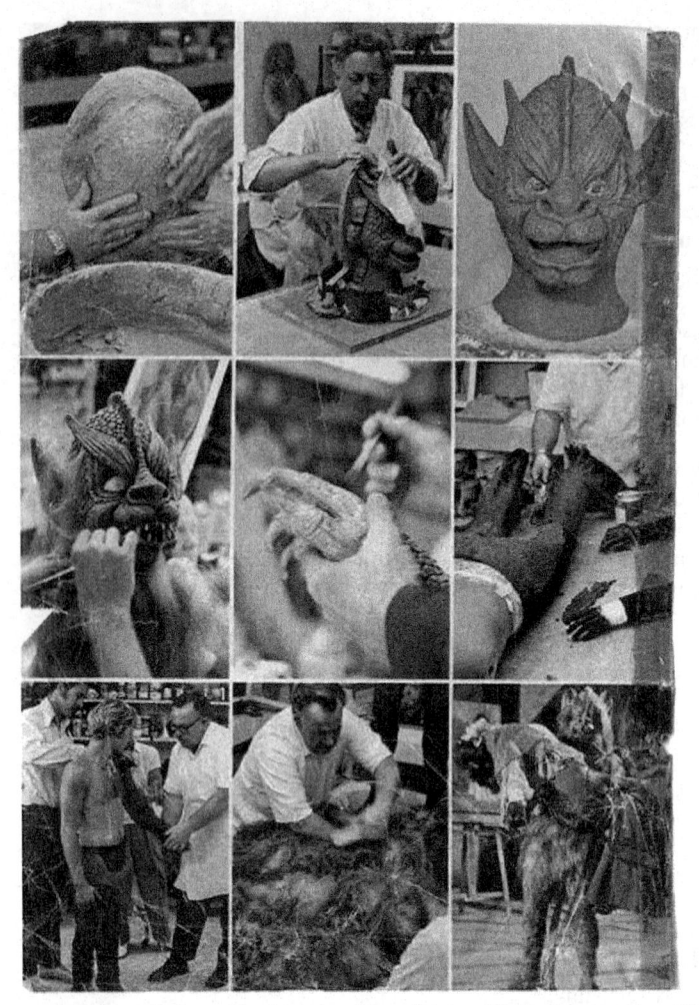

Above: Robert Prohaska played, but didn't create, the *Night Gallery* "Pickman's Model" (images from *TV Guide*, November 27, 1971). **Below & Right:** Janos Prohaska stepped into modified *Outer Limits* Project Unlimited creature costumes for the original *Star Trek* pilot "The Cage" (1965), broadcast as "The Menagerie" (November 17 and 24, 1966)

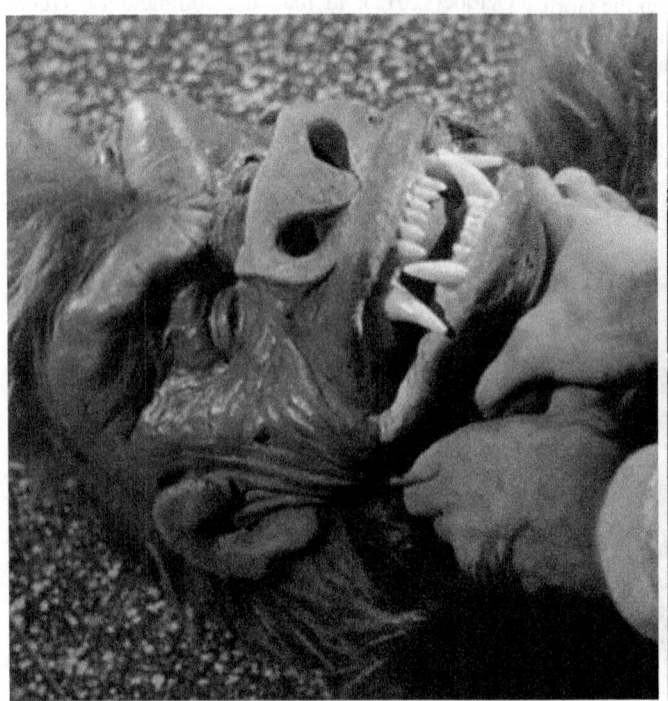

"Why Don't You Give the Bear a Cookie?!"

For 1960s and early 1970s Monster Kids like me, Janos Prohaska was American TV's "monkey man" and monster creator/player extraordinaire—but for most of North America, Prohaska's best-known and most-beloved character creation was "The Cookie Bear" on the popular one-hour NBC-TV musical-variety-comedy show *The Andy Williams Show* (1962-71). Most often coming at the ends of select episodes, Prohaska's man-in-suit comedic bear exasperating the smooth-talking-and-singing Williams became a national sensation between 1969 and the series' conclusion in 1971.

The basic shtick was that Prohaska as Cookie Bear would interrupt Williams singing a song to beg for cookies, until Williams would shout, in near-falsetto, "Not now, not ever—*never!*" which became a catchphrase (this was long before the term 'meme' had been coined). The bear would then speak to the camera and do a pratfall face-first. Prohaska's thick Hungarian accent prevented his providing the voice for his ursine performances (the voiceover was handled by the program's producer, Allan Blye). The show's press releases included photos of Prohaska in-character in his Cookie Bear costume, opening packages of cookies that came flooding into the studio's mailroom; one 1970 article noted, "youngsters yell at Williams in public, 'Why don't you give the bear a cookie?'…"[1]

The same article provided a thorough account of how Prohaska's Cookie Bear became an unexpected celebrity, instrumental to *The Andy Williams Show* usurping *The Jackie Gleason Show* (1952-70, in various formats) in the ratings, just one factor in CBS-TV's decision to cancel Gleason's hit program in the spring of 1970. It also offers more information on Prohaska's practices and work methods than usual:

Janos Prohaska as Cookie Bear, savoring his Andy Williams Show fan mail—and lots of cookies!—in this rare cover photo from the TV Diary section of the *Winnipeg Free Press* (Winnipeg, Manitoba), Saturday, May 2nd, 1970 (SpiderBaby Archives).

"The bear act happens to be the inspiration of Hungarian acrobat Janos Prohaska, who along with Hollywood's George Barrows, makes the best gorilla suits in town. Prohaska and Barrows lead their limited field in animal getups, performing in realistic monsters, anthropoids, bear and monkey suits. Besides being extremely talented in suit building, the two men, especially Prohaska, imitate animal moves with some feeling.

"Working out of his Santa Monica home, Janos constructs his own creatures, then submits photographs of the animal to television companies. He refuses to make a costume on order, preferring to take the risk and have unlimited time. A funny-looking stand-up crocodile is just finished and may debut next fall on the *Williams Show*, and Janos has white gorilla suits, a big glob that swells and recedes,[2] a tall pin head, roosters[3] and a charming female orangutan ready for hire. He is particularly fond of the lady orangutan because she has such a happy countenance.

"'I keep thinking my apes would catch on,' Prohaska said recently. 'The bear fooled me.'

"Janos was hired to play a bear out looking for a room, a one-shot performance last fall on the *Williams Show*. To his surprise Prohaska was called back for the cookie-begging routine. Guest Flip Wilson liked the bear so much he asked Janos to accompany him as co-host of the Hollywood Palace, and

---

2 The albino gorilla appeared in *Voyage to the Bottom of the Sea*'s episode "Fatal Cargo" (November 5th, 1967) and—with a horn affixed to the top of its cranium—as the Mugato (credited onscreen as "Gumato"!) on the *Star Trek* episode "A Private Little War" (February 2nd, 1968), and "the big glob that swells" was either the outsized microbe "The Mikie" from the final episode of the original *The Outer Limits*, "The Probe" (January 16th, 1965), or Prohaska's "Horta" from *Star Trek*'s "The Devil in the Dark" (March 9th, 1967).

3 These "roosters" may have been Prohaska's Giant Cuckoo-Wuckoo Bird from *It's About Time* (1966 episode), the bird monster from *Lost in Space* (1966 episode), and/or the Do-Do a.k.a. Dodo Bird from *Bewitched* (two episodes, 1967 and 1972).

1 "Cookie begging did the trick," uncredited article, *TV Diary, Winnipeg Free Press* (Winnipeg, Manitoba), Saturday, May 2nd, 1970, p.1.

Andy Williams and Cookie Bear (Janos Prohaska) perform together in just two of the many popular The Andy Williams Show comedy skits featuring the ursine character. Prohaska earned part of his living as a TV performer playing bears before and after Cookie Bear's surprise stardom.

hat helped snowball the response. By late January, time of the Andy Williams Golf Tourney, the bear had become a celebrity, and the host was being deluged by cookies.

"Knowing they had a good thing going, producers Chris Beard and Allan Blye were careful not to over-expose the bear, so Janos received less and less air time. He has a meal ticket with the show next season, and that's what counts."[4]

For anyone thinking the Cookie Bear might provide evidence that Prohaska may have created the suit for, and performed as, the Sasquatch in the Patterson-Gimlin footage—perish the thought! Prohaska's simians were always stylized, both in appearance and in Prohaska's performances, as was the Cookie Bear, whose comforting artifice likely enhanced his popularity (i.e., even child viewers recognized the he wasn't a *real* bear but rather a human comedian, and hence wouldn't hurt Andy Williams). Prohaska's Cookie Bear was patently "a fake bear limited in movement and cute facial expression,"[5] and quite obviously such to a TV audience accustomed to Ivan Tors' successful feature film **GENTLE GIANT** ([1967] from Walt Morey's 1965 bestselling Dutton Animal Award-winning novel) and the spin-off CBS-TV series *Gentle Ben* (58 episodes, September 10th, 1967 to August 31st, 1969). Both Ivan Tors production bears were primarily played by the very real PATSY Award-winning black bear Bruno the Bear, who also registered with audiences as the bear in John Huston's and John Milius' **THE LIFE AND TIMES OF JUDGE ROY BEAN** (1972, USA).

4 Uncredited *Winnipeg Free Press TV Diary* article, *Ibid.*

Prohaska *did* appear as a bear, albeit uncredited, in Jan Troell's western theatrical feature **ZANDY'S BRIDE** (1974); he also played bears on episodes of the TV series *The Red Skelton Show* (1965 episode), *The Munsters* (1965 episode), *Honey West* (1966 episode), *Bewitched* (1967 episode), *Mayberry R.F.D.* (1970 episode), *Here's Lucy* (1971 and 1973 episodes), *Love, American Style* ("Love and the Unbearable Fiancé, September 22nd, 1972), *Dusty's Trail* (1973), as well as an uncredited cameo as Cookie Bear on *Pat Paulsen's Half a Comedy Hour* (1970 episode).

Herman Munster (Fred Gwynne) and Olga the Dancing Bear (Prohaska) in The Munsters, "Herman's Child Psychology," Sept. 16, 1965.

Though the Cookie Bear didn't look or act like a real bear even to the untrained eye, it was Prohaska's performances that elevated the skit to its surprise popularity. "You can become a vicious or lovable bear easily… it all depends on how you move. I walk around like a jolly bear since I can't change expression, and everyone is happy."[6]

5 *Ibid.*
6 Janos Prohaska, *Ibid.*

THE LAST BROADCAST
A Foreword

"Found footage" (FF) cryptid movies are with us to stay, it seems.

Of those I've seen, Bobcat Goldthwait's **WILLOW CREEK** (2013, USA) remains the most fun I've had with an FF Bigfoot outing, especially in its opening acts, which essentially serve as a travelogue of key real-world Bigfoot locations any one of us with the time, mileage, and proximity could visit. Leads Bryce Johnson and Alexie Gilmore are the couple out to drive and then hoof-it to the original site of the '67 Patterson-Gimlin Sasquatch sighting/filmed footage—well, *he* is intent on that goal. *She*, being more rational, isn't so sure.

There's not much I can say without spoilers, and it would be unfair to spoil what works in **WILLOW CREEK**. As a vet hiker, I'm once again frustrated by the sheer stupidity of these characters (bring a fucking *compass* and mark your trail, boneheads!!!), but, hey, it's all believable. Idiots do this weekly somewhere in the U.S.—like, around here, in Vermont, New Hampshire and Maine, or wherever.

Suffice to say it's one of the better FF horrors of late. There's one loooooong sustained shot that really cooks (make sure you can *hear* it, though!) and should place this in any upcoming 'long take' film festivals, and the film proves in spades that Bobcat truly knows and loves the core bigfoot lore. **WILLOW CREEK**'s strengths outweighed the weaknesses, for me; Bobcat is an adventurous filmmaker, and I love his features. The overfamiliarity of the *form* (and, for this vet Sasquatch reader, the destination) was a drawback, but if taken on its own modest terms, it's a gem; best of the Bigfoot movies of the past few years, hands-and-feet-down, too.

If **WILLOW CREEK** had existed in, say, 1998, it would have rocked my world; alas, it's 2014, and we've all via shaky-handheld-camera been through a *lot* of fucking woods since '98 (**THE LAST BROADCAST**), and we're in pretty deep in the FF-fearstakes, which simultaneously (and arguably unfairly) raise and dash any expectations. Still, **WILLOW CREEK** remains a solid outing; glad I saw it, but won't likely be back for a revisit.

There have been others: I quite liked Eduardo Sánchez's **EXISTS** and Brett Simmons' **ANIMAL** (both 2014, USA), among others. All this had to begin somewhere, though, and while we can all agree that the Patterson-Gimlin footage was definitely the Ground Zero of the "found footage" cryptid subgenre, I nominate **THE LAST BROADCAST** as the first cryptid FF feature, which requires a bit of back story and an explanation…

Above: Jacob Hope (a.k.a. Norman Jeffries) exhibited the so-called Leed's Devil—the Jersey Devil—in a private museum in Philadelphia in January 1909; it was fraud, of course, a painted kangaroo with fake wings. **Left:** Blu-ray cover art for Bobcat Goldthwait's 'found footage' travelogue **WILLOW CREEK** (2013, USA).

JERSEY DEVILS:
Notes on THE LAST BROADCAST (1998)

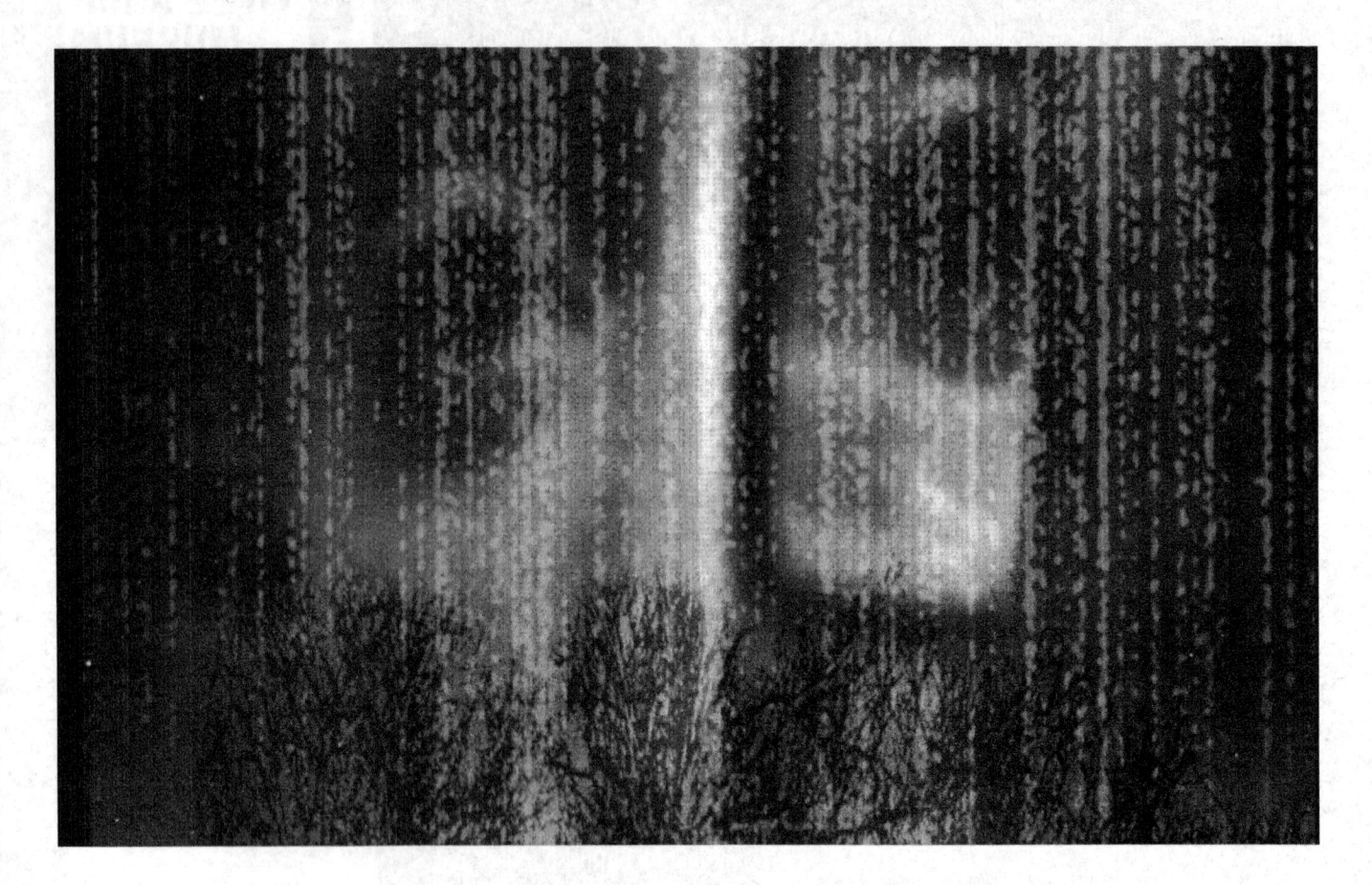

Let's not mince words here: Stefan Avalos' and Lance Weiler's **THE LAST BROADCAST** is **THE JAZZ SINGER** (1927, USA) of the digital era of filmmaking.

Avalos' and Weiler's debut feature stands as *the* first digitally-produced and satellite-broadcast theatrical feature in history—predating the thunder-stealing theatrical presentation via satellite of George Lucas' **STAR WARS: THE PHANTOM MENACE** (1999, USA) by almost a *full year*.

Eventually earning national coverage in *Forbes*, *Wired*, *Entertainment Weekly*, and many other magazines and newspapers, **THE LAST BROADCAST** was made in 1997 for about $900 with borrowed digital cameras (and a kid's toy one!) then edited with available Adobe software and a 166-megahertz personal computer. Through their own distribution firm Wavelength Releasing, Stefan and Lance's film debuted in 1998 in Doylestown, Pennsylvania (long before **THE BLAIR WITCH PROJECT** [1999, USA]!) as a digitally-projected theatrical event. Its successful one-week run was followed by a festival tour and (in conjunction with Cyberstar, Digital Projection, and DLP) momentous satellite-distributed showings in five US cities in October 1998, plus five international showings in May 1999 (New York, Cannes, London, Dublin, and Stockholm). It has since enjoyed a growing cult status, nurtured by its brief '99 video/DVD release (initially self-distributed, followed by innovative finite releases via *amazon.com* and the Hollywood Video national chain-stores), HBO's "New Millennium Horror" showcase, and seasonal showings on IFC.

Make no mistake: Stefan and Lance were and remain heralds of this new age we're now amid, which led to the retirement of 35mm film reels and projection. **THE LAST BROADCAST** forever changed (for better or worse) how films are and will be made and shown. They did so essentially on their own, bucking enormous odds—and they were indeed the first to say that **THE LAST BROADCAST** was (ironically enough, considering its title) only the beginning. In the new digital filmmaking generation, Stefan and Lance stand tall, setting an example for all who followed.

Stefan's and Lance's "Jersey Devil" tale **THE LAST BROADCAST** is also the precursor and blueprint for 1999's independent box-office sensation **THE BLAIR WITCH PROJECT**. In the annals of cryptid cinema, it's also right up there with the original Patterson/Gimlin footage as a wellspring for the plethora of "found footage" (FF) cryptid feature films that have ceaselessly continued to spring-up like mushrooms after a spring rain ever since.

THE LAST BROADCAST is a horror movie, a mystery, and a bit of a sleight-of-hand (camera) shell game with much to recommend it. The story is simple, but the telling is tantalizingly convoluted and intricate. In the context of an imagined 'documentary' by an obsessed filmmaker named David Leigh (David Beard), we are presented with the 'facts' in the case of Jim Suerd (Jim Seward), a young man who was tried and convicted for the murder in the Jersey Pine Barrens of two cable access program creators and their soundman. This amateurish cable "news team" (played by Stefan, Lance and Rein Clabbers) had wandered deep into the Jersey Barrens in search of the Jersey Devil, a legendary demon or monster long-believed to haunt that wilderness area. Though Suerd was convicted for the crime, Leigh believes someone or *something* else—perhaps even the Jersey Devil itself—was the culprit. As the film unfolds its calculating, intriguing tapestry of lies and misperceptions, we discover the horrifying truth of what happened that night.

Stefan's and Lance's decision to cut their teeth on such a film was aesthetically and commercially sound, placing them in a rich pantheon. The often-despised horror genre has provided fertile turf for many debut features: **THE CABINET OF DR. CALIGARI** broke fresh ground in 1919 for its makers and German cinema as a whole. In more recent memory, prominent filmmakers like George Romero (with his "shock felt 'round the world" **NIGHT OF THE LIVING DEAD** [1968, USA]), Steven Spielberg (TV features **NIGHT GALLERY** [1969] and **DUEL** [1970, both USA]), Wes Craven (**LAST HOUSE ON THE LEFT** [1972, USA]), David Cronenberg (**SHIVERS** a.k.a. **THEY CAME FROM WITHIN** [1975, Canada]), and David Lynch (**ERASERHEAD** [1977, USA]) all made their debuts with fresh, bracing explorations of the darker sides of our human nature.

Furthermore, **THE LAST BROADCAST** was based in genuine Americana folklore. The event the film 'documents' is fiction (the disappearance and murder of the *Fact or Fiction* film team, and conviction of Jim Suerd for their murder never actually happened), but Stefan and Lance didn't create the Jersey Devil legend, by any means. They grew up with it. Unlike the completely fabricated Blair Witch invented for their lucrative successor, the Jersey Devil at the heart of **THE LAST BROADCAST**'s narrative and mystery is—or was—'the real McCoy'. The Jersey Devil legend commonly names a woman named Mother Leeds as the wretched mother of the devil, which was born to an impoverished and overburdened family living in the desolate Pine Barrens during the early 1700s. Her child was either deformed or cursed, depending on which version of this oral legend you subscribe to, prompting Leeds to incarcerate the "devil" in her attic or cellar until it broke loose to haunt the Barrens for the next three centuries. Other versions chalk its origins up to a gypsy curse, Revolutionary War treason, or a documented birth in 1855 in Estellville in Atlantic County, among others.

Whatever its origins, the Devil is described as a bat-winged, serpentine monster with the head of a horse, hoofed feet, and taloned forelimbs. It plagued the area sufficiently to provoke an exorcism in the 1740s; to yield a rash of sightings and barnyard mayhem in 1840, the 1850s, the 1890s, and again in 1903. Most astonishing of all remains the cycle of sightings and encounters with the Jersey Devil in the New Year of 1909. Between January 16th and the 23rd, literally *thousands* of people in New Jersey and Pennsylvania (including citizens of southern Philadelphia) reported encounters with the Devil or discovery of its footprints that defy rationalization to this day. Among the witnesses were a Burlington, NJ policeman, a priest in Pemberton, two trolley-car conductors, a Trenton City Councilman, numerous search parties, and firefighters in West Collingswood, NJ, who allegedly actually turned a water hose on the creature and did battle with it!

Thereafter, the Jersey Devil receded into memory. More sightings and encounters followed, though none as dramatic or easily mapped or documented as that aforesaid 1909 week of horrors. Though bounties (ranging from $1,000 to $100,000) were offered and hucksters ballyhooed sideshow Jersey Devil fakery, the Devil was never killed or captured. Reported sightings and encounters periodically hit the newspapers in the 1920s and 1930s, and sporadically in the 1950s and early 1960s too, with the last known report filed in 1966. Whatever it was—*if* ever it lived at all—the Jersey Devil retired to local lore and folkloric circles until **THE LAST BROADCAST** disinterred its almost-forgotten legacy for a new millennium.[1]

Like its oft-cited successor (some would say "imitator," and with good reason) **THE BLAIR WITCH PROJECT** (that '99 film was produced and opened over a year after **THE LAST BROADCAST**; enough said), Stefan's and Lance's **THE LAST BROADCAST** is a fake documentary, a genre also referred to as "mockumentary" or (for its more horrific entries) "shockumentary." Furthermore, **THE LAST BROADCAST** uses the form to dissect, critique and condemn the sort of "reality TV" contemporary networks so recklessly exploit. It also cuts much deeper to probe the psychology and pathology behind the making of such fare. The conceit is central to the film itself; indeed, the opening credits do not acknowledge Stefan and Lance as the directors, but rather announces itself as "A Film by David Leigh", placing the fictional filmmaker at its center right from the beginning.

THE LAST BROADCAST has many precursors, including Peter Watkins' *The War Game* (BBC, 1967; never broadcast at the time of its making, but ironically winner of the Academy Award that year as "Best Documentary Feature") and Ruggero Deodato's notorious **CANNIBAL HOLOCAUST** (1981, Italy), which also attacked the ethics of filmmakers responsible for once-popular "shockumentaries" like Paolo Cavara/Gualtiero Jacopetti/Franco Prosperi's **MONDO CANE** (1962, Italy), and the *Faces of Death* series. And let us not forget

Cover art of the color 12-page *Jersey Devil* minicomic insert, exclusive to the Heretic Films DVD edition of **THE LAST BROADCAST** (released September 26th, 2006), produced by the Center for Cartoon Studies; cover art by Sean Morgan (pencils, splash page 'Devil'), Stephen R. Bissette (who also edited), Josie Whitmore So, scripted by Sarah Stewart Taylor, lettering by Adam Staffaroni. *[©2006, 2017 the respective artists.]*

Orson Welles' hysteria-inducing Halloween 1938 broadcast of H.G. Wells' *The War of the Worlds* that terrified listeners into believing the Martian invaders had landed on American soil!

The forgotten genre precursors to **THE LAST BROADCAST**, **THE BLAIR WITCH PROJECT**, and the entire FF horror genre are the original BBC television serialization of Nigel Kneale's *The Quatermass Experiment* (6 chapters, July 18th to August 22nd, 1953), and Val Guest's and Richard Landau's adaptation of Kneale's teleplay into Hammer Films' theatrical movie sensation **THE QUATERMASS XPERIMENT** (US title: **THE CREEPING UNKNOWN**, 1955, UK). In the original *The Quatermass Experiment* serial, a surviving audio wire-recording of the interior of a rocket's cabin during an experimental flight, for which three astronauts were present within the sealed cabin at lift-off but, inexplicably, only one remained therein upon the rocket's crash-landing in the English countryside. Instead of the teleplay's wire-recording—a visually-impoverished means of exposition—Guest and Landau reconceived the sequence for **THE QUATERMASS XPERIMENT** as a *filmed* record of the rocket's interior during flight. The eerie sequence in which Quatermass and his fellow investigators watch the silent, stuttering footage of the rocket flight unspooling remains a potent pseudo-*cinéma vérité* sequence, still retaining its power to disturb: as the three astronauts move about the cramped quarters of the rocket cabin, a wave of bright light consumes them. One astronauts falls, then another as a second bath of light washes over them; with the third wave, only one man remains standing as the footage abruptly terminates. Val Guest's inventive visualization of Kneale's concept was

---

[1] Actually, *The X-Files* episode "The Jersey Devil" was broadcast on October 8th, 1993. Also note Steven Stockage's and Thomas Ashley's **13TH CHILD: LEGEND OF THE JERSEY DEVIL** (2003), shot in Pennsylvania and Philadelphia's Holmsburg Prison, and Dante Tomaselli's **SATAN'S PLAYGROUND** (2006), shot in NJ's Pine Barrens.

cinema history in the making, the wellspring of the entire so-called "found footage/reality horror" movement we're amidst today. **THE QUATERMASS XPERIMENT** sequence was echoed in Riccardo Freda's and Mario Bava's **CALTIKI THE IMMORTAL MONSTER** (*Caltiki il mostro immortale*, 1959, Italy), when a missing archeologist's camera is found and the film is developed on-site and screened: the compact one minute, 39 seconds of FF echoes the in-ship FF screened in **QUATERMASS XPERIMENT**, and serves the same purpose: a teasing reveal of "what happened" in a hidden chamber from which only a single in-shock survivor emerged, in which the footage hides a lot more than it actually reveals. As Bava scholar Tim Lucas has noted numerous times, this sequence is a significant predecessor to the entire "found footage" wave of horror cinema we're currently overwhelmed with: **CANNIBAL HOLOCAUST, THE LAST BROADCAST, THE BLAIR WITCH PROJECT, PARANORMAL ACTIVITY** (2007, USA) and **[REC]** (2007, Spain), **CHRONICLE** (2012, USA), et cetera, here we come!

There have been plenty of playful "mockumentaries," too, prominent among them being the popular rock parody Rob Reiner's **THIS IS SPINAL TAP** (1984, USA), and **THE LAST BROADCAST** belongs in their ranks. Stefan and Lance acknowledged the inspiration that the genuine documentary **PARADISE LOST: THE CHILD MURDERS AT ROBIN HOOD HILLS** (1996) provided for **THE LAST BROADCAST** and its innovative (and much-imitated) website, supplanting **PARADISE LOST**'s all-too-real child murders with the fictional deaths that fuel **THE LAST BROADCAST**'s narrative.

Stefan and Lance also cite the "autobiographical" independent classic **DAVID HOLZMAN'S DIARY** (1967), in which writer/director Jim McBride and co-author and lead actor L.M. Kit Carson (playing Holzman) targeted the pretensions of student filmmakers with droll precision and wit. The fictional Holzman, a geeky and endearingly earnest youth aching to pierce to the 'truth' of his life via his obsessive filming of every aspect of it, brought a new satiric archetype to the cinema that has been imitated ever since. Thus, McBride (who went on to direct **BREATHLESS** [1983], **THE BIG EASY** [1986], both USA], etc.) and Carson (who later wrote **PARIS, TEXAS** [1984, West Germany/France/UK] and appeared in **RUNNING ON EMPTY** [1988, USA]) mirrored the narcissism of all who followed in their footsteps, anticipating the intrusive effects of bombshells like the PBS documentary series *An American Family* (1973). Clearly, the co-called "David Leigh" is Stefan's and Lance's "David Holzman", albeit with a much *darker* twist relevant to its generation.

In their subsequent solo features,[2] both filmmakers built upon the bedrock of **THE LAST BROADCAST**, further exploring the digital medium—as well as the fearful extremities of memory, obsession, possession, damnation and redemption. As the technology available to these artists continues to expand exponentially, so have their storytelling skills.[3] Still, **THE LAST BROADCAST** remains a seminal work—for its creators, and for all who love cinema. It stands as a historic landmark in cinema history, richly deserving of rediscovery by a new generation.

Revised and expanded from its original publication as "First Run Video Welcomes **LAST BROADCAST** Directors," in *The Brattleboro Reformer* (Brattleboro, VT), January 13th, 2000, and the revised version published in the bonus booklet accompanying the Heretic Films DVD edition of **THE LAST BROADCAST** (2006). The original article has been reprinted in print form in *S.R. Bissette's Blur, Volume 1: Video Views (1999-2000)* (Black Coat Press, 2007) and in digital book form in *Horrors! Cults, Crimes, & Creepers, S.R. Bissette's Best of Blur (Genre Edition) Volume 2: Horror, Cult & Crime Cinema, 1999-2001* (Crossroad Press, 2015).

The Leeds Devil a.k.a. the Jersey Devil has been a fixture of New Jersey folklore since the 18th Century. These comic panels from a 1909 edition of *The Times of Trenton* (Trenton, NJ) parodied the rash of alleged Jersey Devil sightings reported between January 16th–23rd of that year.

---

[2] Stefan and Lance recently wrote and directed solo digital features: Stefan Avalos' **THE GHOST OF EDENDALE** (2004) and Lance Weiler's **HEAD TRAUMA** (which screened for cast and crew on October 8th, 2005, and was released in 2006). Stefan had previously scripted, directed, produced and co-starred in **THE GAME** (a.k.a. **THE MONEY GAME**, 1993), and also executed the Terry Gilliam-like animation for the documentary on Gilliam's scuttled *Don Quixote* project, **LOST IN LA MANCHA** (2003). Lance Weiler later collaborated with David Cronenberg on a remarkable online interactive 'organism' entitled *Body/Mind/Change* (2013), incorporating aspects of filmmaking, videography, game-playing, and more.

[3] Weiler was subsequently co-creator and producer of *Radar* (42 episodes, 2009-2011), and currently teaches 21st Century storytelling at Columbia University, where he co-founded the Digital Storytelling Lab (launched 2013). He's also part of NYU's Cinema Research Institute on the future of film, and is part of the World Economic Forum steering committees on digital policy and on the future of interactive multi-media content creation. After producing visual effects for *Alien Encounters* (2013), *Heist* (2014), *FantomWorks* (2014–2015), *A Haunting* (2015–2016), and associate producing and handling effects work for **TERROR 5** (2016), Avalos debuted his latest feature **STRAD STYLE** (2017) at Slamdance 2017, winning the festival's Documentary Grand Jury Prize and Documentary Audience Award.

A Note on Lovecraftian Crytid Cinema…

Mother's Madness: THE DUNWICH HORROR (1970) affords us a look at Lavinia Whateley (Joanne a.k.a. Joanna Moore Jordan) in her padded cell, foreshadowing the eventual fate of Nancy Wagner (Sandra Dee) after the events depicted in the film.

North American cryptid research long ago traced its roots in First Nation and Native American cultures. As the reader likely knows, the name "Sasquatch" is derived from *sásq'ets*, Anglicized from the British-Columbian First Nation language Halkomelem (that word is itself also an Anglicized term for the language which comprises three distinctly different dialects).

Given the richness and relevancy of such First Nation/Native American lore, and how so many elements of that legacy have been spun into genre fiction and film, it may seem odd at this juncture to shift gears into the wholly-invented "lore" of H.P. Lovecraft. After all, the entirety of a book such as this could instead dedicate itself to the illustrated study of 'adopted' First Nation supernatural beings such as that infrequent-but-memorable 'star' of page and screen the Wendigo, a terrifying cannibalistic being known among Ojibwe, Cree, Naskapi, Saulteaux (or Anihšināpē ["Anishinaabe"]), and Innu people of the Northeastern Great Lakes and Atlantic coastal regions. Short fiction masterpieces like Algernon Blackwood's "The Wendigo" (1910) and August Derleth's "The Thing That Walked the Wind" (1933) fueled later comic book, film, television, and computer/video game incarnations. Invented First Nation/Native American cryptids like the late, great Maine author Rick Hautala's *Unticigahunk*, the titular *Little Brothers* (1988), only expand the menagerie—but those we'll save for *another* book, another day. The unnatural bridge between First Nation/Native American lore and colonial weird fiction was crafted, story by story, by the likes of Blackwood, Arthur Machen, and H.P. Lovecraft, and it's to Lovecraft we now turn in our tour of cinematic backwoods and backwater bogeymen…

There's no way to dig into American rural cryptid cinema without acknowledging the debt to H.P. Lovecraft, a debt which is obvious even in otherwise unrelated films covered in this book, like **ZAAT** and **CREATURE** (the 'mad science' of **ZAAT** and **TUSK** are quite apart from Lovecraft's realm, but **CREATURE** is *absolutely* of it). Lovecraft's invented "Cthulhu Mythos"—a creative playground shared-in and expanded upon by Lovecraft's circle of fellow horror pulp *Weird Tales* authors the likes of Clark Ashton Smith, Robert E. Howard, Robert Bloch, Frank Belknap Long, August Derleth, and others—is what Lovecraft is most renowned for; a mythos that has spilled-over into the 21st Century via a ceaseless stream of new fiction, film/video adaptations and originals, television, comics/graphic novels, music, and all manner of gaming media. Before Lovecraft's mythos congealed into full being, Lovecraft's embellished, partially-reinvented New England took shape, primarily staked-out from his native Rhode Island into the Central and Northeastern regions of Massachusetts—above Boston, bleeding into New Hampshire—and into my own home state of Vermont. Lovecraft's only Vermont-set tale, "The Whisperer in Darkness" (written in 1930, first published in 1931; filmed three times, in 1975, 2007, and most recently by the H.P. Lovecraft Historical Society themselves in 2011), was spiced with Lovecraft mentioning southern Vermont/New Hampshire landmarks like "steep Wantastiquet, about which singular old legends cluster,"[1] but its focal point was Lovecraft's invented cryptid the "Mi-Go". These remain among Lovecraft's *oddest* creations, initially linked by the story's scholarly narrator with "different tribal legends… a marked consensus of belief in certain vital particulars; it being unanimously agreed that the creatures were not native to this earth":

"The Pennacook myths, which were the most consistent and picturesque, taught that the

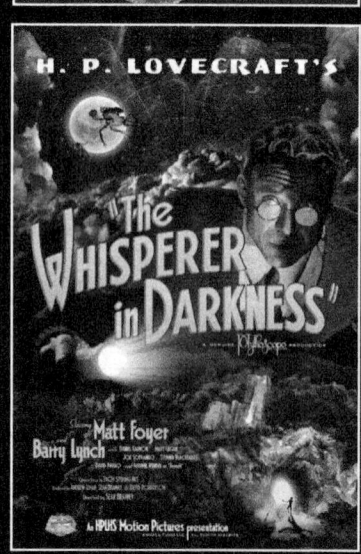

---

1 Lovecraft, "The Whisperer in Darkness."

Winged Ones came from the Great Bear in the sky, and had mines in our earthly hills whence they took a kind of stone they could not get on any other world... They knew the speech of all kinds of men—Pennacooks, Hurons, men of the Five Nations—but did not seem to have or need any speech of their own."[2]

Rather incredible to me still is how Lovecraft's narrator somehow gets from these Native American "Winged One" extraterrestrial miners to not only his Mi-Go—"a sort of huge, light-red crab with many pairs of legs and with two great bat-like wings in the middle of the back"—but also to the Yeti of the Himalayas, yet, all via colonial Vermont lore. Here's the relevant passage, complete; see if *you* can parse where or how these Lovecraftian bat-winged crustaceans mesh with those hominid cryptids which later became known as Yeti:

"Vermont myths differed but little in essence from those universal legends of natural personification which filled the ancient world with fauns and dryads and satyrs, suggested the kallikanzari of modern Greece, and gave to wild Wales and Ireland their dark hints of strange, small, and terrible hidden races of troglodytes and burrowers. No use, either, to point out the even more startlingly similar belief of the Nepalese hill tribes in the dreaded Mi-Go or 'Abominable Snowmen' who lurk hideously amidst the ice and rock pinnacles of the Himalayan summits."[3]

In his helpful and exhaustive 2014 annotation of Lovecraft's fiction, Leslie S. Klinger writes of this passage,

'Mi-Go' means 'man-wild' (or wild man) in Tibetan. It is possible that the narrator encountered the word 'mi-gou,' another Tibetan name for the Yeti or 'Abominable Snowman' of the Himalayas. The term Abominable Snowman did not appear in print until 1922, when Lieutenant Colonel Charles K. Howard-Bury published his account Mount Everest: The Reconnaissance, 1921 *and reported seeing footprints that his coolies [sic] concluded were those of 'The Wild Man of the Snows,' to which they gave the name of Metohkangmi, 'the abominable snow man' [...] The Mi-Go are mentioned again in* At the Mountains of Madness... *and in Lovecraft's sonnet cycle* Fungi from Yuggoth.[4]

As noted earlier, Jack Kirby and Stan Lee posited their four-color comicbook Abominable Snowmen actually being outsized humanoid *reptiles* wearing fur disguises to keep warm. I reckon Lovecraft's conflation of giant fungal-crustacean-beings with wings, and the Yeti isn't much more of a stretch, but it'll never make for convincing Cryptid Cinema if and when someone decides to incorporate that particular aspect into a dramatization. Wisely, the extant **WHISPERER IN DARKNESS** filmed versions have either downplayed or avoided altogether this potentially risible visual 'crossover'.[5]

Lovecraft is better known for his Massachusetts-based horror fiction, particularly the invented villages and towns he posited and positioned along the banks of his invented Miskatonic River. In this, Lovecraft was heir to the folklore-fueled fiction of New Yorker Washington Irving (1783-1859) and especially Salem, Massachusetts-born author Nathaniel Hawthorne (1804-1864). The Miskatonic River and the town of Arkham were first cited in Lovecraft's "The Picture in the House" (written in 1920, first published the following year). Lovecraft scholar Leslie S. Klinger charts this fictional landscape as follows:

It may be seen to follow an easterly course across Massachusetts and... it originates in the hills west of Dunwich. It runs eastward past Dunwich, turns southeast, and flows through the town of Arkham. The river empties into the sea two mile to the

Page 82, Top to Bottom: Distinctive cover art graced many of the Ballantine Books paperback editions of the H. P. Lovecraft stories and Lovecraftian curios, including Murray Tinkelman's cover art for the 1976 edition of *The Mask of Cthulhu by August Derleth* (a collection of Derleth's Lovecraftian stories) and Gervasio Gallardo's covers (1970–1973) like this one for *The Fungi from Yuggoth & Other Poems* (1971, interior illustrations by Frank Utpatel); The H. P. Lovecraft Historical Society's second feature film Lovecraft adaptation **THE WHISPERER IN DARKNESS** (2011) applied contemporary technology to emulate the look, sound, and feel of early 1930s sound cinema, since the story it was based upon was written in 1930 and published in 1931.

2 *Ibid.*

4 Leslie S. Klinger (editor and notes by), *The New Annotated H. P. Lovecraft* (2014, Liveright Publishing Corporation/W.W. Norton & Company), p.394.

5 That said, I have written at length about the 2007 H.P. Lovecraft Historical Society feature film adaptation, and will be gathering that material for revision and republication sometime in 2018–2019.

November 6, 1931: 'About 'Arkham' and 'Kingsport' [...] *They are typical but imaginary places... Vaguely, 'Arkham' corresponds to Salem (though Salem has no college), while 'Kingsport' corresponds to Marblehead. Similarly, there is no 'Dunwich'—the place being a vague echo of the decadent Massachusetts countryside around Springfield—say Wilbraham, Monson, and Hampden.'* [...] [6]

Hereabouts, one would also find on the Atlantic Ocean's Massachusetts shores the Gilman House of Innsmouth—a name evocative in hindsight of **CREATURE FROM THE BLACK LAGOON**'s adopted name of "Gillman"—where guests are confronted by the "strange kind of streak in the Innsmouth folks today...some of 'em have queer narrow heads with flat noses and bulgy, stary eyes that never seem to shut, and their skin ain't quite right"[7] These were the spawn of Captain Obed Marsh's trafficking with the Deep Ones, and arguably any subsequent fish-humanoid monsters in any media are of their lineage, or at least their kin. Nearby, "west of Arkham the hills rise wild," and contagion-carrying meteors from space bring "The Colour Out of Space" (written in 1927, published that same year), creating the tainted "blasted heath" of Lovecraft's personal favorite of his short stories.

But in other stories, Lovecraft wrote of bayous and backwaters far from New England. "The Statement of Randolph Carter" (written in 1919, first published in '20) references a "Big Cypress Swamp," which Klinger admits it is "impossible to determine which of... three southern locations—in Virginia, Georgia, or Florida—is referred to here."[8] Lovecraft's seminal "The Call of Cthulhu" touched upon the investigations of one Inspector John Raymond LeGrasse, leading him into

the wooded swamps south of New Orleans during a raid on a supposed voodoo meeting; and so singular and hideous were the rites connected with it, that the police could not but realize that they had stumbled on a dark cult totally unknown to them, and infinitely more diabolic than even the blackest of the African voodoo circles.[9]

These backwater and bayous—and similar "diabolic cults"—inform the likes of Fred M. Andrews and Tracy Morse's filmed-in-Louisiana gem **CREATURE** (2011), where Innsmouth-like amphibious humanoids and human-monster miscegenation thrive.

Later in his life, Lovecraft pioneered an inventive cross-fertilization of these various threads in the fictional tapestries he'd woven. Everyone is self-franchising today, but Lovecraft was slow and sly about constructing his mythos, most ambitiously laid out in his epic novella *At the Mountains of Madness*. Here, Lovecraft detailed a grand prehistoric backstory in which

...the shoggoths of the sea, reproducing by fission and acquiring a dangerous degree of accidental intelligence... seem to have become peculiarly intractable toward the middle of the Permian age, perhaps 150 million years ago, when a veritable war of re-subjugation was waged upon them by the marine Old Ones... During the Jurassic age the Old Ones met fresh adversity in the form of a new invasion from outer space—this time by half-fungous,

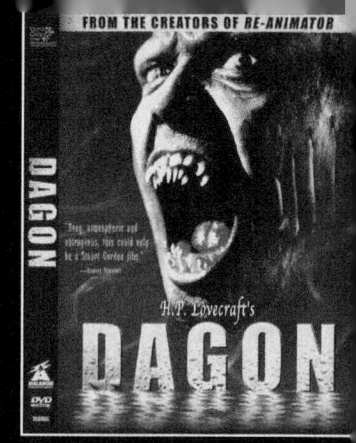

Left: The Gillman was prominently featured in the ad-art for the original 1954 release of **CREATURE FROM THE BLACK LAGOON**. **Above:** US DVD and Thai theatrical release art for Stuart Gordon and Dennis Paoli's **DAGON** (2001), which lifted its title from Lovecraft's 1919 short story but was actually a long-in-the-works adaptation of Lovecraft's classic novella *The Shadow Over Innsmouth* (written 1931, published 1936), in which Innsmouth was inhabited by the rather fishy families named the Waites, the Eliots, the Marshes... and the Gilmans.

Klinger, *Ibid.*, pp.37, 38.
Lovecraft, "The Shadow Over Innsmouth" (written in 1931, first published in 1936).
Klinger, *Ibid.*, p.13.
Lovecraft, "The Call of Cthulhu" (written in 1926, first published in 1928).

...half-crustacean creatures from a planet identifiable as the remote and recently discovered Pluto; creatures undoubtedly the same as those figuring in certain whispered hill legends of the north, and remembered in the Himalayas of the Mi-Go, or Abominable Snow-Men... In the end the Mi-Go drove the Old Ones out of all the northern lands, though they were powerless to disturb those in the sea...[10]

Aside from the unproduced Guillermo del Toro adaptation of *At the Mountains of Madness*, which most recently almost crashed-and-turned-into-turnover in 2011,[11] the closest Cryptid Cinema has come to such an ambitious narrative was another ultimately unproduced genre epic, David Allen's "**THE PRIMEVALS**". Allen's begun-but-aborted opus involved an expedition to remote snowy regions discovering the Yeti, ancient 'lost' tribal cultures, and reptilian invaders from space. Alas, despite repeated announcements by producer Charles Band right up until stop-motion animator Allen's untimely death on August 16th, 1999, "**THE PRIMEVALS**" was never completed.[12]

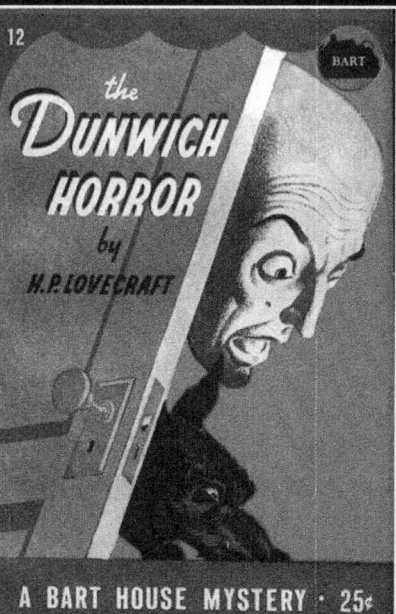

Lovecraftian Cinema has flourished since it tentatively took root in the 1960s. If all goes according to plan, I'll be pulling together a book (or two) on Lovecraftian Cinema in the not-too-distant future, but we're here now to touch upon the crossover between Cryptid Cinema and Lovecraftian Cinema. That juncture seems to me to be the amateur stop-motion animation adventure **EQUINOX** (1967-1970, USA), wherein occult forces bring tusked, Bigfoot-like beings into our dimension, as well as giants, winged demons, and a marvelous land-cephalopod—the former and latter of which are still among my favorite Cinema Cryptids of the 1960s—but we'll get to **EQUINOX** in due time. First, let's steer our compass to Lovecraft's fictional village of Arkham, Massachusetts.

Though it's an uneasy fit in these pages, I decided some cinematic introduction to Lovecraftian Cinema was essential to this overview. I could have gone with the film versions of "The Whisperer in Darkness," but those came late in the game; given the Lovecraft filmography, the backwoods-set "The Dunwich Horror" best fit the bill. The springboard of Lovecraft's "Arkham cycle" (his own term), and still his best-known story, "The Dunwich Horror" (written in 1928, published in '29) remains the only story to offer a rather lengthy passage from Lovecraft's fictional tome, the *Necronomicon*, which many erroneously believe to be an actual book. "The Dunwich Horror" also brings us back to Lovecraft's occasional tapping of First Nation/Native American roots, with its landscape punctuated by inexplicable "noises in the hills... reported from year to year... still... a puzzle to geologists and physiographers," which Klinger associates with the "town of Moodus, Connecticut,"

> *...long associated with spooky noises such as those described for Dunwich. It is thought that several Native American cults focused on Moodus as a place where a god, Hobomock (an evil deity), was actually present. The Algonquins named it Machimoodus, the place of bad noises. Scientists attribute the noises to micro-earthquakes (the region has a long history of quakes).*[13]

Lacking cryptids *per se* but involving human/inhuman hybrids and siblings and establish-

---

Top: Promotional still of two of the stop-motion animated Yetis for David Allen's sadly unrealized feature film **THE PRIMEVALS**; the Yeti also featured prominently in Richard Hescox's preproduction ad art for **THE PRIMEVALS**. **Above:** Cover of the rare Bartholomew House (Bart House) 1945 paperback edition of *The Dunwich Horror*, cover artist unknown.

---

10 Lovecraft, At the Mountains of Madness (written in 1931, first published in 1936).

11 Yoselin Acevedo, "Guillermo del Toro Says He 'Should Have Lied' About the 'At the Mountains of Madness' R Rating," *IndieWire*, April 6th, 2017, archived online (@ http://www.indiewire.com/2017/04/guillermo-del-toro-at-the-mountains-of-madness-r-rating-universal-1201802783/)

12 Charles Band was still touring industry trade shows—including the Video Software Dealer Association (VSDA) trade shows I met him at—with promises of the pending completion of (and even props from) the "**PRIMEVALS**" production; see David Kilmer, "Stop-motion animator David Allen passes away," *AWN.com (Animation World Network)*, Friday, August 20, 1999, archived online (@ https://www.awn.com/news/stop-motion-animator-david-allen-passes-away): "...For ten years he had been working on an independent project, a feature called **PRIMEVALS**. (The film will be finished at Full Moon Studios where the film was being animated before Allen's death.)." Also see the cover story of *Cinefantastique* Winter 1978 (Vol. 8, No. 1), which remains the most comprehensive published account of David Allen's planned epic to date.

13 Klinger, *Ibid.*, pg. 347.

ing many of the templates for so many of the backwoods horror films to follow the story's publication, "The Dunwich Horror" is rich in New England artifacts of the unusual—including pre-Colonial stone chambers and standing stones—and it's also the tale which introduced Lovecraft's now-iconic fictional educational institution, Miskatonic University. Wilbur Whateley is himself arguably a borderline cryptid of sorts, "shabby, dirty, bearded and uncouth of dialect... almost eight feet tall," he cuts quite a startling figure in the first half of Lovecraft's story.

> ...'Inbreeding?' [Dr.] Armitage muttered half-aloud to himself. 'Great God, what simpletons! Shew them Arthur Machen's Great God Pan and they'll think it a common Dunwich scandal! But what thing—what cursed shapeless influence on or off this three-dimensional earth—was Wilbur Whateley's father?...'[14]

The film adaptations inevitably humanize Wilbur Whateley—in Lovecraft, Wilbur was a "bent, goatish giant...like the spawn of another planet or dimension; like something only partly of mankind, and linked to black gulfs of essence and entity that stretched like titan phantasms beyond all spheres of force and matter, space and time..."—but Wilbur's brother is *another* 'thing' altogether. Read on...

Most Lovecraftian filmographies list American-International Pictures (AIP)'s **THE DUNWICH HORROR** (1970, USA) as the third or fourth "official" Lovecraft feature film adaptation,[15] choosing to ignore **LA MARCA DEL MUERTO** ([1961] released cut-and-dubbed by Jerry Warren into **CREATURE OF THE WALKING DEAD** in 1965), the Mexican unofficial/uncredited adaptation of Lovecraft's *The Case of Charles Dexter Ward* (written in 1927, published in '41), the same novella from which the first American Lovecraft film adaptation **THE HAUNTED PALACE** (1963) was derived. However, **THE HAUNTED PALACE** was actually sold as an *Edgar Allan Poe* film, and AIP's adaptation of "The Colour Out of Space," **DIE, MONSTER, DIE!** (a.k.a. **MONSTER OF TERROR**, 1965, UK/USA), downplayed the Lovecraft source material, since HPL's name at that time meant next-to-nothing at the box-office. I was fourteen years old when **THE DUNWICH HORROR** opened, and it was the first theatrical feature film ever to be *sold* as a Lovecraft film...

---

14 Lovecraft, "The Dunwich Horror."

15 (See *http://www.yankeeclassic.com/miskatonic/dcommunications/films/thefilms01.htm*). It depends, too, on whether you count **THE SHUTTERED ROOM** (1967, UK), which was adapted from one of the short stories that August Derleth constructed around fragments of stories discovered among Lovecraft's personal papers, or **CURSE OF THE CRIMSON ALTAR** (a.k.a. **THE CRIMSON CULT**, 1968, UK) as "official" Lovecraft films or not.

Above, Left & Right: Leave it to Jerry Warren—who you've already met in these pages—to add the patently-phony actor credit from **MAN BEAST**, "Rock Madison," to **LA MARCA DEL MUERTO** (1961, Mexico) when he hacked-and-dubbed it into **CREATURE OF THE WALKING DEAD** (1965), further obscuring the film's debt to Lovecraft's *The Case of Charles Dexter Ward* (written in 1927, published in '41). **Left:** Cover art for the 1964 Lancer Books paperback edition of *The Colour Out of Space and Others*, one of three editions from Lancer (1964, 1967, 1969). **Bottom Left:** Italian *locandina* for **DIE, MONSTER, DIE!** (1965); art by Mario Piovano / Studio Paradiso.

DEAN'S DUELING DUNWICH HORRORS:
Or; A Meandering Meditation on How One Actor Shook Both Sides of the Gate

Sometimes, genre history is made in mere seconds.

It's a fact harder to digest in the moment, more often than not, but transparently simple to spot with 20/20 hindsight. Sometimes, those moments blaze like comets the second they are first experienced, in their initial theatrical release: the gate opening to Kong's realm in **KING KONG** *(1933, USA), the Thing at the doorway in* **THE THING FROM ANOTHER WORLD** *(1951, USA), the shower curtain torn open and subsequent murder in* **PSYCHO** *(1960, USA), the zombies tearing into human flesh in* **NIGHT OF THE LIVING DEAD** *(1968, USA), the metal door thrown open, the plunge of the hammer, the dragging of downed prey into the abattoir and slamming shut of the door in* **THE TEXAS CHAINSAW MASSACRE** *(1974, USA).*

Doors, so many doors…

Other transformative moments we recognize only years, perhaps decades, later.

Swedish poster (artwork by Fuchs) for **THE INVISIBLE RAY** (1936), which the late, great horror author and scholar Les Daniels considered to be the first-ever Lovecraftian-themed film.

Topless promo shot depicting a scene not seen in the film itself.

Much has been written over the past half-century about H.P. Lovecraft, Lovecraft's fiction, the Cthulhu mythos, and the apparent impossibility of adapting Lovecraft's unique stories to cinema. Lovecraft himself had little regard for the genre movies of his day, though few scholars (of either Lovecraft or cinema) have noticed that what is arguably the first example of "Lovecraftian cinema" was released in Lovecraft's lifetime. The late, great Les Daniels argued that the Universal Pictures Boris Karloff/Bela Lugosi vehicle **THE INVISIBLE RAY** (1936, USA; directed by

Dell comics adaptation of the Karloff/Lovecraft film DIE, MONSTER, DIE!

Lambert Hillyer) lifted the premise of Lovecraft's "The Colour Out of Space", with Karloff playing much the same role he would later in his career in the first official screen adaptation of the story, DIE, MONSTER, DIE! (1965, USA).

Directed by Roger Corman's ever-inventive art director Daniel Haller, DIE, MONSTER, DIE! was and remains a pedestrian but entertaining outing with a least one imaginative set-piece—the hero's (Nick Adams) fleeting glimpse of the mutant creatures caged in Karloff's lab, looking like "a zoo in hell!"—but precious little that looked, felt, or played as being remotely Lovecraftian.[1]

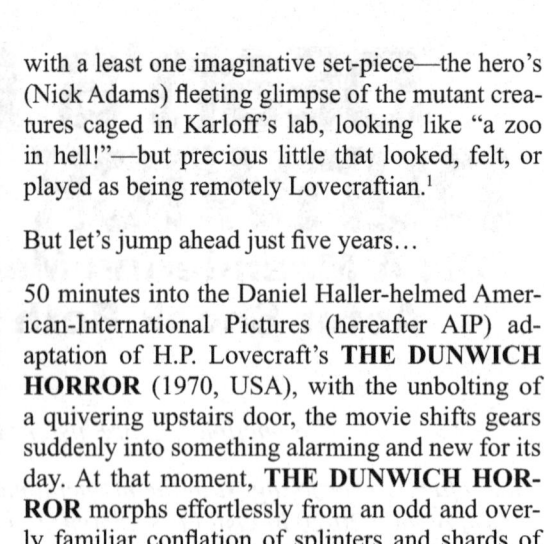

But let's jump ahead just five years…

50 minutes into the Daniel Haller-helmed American-International Pictures (hereafter AIP) adaptation of H.P. Lovecraft's THE DUNWICH HORROR (1970, USA), with the unbolting of a quivering upstairs door, the movie shifts gears suddenly into something alarming and new for its day. At that moment, THE DUNWICH HORROR morphs effortlessly from an odd and overly familiar conflation of splinters and shards of the classic H.P. Lovecraft short story with tropes from Satanist movies dating back to the silent era, ROSEMARY'S BABY (1968, USA), and "crazy relative in the attic" potboilers to—apologies for the crude wording—*tentacle rape!*

Suddenly, that which was only hinted at in Lovecraft's fiction was made explicit. AIP even made it the center of their ad campaign, in poster and advertising art painted by vet studio artist Reynold Brown. It was rape imagery, pure and simple, and Brown himself reportedly found it so distasteful a job that he soon retired from the field he'd worked in for over two decades. Such imagery was always implicitly sexual, as in Brown's iconic art for the trio of CREATURE FROM THE BLACK LAGOON films and nearly every monster movie poster Brown painted thereafter (including Brown's art for the previous AIP Lovecraft adaptions, THE HAUNTED PALACE and DIE MONSTER DIE). But DUNWICH HORROR's ad art was unequivocally a monster-rape image, the most explicitly staged of any Brown had ever painted. THE DUNWICH

---

[1] That same year—1965—an unofficial appropriation of Lovecraft themes did play in theaters as a second feature accompanying William Castle's I SAW WHAT YOU DID. It was DARK INTRUDER (1965, USA), produced by Alfred Hitchcock's TV production wing Shamley Productions as a pilot for NBC originally entitled *The Black Cloak*, featuring Leslie Nielsen as a turn-of-the-century occult investigator in San Francisco. Clocking in just shy of an hour, the script, by genre vet Barré Lyndon (pseudonym of Alfred Edgar, who also scripted NIGHT HAS A THOUSAND EYES [1948, USA], MAN IN THE ATTIC [1953, USA], and the George Pal THE WAR OF THE WORLDS [1953, USA]), involved a demonic killer named Malachi (Werner Klemperer, soon to gain fame as Colonel Klink on *Hogan's Heroes*) evoking the names of deities from Lovecraft's Cthulhu mythos in its bid to take over its human host (Mark Richman). The relationship between man and demon recalls that between the Whateley siblings—man and demon—in "The Dunwich Horror", and dialogue citing "gods older than the human race", Dagon, Azathoth, and Nyogtha made DARK INTRUDER a far more Lovecraftian cinematic shadow than DIE, MONSTER, DIE!

A 1969 pre-production ad featuring a different name and star for the film.

A trio of ROSEMARY'S BABY posters:

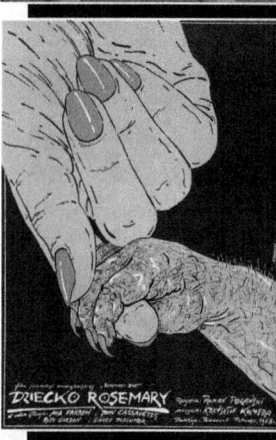

From Top to Bottom: 1984 Polish reissue poster (art by Wieslaw Walkuski), original release Polish poster (art by Andrzej Pagowski), and a rare alternate US one-sheet poster design.

Stockwell's Wilbur is an aloof, obsessed, and oddly urbane young warlock, praying to "Yog-Sothoth".

"Aleister Crowley and his belief in Ordo Templi Orienti; he created the Signs of Nox as a counterpart to the Golden Dawn's Signs of Lux; the earliest example of it that I know of is from Crowley's Book of Lies.
I do find it interesting that it doesn't, of course, appear in HPL's Dunwich Horror but Stockwell uses it in the movie version, since Dunwich Horror is essentially HPL's take on Machen's (himself a Golden Dawn member, of course) Great God Pan, though I believe it more likely that someone just threw that in to the script because they saw a pic and thought that it looked cool."

~ Paul Hyson
(quoted with permission)

HORROR was the straw that broke the camel's back for Reynold Brown; this was his final movie promo art.

Creaky as it is, there's more to **THE DUNWICH HORROR**, than contemporary audiences necessarily recognized or responded to. The film had been announced for some time, with early trade magazine ads from AIP announcing Peter Fonda as the lead and Mario Bava as the director. Well, we didn't get *that*, but this still wasn't a studio "establishment" movie; there was more percolating here than easily met even the most receptive eyes, circa 1970. This was, after all, reflecting in part the input and sensibilities of young up-and-coming screenwriter (and future director) Curtis Hanson, who at the time was editing *Cinema* magazine; Hanson co-scripted the adaptation with Henry Rosenbaum and Ronald Silkosky. From its animated opening title sequence—still eye-catching and audacious, however crude the design and actual animation—**THE DUNWICH HORROR** was carrying on a tradition Corman had established as such in the 1950s (remember, Corman's films often sported arresting animated titles by vet animator Paul Julian, beginning with **SWAMP WOMEN**, 1955, USA), and pushing a few envelopes further. **THE DUNWICH HORROR** may not have been "Lovecraft enough" for Lovecraft devotees, but it handily summarized and dispensed with the previous generation's genre tropes before the opening titles were over. Conservative enough to satisfy AIP's honchos while incorporating, anticipating and setting new thresholds for the shocking 1970s, **THE DUNWICH HORROR** was among the most interesting of the post-**ROSEMARY'S BABY** spinoffs. The 1970 film is as handy a crossover point from Aleister-Crowley-to-Charles-Manson cult horror as any, with Dean Stockwell playing Wilbur Whateley, the sire of a birth orchestrated by his father (Sam Jaffe) that left his mother insane, and his brother the-thing-behind-the-door upstairs. Thus, the boy actor who had played Joseph Losey's **THE BOY WITH THE GREEN HAIR** (1948), the young D.H. Lawrence hero (in **SONS AND LOVERS** [1960]), and the doomed lover of **RAPTURE** (1965) brought something fresh to his role, an approach taken hot off the tabloid presses, as it were. *This* Wilbur Whateley bore precious little resemblance to the weird Massachusetts halfbreed (half—*what?*) of Lovecraft's story: Stockwell played Wilbur as a pseudo-hippie on a bizarre religious "trip", seeking either an acolyte or a birth mother (for *what?*). Instead of Lovecraft's surly inbred, *this* Wilbur is a surrogate Charles Manson: a fanatic able to "pass" in proper company… for a little while; a bit of a womanizer; an initially attractive if furtive man with a zealot's agenda.

Stockwell's Wilbur is an aloof, obsessed, and oddly urbane young warlock, praying to "Yog-Sothoth", bracing his finger rings at odd angles to his temples before deflowering Sandra Dee on an ancient altar by the sea (echoes of Corman's Poe films; no surprise, since both AIP and Haller were essential partners in Corman's procession of 1960s Poe adaptations). In fact, Stockwell's Wilbur Whateley was an immediate contemporary to Andrew Prine's lead role in **SIMON, KING OF THE WITCHES** (1971, USA), and the two look, sound, and unreel as brothers in far more than their early 1970s timeframe. They are the new Hollywood's instant-Polaroid of Charles Manson, the brand-new incarnation of satanic cult mind-control and cultural bogeyman, supplanting Crowley's dominion over the archetype since the

89

Mary Louise Brown, wife of poster artist Reynold Brown, recalled: "One day Reynold was working on a drawing that featured some sexual images for one of AIP's movies and he heard the kids coming up the stairs and he hid the drawing under a stack of papers because he was embarrassed by it. He told me later that day that he wanted to stop doing that kind of work." Hiding work-in-progress on the poster art as he completed the job, Reynold also "filed" all his rough sketches for **THE DUNWICH HORROR** to the trash, noting, "When you have to do that, it's time to quit." Reynold Brown and Mary Louise Tejeda-Brown are quoted from the biography *Reynold Brown: A Life in Pictures* by Daniel Zimmer and David J. Hornung (2009, The Illustrated Press), page 103.

Above: Art director Daniel Haller's set design was a vital design element in Reynold Brown's poster art for **THE HAUNTED PALACE** (1963), and an overt sexual innuendo suggesting interspecies rape informed its ballyhoo.
Below: Australian daybill poster for the H.P. Lovecraft/August Derleth adaptation **THE SHUTTERED ROOM** (1967). **Below Right: DUNWICH HORROR** director Haller—former art director for Roger Corman's American-filmed Edgar Allan Poe adaptations—introduced ersatz Native-American motifs into the Whateley abode, as seen here.

early 1900s. As that transitional figure, Stockwell was the incarnation of that archetypal transformation. It was a new age, and what was dawning, according to the new Manson cult leader archetype, was hardly the Age of Aquarius.

THE DUNWICH HORROR is also a sterling example of an early independent-studio horror opus lifting experimental cinema imagery and kinetics to evoke "the unspeakable"—in this case, adopting and adapting recreations of imagery from Jack Smith's infamous **FLAMING CREATURES** (1963, USA). Smith's film was an often-busted experimental/underground film which **DUNWICH HORROR** executive producer Corman had already pillaged/ pastiched for his own **MASQUE OF THE RED DEATH** (1964, USA) and **THE TRIP** (1967, USA). In this, Haller's **THE DUNWICH HORROR** is also significant. Later horror films like the Japanese **RINGU** (a.k.a. リング, 1998) and its US remake **THE RING** (2002) appropriated imagery and kinetics from underground cinema to evoke the unspeakable: in both (and all) *Ring* films, another experimental cinema pastiche opens lethal dimensional portals, too. The die was cast here, in Corman's Poe films and **THE TRIP**, and more so in **THE DUNWICH HORROR**. In this, I am not claiming that Haller was an innovator. He was merely following and building upon an already-mainstreamed new genre template: before **FLAMING CREATURES**, Corman had sown the seeds in the Poe film dream sequences (beginning with **THE FALL OF THE HOUSE OF USHER** [1960, USA]); contemporary to Smith, John Frankenheimer's **SECONDS** (1966, USA) had adopted similar distortion-lensed nightmare imagery (thanks to cinematographer James Wong Howe), *sans* Smith's sexualized androgyny. By 1970, directors like Paul Wendkos were using the trope even on television: see, for example, Wendkos' **FEAR NO EVIL** (1969, USA) and theatrically-released **THE MEPHISTO WALTZ** (1970, USA). **THE DUNWICH HORROR** took it just a little further, with its "trip/orgy" visions/dreams sporting more **FLAMING CREATURES**-like androgynes among their numbers.

Other flourishes incorporating what straight-AIP-production-teams *thought* echoed the counterculture grace the film's visual design. Wilbur/Stockwell's chest tattoos were created by Los Angeles artist George Herms (those chest tattoos were later echoed in Kim Henkel's **THE TEXAS CHAINSAW MASSACRE. THE NEW GENERATION** [a.k.a. **THE RETURN OF THE TEXAS CHAINSAW MASSACRE**, 1994, USA], and in Clive Barker's **HELLRAISER** [1987, UK] and **LORD OF ILLUSIONS** [1995, USA]; weird how all this stuff resonates around).

Even to 1970 movie audiences "in the know", this was perhaps more Bradbury than Lovecraft—after all, Jack Smight's Ray Bradbury adaptation **THE ILLUSTRATED MAN** (1969, USA) was a fresh memory, still playing in drive-ins and theaters. The floor patterns in the Whateley abode and the designs on the scepter the elder Whateley (Sam Jaffe) totes around are ersatz Native-American patterns. **THE DUNWICH HORROR**'s art direction is a real 1970 mash-up of "this is what we think *you* think magick symbols look like!" art director lunacy. What a crash course!

Up to this point in the movie, Sandra Dee's ersatz-**FLAMING CREATURES** nightmares, visions, and violation mesh the AIP/Corman aesthetic with the still-fresh transgressions of Roman Polanski/Ira Levin's **ROSEMARY'S BABY** (i.e., Mia Farrow/Rosemary's vivid sexual encounter with the devil). But Haller took this further at the 50-minute mark in **THE DUNWICH HORROR**. The eruption was bracing but oh-so-fleeting at the time: a woman (Elizabeth Hamilton) searching for Sandra Dee opens the forbidden/forbidding door, she screams as the screen flash-flames scarlet, and something with tentacles assaults her in a spasm of rubbery thrashing. Even in 1970, it was an assault both familiar and unfamiliar—how many forbidden/forbidding doors had been opened since **THE THING FROM ANOTHER WORLD** (1951, USA) two decades before, or **PSYCHO** a decade before? The two earlier Lovecraft films that acknowledged they were based on Lovecraft stories had *their* forbidden doors, hiding hidden horrors: Corman's own **THE HAUNTED PALACE** (1963, USA; based on Lovecraft's novella *The Case of Charles Dexter Ward*), David Greene's **THE SHUTTERED ROOM** (1967, USA; based on a short story August Derleth extrapolated from Lovecraft's notes for a never-scribed short story).

But **THE DUNWICH HORROR**, in mere sec-

Artist Lee Brown Coye's Wilbur Whateley as he appears on the dust jacket of the 1963 Arkham House edition.

onds—and only for a few seconds—went further than any genre film before. We see enough perhaps to divine the similarity between the attacking creature and the Reynold Brown image on the one-sheet poster, *if* we'd seen the newspaper ad or the poster before seeing the movie. Regardless of that reference point, *any* viewer can see this is a violent (not dreamlike) monster-rape: the screaming victim's clothing is torn off, leaving no doubt she has been stripped nude for the assault (the new paradigm of Roger Corman's post-1970 market template apparent: a breast, a nipple, barely but definitely visible, the first onscreen Corman monster-rape).

Weak tea today, but this was something fresh, even alarming in 1970. It was enough to prompt Reynold Brown to abandon painting for the movie studios ever again. It was enough to provoke uneasy laughter—but not enough to provoke the censors. This was, after all, still "safe enough" for AIP's market at drive-in and neighborhood hardtops—rated "M" for "Mature", the forgotten MPAA rating that later became "GP", then "PG", then bifurcated into "PG" and "PG-13", and far more accommodating of nudity and sexual content than it would be only a year or two later—but it was still a violation unlike any shown before on an American movie screen.

Make no mistake. Haller's red-tinted flash-frame "tentacle rape" sequence set the standard for later such violations—following through, **THE DUNWICH HORROR** to 1979's **ALIEN** (that horrific shot of the tail slithering up female Nostromo crewmember Veronica Cartwright's leg, poised for penetration) to **INSEMINOID** (a.k.a. **HORROR PLANET**, 1981, UK), full circle to Corman's 1981 New World Pictures **ALIEN**-riff **GALAXY OF TERROR** (the giant-maggot-rape) and on to artier genre fare like **POSSESSION** (1981, France / West Germany) and **JACOB'S LADDER** (1990, USA), and what was, by then, an entire subgenre of Japanese horror manga/anime/live-action cinema, 触手強姦 / *shokushu goukan*.

I know, I know, this is all weird shit. But such is the lumpy legacy of Lovecraftian cinema.

There are other elements that emerge in hindsight. For many, this was the first time they heard passages from Lovecraft's invented *Necronomicon* read aloud; according to James Paul Harless, the audience he first saw the film with in 1970 laughed aloud at some of those passages, especially at the point that Dr. Henry Armitage (Ed Begley) messes with Wilbur's climactic recitation from the *Necronomicon* to complete the insemination of Dee on the stone altar. According to Harless, some of that laughter was prompted by Stockwell's facial contortions; he hams it up shamelessly without breaking character, and wouldn't be this creepy a screen presence again until David Lynch had him lip-synching Roy Orbison's "In Dreams" in **BLUE VELVET** (1986, USA).

Italian newspaper ad (from *Il Corriere della Sera*, 9/76) ... forgoing the monster and forging straight ahead in the salacious.

Artist Lee Brown Coye was the premier cover artist for much of the collected weird fiction published by Arkham House in the 1950s and 1960s.

Same Title, Different Works! **Above:** German A1 poster art for the British/American co-production **NIGHT OF THE EAGLE** (US title: **BURN, WITCH, BURN**, 1962), based on Fritz Leiber's novel *Conjure Wife* (1943), which was also adapted to film as **WEIRD WOMAN** (1944) and **WITCHES' BREW** (1980). **Below:** Vintage Spanish edition of A. Merritt's novel *Burn Witch Burn!* (1932), which was adapted to film as Tod Browning's **THE DEVIL-DOLL** (1936) and Benito Alazraki's **MUÑECOS INFERNALES** (1961).

Speaking of future star turns and demon births, almost a decade before she feared what might be growing in her womb in John Frankenheimer's **PROPHECY** (1979, USA; ballyhooed as "The Monster Movie"), Talia Shire appears in **THE DUNWICH HORROR** (as "Talia Coppola") playing the Dunwichs' country doctor's nurse/secretary (she, too, is ravished by the demon creature/brother, but off-screen—we get the buildup and scream, but Haller cuts away from the violation this time). There are other points of interest (Curtis Hanson's script nods to vet director and friend Sam Fuller, via the reporter named "Fuller"), but I'll leave further analysis for a future time and venue.

I don't mean to pile too-intensive analysis or high expectations onto **THE DUNWICH HORROR**, or give the movie too much credit—but it is what it is, and it was what it was. Haller was a solid enough director, continuing with a pair of action movies (**DEVIL'S ANGELS** [1967, USA], **THE WILD RACERS** [1968, USA]) between his Lovecraft AIP adaptations, and soon after helming a couple genre gems (like *"I'll Never Leave You—Ever"* for *Rod Serling's Night Gallery*)—and the film has been ignored, ridiculed, and/or dismissed for far, far too long.

Almost a half-century later, Dean Stockwell was back in Dunwich, on the other side of the struggle to resurrect the Old Ones...

Leigh Scott's **THE DUNWICH HORROR** (a.k.a. **WITCHES: DARKEST EVIL**, 2009, USA/Germany) adapts one of the greatest of all H.P. Lovecraft stories—loosely, very loosely—into a fresh concoction involving traveling exorcists/occultists Dr. Henry Armitage (Dean Stockwell) and female sidekick (Sarah Lieving) scouring the Louisiana bayous for the "open portal" they're initially alerted to during an exorcism (involving a Sumatran demon and portable pyramid, the latter recalling the Lament Configuration of Clive Barker's **HELLRAISER**). Who has been dabbling with opening the portal? Surly, jut-jawed Wilbur Whateley (Jeffrey Combs), that's who! Griff Furst plays the academic refuting all this as "clap trap" until he gets pulled into the escalating shenanigans, which eventually leads to the first extensive use of belly-dancers in Lovecraftian cinema.

I couldn't resist tracking down this curio given the one-two punch of (1) Dean Stockwell, the Wilbur Whateley of the 1970 AIP **THE DUNWICH HORROR**, now in the role Ed Begley played earlier, and (2) Jeffrey Combs as Whateley, savoring yet another eccentric Lovecraft-inspired rube in Combs' cinematic rogue's gallery.

Stockwell's Dr. Armitage is an occult detective/warrior here, shooting CGI laser effects from his fingertips

Stockwell's Dr. Armitage is an occult detective/warrior here, shooting CGI laser effects from his fingertips more than once, taking us further afield from the source material than even the change of locales from rural Massachusetts to Louisiana flatlands and backwaters (there's occasionally good use of the locations, which echoes "The Call of Cthulhu" but the Whateley mansion looks as out-of-place as the Mendocino, California locales of the 1970 Daniel Haller opus). Alas, it's Furst and Lieving—estranged couple bonding anew thanks to joining forces against "the Old Ones" and "the portal" (feminist academics, take note!)—who dominate the proceedings, with Furst essentially replaying the pragmatist academic of **NIGHT OF THE EAGLE** (a.k.a. **BURN, WITCH, BURN**, 1962, UK) being put in his place when confronted by truly occult forces manifesting against him, which writer/director Scott uses as his narrative anchor and frame here.

93

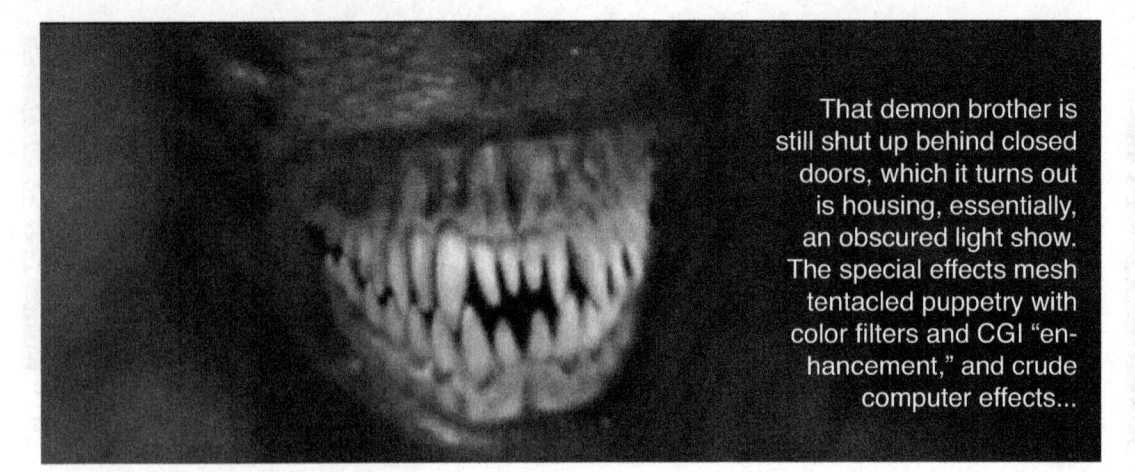

That demon brother is still shut up behind closed doors, which it turns out is housing, essentially, an obscured light show. The special effects mesh tentacled puppetry with color filters and CGI "enhancement," and crude computer effects...

Like the 1970 AIP adaptation and far too many "Lovecraft films" since, the immediate fusion of Satanism and older demonic pantheons and exorcism with Lovecraft's invented cosmos derails this from Lovecraft's fiction and true legacy from the get-go, and Scott's decision to incorporate faux-Louisiana-voodoo trappings en route only compounds the heresy. As in the AIP version, there's also some fun to be had with the verbal tongue-twisting with Yog-Sothoth (mispronounced "Yog-Soshoth" time and time again here), and we just haven't come any distance when Leigh Scott is essentially still reliant on the same flashy smoke-and-mirrors approach Daniel Haller did in 1970 to picturing Wilbur's sibling. That demon brother is still shut up behind closed doors, which it turns out is housing, essentially, an obscured light show. The special effects mesh tentacled puppetry with color filters and CGI "enhancement", and crude computer effects are even more apparent in the depiction of the creature's storm-like wake once it's unleashed.

That duly noted, this version opens (as did the Haller version) with the birth of the Whateley "twins", though it's more graphic than would have been tolerated by the MPAA in 1970. This is a grabber for the uninitiated and frustrating—laying cards on the table Lovecraft buried in the closing line of his story—for the initiated. This is also the *only* live-action version thus far to include Wilbur's unveiling/transformation as part of the adaptation (one of the original short story's most effective passages), but even that is fudged and far too fleeting. In fact, one of the most glaring disappointments of the film are the perfunctory write-offs of both Wilbur and Armitage—the characters and the actors deserved more, and one cannot help but wish something (*anything*) more devastating or satisfying had been staged for their exits.

Combs gives his all, per usual, but deserves better, per usual. I'll remember the set of Combs/Wilbur's jaw and drawl long after the rest of this movie fades from memory, and his perverse lip-smacking, v-smiling supping of the word "brother" to Stockwell. Brownie points, too, for including the mad Arab Abdul Alhazred in a post-9/11 cameo, and despite the prosaic trotting out of facsimile *Necronomicon*s (all missing "page 751", dammit! Funny conceit, that); score a further brownie point for an imaginative twist with what the *Necronomicon* "is" and where it's hidden.

Leigh Scott's dedication to the genre is commendable, his work very much in the exploitation tradition of Corman *circa* the direct-to-video/DVD marketplace of today for Asylum and Imaginarium (**BRAM STOKER'S DRACULA'S CURSE** [2006, USA], **H.G. WELLS' WAR OF THE WORLDS** [2005, USA], **THE BEAST OF BRAY ROAD** [2005, USA], **THE PENNY DREADFUL PICTURE SHOW** [2013, USA], etc.). As with Brett Piper's films (I never miss a one of 'em!), you take these as they come for what they are, and no more, or you don't take 'em at all. Scott's **DUNWICH HORROR** was a step up from his previous genre efforts, and the extras on the Aussie DVD release (read on) demonstrate the energy and work he and his team poured into the movie, however tight the timeframe, budget, and aspirations.

Lovecraft junkies, you know you want to see it—it's streaming on YouTube complete as of this writing, but if you've got an all-region player, the still-affordable eBay access to the Australian DVD of **WITCHES: DARKEST EVIL** (the title on the back cover is listed in the credits as "**HAUNTED HOUSE** a.k.a. **WITCHES**" [sic]; Reel DVD, PAL Region 4, C-109436-9) is the way to go It's worth the search and a viewing for Stockwell and Combs alone; recommended only as fun-but-sad double-bill fodder with the 1970 AIP version.

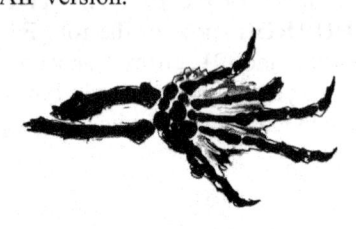

SIDEBAR: MUSIC OF THE DEVIL GOD CULT

American-International Records released a full LP entitled *Music of the Devil God Cult: Strange Sounds from Dunwich* (1970, ST-A-1028), and it's a pretty amazing record. I've had it in my collection for a long while, and used to spin it on Halloween. It features six cuts on side one ("Dunwich", "Sacrifice of the Virgin", "Black Mass", "Sensual Hallucinations", "Strange Sleep", and "Cult Party") and five on side two ("Necronomicon", "Reincarnation", "Devil Cult", "Strange Sleep", and "Devil's Witchcraft"), all of which sport titles which play up the titular "Devil Cult" aspect. Lovecraft collectors note: other than the tune entitled "Necronomicon", nothing on the LP cover art beyond the film credit byline "based on a story by H.P. Lovecraft" chooses to exploit any association with Lovecraft.

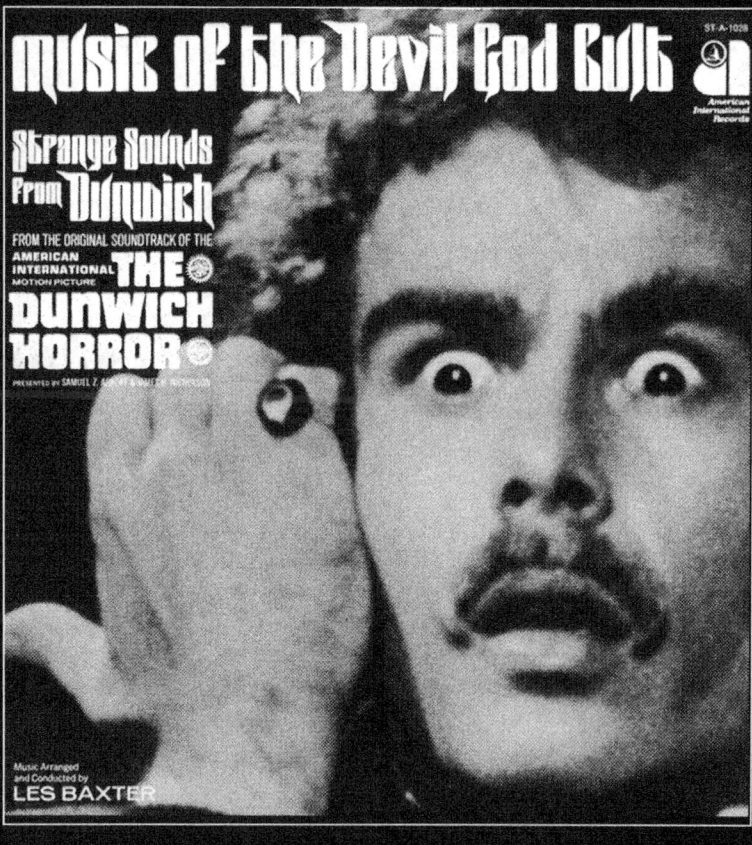

"On picture postcards Dunwich looks like a pleasant village..." the back cover text begins, teasing out the usual AIP ballyhoo to its crescendo:

"Only the courageous will listen to this record alone. Only those with nerves of steel will dare to experience these strange sounds in the closeness of a darkened room...for darkness is the playground of the devil.

"Where is the Dunwich Horror? It exists in the furthest reaches of your mind...it is all around you, watching, waiting...it lurks uneasily behind bolted doors, eager to explode its terror on an unsuspecting world.

"Be warned. When you listen to the sounds of the unspeakable your thoughts may unlock the door to the Dunwich Horror, giving freedom to mystical forces far beyond the realm of your imagination... and Dunwich may yet again become chilling reality." [all ellipses in the original text]

Note the references to the "bolted doors", the sexualized "eager to explode"—in hindsight, even that transgressive moment of the movie is slyly acknowledged on the LP!

American International Records was incorporated on March 19, 1958. From all available evidence, this *Dunwich Horror* LP was part of a sudden resurgence of record market synergy from AIP/AIR after a long fallow period of inactivity in the 1960s. *Music of the Devil God Cult* was distributed by the Transcontinental Record Corporation out of Los Angeles, an imprint of MGM Records. For a time in the 1970s, MGM distributed the AIP label offerings. There's a discography online at *http://www.discogs.com/label/81511-American-International-Records* which states, "Throughout its existence, AIR was distributed exclusively first by Forward Records, then by MGM Records, and finally by Casablanca Record & FilmWorks (Casablanca Records) in 1978 and 1979." There's another at *http://www.bsnpubs.com/mgm/airtogether.html* Alas, neither is a complete discography, as I know for a fact there were Les Baxter soundtrack LPs for one of their early 1960s imports, **GOLIATH AND THE BARBARIANS** (*Il Terrore dei Barbari*, 1959, Italy) a.k.a. *Les Baxter's Barbarians* (issued by AIR as a Les Baxter title, AIP LP 1001-M and 1001-S), and the Jules Verne adaptation *Master of the World* (Vee Jay SR 4000). Both were from 1961—I used to own them, but long ago traded them off (stupid, stupid Bissette creature!). These were reissued on vinyl in 1978 by Varese Sarabande, and later on a very limited-pressing CD by Intrada Signature Editions (ISE-1029). All are long out-of-print and highly sought after by collectors; a recent CD entitled *Les Baxter Vol. 4: Eight Classic Albums* (Real Gone Jazz, UPC #5036408136022) offers the LP tracks anew at an affordable price. There are also rumors of a privately-issued AIP Les Baxter soundtrack LP for either Mario Bava's **BLACK SABBATH** or **BLACK SUNDAY**, or of **BLACK SUNDAY**'s Baxter score with a cover image of Boris Karloff from **BLACK SABBATH**; I've only heard rumors—I've never seen a copy.

For another discography of AIP Records 45s dating back to their 1959 launch, see *http://www.globaldogproductions.info/a/american-intl.html* and note that they include a 45 RPM single release of Les Baxter's *The Dunwich Horror* from the LP. "Dunwich (Main Theme)" (A-1055) and "Necronomicon" (A-1056) were issued as A-143, and it's even more collectible and tougher-to-find than the LP. The 1959 AIP singles included Tony Casanova's "Diary of a High School Bride" and Jimmy Maddin's band "The Nightmares" playing tunes from the Herman Cohen productions **THE HEADLESS GHOST** and **HORRORS OF THE BLACK MUSEUM** (entitled "[Oooh, I'm Scared of] Horrors of the Black Museum," both Cohen cuts are archived on Michael H. Price's *The Music of Forgotten Horrors Vol. 2* [2013, CRM07804]), and a Bill Anson single offering "Bucket of Blood" with "The Leeches"—oh, man, I'm drooling! Also see *http://monsterkidclassichorrorforum.yuku.com/topic/35699/AMERICAN-INTERNATIONAL-RECORDS-releases#.U5tBWxzDZIY* for more info.

Their other 1970s soundtrack LPs and singles included full soundtracks and/or cuts from **BLOODY MAMA, A BULLET FOR PRETTY BOY, 3 IN THE CELLAR, ANGEL UNCHAINED, BORA BORA, BUNNY O'HARE** ("The Ballad of Bunny O'Hare" by Mike Curb "with Orchestra") and Michel Legrand's romantic themes for the Robert Fuest **WUTHERING HEIGHTS** (1970, UK), wrapping up with "Amityville Frenzy" and "Theme from *Amityville Horror*" (4012) at the end of AIP's reign. *CC* readers may want to track down (*if* they can afford a copy...) the AIR LP of Basil Kirchin's score for **THE ABOMINABLE DR. PHIBES** (1971, UK/USA; A-1040), which is arguably the best and most-beloved of the lot.

There was also another 1970s *Dunwich Horror* LP that wasn't associated with the movie. *H.P. Lovecraft The Dunwich Horror (Slightly Abridged) Read by David McCallum* was issued by Caedmon in 1976 (TC1467), with back cover text by L. Sprague de Camp. The Dunwich Horror is now the name of an American heavy metal "black mass horror" band; a number of other bands (Malhavoc, etc.) have recorded songs named after the Lovecraft story.

The single "Dunwich Horror" by the Symphonic Deathcore rock band Lorelei.

Big Foot Goes Supernatural

The La Canada woods area known as Big Foot was the location used by director Jack Woods when he photographed the supernatural color adventure EQUINOX.

Famous for its un-tropical foliage this unpopulated scenic retreat received its share of the 1969 rain deluge causing many problems for the construction crew since shooting of this Jack H. Harris production took over three years to complete and the rain had greatly altered the topography.

*[Press release from the original 1970 **EQUINOX** pressbook.]*

EQUINOX

THE OCCULT BARRIER BETWEEN GOOD AND EVIL!

Was **EQUINOX** (1967/70, USA) real? Did it exist—had we seen it, or was it something that might exist? For decades, we weren't sure.

It wasn't until Criterion released **EQUINOX** in a 2-disc DVD edition that those of us who grew up with **EQUINOX** could see the original edit of the movie—the amateur labor-of-love feature that launched so many careers—alongside the Jack H. Harris version my generation found at the drive-in or on late-night television. **EQUINOX** was the amateur monster movie "that could"—the Monster Kid "Pinocchio" that became "a real movie," playing real movie theaters. It was odd, as if it had existed before it existed; like some John Keel cryptid, **EQUINOX** seemed to herald from some alternate dimension.

After all, from 1969 on, **EQUINOX** was a rumor, a whisper, an image, a *dream*...

Above: Jim Duron as the live-action not-so-jolly green giant demon in Dennis Muren/Mark Thomas McGee/Jack Woods' **EQUINOX** (1970), which also featured stop-motion monsters animated by the late, great David Allen (1944-1999). **Below:** German DVD cover.

EQUINOX was known to most of us, at first, only as a title—evocative in and of itself—and an image. Depending on which newsstand monster magazine or which fanzine you'd lucked into in the late 1960s or early 1970s, the image was most likely either a tantalizing photo of the winged Satanic demon or of the stop-motion ape-like tusked demon. In either case, it was a definite hook, and in subsequent months and years these were all the more alluring for how completely out-of-reach, out-of-sight the movie remained.

Famous Monsters of Filmland ran two images early on—a full-page "You Axed For It" shot of the winged demon (in *FM* #53, January 1969), and later a full-page black-and-white shot of that glorious **EQUINOX** advertising art (in *FM* #81, December 1970). The latter sported a caption citing Fritz Leiber (already a favorite author for me) as having a role—specifically as a "Lovecraftian Seeker of Forbidden Knowledge", the first overt association of H.P. Lovecraft with this film to see print—and mention that *FM* editor Forrest J. Ackerman was in the movie, too, as a voice delivering "the Tape Recorder's Message of Terror!"

Mountain Stream Goes Hollywood

A stream in the Tujunga mountains got the Hollywood touch during filming sequences on the Southern California location for EQUINOX the exciting new adventure drama opening........at the ....theatre.

When director of photography Mike Hoover discovered the waters of this famous mountain stream did not photograph properly for his sensitive color cameras, he and his technical staff got together for some colorful thinking.

The solution was to dump 40 gallons of special dye into the water to make the stream more photogenic each time they rolled the cameras.

A New Style Producer on the Hollywood Scene

A producer who made two top-grossing movies for the screen before he ever saw the inside of a Hollywood sound stage has now embarked on a one-man campaign to restore science-fiction films to the status of family entertainment.

JACK H. HARRIS, who made THE BLOB, 4-D MAN and DINOSAURUS has poured the profits from these and other productions into a spine-tingler titled EQUINOX opening........at the........ theatre. It's a big and lavish production, complete with Color by De Luxe, and its aim, according to Harris, is to reunite mom and dad with the kids in a row of moviee theatre seats.

How does he plan to do it?

"By cutting down on sex and violence", Harris explains. "Overemphasizing these two elements has been the main cause of a decrease in popularity of movies about science-fiction, horror, and westerns, too".

"Film producers have tried to outdo each other in the field of sensationalism, adapting the raw approach to love and engulfing the story with the blood of overdone scenes of violence. The former makes a movie unacceptable for children; the latter makes it unpalatable for adults."

Harris, who confined his moviemaking to the East before coming to Hollywood to make "DINOSAURUS", has been making films for ten years, but 41 of his 47 years have been spent in show business, beginning with his trouping at the age of six as a member of the Gus "Ukelele Ike" Edwards' Kiddie Revue, and maturing via a successful career in film exhibition and distribution.

"I believe I know what folks want on a movie screen", says the producer. "I've been listening to their comments in theatre lobbies for more than twenty years."

To give EQUINOX that much sought after family flavor, Harris has concocted some unusual approaches to the characters of such supernatural hair raisers as The Blue Giant, The Ape Monster and The Occult Forest Ranger who share star billing with his four attractive screen newcomers Edward Connell, Barbara Hewitt, Frank Boers jr. and Robin Christopher. The film directed by Jack Woods is a VIP distributors release.

The Story

Dr. Waterman, famed archaeologist, is mysteriously missing, Dave, Susan, Jim and Vicki set out to search for him.

The foursome arrive at Dr. Waterman's mountain retreat to find his house completely demolished. They report the disaster to Ranger Asmodeus who promises to investigate.

The teenagers further discover a weird castle in the hills, strange gigantic footprints and a mysterious cave which they enter and explore. In the cave a babbling old man provides no information about the missing Dr. Waterman, but hands them a strange ancient book.

Back outside the cave the girls set a picnic and the boys pry open the 1,000 year old Book containing formulas and facts of devil worship. Someone dashes into the picnic area, snatches the book, and runs off with it. It is Dr. Waterman but a crazed, frenzied Dr. Waterman. Dave and Jim give chase and tackle the doctor who falls suddenly dead at their feet in the forest. The boys are undone by this strange happening and start for help, but turn back to cover the body, which has suddenly vanished.

Ranger Asmodeus appears but is told nothing of the Dr. Waterman occurrence. Dave and Jim, Book in tow, rejoin the girls and the foursome starts back for their car. They are arrested in their tracks by the appearance of a 30 foot mutant apelike creature. The teenagers dash madly through a narrow mountain pass, which prevents the great ape from following. The boys fashion a spear which finds its way into the monster's chest. It is demolished, but it has become clear that the monster was after the ancient Book. The foursome head for a meeting place by separate routes and Jim meets Ranger Asmodeus (his name is the Greek derivation of the word "devil") who explains he will have the Book, then threatens to bring down more monsters in order to acquire it. Asmodeus bribes Jim with promises of untold riches in exchange for the Book. Jim agrees, and heads for the prearranged meeting place to get the Book from Dave.

A fearsome blue giant stalks the foursome. Jim knows what the giant is after: the Book. Jim grabs the Book and dashes with it to the giant who carries off the Book and Jim through the invisible barrier into the world of the Supernatural. Dave follows Jim and the giant beyond the barrier where he finds Jim lying dazed, the Book is gone. Dave helps Jim out of the devil's area through the barrier back into the forest but discovers that the man he has helped is not really Jim. Instead he has helped Asmodeus who has adopted Jim's form. Asmodeus stuns Dave and kills Susan and Vicki. Dave regains consciousness sees the girls dead bodies and runs wildly toward the road out of breath and exhausted. Dave hails an oncoming car which accelerates speed and smashes into Dave. The car rolls to a stop and we see it is driverless.

As with many movies Forrest J. Ackerman would reference with a single photo and teaser caption, what was most confounding was FJA's phrasing or framing of every fleeting reference, as if this mysterious movie was somehow a known quantity to some of the readership. I mean, there was a list of names under that *FM* #53 "You Axed For It" photo—*somebody* had seen it, apparently, so it was "see-able." *But what the hell was this movie?* What was I missing? Why was there never *any* information, however vague, about what **EQUINOX** could possibly be? It was as alluring and baffling as such *Famous Monsters of Filmland* "constants" as **MUTANO THE HORRIBLE**: an exotic movie title cited, again and again; rarer still, a photo linked to the title, sans any explanation or context.

What gradually became manifest, though, was that *this* was a monster movie made by fellow fans, for monster lovers.

By the time I was in high school, a wee bit more of the movie was finally in reach—it was in my own collection of 8mm monster movie reels, and frequently threaded up in my projector for another viewing.

As an avid collector of 8mm monster movies, I somehow found and screened the 50-foot short reel of **EQUINOX** first. It wasn't much, really, but it was something, and I quickly tracked down a copy of the 200-foot longer reel by mail-ordering it directly from Ken Films.

Like most 8mm and Super 8 movie "cutdowns", the reels were silent—and in black-and-white. The 50-foot reels were mere minutes in duration, the 200-foot reels almost 12 minutes long: more than a preview trailer, less than a movie.

Whoever was behind the selection and editing of these stripped-down highlight reels rarely demonstrated much passion for the presentations, though the labels themselves evidenced different levels of care in that department.

Blackhawk Films was the aristocracy of 8mm collecting: complete, incredibly rare films, mostly from the silent era, lovingly restored from whatever elements still existed. Those were available *only* via direct mail order from Blackhawk.

Those were entirely different from the rest of the 8mm and Super 8 films available. What we found in department stores in the 1960s—the first attractively packaged consumer-targeted sales of movies in public retail venues, predecessor to the video rental revolution of the 1980s—were the mass-market 8mm and Super 8 offerings from Castle Films, Ken Films, and (harder to find) Republic Pictures. There was also a label that sold a few movies with soundtrack records (!) that you would cue up to synchronize the sound and the movie; I had a few of their titles, too (**THE CURSE OF FRANKENSTEIN**, **HORROR OF DRACULA**, **COSMIC MONSTERS**, etc).

Castle Films reels, complete with subtitles and even explanatory intertitles at times, offered the most satisfying selections, delivering more story content and more spectacle than, say, Ken Films usually did. Ken Films offered rather confounding edits, selected and patched together with little apparent rhyme or reason, often leaving out the meat of the movie being excerpted, so to speak. I learned this very early in my 8mm collecting years, with Ken Films' reel of **THE GIANT BEHEMOTH** (1959, UK; released on 8mm film as early as 1961), which was blissfully free of much Willis O'Brien/Pete Peterson animation footage (I recall only the clumsy shots of the dinosaur swimming underwater). The bulk of the **BEHEMOTH** reel (both 50-foot and 200-foot) comprised the risible rod-puppet "Behemoth" ferry-boat sequence.

EQUINOX was a Ken Films release.

The bulk of the excerpted footage was nonsensical, but entertaining enough—introduction of the 20-something-year-old "teenage" heroes on their picnic, glimpses of the Necronomicon-like book responsible for all the hubbub, and the giant that was an actor in makeup and shaggy caveman-like

Cover to one of the mail-order *Blackhawk Films Bulletin*s, from which one could order rarities like Georges Méliès short films, F.W. Murnau's **NOSFERATU**, and much more

Top: Image from the German amateur genre film **MUTANO THE HORRIBLE** (1961?); for more on this "lost" film that may never have really existed at all, see *Monster!* #14 (February 2015, pp.103–105) *[cover depicted above]*, which also features a 'roundtable' analysis of **EQUINOX**.

100

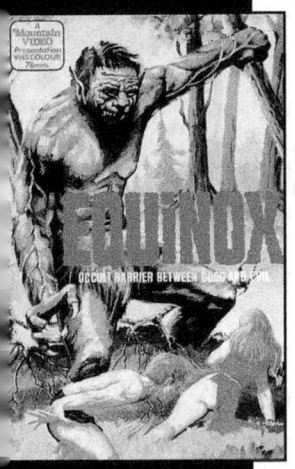

garb attacking our heroes, intent on recovering the book—but the climactic winged demon stop-motion animation sequence was the absolute highlight. *That* was what I ran the reel to watch again and again, despite the brevity of the stop-motion on view.

Still, Ken Films packaging was always sweet eye candy. It was the **EQUINOX** cover art that *really* grabbed me, promising action and monsters that were M.I.A. from the 8mm reel itself. This was the full-color version of the promo art shown in *FM* #81. The cartoony color graphic looked like a Matt Fox *Weird Tales* or 1950s Pre-Code comicbook cover, the title block lettering practically shouting *"Eeeeeqqqquuuiiinoxxx!"* Front and center was that wonderful Kong-like tusked ape-creature, arms raised with a victim clutched in one fist, its chest bloodily pierced by a spear—a creature frustratingly not included in the Ken Films 8mm footage—and so this further taste only whet my appetite for the Real McCoy.

EQUINOX was still a great unknown. Only a little of its mystery had been resolved, enhancing the promise of what was still unseen, unheard, and unknowable.

I still can't sort out how it would have been so that the Ken Films 8mm reels were sold before the movie itself played in our neck of the woods, but there ya go. That's how it happened.

My jaw fell open when I saw the newspaper ad for **EQUINOX** in *The Times Argus* (Barre, VT). It had at last arrived! There, in black and white, was a fragment of that artwork I'd studied in *Famous Monsters* and on the Ken Films cover art—the Jack Harris advertising art, as it turned out—and that title graphic:

EEEEQQQUUUIIIINNOOOXXXX!!!

Lucky me, at sweet sixteen years of age I had my driver's license, so I could drive myself the fifteen or so miles from home to the Twin City Drive-In on the Barre-Montpelier Road and see it that very night, double-billed with **BEWARE! THE BLOB**

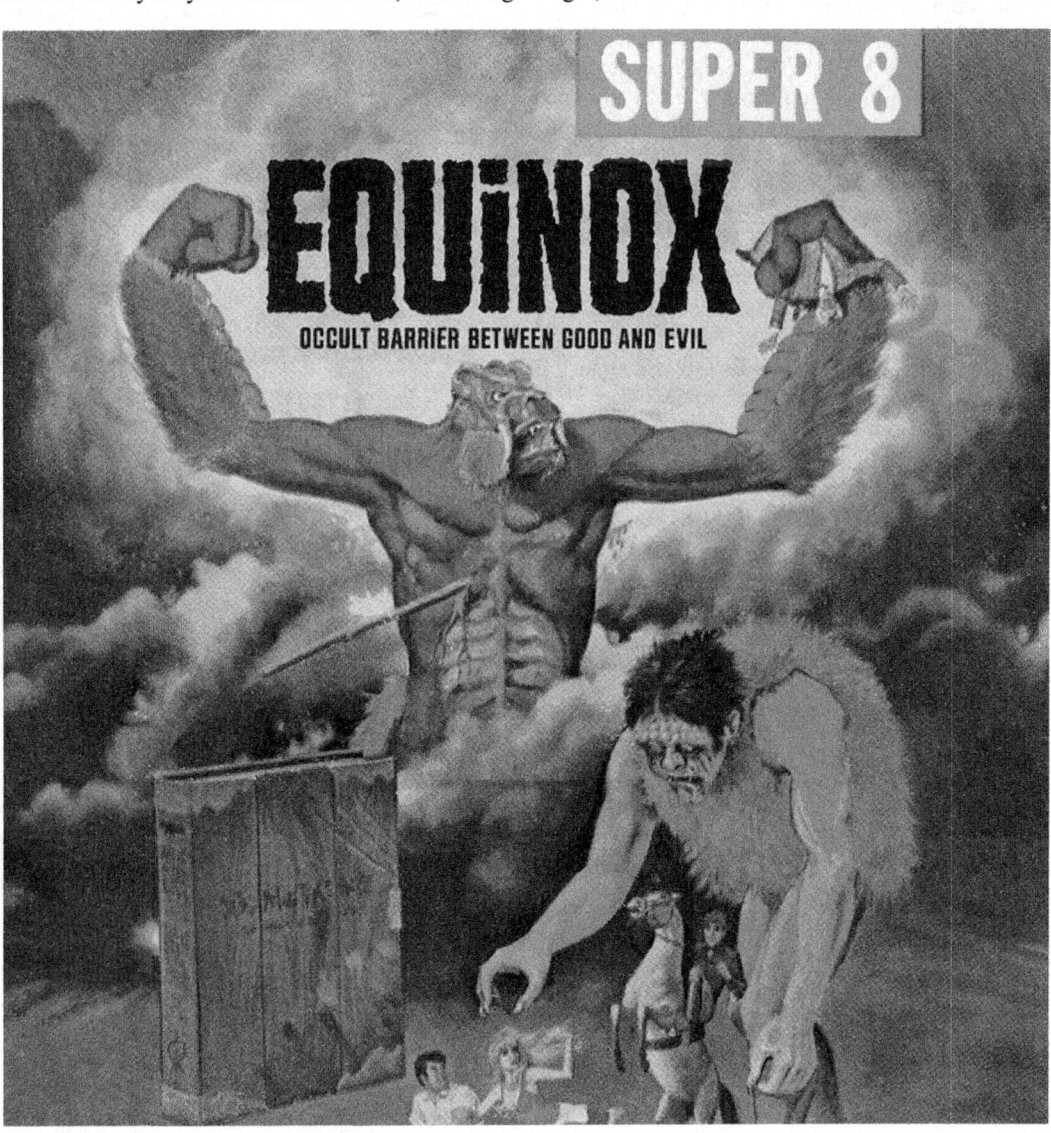

Above: British VHS artwork for **EQUINOX**. **Right:** The film's original poster art was used to package Ken Films' American Regular/Super 8mm 'cutdown' reel. **Below:** Jack H. Harris also produced and distributed Larry Hagman's "blob-come-lately" sequel **BEWARE! THE BLOB** (a.k.a. **SON OF BLOB**, 1972).

101

(a.k.a. **SON OF BLOB**). Jack H. Harris rolled that sequel out in 1972, so that's the year I finally saw **EQUINOX**, sometime in late June or early July.

Going it alone—none of my friends cared to go with me—I arrived early, snagging the perfect central spot for the car for the optimum windshield visibility, popping out to get sufficient popcorn and soda for the duration, then hooking up the speaker to the car window and settling in for whatever was to come.

Having grown up with the Holy Trinity of Jack Harris monster movies—**THE BLOB** (1958), **THE 4D MAN** (a.k.a. **MASTER OF TERROR**, 1959), and **DINOSAURUS!** (1960, all USA), all via TV (and in color, since we had one color TV set in our front room)—there was a look, sound, and feel to movies produced by Harris that shaped whatever expectations I harbored that night.

Both movies confounded those: this was, after all, the early 1970s, and even the Blob went with the flow. **BEWARE! THE BLOB** was weird, staccato, abrasive and at times funny, starring Godfrey Cambridge (who I'd recently seen in **WATERMELON MAN** [1970, USA]; he's devoured by the Blob in his living room chair in the opening minutes), Robert Walker, Jr. (indelibly, iconically *Star Trek*'s dangerous "Charlie X" to my generation, though he was also one of the commune hippies I'd recognized in **EASY RIDER** [1969, USA]), and even Burgess Meredith (The Penguin!) in a cameo as a wino (with director Larry Hagman, recognizable in those pre-*Dallas* days only for *I Dream of Jeanie*). The pitch-black humor of **BEWARE! THE BLOB** had almost nothing to do with the Harris movies of yore. Only the bright-red blob itself was a touchstone to the Harris/Irvin S. Yeaworth, Jr. era, and there was very little of Yeaworth's Christian conservatism on view in **BEWARE! THE BLOB**.

My heart raced a little as the second feature splashed across the drive-in screen. Fun as **BEWARE! THE BLOB** had been, I was here for **EQUINOX**.

I was not disappointed.

What no doubt put off most audiences about **EQUINOX** on the big screen lit candles in my heart: it *looked and felt like a student movie*, and that wasn't a bummer for me, it was a joy. I was transfixed, mesmerized. I wasn't going anywhere except where **EQUINOX** led me.

Needless to say, as a stop-motion animation junkie from childhood, I was in 7th heaven whenever the movie's effects graced the screen. The story, such as it was, did its job linking the monster set-pieces,

The pressbook cover for **EQUINOX**'s "X"-rated (!) UK theatrical release, double-billed with **BIGFOOT**

which couldn't last long enough for me. The blue simian (Taurus by name, I at some point divined over a decade later when a copy of the 1970 movie fanzine *Ready for Showing* Vol. 1, No. 1 fell into my hands) was my favorite by far, succumbing

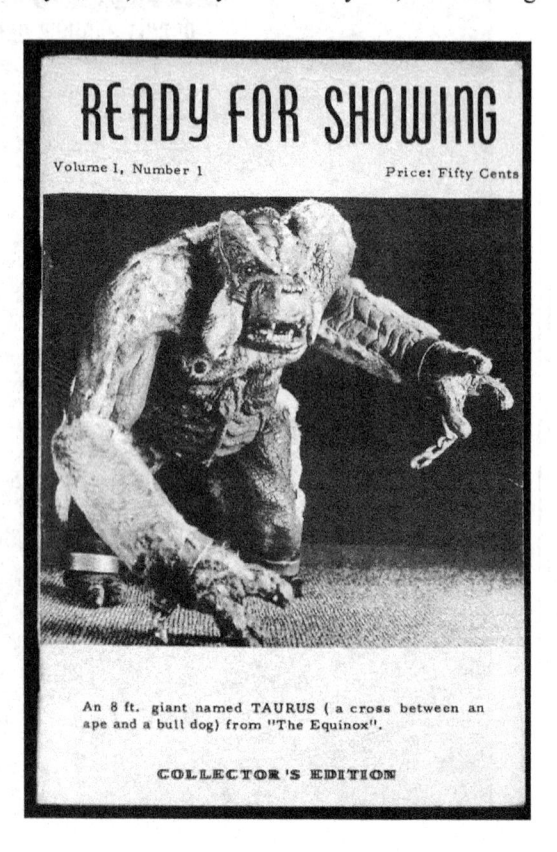

An 8 ft. giant named TAURUS (a cross between an ape and a bull dog) from "The Equinox".

COLLECTOR'S EDITION

102

much too quickly to that spear in the chest. Even the green fur-clad ogre from the Ken Films cutdown was more appealing in full color. These creatures were all intent upon recovering The Book from the picnicking "kids," and for their trespasses the hapless picnic quartet would pay with their souls and their lives before the film's grim coda (which wasn't much of a surprise by 1972, since George Romero's **NIGHT OF THE LIVING DEAD** and Bob Kelljan's **COUNT YORGA, VAMPIRE** had popularized the downbeat twist finale for almost all subsequent drive-in horrors).

Whatever Jack H. Harris and director/packager Jack Woods did to and with the original Dennis Muren/Mark McGee feature film (changes we now know and can identify, but at the time there was nowhere or no way to find out), **EQUINOX** matched and transcended any and all of my expectations. A couple of cars gave up and drove out of the drive-in lot during the film, giving up; well, it was getting late, but I doubt it worked for the average audience. I loved and responded to its roughhewn nature. Its very crudity—including the crass addition of the demonic "forest ranger" Mr. Asmodeus, played by Jack Woods—was intoxicating. This was a bizarre crash-course in filmmaking, *if one only had eyes to see*. And oh, I did—I did. The crazy-quilt shift of old and newer footage was readily apparent, emphasized by the ever-changing color palette. The characters changed dramatically without rhyme or reason, despite the roles being played throughout by the same quartet of lead players: their hairstyles and hair-lengths changed and they'd look younger, then older, in various shots and sequences. Was anyone else in the cars surrounding me noticing this? Would they care if they did? The whole confection was off-kilter and disorienting, but it was a lot of fun.

Still, it was hard to nail down what precisely **EQUINOX** was, or was even *like*. I'd read a lot of H.P. Lovecraft by this point in life, and it initially struck me that the Lovecraftian angle FJA had cited in *Famous Monsters* was honest enough. I dug the discovery and narrative role of the *Necronomicon*-like book responsible for all the interdimensional passages, portals, and transgressions. Then again, this *wasn't* Arkham, Massachusetts: it was southern California, already overly-familiar after a lifetime of movie and prime-time TV viewing.

In short order, the movie took a more playful path. These protagonists weren't obsessed scholars uncovering dark secrets of primordial God-like beings; they were clean-cut college students on a picnic, utterly chaste in their relationships with one another, and the creatures they accidentally conjured or encountered were movie monsters,

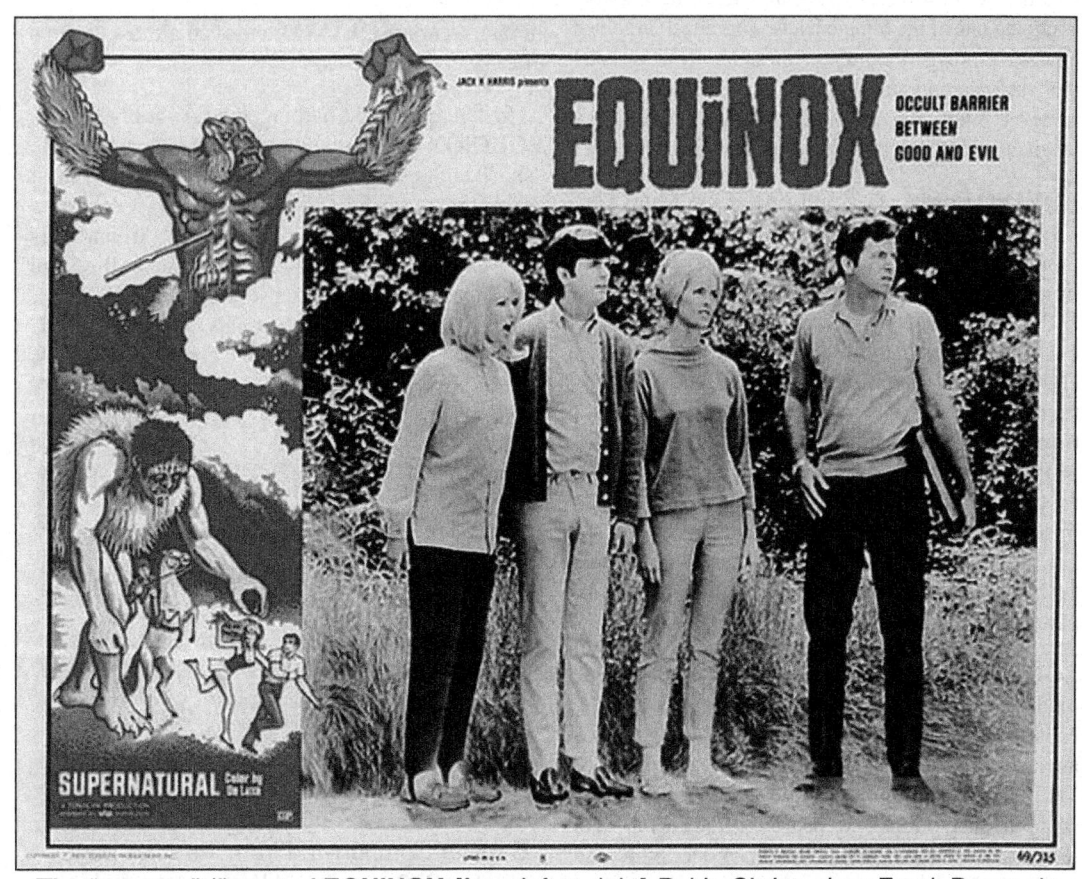

The "teenage" (!) cast of **EQUINOX** *[from left to right]*: Robin Christopher, Frank Boers, Jr. (better-known later in his career as Frank Bonner), Barbara Hewitt and Edward Connell

103

pure and simple. The most demonic of them all—the true form of the sneering, drooling Asmodeus—spread its bat-wings and soared from more classical mythological and Judeo-Christian iconography, recalling Doré's Biblical Fallen Angel and Harryhausen's reptilian harpies.

The permeable dimensional barrier/portal, the fairy-tale castle, odd eruptions of magic, and the frantic back-and-forth shenanigans of the put-upon heroes smacked of fantasy rather than horror, with nary a goosebump or hackle raised. It was entertaining enough and had its own flavor, but it was hardly Lovecraft. For me, only one image in the entire movie truly echoed what I loved most about Lovecraft's fiction: the all-too-fleeting glimpse of a stop-motion-animated land cephalopod attacking Fritz Leiber's country cottage in a flashback. In those precious seconds of screen time, **EQUINOX** proved budget wasn't what stood in the way of Lovecraft's stories being properly translated to the silver screen. If only **THE HAUNTED PALACE** (1963) or **THE DUNWICH HORROR** (1970, both USA) had briefly incorporated such startling imagery!

Mr. Asmodeus and the deranged old man laughing in the cave (played by Dennis Muren's grandpa) were the silliest characters. Mr. Asmodeus—with his garish makeup, park ranger's uniform, and his magic ring—was the goofiest of all, especially when he sexually assaulted one of the female leads. This attack involved hilarious, exaggerated close-up shots of Woods/Asmodeus mugging and slavering for the camera. Rape is never funny, but it was hard to do anything but laugh at such shamelessly over-the-top ham.

EQUINOX was, above all, inspiring. Mind you, I'd been experimenting with making my own 8mm and Super 8 movies for a few years by that time, primarily working with my high school pals Bill Hunter and Alan Finn. Our antics included our timid experimentation with crude stop-motion clay animation and effects, the most elaborate and time-consuming of which was staging the climactic decay of M. Valdemar for a planned adaptation of the Edgar Allan Poe tale. Alas, what took days to film, frame-by-frame, passed by in seconds once the developed film arrived and prompted high hilarity (as Valdemar's clay face—constructed by me on a Renwall human skull model—appeared to vertically unzip and flop apart).

EQUINOX unreeled like the best-ever homemade monster movie, better than the one I'd long been concocting in my own noggin. All the telltale signs of its amateur origins were evident, but this was the **GONE WITH THE WIND** of amateur monster movies. As such, it was glorious and inspiring. It made me want to tinker with making my own movies once more, and definitely fired-up the desire to write and draw my own stories and comics with more determination.

Point-Of-View Rape: Woods as Asmodeus

I went back to catch the entire double-bill again the following night. I was trying to brand every frame of **EQUINOX** into my brain, certain that I'd never see it again in my lifetime. It played one more night—a Sunday—but I couldn't justify borrowing my parent's car again to revisit movies I'd already seen twice.

Then it was gone.

Gone... *forever?*

———

Hardly.

In later years, **EQUINOX** enjoyed a most curious afterlife.

At first, it remained a harbinger in *Famous Monsters*. **EQUINOX**'s (soft) bummer finale was among the "shock endings" detailed in the solid article on twist horror movie finales and codas in *Famous Monsters of Filmland* #94 (November 1972). Around this time, **EQUINOX** was advertised as one of the 8mm and Super 8 monster movies (along with Willis H. O'Brien and Ray Harryhausen's **MIGHTY JOE YOUNG** [1949], Harryhausen's **EARTH VS. THE FLYING SAUCERS** [1956] and **20 MILLION MILES TO EARTH** [1957, all USA], and Jim

Captain Company ad from the back pages of late 1970s issues of Warren magazines, including *Famous Monster of Filmland*

EQUINOX ad-art, for the original US [above] and UK [below] theatrical releases.

104

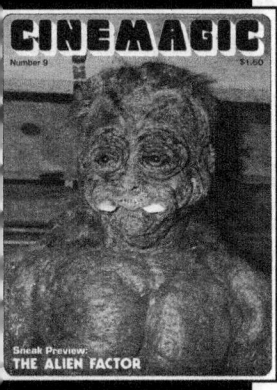

Danforth's **WHEN DINOSAURS RULED THE EARTH** [1970, UK]) in the back pages of late issues of *Famous Monsters* and all the Warren magazines, specifically spotlit as a choice title among "Animated Monster Home Movies". However, that damned green-skinned live-action ogre was pictured in the ad (accurately enough, since that beastie dominated the Ken Films cutdown reels). Only much, much later would I learn that **EQUINOX**'s production essentially began in the pages of *Famous Monsters* in the early 1960s, reportedly via a catalytic "Graveyard Examiner" ad that brought the original teenage filmmaking team together.

Don Dohler's *Cinemagic* magazine became a staple of my reading, expanding upon the legacy of **EQUINOX** and adding a rogue's gallery of subsequent amateur SF/fantasy/horror/monster movies and filmmakers to my "must-see" list. By the time Dohler's self-published slick zine made the leap to the newsstands as a companion to *Starlog* and *Fangoria*, **EQUINOX** had become a somewhat sacred artifact, a touchstone of a new generation of filmmakers at all levels of amateurism and professionalism.

Amid all this, I did my small part to expand its do-it-yourself legacy while at Johnson State College. Though I couldn't locate a 16mm rental print of **EQUINOX** to include in the busy film programming I spearheaded from 1974-76, I *did* manage to convince JSC campus radio station manager William Price to let me script and codirect a (very) short-lived original radio TV horror anthology program entitled **EQUINOX**. Bill Price and his right-hand tech Laird worked up a dandy title spot, in which Price's Rod Serling-like introduction led into the program's title, booming over the airwaves with an echo-chambered resonance: *"The Occult Barrier Between Good and Evil: EEEEEQQQQUUIIINNNOXXXXX!!!"* Alas, the show only lasted three episodes; the first, in which excerpted phone conversations between two mothers end with one of their children being found dead—having been partially devoured by his *teddy-bear*—was considered pretty effective. Nevertheless, it bombed. For me, though, it was a hoot for as long as it lasted.

Then **STAR WARS** hit, and Dennis Muren became a name to conjure with in the science-fiction and special effects fan communities. "Hey, didn't Muren make a monster movie in his youth?"

Then *WKRP in Cincinnati* was a primetime TV hit (from 1978 to '82), and Frank Bonner a.k.a . Frank Boers, Jr. became a familiar face, enjoying celebrity far, far beyond his heroic turn in **EQUINOX**. Thereafter, whenever friends mentioned to me their having caught **EQUINOX** on late-night TV, it's Bonner/Boers' performance they chuckled over more than anything else.

Don Dohler's original self-published DIY special effects zine *Cinemagic*, issues #5, 9, 10 (1976-1977).

From top: "Taurus", the stop-motion-animated simian demon; Asmodeus reveals his true demonic form at the climax of **EQUINOX**; Jim Hudson (Frank Bonner) uses an arcane symbol to ward off evil; Bonner as Jim's evil *doppelgänger* (actually Asmodeus in disguise)

105

When my friend Jack Venooker and I made the pilgrimage to the still-standing VT/NY state border Hathaway's Drive-In (in North Hoosick, NY, on Route 67) to catch the area premiere of **THE EVIL DEAD** (1981, USA), more than one associative link with **EQUINOX** came to mind as Sam Raimi's breakthrough "Ultimate Experience in Grueling Horror" sent folks reeling from their cars. From the discovery of the *Book of the Dead* to the subsequent unleashing of ancient demons to the critical role of an old tape-player and use of stop-motion animation (albeit for gore effects instead of Harryhausen-like creatures), I couldn't help but wonder if the **EVIL DEAD** do-or-die creative team had been inspired by **EQUINOX**. I tried to explain this to Jack, but he'd never heard of **EQUINOX**—"Only *you* see that, Bissette", I was told. Ya, well, maybe so, Jack.

Soon afterwards, as videocassettes popped up in Mom and Pop electronic shops and grocery stores throughout New England like mushrooms in cowpies after a morning rain, countless "lost" movies became accessible. This was *way* better than collecting 8mm cutdown reels! And, lo and behold, there was **EQUINOX**! I occasionally stumbled on the sun-faded box art for Charles Band's lackluster early Wizard Video release (*"Four Teenagers Fight a Devil Cult in EQUINOX"*), spending more than one afternoon revisiting the movie I'd once thought I'd never see again. The more picturesque 1985 big-box Wizard release under a new moniker, **THE BEAST**, was even more eye-catching. The big blue ape-critter on the front cover gave away the truth, and I later convinced the shop owner to sell me the tape. It holds a place of honor in my collection, still in surprisingly good shape.

When the original arcade video game *Primal Rage* hit in the 1990s, its simian monster characters (lovingly recreating the look and movement of classical cinematic stop-motion-animated creatures) sure looked like they might have been kith and kin to **EQUINOX**'s azure-blue primate-spawn demon, Taurus.

In June 2006, the unlikeliest event of all—a Criterion DVD edition of **EQUINOX**—cinched the film's stature for all time. *Finally!* Now we could experience the original movie, in its original form, as well as revisit the Harris/Woods revised theatrical version, and savor each on their own terms.

By then, **EQUINOX** was surfacing in a marketplace hip to its origins and status as the ultimate pre-**EVIL DEAD** horror "home movie". Though many expressed surprise, the Criterion treatment seemed apropos to me, given Criterion's 2001 release of Richard Gordon/Arthur Crabtree's **FIEND WITHOUT A FACE** (1958, UK). Moreover, Criterion was more attuned to marketplace

THE CALL OF CTHULHU (2005)

than anyone acknowledged, given the immediate company of DVD revelations like **MONSTER KID HOME MOVIES** (2005), **I WAS A TEENAGE MOVIEMAKER: DON GLUT'S AMATEUR MOVIES** (2006), **THE SCI-FI BOYS** (2006), and the H.P. Lovecraft Historical Society's magnificent "amateur" faux-silent-movie **THE CALL OF CTHULHU** (2005, all USA). Now we could screen a lot of amateur monster movies dating back to the early 1960s—the very movies we'd only read about or seen photos of in the pages of *Famous Monsters*, *Castle of Frankenstein*, and Larry Ivie's *Monsters and Heroes*—the creative continuity **EQUINOX** emerged from and belonged to wholeheartedly.

Furthermore, building on that bedrock, HPLHS/Andrew Leman's **THE CALL OF CTHULHU** proved once and for all time that **EQUINOX**'s recipe for "homemade monster movies" was *the* correct province of truly Lovecraftian cinema, delivering the most delicious of all Lovecraft film adaptations ever. Proving lightning could strike twice, the HPLHS team upped the ante and delivered their first sound (*circa* faux-1930s cinema) Lovecraft adaptation, **THE WHISPERER IN DARKNESS** (2011, USA).

About the same time, the theatrical rollout of J.J. Abrams' **SUPER 8** (2010, USA) was plundering and providing an even richer cultural contextual companion in a much more populist arena. Set as it was in 1979—a decade after Jack H. Harris snapped up **EQUINOX** and began reshaping it into something that could play in theaters and drive-ins—**SUPER 8** more than vindicated **EQUINOX**'s standing in cinema history: it arguably sanctified it.

EQUINOX had achieved immortality, of a kind, and that's more than OK by me.

And here we be, still talking about it...

DVD packaging art for **MONSTER KID HOME MOVIES** (2005), **I WAS A TEENAGE MOVIEMAKER** (2006), and the H. P. Lovecraft Historical Society's debut feature **THE CALL OF CTHULHU** (2005).

106

CREATURE, SANS COMFORTS

Or; How One of My Favorite Monster Movies of 2011 was The Most Despised Movie of 2011

Everybody seems to already have an opinion about the next GODZILLA movie before it's even kissed a single public screen anywhere on Earth.

How is that?

It's the way of the world in the 21st century, it seems.

And it brings to mind 9/11 for me.

Not the way the makers of the new Godzilla movie want us connecting monster movies and 9/11, mind you. Let me explain…

Remember 9/11?

Sure you do.

On September 11th, 2011, I had some fun for the first time in an entire decade.

I caught **CREATURE** (2011).

I was the only person in the theater.

I *loved* it.

First of all, credibility check and a little context, especially for readers of this tome:

Look, I *love* monster movies. It seems fair to assume you do, too, or you wouldn't be reading this in the first place.

Like most monster-lovers of my generation, I grew up with movies that dragged ass for 77 minutes to reward me with about four minutes of rubber-suit monsters with visible seams up their back, and I savor revisiting those clunkers today; you CGI-fed-cats are spoiled rotten. Furthermore, I drew *Swamp Thing* for DC Comics after steeping for at least two decades in steamy "bayou hussy" paperbacks, ink-staining-your-fingers Pre-Code horror comics reprints in the shoddiest-looking horror comic 'zines on the newsstands, and I love nothing more than stumbling on a movie I've never heard of before— particularly if I'm stumbling upon it *in a theater*.

In that category, it's better still if I've been lured into the theater due to a "what the fuck is this?" one-sheet poster, like the original Wes Craven **THE HILLS HAVE EYES** (1977), which snagged me as soon as I spotted what turned out to be Michael Berryman's mug glaring at me from across Blackwell Street from the poster display under the old-school marquee at the Baker Theater in downtown Dover, NJ (back in my Kubert School daze). Thirty years later, in New

Cover art for the German DVD release of CREATURE (2011).

107

Hampshire, a one-sheet movie poster prompted me to pay my $8 to see something I'd never heard of, **DRAGON WARS** (2007, onscreen title: **D-WAR**) based solely on the poster which looked like a cheesy CGI giant monster pic, a theatrical **BOA VS. PYTHON** (2004) pastiche (rip-off of a rip-off) released by a distributor I've never heard of (Showbox) from a production company I didn't recognize (Younguu Art).

That was back in September of 2007, and damn if lightning didn't strike again for me: same local theater, too!

OK, now that I've put all that in context, and forever scotched any chance of your considering me a "man of taste," let's dance.

CREATURE opened nationwide on Friday, September 9th, 2011—and closed, *everywhere*, within the week.

CREATURE was reviled, pilloried, ridiculed, and taunted, coast to coast. It also bombed, brutally, worse than any theatrical film of the decade up to that point in time, which was incredible—I mean, if the boxoffice had represented *only* the number of posts savaging the movie in its opening weekend, it would have earned more at the boxoffice than it did.

Curious thing: most of those shitting on **CREATURE** never saw it.

No, that's not my supposition: that's what was everywhere on all social networks. People—self-described "horror fans"—were positively boastful about that fact: they hadn't seen it, and they *wouldn't* see it. It was beneath them to see it. See it? Never. Shit all over it? *Eeeeeehaaaaa!* Shitting on the unseen **CREATURE** was one of *the* American indoor sports highlights of 9/11 weekend.

After collectively complaining about the millions upon millions of dollars spent on "faux-low-budget" homages (**GRINDHOUSE**, **PIRANHA 3D**, Michael Bay-produced-remakes of 1970s/'80s classics, etc.), here's the real steamer—a genuine low-budget regional oddity inexplicably popped up theatrically—and every genre site, post, and fan I found the morning after **CREATURE** opened was bitching about the film. Again, mostly sight unseen.

Well, yep, it tanked: no promo, unexpected arrival, no pre-sell. No surprise to me, I was the *only* person in the theater (first evening show, Sunday night). In fact, when I went *back* (read on), the local theater manager said, "*Why* are you seeing *that?*" as if the money I'd just dropped at his ticket counter was money badly spent. When I grinned and told him it was my second time, he said, "Oh, so *you* were one of the four people who've paid to see it!" (By the way, one of the four *other* people that *were* there when I went the second time walked out ten minutes into the movie—ah, well, no accounting for tastes.)

Within about 24 hours, **CREATURE** was clearly separating the ranks (choose your metaphor: "the men from boys," whatever) when it comes to "I love cheapjack hardscrabble regional horror movies," and **CREATURE** set a new barometer.

Folks who claimed to "love" horror movies "the raunchier the better" or "the more despised the better" were avoiding it. They were crowing over, *celebrating* its failure; well, fuck 'em.

I saw it, I loved it, and now I love it *more*, for what it is.

CREATURE was not to be missed. If you truly love 1970s/'80s drive-in/nabe genre fare, **CREATURE** (for the first time in years) is the Real McCoy: regionally-shot, roughhewn, brain-and-moral-addled potboiler, and I had a grand time with it. It's a rude, clunky, grand and glorious unabashed tits-ass-blood-grue-man-in-suit-monster joyride, and it's wonderful if you love exploitation—a breath of fresh air after years of "multi-millions spent to emulate low-budget" fare. After so many mega-buck mock-1970s/'80s horror pastiches, this rang my bell: shot in Lou-

*The out-of-nowhere US theatrical release of **DRAGON WARS** a.k.a. **D-WAR** (2007) had eye-catching posters, as did the international release of **GRINDHOUSE** (2007), a faux-1970s double-feature comprised of two features: Quentin Tarantino's **DEATH PROOF** (here is the Japanese B2 poster) and Robert Rodriguez's **PLANET TERROR** (here represented by a hand-painted Ghanaian poster)*

108

In 2011, **CREATURE** famously tanked—while lesser also-lensed-in-Louisiana (and Texas) genre offering, Will Hayes, Jesse Studenberg, and the late David R. Ellis (**SNAKES ON A PLANE**)'s **SHARK NIGHT 3D** played for weeks domestically and raked in $40 million worldwide (here is the film's Thai release poster art).

isiana, weird, sick, lumpy, dumb, down, dirty, rude, crude, lewd, nasty, wonky, twisted swamp critter sleaze-fest, for real. *This* was what drive-in fodder used to be—better, in fact, than most of those films actually were.

Give me the genuine cheapies on the big screen any day—and those have been few and far between since the early 1980s.

The pity is the tepid, tame, lame-ass, by-the-numbers **SHARK NIGHT 3D** (2011; which I also saw the week before, and enjoyed as much as I could; two good villains, one good nurse shark attack, one twist in the tail that worked well enough) played for a *full month* in theaters hereabout. The afternoon matinee of **SHARK NIGHT 3D** I caught was about a third full. Sigh. Why? Why was **SHARK NIGHT 3D** racking up business, and not **CREATURE**?

Welcome to the mysteries of 21st Century horror movie "fandom", contemporary theatrical film distribution, and what passes for "entertainment news" and movie-mob-mentality in lock-step these days.

CREATURE cost me $7 to see and it was worth every nickel. I went back that Tuesday night with my pal Denis St. John (*Monsters & Girls*), and had an even better time. **CREATURE** was well worth $14 out-of-pocket for me to see on the screen—and given the crap the filmmakers had to have been writhing over this fall, I'm *honored* to have paid $14 for their movie. They *need* it. I bought the DVD, too, and extra copies for Christmas gifts for friends (and if they didn't like it, they got nothing for Christmas the next year).

Let's put it this way: **CREATURE** was more fun than all but four of the 3D movies I've paid a bundle to see theatrically in the past few years (and yes, that includes **HARRY POTTER 3D** on the *"less entertaining to Bissette than CREATURE"* 3D list).

Then, why the hate fest?

There were some theories floating around in those first 24 hours of **CREATURE**'s short, brutal screen life…

The slim, fleeting weekend **CREATURE** was in theaters, Steven Barnes wrote on Facebook:

> "I noticed a horror film called **CREATURE** where the lead is a black ex-SEAL…and he's with a white woman. He might well survive, but my position is that the audience would have rejected him even if he'd been with a black chick. White girl?

*Instant mega-doom. The result? **CREATURE** opened Friday, earned $331,000, the LOWEST BOX OFFICE EVER for a film opening in at least 1500 theaters. What in the hell were they thinking..? Jeeze, if someone had just asked me…"*

To which I replied:

"I'd point—and am pointing—the finger at (a) it was cheap, (b) it came outta nowhere, (c) it has almost no promo, (d) it has absolutely no pre-sell (save a Fangoria *cover), (e) it's been dumped on 9/11 weekend in a traditionally awful weekend fall slot under the best of circumstances, (f) it's a fucking gator-man movie that (g) nobody ever heard of and (h) doesn't want to know about. If I had to play a race card, it would be somewhere down around (q), because none of the promo even implies a black hero, much less a black hero enjoying (and he does) sex onscreen. If that were an issue,* **SHARK NIGHT 3D** *wouldn't be in its third week (black supporting character with white girlfriend is the only likable cat in the cast), and* **CREATURE** *wouldn't have even found* one *theater slot, much less popped up nationally and in NH, yet. … [as for its release,] "haphazard" is an understatement. To me, it's a miracle this is in theaters at all!"*

Did race and miscegenation dread kill **CREATURE**? I think not, but others think so. Serinda Swan and Mehcad Brooks were easy on the eyes and likeable enough as the mixed-race couple hero/heroine of the film.

Without even a poster (I asked the theater manager; the film arrived *sans* a one-sheet, with only one of those plastic title cards for over the ticket counter), you can't chalk up **CREATURE**'s dismal weekend to the race card. There was no way to tell *who* was in the movie, much less what color they were! Besides, the miscegenation of the movie isn't black/white: it's the typical gator-man/human miscegenation (okay, I'm being glib, but really—monster/girl miscegenation has been a movie staple since **KING KONG** [1933]).

What was even crazier to me than that theory, though, was the utter disconnect between the reality of **CREATURE**—what it was, is, as a movie—and the shit being said about it.

After all the dung flung about *anything* new by George Romero, Wes Craven, Tobe Hooper, etc.;

109

all the griping, bile, and belittling of **GRINDHOUSE, PIRANHA 3D**, etc.; the endless sniping at the ongoing cycle of **TEXAS CHAIN SAW MASSACRE/NIGHTMARE ON ELM ST./FRIDAY THE 13TH/LAST HOUSE ON THE LEFT/THE HILLS HAVE EYES/I SPIT ON YOUR GRAVE** et al 1970s/1980s remakes of originally-low-budget movies, and other big-budget attempts to "recreate" the cheapie creepies of earlier era (Rod Lurie's about-to-open-the-next-week **STRAW DOGS** [2011] remake was taking an online pasting, also as-yet sight unseen at that point)—those now-sacred texts that scored "reviews" like *"peel grapes, not people"* (I shit you not) when they opened in their day—well, here was an honest-to-God out-of-the-bayou batshit cheapjack coonass horror movie, and you'd think there'd be some wee bit of misfit mutant love showing.

Nope—with the exception of only two reviews I found online, it was all jeers and sneers, whether they'd seen it or not.

The same cold shoulder treatment has gone to some of my favorite films of 2011, from Kevin Smith's self-distributed **RED STATE** (now on DVD from Lionsgate) to Jennifer Lynch's made-in-India gem **HISSS** (now on DVD) to Simon Rumley's searing **RED, WHITE AND BLUE**. These, and more, made 2011 a great year for horror movies, and **CREATURE** added to the rum punch.

I really don't get most genre "fans" these days: what do you *WANT???*

This was BleedingCool.com's screed:

"This weekend's horror dud, **CREATURE** averaged SIX people per screen in its nationwide release.

"Record-Breaking Box Office Disaster for Epic Failures **CREATURE** and **BUCKY LARSON**.

"We spend a lot of time dedicating front page headlines to movies at the top of the box office, but for now, it's time to honour a couple of films to turn heads with truly catastrophic bum-to-seats ratios.

"First up is **CREATURE**, the directorial debut from production designer Fred Andrews. It opened on 1,507 screens and made an estimated $331,000 off a $3,000,000 budget. It slides comfortably into place as the fifth lowest-grossing opening on record for a nationwide release, second worse in terms of per-location average and the worst ever gross for a film screening at over 1,500 cinemas, with an average per-screening attendance of six people.

"**CREATURE** currently has a Metacritic score of 27/100 and has been described as 'Absurdly plotted, ineptly scripted and haplessly acted' by the Orlando Sentinel and 'devoid of scares, imagination and basic technical and screenwriting competence' by Box Office Magazine.

"Ouch.

"But don't let others make up your mind for you. Take a look at the trailer and decide for yourselves if this looks like a work of undiscovered genius..."

"Undiscovered genius"?

Mehcad Brooks survives against all odds as **CREATURE**'s put-upon hero

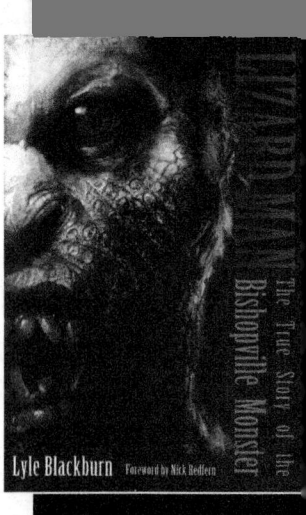

The wellspring for the **CREATURE FROM THE BLACK LAGOON** was reportedly a story actor/producer William Alland heard in 1940 from Mexican cinematographer Gabriel Figueroa (see Tom Weaver's complete account in his excellent recent books *The Creature Chronicles* and *Universal Terrors, 1951–1955*), but humanoid 'lizard man' and amphibious cryptids continue to emerge from all corners of the globe. Lyle Blackburn's *Lizard Man: The True Story of the Bishopville Monster* (2013, Anomalist Books) details Blackburn's investigation of just such a creature reported in South Carolina in the late 1980s; along the way, Blackburn offers an overview of similar 'swamp monster' sightings and lore, and includes a a handy swamp monster filmography (including **ZAAT**). Recommended!

Right: The titular **CREATURE** (Daniel Bernhardt)'s 'courtship' of Karen (Lauren Schneider, of **AMONG BROTHERS** [2005] and **RED WHITE & BLUE** [2010]).

The breeding of deep-sea-dwelling humanoids at Cobb Seamount is essential to the survival of intelligent life on a ravaged Earth in D. D. Chapman and Deloris Lehman Tarzan's *Red Tide* (1975), second entry in the second of three series of Ace Science Fiction Special titles published from 1968–1990.

No. 'Twarn't that at all.

Genius has nothing to do with it.

CREATURE was fueled by desperation. Make it or break it. Base commerce. Crass, down-and-dirty exploitation. That's the lowest common denominator shit that fueled almost *all* of those now "sacred" 1960s/'70s/'80s horrors, too.

CREATURE? Genius? Fuck you, *Bleeding-Cool.myass*, for even setting that false bar.

CREATURE wasn't "genius."

But it sure was *fun*.

And it sure was a *real* slice of what we used to catch on the drive-in and nabe screens in the 1970s and early 1980s.

But hey, *BleedingCool.com* "movie fans," particularly self-proclaimed "horror/SF fans", *what the fuck do you WANT?*

Let's stack up your equations, based on what I read weekly online from so-called "devoted horror fans" and "movie lovers," those with or without followings. The lock-step echoes like military marches many days:

Big-budget horror movies=suck.
Low-budget horror movies=suck.
Any remake of anything=suck.
Any movie "not living up to potential"=suck.
Any big-budget pastiche of low-budget original=suck.
Any genuine low-budget-snuck-into-theaters=suck.
Any direct-to-DVD=suck.

Any SyFy movie=suck.

Biggest bullshit, to me: Any movie by once-revered geezer=suck.

I've found plenty to enjoy, even savor and revisit, in new work by Romero/Craven/etc.

Well, fuck y'all.

I'm having fun, and looks like "faux-fan"=suck from here.

Hey, maybe you *just don't like movies*. Could that be it?

They/you hate big-budget fare, "where'd that come froms" like **SPLICE** (2009), mainstream studio genre surprises like **RISE OF THE PLANET OF THE APES** (2011), anything from the vets (Romero, Craven, etc.), anything genuinely low-budget that somehow escapes… well, fuck it. The hell with y'all.

I *love* seeing genre films in the theaters; I *miss* having access to the sleaziest of 'em.

I enjoyed **CREATURE** for what it is: a cheap, grubby, effective coonass/monster exploitation flick with some juice, shot on location with on-camera monster and mayhem, efficiently edited rough and ready, without apologies or pretensions or much of a catering budget or even half-a-brain in its skull.

Genius? Fuck you. Down-and-dirty grub-fest with a monster, here I come!

Sid Haig fueled the fun; correct me if I'm wrong, but has Sid Haig *ever* been in a single theatrical movie (other than perhaps Rob Zombie's **THE DEVIL'S REJECTS** [2005]) that got a *single* good review when it opened? Ever? His track record is solid now! The Creature (Daniel Bernhardt) itself was a hoot. Lauren Schneider delivered one of the best performances of the year in a genre flick right here, folks, and co-star Amanda Fuller (both from the scathing, sorely underseen, underrated **RED, WHITE AND BLUE**) was even better.

CREATURE was the most unexpected fun I'd had in a theater since **DRAGON WARS** (which also caught me completely off-guard when it popped up locally), **SPLICE** (which was the best recent indie horror/SF, for my money), and **INSIDIOUS** (one of 2011's best horror movies, period). Man, I loved **INSIDIOUS**: a great little movie, caught it in the theater and glad I did (it only started getting cheers from "horror fans" when it finally hit DVD; d'oh!). Sent a chill right up my spine at one point, and that's rare and lovely. I loved **SPLICE**—went twice while it was playing in the theater. I hadn't experienced anything quite like it theatrically since David Cronenberg's **THE BROOD** (which I actually caught on its second run, at a drive-in double-bill); it's a genetic *Frankenstein* by way of Charles Burns, Cronenberg, and its actual filmmakers, who should be household names among genre buffs already for their earlier works (**CUBE**, **CYPHER**, **NOTHING**, etc.; that's Vincenzo Natali's track record, joined here by writer Antoinette Terry Bryant). Absolutely enjoyed **RISE OF THE PLANET OF THE APES**, and convinced my wife to go with me on the return, and *she* liked it (and she *hates* horror/SF). **CONTAGION** (2011) was as good as Robert Wise's 1970 adaptation of Michael Crichton's *The Andromeda Strain*. I would have killed to catch George Romero's **DIARY OF THE DEAD** (2007) and **SURVIVAL OF THE DEAD** (2009) on a big screen; loved 'em both, once I could see them (DVD)—particularly the latter. Hell, Romero is *still* a great storyteller, we're lucky he's still with us and should cherish everything left he's permitted (by budgets/powerbrokers) to share with us.

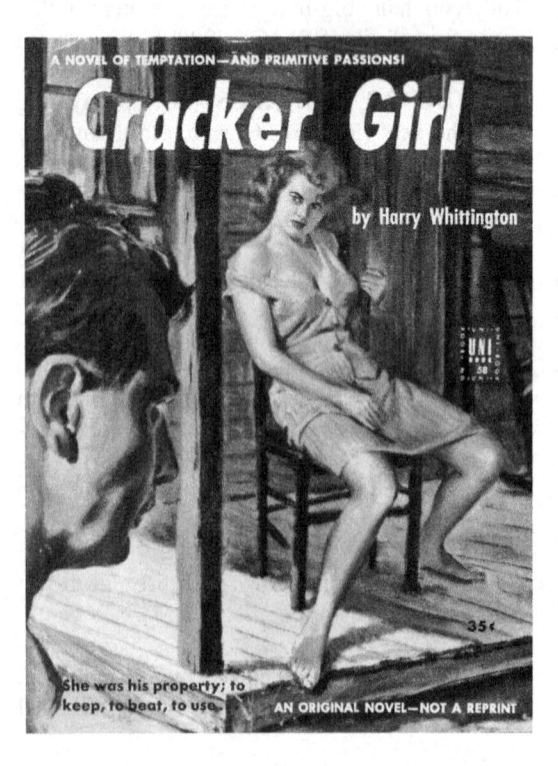

There's been a *lot* of good and even great genre fare to enjoy—each on their own terms—but you wouldn't know it from the online chatter or piss-poor reviews.

Why is that?

I enjoy movies. I enjoy revamps and remakes and reboots and originals and "where'd that come from?" and sequels and monkeyfuckfests.

It's incredible how precisely the current bitching matches the bitching from the 1970s about the very films contemporary "fans" rhapsodize over like Holy relics. As video artist Matt Bucy says: *"Hats off to anyone who tries to make anything!"*

I couldn't wait to drive back to **CREATURE** to savor one more time a genuine cheapjack regional cracker-baiting low-budget roughhewn nasty horror flick on the big screen. It's been too long, and these were staple diet fare in my teen and college years, when such films still landed theatrical play. I loved and still love **THE WITCHMAKER** (1969), **TOURIST TRAP** (1979), **GATOR BAIT** (1974), **HUMANOIDS FROM THE DEEP** (1980), **SWAMP THING** (1982), etc., and **CREATURE** was as engaging as any one of those (which were hated in their day, too).

CREATURE was a rare opportunity to be seized, and "horror fans" instead bragged about missing it. **CREATURE** was *precisely* the kind of film that used to grace drive-ins in the 1970s and 1980s, in all its shoddy, ramshackle, twisted bayou glory. This was like seeing **ATTACK OF THE GIANT LEECHES** (1959), **THE BROTHERHOOD OF SATAN** (1971), or **THE FUNHOUSE** (1981) for the first time. And, I shit you not, once the "local yokels gathered to chant to their unholy swamp deity" sequence arrived, I'll be damned if it was actually a fairly spot-on dramatization of H.P. Lovecraft's "The Call of Cthulhu":

> *"...In a natural glade of the swamp stood a grassy island of perhaps an acre's ex-*

Lizard Man of Scape Ore Swamp is a reptilian humanoid that first made itself known in 1987. The tall, scaly bipedal critter has often been sighted in adn around the state of South Carolina. The monster struts its stuff in this popular image which later proved to be hoaxed.

"Swamp Monster", toy, 1989. Monster in My Pocket was best known as a toy-line released by Matchbox in 1989. Monster in My Pocket is a media franchise developed by American company Morrison Entertainment Group, headed by Joe Morrison and John Weems, two former senior executives at Mattel.

Facing Page: Backwoods / hillbilly / 'swamp tramp' sexploitation was a staple of 1950s-1970s pulp paperbacks (here, *Cracker Girl* by Harry Whittington a.k.a. J.X. Williams, 1953) and movies. **Right:** Serinda Swan and Mehcad Brooks, heroine and hero of **CREATURE**.

Artist's rendition of Louisiana's Honey Island Swamp Monster, which has been active since around the mid-1940s, although published reports started in the early 1960s. The critter is what could be called an "aqua-bigfoot": hairy, with a crocodilian head, webbed hands, and three (sometimes four)-toed feet (plaster casts have been made of various footprints found at scenes of the monsters' appearances). At least one report gave the Honey Island cryptid a thick, T-Rex style tail.

tent, clear of trees and tolerably dry. On this now leaped and twisted a more indescribable horde of human abnormality than any but a Sime or an Angarola could paint. Void of clothing, this hybrid spawn were braying, bellowing, and writhing about a monstrous ring-shaped bonfire; in the centre of which, revealed by occasional rifts in the curtain of flame, stood a great granite monolith some eight feet in height; on top of which, incongruous with its diminutiveness, rested the noxious carven statuette. From a wide circle of ten scaffolds set up at regular intervals with the flame-girt monolith as a centre hung, head downward, the oddly marred bodies of the helpless squatters who had disappeared. It was inside this circle that the ring of worshippers jumped and roared, the general direction of the mass motion being from left to right in endless Bacchanal between the ring of bodies and the ring of fire...."

When **CREATURE** finally got underground, scrabbling around in the overlit-but-still-atmospheric critter's lair, I was indeed in **BEAST FROM HAUNTED CAVE** (1959) and **ATTACK OF THE GIANT LEECHES** heaven (both movies I caught on bad-reception late-night TV broadcasts initially, where not being able to see too well but hearing the soundtrack perfectly only made the "things feeding on their stashed human prey in their caves" even more unforgettably disturbing). It stuck with its nastiest turns right to the final shot, in a hardly-unexpected coda that satisfied in the way grotty pre-Code Iger Studios and Eerie Publications horror comics used to. What's not to love?

Anyhoot, back to Steven Barnes and that race card:

So, Steven and I had a chat on Facebook. Here's some of it:

Barnes: *Stephen–oh, I think race was a factor...but it wasn't just that the audience would tend to stay away even if it was good. I also think it speaks to a lapse in judgment on the part of the producers, and I think that others connected with such projects have more tendency to "phone it in." But the article misses the real point: black or Asian men can't have sex with ANYONE without trashing their box office. It fascinates me how hard it is for people to see it.*

Bissette: *Well, now, wait.* **SHARK NIGHT 3D** *(which was just as dismal a shot-in-Louisiana low-budget effort, sans the juice, and is knocking 'em dead in its third week, so to speak) also has a black character with white girlfriend prominent in the cast. It's not like* **CREATURE** *has a one-sheet or ad campaign like* **BLACK SNAKE MOAN** *(2006), Steven—I'm the target audience for* **CREATURE***, have been since age 6, and there's not a clue in anything that got my ass into that theater seat about the race of any character in the film, save completely fictional gator/human hybrid.* **NIGHT OF THE LIVING DEAD** *didn't wear that card on its promo's sleeve, either; I just think you're misattributing the failure of a not-pre-sold, not-promoted, seasonal-dump-into-theaters-in-the-worst-season unknown regional low-budget clunker to the race of its hero.* **TWIN PEAKS: FIRE WALK WITH ME** *did just as badly upon its release (check the record); I could cite countless others, none of which had the race issue even remotely involved.*

*PS: Forgive me, please, but having seen the movie (***CREATURE***), it might also be (not to be crass, the movie is) that audiences didn't want to see a white sister give a hand-job to her white brother shooting voyeuristic photos while they spied on the black hero having swamp sex with his "what race is she?" girlfriend.*

PPS: Mehcad Brooks gives a solid performance in **CREATURE***, makes his hero likable and a man clearly in love (rare in such fare), and survives. That's all rare, too.*

Another fellow (**Michael Michalchik**) chimed in: *Wait I thought audiences*

E. R. Burroughs's East Indies isle Dr. Moreau-spin *A Man Without a Soul* (1913) became *The Monster Men* (1963 edition, Frank Frazetta art)

were supposed to hate Male black female white miscegenation?

Bissette: *The clear evidence, this dismal 9/11 weekend, is audiences rejected implicit gator-man/white woman miscegenation.*

Matthew Damon added: *"in order to pack theaters this weekend they would've had to have the Gator-man have sex with a black dyke and white transsexual at the same time while getting married and flying an airplane shaped like Jesus into Ground Zero during a memorial celebration FULL of firemen and cops…"*

Maybe Matthew's right. Hell, maybe Steve's right—but I don't think he is. I just think **CREATURE** was the ideal scapegoat, whipping-post at the ideal time: something *easy* for *everyone* to hate on the tenth-anniversary, loaded-for-bear 9/11 weekend. Something *everyone* could comfortably lambast, loathe, and righteously spit on without even pretending to care, much less pretending to have debased their precious eyes by *seeing* it.

OK, junk horror/monster junkies—if **CREA-TURE** pops up again on screens anywhere in driving distance, do *not* miss it.

As I say, it's incredible to me **CREATURE** played *any* screen *anywhere*, any time, much less the wide opening it enjoyed. It was distributed by an outfit named "The Bubble Factory" (I kid you not), and it somehow slipped into theaters.

Somehow? Well, there's some dollars, power, and incredible Hollywood muscle behind **CREATURE**, though you wouldn't know it from the movie, the paucity of production or promotion, or *any* published or online review—it's the **CREATURE** story everyone ignored or missed, and explains how **CREATURE** landed so many simultaneous national playdates. However, given the lack of promotion, it's also a cautionary case history revealing how hard and expensive it is to open *any* movie in 2011, much less in such a hostile media environment (and it's harder to imagine a faster, more furious piranha-feeding-frenzy than that which rendered **CREATURE** into almost instant mincemeat). Vet production designer Fred Andrews took most of the heat for directing (his debut) and co-scripting (with actor/director/writer Tracy Morse) **CREATURE**—and believe me, I'll now check out everything and anything he and Tracy does hereafter—but Bubble Factory is the *real* story here.

The Bubble Factory has an interesting, truly weird track record.

They were the production outfit behind the **FLIPPER** remake (1996), followed by the ambitious roster of **THE PEST**, **THAT OLD FEELING**, **McHALE'S NAVY**, **A SIMPLE WISH**, **FOR RICHER OR POORER** (all in 1997, their busiest year), **SLAPPY AND THE STINKERS** (1998)—then, *phhhhht*. And believe me, **MCHALE'S NAVY** was a *real* stinker. They got only three films out over the following decade (**PLAYING MONA LISA** [2000], **BAD GIRLS FROM VALLEY HIGH** [2005], and **MADE IN BROOKLYN** [2007]), and I'd love to know more. There's a book to be written here, no doubt, but who would buy it?

CREATURE was their shot at getting back into theaters, and their first film as producers and distributors—what a weird revival shot, but there's no denying they did get it into theaters, sans any ballyhoo or promotional support. *Plop. Thud.*

Now, Bubble Factory belongs to—*is*—the Sheinbergs. Who are the Sheinbergs, you ask? Let's start with legendary father Sid Sheinberg, former confidant of the more legendary (and

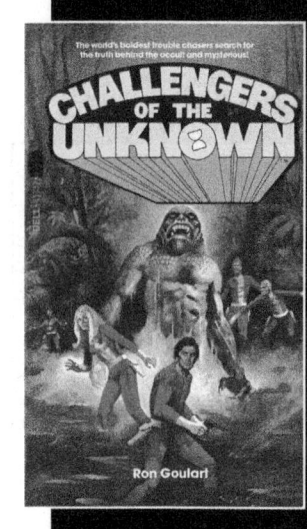

Challengers of the Unknown (1977) Another Gillman-like reptilian humanoid lurked in the South American Lake Sombra in Ron Goulart's *Challengers of the Unknown* (1977, Dell Publishing Co., Inc.), an original novel licensed by National Periodicals Publications/DC Comics from the Jack Kirby-created comic book series.

feared) late Lew Wasserman and himself former head of Universal Studio. Sid Sheinberg is the man popularly cited as having discovered Steven Spielberg (they co-own an entire floor of the Trump Tower in NYC). He's also the man who fucked with Ridley Scott's **LEGEND** (1985), among other films, and who Terry Gilliam went nose-to-nose with over **BRAZIL** that same year. Sid is married to actress Lorraine Gary (from **JAWS, JAWS 2, JAWS: THE REVENGE**, and many other credits going back to 1967)—and their two sons, Bill and Jonathan, *co-own* the Bubble Factory with pop-a-roonie.

Got that?

Jonathan has executive producer and producer credits going back to Steven Seagal's **HARD TO KILL** (1990); to date, brother Bill only has the Bubble Factory credits to his name. Working with the Sheinbergs on **CREATURE**: the film was executive produced by executive-in-charge-of-production super-vet Paul Mason (of *Welcome Back Kotter, Key West, Matlock, Sabrina*, etc.), produced by former production accountant Kerry Andrews, and the associate producers were former executive ass't/ass't to producers Brian K. Aspinwall and vet post-production supervisor Anthony Gore.

That's quite a formidable production team and package, which only adds to the mystery and allure of what, exactly, pulled all these elements together to make and then slam-dunk-cram **CREATURE** into theaters.

Why isn't anyone writing about *that*?

Ah, it's easier, quicker to just bitch and blister a movie instantaneously blasted as a turkey, in't it?

Above all, **CREATURE** is a cautionary case history of passive promotion utterly failing to promote to its target audience. Let's face it: other than the *Fangoria* cover/article and the trailer being online, all most of us saw (and saw first on September 9th) was a bland, typeset title in the listing for our local theater: **CREATURE**. That's it.

Showmanship is dead. William Castle and David Friedman would never survive in 2011.

The theaters didn't even have anything to catch the eye of monster-movie lovers. It costs a lot—too much—to open a low-budget horror movie these days—much like 20th Century Fox's **WRONG TURN** (2003; a great little movie I also caught theatrically, which at least had a one-sheet poster), **CREATURE** was simply and unceremoniously dumped into release. Regardless of the money, power, and clout implicit in the Sheinberg family name, **CREATURE** benefitted from that not a whit—they may, in fact, have regarded it as nothing other than a tax write-off (who knows?).

Had **CREATURE** opened in the 1970s, there would have been eye-catching newspaper ads, a corker of a pressbook (even if it had been only four pages), plus one-sheet posters and a trailer we'd have seen on theater screens for at least a week prior to release. In 2011 (as with 2007's **DRAGON WARS**, and 2010's **SPLICE**, or 2013's **INSIDIOUS 2**—at least the latter two enjoyed more ballyhoo than **CREATURE**), we're lucky to even see the title.

Anyhoot: my ass was in a theater seat. **CREATURE**, the title alone, did it for me. **CREATURE**? I'm there.

The Bubble Factory logo had me going, *"what the fuck?"*

Instant galvanizer.

Then:

No boutique Michael Bay/studio-faux-low-budget homage here.

30 seconds: nude woman swimming in the swamp.

1 minute: gator attack.

2 minutes: dismemberment.

Vintage American sideshow poster for "Jake the Alligator Man".

115

Titles.

Heaven.

Horror Movie Heaven.

Then: three couples (including weird bro/sis thang), two grunts, black hero, incest, miscegenation, bogus/lurid monster origin story, Sid Haig, Pruitt Taylor Vince (a great actor, wasted here —but still, he added spice), and they're the "lighter" bayou faux-coonasses. Next to Haig, the heavy coonass crazies are Wayne Pére (character actor with over seventy movie and TV credits to his name, in top form) and the amazing David Jensen (ditto, here also a bit of mutant: check out his hand!), who are indelibly reprehensible cajun caricatures.

Look, I've already said too much, and I haven't given away anything, really. Co-creators Tracy Morse and Fred Andrews have done the deed—don't want to build expectations, though, because the creaky/hokey/choppy/roughhewn lumpiness of the whole sick puppy was part of the hoot for me.

It's the catching of this, sans prep, in a theater that made the evening such an unexpected treat. I know "they" still make 'em like this, but "they" don't get 'em in theaters anymore—well, like **DRAGON WARS** and **SPLICE**, this weird scaly freak slipped through somehow, and I couldn't be happier!

As I say: said too much already. Just, if you love genuine regional clunky/fucked up horror/monster movies, this is gravy.

CREATURE has its oddest character (and that's saying something) drop a slang reference to "spider baby" at one point—a nod to one of Sid Haig's first screen roles that caught my generation's eye. I've grown up watching Haig in made-in-Philippines women-in-prison movies, on TV, in 1981's **GALAXY OF TERROR** (another beloved night at the movie theater, that I rushed to see twice that week; another movie that was universally reviled when it opened, now beloved), and in Rob Zombie's movies—and all but **SPIDER BABY** (1968) and the TV fare I was lucky enough to catch on the big screen, theatrical.

Also of interest to this ol' *Swamp Thing* co-creator and friend/fan of fellow cartoonist Rick Grimes: Shreveport, Louisiana provided locations for at least three theatrical films I saw last year: **BATTLE LOS ANGELES**, **SHARK NIGHT 3D**, and **CREATURE**. Guess which one I had the most fun with.

> **Dan Bailey** noted on Facebook, *"I grew up about 20 miles from the La. border, & my dad's family are all from the Shreveport area, & beyond that I lived for 18 months in the New Orleans area ... so I'm wondering how "weird, sick, lumpy, dumb, down, dirty, rude, crude, lewd, nasty, wonky, twisted" doesn't describe the normal denizen of that part of the world."*

Shreveport was where my old Kubert School/comics pal Rick Grimes heralds from; not sure where **CREATURE** was specifically shot, but it was definitely thereabouts. The Louisiana Film Commission even has their logo on the final credits crawl, which given the irredeemable portrait of bayou scum and Louisiana inbreeding and cross-species miscegenation in general that populates the movie, should provide some political capital for *someone* in the coming elections.

All of which, of course, vastly improves the sick puppy entertainment quotient for **CREATURE**.

The real pisser with the buzz-kill on **CREATURE** was that we'd never have had a single one of the drive-in/exploitation gems of yore had we all tracked "entertainment news" thus.

It used to be this kind of buzz-kill only popped up in *Variety* or *Boxoffice*, the trade publications for theater owners. Now, every online poka-doke struts like they're in that catbird seat.

2011's **CREATURE** *[top left]* owes a debt to **CREATURE FROM THE BLACK LAGOON** (1954) *[above, and on p.118* in more than just title alone.

116

If they'd been around then, we'd have had no exploitation films to celebrate today. *"TWO THOUSAND MANIACS tanked in two venues this Friday, skipping it"—"Something called WHAT! opened in only four venues, to no boxoffice, why bother?"—"MICKEY LION'S HOUSE OF EXORCISM isn't even directed by 'Mickey Lion'! It's Italian. Piece of shit, no doubt"—"Hallmark's Boston rollout of TOMBS OF THE BLIND DEAD clunked; who cares about this crap?"*—well, you get the idea.

Tue Sorensen weighed in on the Facebook conversation: *"You're complaining that other people don't think that bad movies are good enough? Well, you should get together with other people who specifically love movies that are so bad that they're good. Seems like your crowd... It may be true that there is a tendency today to bash bad movies extra hard (and, similarly, praise good movies even higher than they deserve), but I think that's because people are tired of having their time wasted again and again by crappy product. As a movie buff myself, I have to say I understand that attitude. Eventually, most people get sick of bad movies."*

No, I just enjoy movies for what they are. Anyone entering anything completely unknown named **CREATURE** with high expectations (or, in my case, *any* expectations) is asking for disappointment.

My friend Joe Citro and I have a scale: *"Good Movie/Entertaining—Bad Move/Entertaining—Good Movie/Not Entertaining—Bad Movie/Not Entertaining"*—that covers it all in shorthand. I loathe 'star' ratings and number ratings. Tell me something useful. Shorthand on **CREATURE**: For me, *"Bad Movie/Entertaining."* That's worth my theatre visit every time.

"Good"? Who said anything about "good"? I just want to enjoy myself with a movie. Anything else is gravy.

No expectations is key. I now avoid reading reviews, promo, etc. and just *go* to what catches my eye or fancy.

Look, the really fun genre movies rarely ever get any love when they open. For the most part, mainstream reviewers never grok the genre, and rarely have or did or do. From the likes of **THE BRAIN THAT WOULDN'T DIE** (1962; a *perfect* movie) to **KILL BABY, KILL** (1966) to **FASTER, PUSSYCAT! KILL! KILL!** (1965) to **THE BLOOD SPATTERED BRIDE** (1972) and **THEY CAME FROM WITHIN** (1975) to **THE TEXAS CHAIN SAW MASSACRE** (1974) to **HALLOWEEN** (1978), the films I grew up loving were spat upon in opening reviews, if and when they were reviewed at all; it didn't matter, the audiences that wanted to see 'em saw 'em.

I laughed the week before **CREATURE** opened when I read someone in a FB thread asserting Larry Cohen's **THE STUFF** (1985) as a holy relic: look, I just don't believe the writer would have argued that when **THE STUFF** was in theaters. I was there; folks fucking hated **THE STUFF**. I caught that in a Revere, MA theater the weekend it opened (to terrible, blistering reviews). I loved it, but the folks I went with *insisted* we duck into the end of another movie

Exploitation vet character actor Sid Haig *[right]* boasts a career dating back to vaudeville revival stage shows and theater, debuting in cinema in Jack Hill's UCLA student film **THE HOST** (1961) and Hill's **SPIDER BABY** (1967), retiring in 1992 after decades of movie and TV roles, returning to appear in Quentin Tarantino's **JACKIE BROWN** (1997) and star in Rob Zombie's **HOUSE OF 1000 CORPSES** (2000/2003).

"Piss on y'all!"

after so they could say they'd *"seen part of a real movie."*

Man, when they're actually "here" and on the big screen, so few recognize these gems for what they are.

To paraphrase the Bible circa Roger Corman's *"oh it's not that good though it won a prize at Trieste not as good as it should have been oh it's low budget"* now revered **X: THE MAN WITH THE X-RAY EYES** (1963): *"If thy eye offend thee, PLUCK IT OUT!!"*

Or, as Sid Haig damn near says more than once in **CREATURE**, *"Piss on y'all!"*

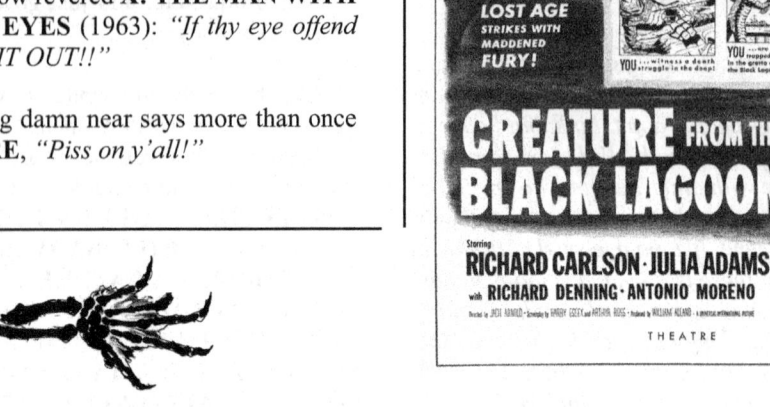

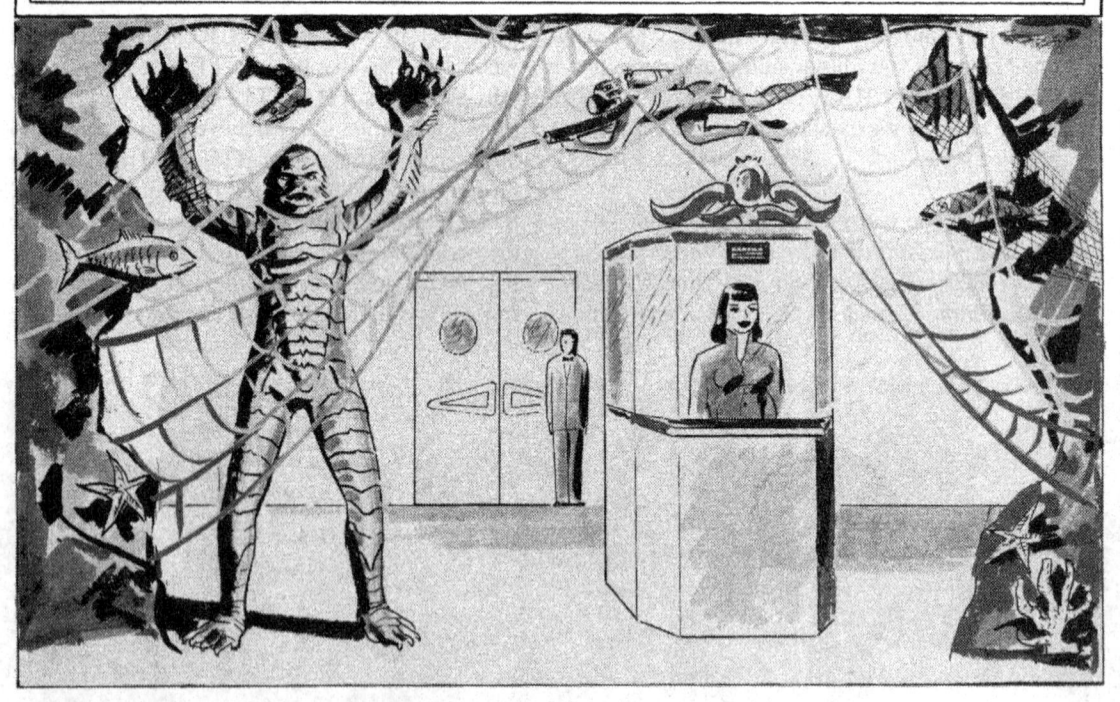

AQUARIUMS IN YOUR LOBBY

Dealers in tropical fish and aquarium supplies in general should be interested in this picture which shows many underwater fish. As part of the tie-up, offer dealers the opportunity of displaying aquariums of tropical fish in your lobby. Add dealer credit cards. The aquariums will ad an interesting touch, particularly if you place them behind a 40 x 60 display. Cut out an aperture in the display through which the fish may be seen. Add decorative touches to suit your needs.

WHAT'S ZAAT?

You could say my working in collaboration with writers Marty Pasko and Alan Moore and fellow artists Tom Yeates, John Totleben, Rick Veitch, and Alfredo Alcala (and fellow Kubert School alumni Ron Randall) on the comicbook *Saga of the Swamp Thing* in the 1980s informed my own affection for the most mongrel dogs of all monster movies. Well, that's not the case, though it certainly didn't hurt.

Truth to tell, I loved 'swamp monster' movies before I was knee-high to a nutria.

The Gillman—the **CREATURE FROM THE BLACK LAGOON** himself—was among my all-time favorite monsters as a kid, and from the happy hours spent assembling the Gillman's Aurora monster model kit in the early 1960s to savoring obscurities like **BOG** (1979) and **TERROR IN THE SWAMP** (a.k.a. **NUTRIA-MAN: THE COPASAW CREATURE**, 1985, both USA) during video store rental binges in the 1980s, my affection for swamp creatures predated and lasted long, long after my official stint on *Swamp Thing*.

Swamp monsters have inhabited some truly wretched but often inventive cinematic sleaze. I'd caught a few on TV while growing up, including Bernard L. Kowalski's **ATTACK OF THE GIANT LEECHES** (1959), which was always worth a revisit just to spend more screen time with Yvette Vickers and Bruno VeSota (and oh, the gruesome horror of that 'feeding scene' in the leeches' grotto lair!). While low-budget, none of these were more impoverished than Larry Buchanan's **CURSE OF THE SWAMP CREATURE** (1966, USA), which I caught one Saturday afternoon during my teenage years. There was also Florida-based William Grefé's swamp monster movies from 1966, the double-bill of **STING OF DEATH** (a jelly-fish man) and **DEATH CURSE OF TARTU** (a resurrected skeletal Seminole shaman); documentarian Daniel Griffith recently immortalized Grefé's legacy in the loving doc **THEY CAME FROM THE SWAMP: THE FILMS OF WILLIAM GREFÉ** (2016, USA), which is highly recommended.[1]

In my adult years, my "taste" for dredging the cine-swamp had only increased. After having dragged my entire family to Houma, Louisiana in the winter of 1984-85 to location-scout to im-

---

1 See *http://www.theycamefromtheswamp.com*

prove my ability to draw that bayou country in *Saga of the Swamp Thing*, I of course had to track down the only filmed-in-Houma cryptid opus in history, **NUTRIAMAN: THE COPASAW CREATURE**, which turned up on home video as **TERROR IN THE SWAMP**. It's also to date the one-and-only Nutriaman movie *in the whole world*. **NUTRIAMAN** a.k.a. **TERROR IN THE SWAMP** must have enjoyed a regional premiere of some sort in 1984 (the year of its copyright; there are movie poster images online for **NUTRIAMAN: TERROR IN THE SWAMP**, with the ballyhoo *"Hunting Season's Open...On You!"* and an official MPAA "PG" rating tag affixed), but the film's officially-listed (at least by the IMDb) debut is its July 1985 home videotape release via New World Video.

Enticing as the cast credit "introducing Michael Tedesco as 'T-Bob'" sounds today, Roger Corman knew direct-to-home-video fodder when he saw it, and when the man who produced **ATTACK OF THE GIANT LEECHES** tags your labor-of-love as direct-to-video fare, well—there you go.

Given the fact that the semiaquatic Nutria, a.k.a. the Coypu (*Myocastor coypus*), isn't nearly as well-known outside of the deep South as, say, its semiaquatic "cousins" the muskrat is (in fact, nutria is the only member of the *Myocastoridae* family), it's also obvious why the film's **NUTRIAMAN: THE COPASAW CREATURE** title had to go. Co-directed by Joe Catalanotto and Martin Folse from a script and story by Folse, Henry Brien, Terry Hebb, and Billy Holliday (no, not *Billie* Holliday, may she rest in peace), **TERROR IN THE SWAMP** is a curious specimen, a fairly well-done regional mash-up of mad science—a renegade scientist trying to breed a bigger nutria to boost the local fur trade inadvertently unleashes the titular humanoid Nutriaman (Keith Barker) on the locals—and the kind of 1970s Sasquatch/Skunk Ape/Bigfoot fare spawned by the surprise success of Texarkana native Charles B. Pierce's made-in-Arkansas "Fouke Monster" movie, **THE LEGEND OF BOGGY CREEK** (1975). It's also one of those regional genre offerings too competently made to render it desirable: by both mainstream and "bad film" connoisseur standards, **TERROR IN THE SWAMP** is "just okay" at best, nothing exceptional, too-well-made and neither laughable nor abysmal enough to score a devotional following. Fellow *Swamp Thing* writer Nancy Collins—the *only* bayou-country-raised *ST* creator ever to work on the character[2]—has a soft spot for the film, which can be chalked-up to local pride and a healthy affection for low-budget regional genre fare of any kind. "All I can say about nutrias," Nancy says, "is that they were once a thriving industry in Louisiana (they were a beaver pelt substitute) in the 19th Century, and thereby encouraged to thrive. And that we once had one get inside our house when I was in high school and had to chase it with a broom."[3]

But I daresay none of these cheapjack swamp monster movies holds a candle to a certain made-in-Florida wonder.

Was he man... fish... or devil?

Video packaging art for the made-in-Houma, Louisiana **NUTRIAMAN: THE COPASAW CREATURE** a.k.a. **TERROR IN THE SWAMP** (1984/1985), the one-and-only Nutriaman movie on planet Earth: New World's original US VHS release, and the German edition (via CBS Fox).

[2] Nancy notes, "I wasn't born in Louisiana. I was born in the ArkLaMiss, which is the Arkansas/Louisiana/Mississippi corner of the Mississippi River delta—same as Jim Henson and Levon Helm. I'm from Arkansas. But I did grow up in bayou country and live in New Orleans for ten years. Seven Devils Swamp used to belong to my family until the 1950s. It's now a state park. Seven Devils is the name I gave the fictionalized version of my home town, which serves as the locale of several of my Southern Gothic stories. It's my Arkham or Castle Rock." For more on the Seven Devils Swamp—now, *there's* a title for a horror movie waiting to be made (with Nancy's involvement/screenplay/permission)!—see https://youtu.be/00hXqZhJjSA

[3] Nancy Collins, personal message to the author, August 12th, 2017; quoted with permission.

I. Bringing the ManFishDevil Home

So, given my own affection for all things moist and mossy on the media landscape, it's high time I acknowledge the most adorable and philosophical of all immediate cinematic contemporaries to Len Wein and Berni Wrightson's original *"Swamp Thing"* outings.

I speak of the wonder and the glory of **ZAAT** (1972), or, more precisely given the fleeting on-screen "explanation" for the title, "Z_aA_t" (Z-sub-A, A-sub-T), the chemical compound "formula" that yields the man-into-walking-catfish-man transformation.

The ads asked, *"Was he man... fish... or devil?"* but the truth is he was the world's first and only Walking Catfish humanoid—well, that we *know* of, anyway.

Walking Catfish were new to Florida in the late 1960s (the earliest reports I recall reading were around 1968 or 1969); they're now *everywhere* in Florida, and they've got their own pages all over the internet. The Smithsonian Marine Station at Fort Pierce is online, and has all you'd care to know about *Clarias batrachus*:

"As early as 1970, researchers were reporting *C. batrachus* abundance in small Florida ponds in excess of 3,000 pounds per acre (Lachner 1970)."[4]

Clarius batrachus also enjoys ample screen time on YouTube.[5] One particular YouTube video comes from Ed a.k.a. "Seaheart88", posted on August 20th, 2008,[6] who wrote,

"This is a walking catfish; exotic in Florida (not supposed to be here). They have been walking/swimming up and down my street the last two days. I am flooded-in today... Walking catfish move around from pond to pond, ditch to ditch when it is wet and rainy. They can live out of the water quite a while and use this advantage to expand their population areas. I got good video of him walking down my driveway but too large to send."

Now, exploitation filmmakers thrive on newsworthy critters like these, and Walking Catfish *were* news in 1969-71. Walking Catfish landed the cover spots on newspapers and sensationalistic tabloid sleaze publications alike—so, you might say that **ZAAT** was... well, *inevitable*.

The 1970s tabloids were buzzing about Killer Bees invading America, so Killer Bees invaded made-for-TV movies and big-screen movies until Irwin Allen killed 'em with the massive bug-bomb entitled **THE SWARM** (1978, the same year the Killer Bee movie with the greatest one-sheet poster of all Killer Bee movies—Alfredo Zacarías' **THE BEES**—hit theaters, too).

Applying that logic, I reckon you could say that **ZAAT**, the first of the Walking Catfish movies, killed that movie genre right at birth—truth in advertising, given the **ZAAT** ballyhoo that read, *"Zaat is Death!"*—but that would be like claiming **THE GOD-MONSTER OF INDIAN FLATS** (1973, USA) killed-off the sheep-monster genre for, like, three decades!

Oh, wait, it did... and that one barely even got a theatrical release. That's toxic cine-stuff.

ZAAT *did* kiss theater screens, under more than one title, and we've got the proof to show you. And **ZAAT** *did* kill the Walking Catfish subgenre, deader than a drowned lungfish. But I'm getting ahead of the story here...

---

4 "Indian River Lagoon Species Inventory: Species name: *Clarias batrachus*," Smithsonian Marine Station at Fort Pierce, archived online (@ http://www.sms.si.edu/irlspec/Clarias_batrachus.htm)

5 See https://www.youtube.com/watch?v=m4a-ckzpD0I , https://www.youtube.com/watch?v=84rqMzH4Nvw, https://www.youtube.com/watch?v=MOS6473PS0I , etc.

6 See https://www.youtube.com/watch?v=crw-1rO-rhQ

Left: ZAAT's original release played up the walking catfish exploitation angle in ways the film never did!
Right: Photo of Wade Popwell hitchhiking in full Zaat regalia from the *Fort Lauderdale News* (Fort Lauderdale, FL), Friday, December 22, 1972, page 56, and (on the next page) in the *Daily Star* (Annistan, Alabama), March 11, 1973; special thanks to David Szulkin for providing access to this material.

II. Zippin' Up ZAAT

Producer/director/writer Don Barton drafted the final **ZAAT** script from a story by Ron Kivett and Lee O. Larew; Kivett's input included the Zaat-created monster design and construction that stood almost six feet in height and weighed well over 100 pounds. Like other regional genre filmmakers, from Herk Harvey to George Romero, Don Barton had cut his teeth on industrial films; just prior to **ZAAT**, Barton had helmed the cautionary 'watch-out-for-shoplifters' retailers' instructional short *They're Out To Get You* (1969) in Kansas City and the Kansas City Prison in Missouri. According to some sources, an uncredited Arnold Stevens worked with Barton on **ZAAT**'s screenplay and direction.

After preproduction prep—including Kivett completing construction of the Walking Catfish Man full-body suit, working with Martha Fillyaw and Les Lancaster (which, like most low-budget monster movie suits, constantly fell apart and required reconstruction throughout the filming)—the cast and crew of **ZAAT** labored with a reported budget of $75,000. **ZAAT** was completed during a single month in 1970. Filming locations included Marine Land (i.e., Marineland) of Florida, where the laboratory and tank room sets were constructed within standing Marine Land facilities; Silver Springs, for the underwater sequences; and Green Cove Springs for townie locales. Horror author James Robert Smith cited the magnificence of these springs "in the limestone karst region of Florida. My wife and I head down there to kayak and snorkel every year and we've hit a lot of them where many movies and TV shows were filmed (including Tarzan movies, **CREATURE FROM THE BLACK LAGOON**, *Sea Hunt*, etc.)."[7] I later found out from my (late) pal Bill Kelley[8] (who wrote a lengthy article about Florida's checkered cinematic legacy back in the 1980s for the *Fort Lauderdale Sun-Sentinel*) that the curiously-named—well, to *me*, it's curious—Switzerland, Florida in the state's northeast corner also provided a location or two for the filming along the banks and in the waters of the St. Johns River, just south of Jacksonville, as well as the house in which Leopold's second victim is murdered by the creature.

ZAAT opens with (and intercuts throughout the film) intimate

---

[7] James Robert Smith, comment posted to *Myrant*, December 13th, 2011, 8:28 pm, archived online (@ *http://srbissette.com/whats-zaat-part-1/*)

[8] Bill passed away on August 12th, 2003 at the too-young age of 54. See Bill's *Sun-Sentinel* obit, still archived online (@ *http://articles.sun-sentinel.com/2003-08-13/news/0308120560_1_mr-kelley-movies-bill-kelley*)

shots of marine life footage filmed and acquired from Marine Land; extensive use of marine life stock footage in genre features dates back to the silent era, with particular abuse of the silent shark vs. octopus footage that seems to have debuted in the semi-documentary **SEA KILLERS** (1933) and later turned up in countless other filmic fare (including serials like **FLASH GORDON** [1936] and **THE SEA RAIDERS** [1941], etc.; as well as feature films like the *Tarzan* series and **STRANGE VOYAGE** [1946], **THE BEAST FROM 20,000 FATHOMS** [1953, all USA], etc.). The year when **ZAAT** was released, Walon Green and David Seltzer's insect mockumentary/documentary **THE HELLSTROM CHRONICLE** (1971) scored multiple awards, including an Academy Award for Best Documentary Feature, codifying the use of nature macrophotography in theatrical features to an extent never before seen in mainstream American commercial film. Thus, Barton's extensive use of the Marine Land footage was of its time, bizarre as it may seem to contemporary viewers. Ivan Tors had standardized the conceit with his 1960s *Flipper* franchise (also based in Florida) and Tors' features like **AROUND THE WORLD UNDER THE SEA** (1966), and TV viewers grew used to the abundant sea life imagery essential to the *National Geographic* Jacques Cousteau primetime specials, but later 1970s genre films—e.g., Saul Bass's **PHASE IV** (1974), Jack Cardiff's **THE MUTATIONS** (a.k.a. **THE FREAKMAKER**, 1974, both UK/USA), etc.—really codified the use of such footage. Anyone accusing **ZAAT** of abusing the practice owes it to themselves to endure the embarrassing Canadian/US SF feature **THE NEPTUNE FACTOR** (1973), which wed absurdly out-of-scale miniatures with marine life macrophotography by Paul Herbermann.

What makes Barton's initial use of the Marine Land footage risible is the rambling misanthropic, and quite passionate fish-love narration by Dr. Kurt Leopold (Marshall Grauer, who also does his character's voiceover here). Leopold comes across like a nappy-haired, batshit-crazy version of Don Knotts fish-lovin' bookkeeper Henry Limpet in Arthur Lubin's live-action-combined-with-cel-animation fantasy **THE INCREDIBLE MR. LIMPET** (1964).[9] Forget about any possible association with

---

[9] Horror novelist and kindred *Swamp Thing* writer Nancy Collins reminds me that the author of the novel **THE INCREDIBLE MR. LIMPET** was based on—*Mr. Limpet* (1942)—was Theodore Pratt, also wrote *The Barefoot Mailman* (a.k.a. *Danger Trail*, 1943), the "historical novel about the barefoot mailmen of Florida, who carried mail by foot through the Everglades. This one was eaten by alligators or a shark and they built a statue dedicated to him. Pratt wrote about a lot of stuff set on the ocean and Florida. He also wrote about nymphomaniacs." (Nancy Collins, 8/12/2017 message to the author, quoted with permission). The creator of *Mr. Limpet* also wrote science-fiction stories for the SF digest/pulp *Fantastic Universe* in the 1950s, and Pratt's other novels include *Big Blow* (1937), *Mercy Island* (1941), *Mr. Winkle Goes to War* (1943), *Thunder Mountain* (1944), *Miss Dilly Says No* (1945), *Murder Goes Fishing* (1945), *Valley Boy* (1946), *Mr. Thirtle's Trolley* (1947), *My Bride in the Storm* (1950), *The Tormented* (1950), *Cocotte* (1951), *Handsome* (a.k.a. *Handsome's Seven Women* [1951]; in contrast to his 'nympho' novels, an analysis of satyriasis), *The Big Bubble: A Novel of the Florida Boom* (1952), *The Golden Sorrow* (1952), *Escape to Eden* (1953), *Smash-Up* (1954), *Seminole* (1954), *Florida Roundabout* (1959), *The Lovers of Pompeii* (1961), *Tropical Disturbance* (1961), *Without Consent* (1962), *The Story of Boca Raton* (1963), *The White God* (1963), *The Money*

Star photo by Harold Nichols

VISITOR TO ANNISTON GETS DIRECTIONS

'Green monster' seen on Noble

By PATRICIA GREENE
Star Staff Writer

I talked with a green monster last week. He seemed like a fairly nice fellow except for that funny green hair on his chest.

But he had a nice voice. Zaat is his name and he was appearing at a local drive in movie.

That day he was wearing a 75-pound solid rubber suit, no tie, and was spatterred with a tinge of blood. Not exactly the neatest monster around but cordial.

He was hanging around the corner of 10th and Noble Streets, calmly enduring jeering screams from passersby and a few laughs from sidewalk critics.

He was drawing a lot of attention, though, in that get-up.

Zaat in real life is Wade Popwell of Jacksonville, Fla., an actor who plays the role of a half man, half fish in his first movie. He is touring the Southeast promoting it.

Popwell said it was interesting being a monster but it sure was hot in that suit. In one scene of the movie he wore the rubber suit plus 45 pounds of lead weights while he walked on the bottom of the ocean. He enjoyed his first film experience, but hopes to move into other types of movies.

Popwell was cast as the monster because he fits the six-foot-five suit and is an experienced swimmer and scuba diver. He answered a newspaper ad listed "Monster Wanted."

Zaat ended Saturday at the Bama Drive-In.

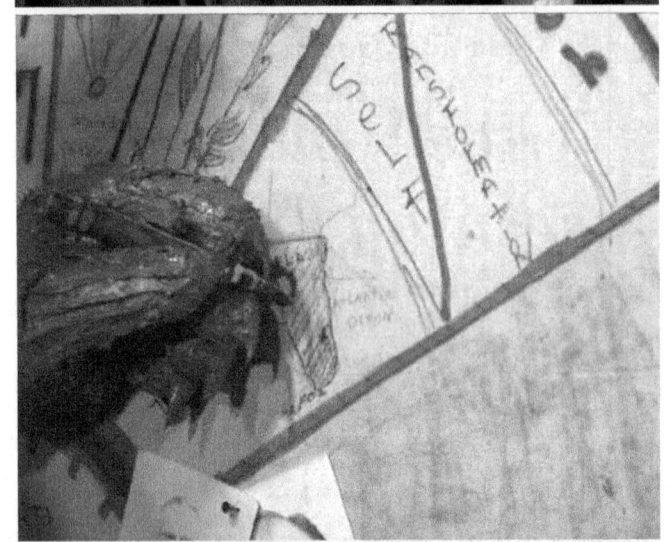

H.P. Lovecraft or the denizens of Innsmouth: Dr. Leopold's somber rant/screed (including a reference to "Sargassum, the weed of deceit") segues into shots of the sullen, slump-shouldered, shabby-looking doc shambling around the beach and dragging his feet through the ramshackle grounds he's been living amid. Instead of Don Knotts singing **MR. LIMPET**'s Sammy Fain/Harold Adamson tune "I Wish I Was a Fish", the **ZAAT** credits roll accompanied by a grim song from local acoustic guitarist/singer Jamie DeFrates[10] (*"...tombstones are piling up your last mistake / We all wait for you to give us a break / Give us a break... Stalking, skulking through the Sargassum / A plan of revenge on your friends..."*), ending with Dr. Leopold going into his secret laboratory.

The morose Dr. Leopold's narration reveals he has lived and worked alone in this rundown lab for two decades; later in the film, we learn of Leopold having graduated MIT *cum laude* in 1934 before joining the Nazi Party. This handily bridges *two* madmen of 1964 genre films: Mr. Limpet *and* Martin Kosleck's Professor Peter Bartell of Jack Curtis' and Arnold Drake's seminal SF/splatter opus **THE FLESH EATERS**. **ZAAT** also owes a major nod to the scientifically-spawned Atlantic Portuguese Man o' War (*Physalia physalis*)-man, or (to use the less redundant, more common moniker) the "jellyfish man" of William Grefé's previously mentioned **STING OF DEATH** (1966), a mutant created by a not-mad marine biologist's mad assistant, Egon (played by John Vella), with the erstwhile Doug Hobart (who also played Tartu in Grefé's co-feature **DEATH CURSE OF TARTU**) playing the garbage-bag-headed Man o' War Man in cut-price special effects makeup of his own design. *All Hail Hobart!*[11]

In another staple of low-budget genre fare, we never actually *see* Dr. Leopold speak on-camera; his lips never move. He just thinks aloud to us as he bums around his rather ordinary-looking improvised lab equipment and his absolutely extraordinary outsized circular calendar/chart of his personal "Master Plan" to become a form of marine life himself and lead a multi-spe-

---

(1965), *Florida's Spanish River Area* (1969), et cetera.

10 Jamie DeFrates is still recording music; his CD releases are *Gypsy Valentine* (2002) and *Winterhawk* (2007), and DeFrates' earlier vinyl releases include *Pegasus Inflight* (1976) and *Son of Dust* (1978).

11 See Charles Kilgore, "Swamp Trash and Bayou Blues" (*Ecco: The World of Bizarre Video* #15, 1991, pp.9-15), and Charles Kilgore, "The Wild World of Doug Hobart" (*Ecco: The World of Bizarre Video* #17, 1992, pp.14–22); also see Jon Kitley's "Interview: Doug Hobart", Kitley's Krypt: Discover the Horror," April 4, 2015, archived online (@ https://kitleyskrypt.wordpress.com/2015/04/04/interview-doug-hobart/)

Left, Top to Bottom: Warner Bros. promoted their ingenious fusion of live-action and animation with this image featuring Don Knotts as *both* incarnations of **THE INCREDIBLE MR. LIMPET** (1964); **ZAAT**'s sad-sack "Mr. Limpet" who wish, who wish, who wish he was a fish is Dr. Kurt Leopold (Marshall Grauer), who keeps track of his "self-transformation" and glorious master plan with his oversized circular calendar/chart (bottom two photos) in some of **ZAAT**'s most quietly audacious scenes.

cies revolution against all land-dwelling civilization (!). Leopold's colorful chart is the most ingenious aspect of **ZAAT**: it's a six-foot-in-diameter pie chart the that monstrous Leopold keeps periodically consulting, crossing-out the names of his target victims and marking-off his accomplishments of various tasks as the story unfolds. Oh, did I write, "target victims"? Yes, I did. In classic 1930s-to-present mad scientist fashion, Leopold is brooding obsessively over his former scientific colleagues mocking his "formula" to achieve his scheme, a mutagenic compound which Leopold has named "Z_aA_t" a.k.a. "Zaat" (thus, like the Frankenstein/Frankenstein's Monster conflation in our pop culture, Zaat is the name of the formula which creates it, *not* the humanoid Walking Catfish man Leopold turns himself into itself).[12] The combination of Leopold's chemical compound injected directly into his bloodstream and immersion into his lab tank filled to the brim with some unspecified seething liquids successfully transforms him into a man/fish hybrid. This happens just minutes into the film; in this new form (monster suit worn by Wade Popwell), he immediately sets out with a little spritz bottle full of Zaat to "mutate all sea life".

The now-monstrous Leopold launches his reign of terror by unleashing several wriggling, real Walking Catfish on the local backstreets and waterways. He then submerges himself in the St. Johns River and sprays a milky substance (i.e., Zaat) out of that little spritz bottle, which looks pretty ineffectual when industrial-strength polluting of waterways is more likely called for if polluting "the entire planet" is indeed the Master Plan. Later in the film, we're given a glimpse of a number of Walking Catfish slithering over lawns, roads, and (in one enigmatic shot) a miniature landscape, inferring rather obliquely that the mutagenic Zaat compound has somehow increased the size of at least one of the Walking Catfish.[13]

Nevertheless, Leopold's fouling of the waters makes local townspeople ill, while Leopold shifts gears into more traditional genre mode and starts killing-off those of his former colleagues who dared to scoff at his life's work. Also in classical genre form, Leopold pines for *a mate*, like the Frankenstein's Monster and Brazil's Zé do Caixão (José Mojica Marins) before him—only he'll have to turn his potential mate into a Walking Catfish Woman first. Leopold spies a lone female (Nancy Lien) camping on a nearby beach—her yellow shirt perfectly matching her lemon-yellow Volkswagen Beetle—and he dreams of dispatching her damned dog and taking her back to his lab, which he later does. Alas, she succumbs either to his manhandling or the transformation process, dying in his lab tank while evidencing skin eruptions that indicate his process *almost* worked before her death. Well, if at first you don't succeed, try, try again, as they say!

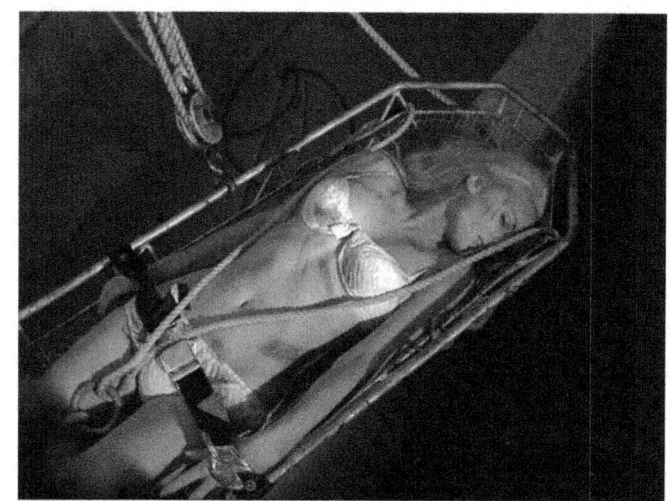

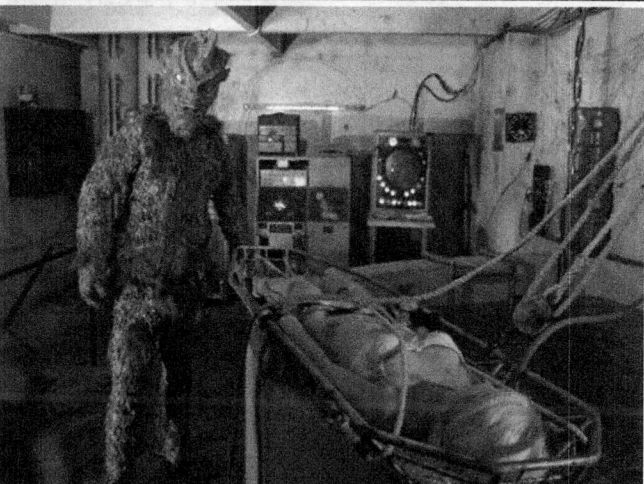

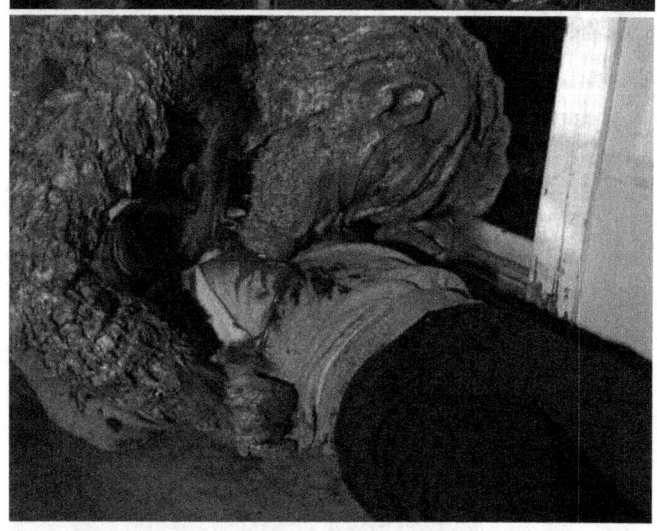

Top: The transformed Dr. Leopold tries to manufacture a mate by kidnapping the Women in Yellow ((Nancy Lien), but she dies in the process. **Above:** Leopold murders and apparently suckles the chest wounds of his teenage victim (Jim Merrill).

---

12 My favorite variant on this title is the Russian release title/translation: Заат. I mean, just *look* at that lovely word as a graphic object!

13 This shot appears 39m, 48s–54s into the film; the wriggling catfish knocks over a portion of a miniature fence in a shot that passes too quickly to really register as being indicative of the fish being of any great size, crosscut as it is between shots of Rex and Walsh collecting water samples and other normal-sized Walking Catfish slithering on what are clearly normal-sized roadways and lawns.

Leopold's subsequent murder of yet another hated former colleague establishes a pattern to the killings that leaves local Sheriff Lou Krantz (Paul Galloway) and Marine Biologist Rex Baker (Gerald Cruise) stumped. Adding to their confusion is Leopold's savage murder of a teenager (Jim Merrill) and apparently suckling on the dead teen's chest wounds; this, after vandalizing a drug store while unsuccessfully searching for something to ease the pain of the mutagen's toll on his transformed body. Sheriff Krantz and Rex Baker's earnest but clumsy detective work lends **ZAAT** its necessary police procedural elements, culminating in two things: (1) the arrival of Inter-Nations Phenomena Investigations Team (INPIT) agents Walker Stevens (Dave Dickerson) and Martha Walsh (Sanna Ringhaver), and (2) Krantz's peculiar interlude with a group of long-haired hippy 'Jesus Freaks' playing religious folk music. These Jesus Freaks are led by **ZAAT**'s title-tune acoustic guitarist, Jamie DeFrates. Presumably for their own protection, Sheriff Lou leads DeFrates and the Jesus Youth through town and locks 'em all up in the town's jail. This long sequence is cut from some versions of the film, and was presumably trimmed from the **BLOOD WATERS OF DR. Z** rerelease (read on).

The arrival of INPIT agents ups the ante in a couple of ways. First off, INPIT echoes not only the 1960s spy and cover government agents action-adventure cycle spawned by the 007 James Bond films and *The Man From U.N.C.L.E.*, but more to the point is yet another ripple from producer Ivan Tors' legacy, predating Tors' Florida filmmaking and TV production years. Ivan Tors and George Van Marter's production of Curt Siodmak's **THE MAGNETIC MONSTER** (1953, USA) kicked-off a trio of feature films chronicling investigations by the Office of Scientific Investigation (O.S.I.), embodied by "A-Man" agent Jeffrey Stewart (Richard Carlson); the O.S.I. trilogy was completed with **RIDERS TO THE STARS** (co-directed by Carlson himself) and the 3D widescreen color feature **GOG** (both 1954, USA). Like the O.S.I., INPIT also looks forward to Chris Carter's *The X-Files* (September 10th, 1993 to May 19th, 2002 and January 24th, 2016 to present). This may seem like a stretch, but it's the finest genre pedigree that **ZAAT** can boast.

The INPIT agents' arrival also ups **ZAAT**'s narrative imperative when Walking Catfish Man Leopold decides to give the kidnap-and-transmutation of another potential female mate another spin, this time with INPIT Agent Martha Walsh.

Fellow INPIT agent Walker Stevens feels responsible—having left Martha alone while he tracked Leopold from the most recent sighting/crime scene with Sheriff Lou and Rex—and he gets to tracking the creature with a Geiger Counter. After a prolonged tracking sequence and the inevitable "let's-double-back-to-the-lab-when-they-realize-Leopold-kidnapped-Walsh" padding, Stevens eventually goes hand-to-hand with the monstrous Leopold during his failed rescue attempt. Leopold savages and cripples Stevens, then kills the sheriff and mortally wounds Rex once he's returned to the lab with the unconscious Walsh over his shoulder. Leopold injects the Zaat formula into Walsh and preps her for immersion into the tank to complete her transformation, but the dying Rex rescues Walsh before she is fully-submerged, interrupting the process. Leopold flees with the two surviving canisters of Zaat to spread the compound into the sea. Stevens shoots Leopold before he

Top: Scaly Dr. Leopold draws a portrait of his new crush, NPIT Agent Martha Walsh (Sanna Ringhaver). **Center:** Clippings of a 1973 Santa Fe, NM drive-in showing and an Orlando, FL ad, compliments of David Szulkin (*Thanks, David!*). **Above:** Marine Biologist Rex Baker (Gerald Cruise) tangles with the monstrous Dr. Leopold in the mad doctor's no-longer-secret laboratory.

can complete the task, but a zombie-like Walsh wanders from the lab in a trance and ignores Stevens to follow the bleeding Leopold into the surf.

This pleasingly ambiguous finale—with Leopold suffering severe gunshot wounds but not yet dead, and Walsh joining Leopold to disappear into the ocean waves—recalls the endings of **I WALKED WITH A ZOMBIE** (1943), **THE MUMMY'S GHOST** (1944), **THE CREATURE WALKS AMONG US** (1956), **THE SHE-CREATURE** (1956, all USA), **EYES WITHOUT A FACE** (*Les yeux sans visage*, a.k.a. **THE HORROR CHAMBER OF DR. FAUSTUS**, 1960/62, France), **THE BRAIN THAT WOULDN'T DIE** (1959/1962, USA), and others. You could argue that contrary "I'm with It" endings were pretty much *de rigueur* by 1971 (after the twist endings of **DANCE OF THE VAMPIRES** [a.k.a. **THE FEARLESS VAMPIRE KILLERS**, 1967, UK/USA] and **COUNT YORGA, VAMPIRE** [1970, USA]), but the open-ended imagery and action—and Walsh's utter indifference to/rejection of Stevens—makes for a memorable fade-out.

The ballyhoo from the original theatrical release of **ZAAT** tells the production story the filmmakers and their initial distributor crafted for public consumption. That is, what they *wanted* to present to theater owners and potential audience members, via press releases and sample articles to be sent to local newspapers to promote exhibition. This is what they *wanted* viewers to know, to lure dollars into the boxoffices and asses into movie theater seats.

Here are sample press releases from the original pressbook:

"How do you cast a seven foot underwater creature for a monster movie?

'Simple,' says producer-director Don Barton of ZAAT. 'Put an ad in the paper.'

Barton did just that, and it read... 'WANTED: 6'5" or taller male to play role of Monster in Horror movie. Must be experienced swimmer, scuba diver. ACTING ABILITY not required.'

'The response was gratifying,' says Barton. 'We interviewed forty prospects before we chose Wade Popwell.'

What made Wade the most acceptable to play the role?

'Wade fit all the requirements,' Barton added. 'In addition, he is a professional actor. During auditions, when I told him to attack an imaginary victim, Wade did it with such realism there was no doubt in my mind he was the man for the job.'"

———

"When underwater filming was being done at Marineland, Florida, for the monster movie ZAAT, customers were allowed to file through the Amazon porpoise exhibit as usual. Much to their amazement, what they saw was far-removed from a placid porpoise setting.

The original **ZAAT** pressbook herald 'template sheet.' Heralds used to be a key promotional tool for ambitious exhibitors eager to promote the opening of a given film locally (note the printing fee: a little over $11 in 1970s dollars got you 2000 to advertise the movie).

Action varied, from a giant, slimy green sea monster thrashing wildly, to a beautiful bikini-clad blonde strapped to a basket being lowered to the depths.

Commented one elderly gentleman, 'I've seen porpoises before, but these Amazons are absolutely delightful.'"

———

"Sanna Ringhaver is the feminine lead in the new monster movie ZAAT. A veteran model in both Europe and the States, this is Sanna's first dramatic movie role.

As INPIT agent Walsh, she travels the globe as a member of an international agency specializing in solving unusual phenomena.

In ZAAT she teams with veteran actor Dave Dickerson in tracking giant killer catfish."

———

127

PRESS RELEASE #4

In the creature movie ZAAT, opening .... at the .... theatre, walking catfish are introduced to movie fans the world over for the first time.

The fact is, walking catfish — the 18-inch variety — are a way of life in Florida. They move overland from lakes to ponds to rivers, devouring practically all other fish life.

While primarily a warm weather fish, they are migrating north to Georgia and Alabama, apparently adapting to the cooler climates as they go.

Says Vernon Ogilvie, Florida Game Commission specialist, "There are millions of them. There's just no way to stop them. It would take an atom bomb that would completely eliminate all life."

Walking catfish creep away from poisons and they seem to have no known natural enemy in this country.

PRESS RELEASE #1

How do you cast a seven foot underwater creature for a monster movie?

"Simple," says producer-director Don Barton of ZAAT. "Put an ad in the paper."

Barton did just that, and it read... "WANTED: 6'5" or taller male to play role of Monster in Horror movie. Must be experienced swimmer, scuba diver. ACTING ABILITY not required."

"The response was gratifying," says Barton. "We interviewed forty prospects before we chose Wade Popwell."

What made Wade the most acceptable to play the role?

"Wade fit all the requirements," Barton added. "In addition, he is a professional actor. During auditions, when I told him to attack an imaginary victim, Wade did it with such realism there was no doubt in my mind he was the man for the job."

PRESS RELEASE #3

Sanna Ringhaver is the feminine lead in the new monster movie ZAAT. A veteran model in both Europe and the States, this is Sanna's first dramatic movie role.

As INPIT agent Walsh, she travels the globe as a member of an international agency specializing in solving unusual phenomena.

In ZAAT she teams with veteran actor Dave Dickerson in tracking giant killer catfish.

ZAAT opens .... at the .... theatre.

Pressbooks also featured press releases, articles, and even manufactured 'reviews' for placement in local newspapers to promote the film's opening; here is a sampler of the original **ZAAT** pressbook suggested press releases.

---

*"In the creature movie **ZAAT**... walking catfish are introduced to movie fans the world over for the first time.*

The fact is, walking catfish—the 18-inch variety—are a way of life in Florida. They move overland from lakes to ponds to rivers, devouring practically all other fish life.

While primarily a warm weather fish, they are migrating north to Georgia and Alabama, apparently adapting to cooler climates as they go.

Says Vernon Ogilvie, Florida Game Commission specialist, 'There are millions of them. There's just no way to stop them. It would take an atom bomb that would completely eliminate all life.'

Walking catfish creep away from poisons and they seem to have no known natural enemy in this country."

Boy, howdy, that'll bring in the Yahoos!

ZAAT has taken a lot of heat since it's been enshrined by *MST3K* (*Mystery Science Theatre 3000*, natch) acolytes as a sacred "bad movie" artifact. For all the pejorative "worst movie ever" text lavished on **ZAAT**, precious little attention has been given to its competent technical credits, or the role it played in launching cinematographer Jack McGowan's impressive 1970s genre track record. McGowan's cinematography and lighting is crisp and far more effective than it has ever been given credit for, especially given the tight 30-day shoot. Without doubt, **ZAAT** looks much better than a multitude of low-budget exploitation films from the period. This was McGowan's first big-screen credit, but he immediately went on to do camerawork on far more atmospheric, gruesome, and effective horrors. McGowan worked with Bob Clark and Alan Ormsby to lense their Coconut Grove/Miami, Florida-shot **CHILDREN SHOULDN'T PLAY WITH DEAD THINGS** (1972), Alan Ormsby's **THE GREAT MASQUERADE** ([1974] also filmed in and about Miami at the Flamingo Hotel, the S.S. Emerald Seas, and Studio Center), then head north to Ontario, Canada with Clark and Ormsby to shoot the Ed Gein biopic **DERANGED: CONFESSIONS OF A NECROPHILE** (1974). McGowan returned to Brooksville, Florida with Clark and Ormsby to lens the American-Canadian-British co-production **DEAD OF NIGHT** (a.k.a. **DEATHDREAM**, 1974), including location work at Brooksville's 41 Drive-In for that sleeper gem's horrific finale. McGowan was also cinematographer for Chris Robinson's once-long-lost, recently-rescued-for-Blu-ray slasher **THE INTRUDER** (1975), Steve (**BLOOD FREAK** [1972]) Hawkes' Florida-filmed family flick **STEVIE, SAMSON AND DELILAH** (1975), Jack Weis' New Orleans-set slasher **MARDI GRAS MASSACRE** (1978), and Ken (**SHOCK WAVES** [1977], **EYES OF A STRANGER** [1981]) Wiederhorn's college sex-comedy **KING FRAT** ([1979] filmed in Miami and Coral Gables, Florida).

Local 16mm editor and sound technician George Yarbrough saw to the edit and sound mixing and sound editing chores on **ZAAT**. Barton recalls,

"...he was an independent producer and sound engineer out of Orlando, Florida, and he did not have 35mm editing equipment. We actually reduced the 35mm negative to a working 16mm print. So, he edited the 16mm, then we transferred it back—not the easiest way, but that's the way we adapted to the talent we had available, and I was very, very pleased when I saw the cut. I had very little to do, very little input in the editing; he did it mostly all on his own."[14]

---

[14] Don Barton, **ZAAT** Blu-ray (2012, Cultra/HD Cinema Classics, HDCC-010), commentary track, 29m 33s–30m 14s.

MAN...FISH...OR DEVIL?
"IT WOULD TAKE AN ATOM BOMB TO WIPE OUT THE WALKING CATFISH!
— Vernon Ogilvie, Specialist for the FLA. GAME COMMISSION
"A CREATURE LIKE YOU'VE NEVER SEEN BEFORE."
— KIPP, News Journal
ZAAT
...IS DEATH!
IN EASTMAN COLOR
starring
DAVE DICKERSON
SANNA RINGHAVER
PAUL GALLOWAY
GERALD CRUSE
MARSHALL GRAUER
and
WADE POPWELL
as the Creature.
FILMED ENTIRELY ON LOCATION IN FLORIDA
WARNING!!
POSITIVELY NO ONE ADMITTED DURING LAST 15 MINUTES!
PG PARENTAL GUIDANCE SUGGESTED
Produced and directed by DON BARTON
Story by LEE LAREW & RON KIVETT
A BARTON FILM PRODUCTION • A HORIZON FILMS RELEASE

Producer/director Don Barton appears in this promotional photo for **ZAAT**, exchanging barbs and needling Wade Popwell on the finer points of handling oversized hypodermic syringes before tackling another shot (we grew up reading *Famous Monsters of Filmland*—what do you want, no pun-filled captions?).

Prior to **ZAAT**, Yarbrough had also worked the industrial film market; he'd filmed, edited, scripted, produced and directed the promotional short *The Wonderful World of Tupperware* (1965), and who else has *that* claim to fame? Yarbrough also saw to the sound and/or sound edits on two previous filmed-in-Florida commercial features, Bob Welborn's **DAYTONA BEACH WEEKEND** (1965, USA) and a Universal Pictures theatrical feature, Paul Wendkos' **JOHNNY TIGER** ([1966, USA] starring Chad Everett as the titular Seminole renegade). Among the elements Yarbrough dealt with in his **ZAAT** sound mix was the musical score by Barry Hodgin, punctuated with bemusing electronic music atonalities, blips and blurps by Jack Tamul and songs by Jamie DeFrates (already mentioned). Yarbrough and Barton also spiced Hodgin's score with stock music (composed by the uncredited Trevor Duncan). To the vet monster-movie lover, the stock music only enhances the *déjà vu* pleasures of **ZAAT**'s score.

Even Ron Kivett's oft-ridiculed monster design has its attributes, believe it or not. Kivett built a CO2 bottle into the head piece (presumably refilling it with oxygen for Wade Popwell's use during filming?), and the exterior skin detailing appears to be a plastic or rubber compound using its original color as the Zaat Leopold's off-green pigmentation. Though it never looks remotely like an actual living being, the surface/skin was rather carefully textured, with downward-tilted, pointed 'drip' scales; all in all executed with a curious eye for detail, given the resources at hand. As with many of Paul Blaisdell's once-reviled, now-revered monster creations for the American-International Pictures (AIP) 1950s monster movies, **ZAAT**'s direction and rather maladroit staging of the action sequences obscures certain components of the Leopold monster's design: the venomous 'spurs' or spines on his forearms, for instance, aren't played-up for all their worth. Only the tame gore makeup by Lee J. O'Donnell (credited here as "Lee James O'Donnell") suggests the nature of the wounds inflicted by those spurs. Zaat Leopold's spurs or spines are extrapolated from actual catfish anatomy: catfish sport a hard spine that runs the length of the dorsal and pectoral fins, the tips of which do not 'sting' but can be quite pointed and sharp, particularly on smaller catfish and channel cats. In handling, if these spines puncture a fisherman's skin, the venom in the dorsal and pectoral fin can cause edema and a hemolytic reaction (the source of the belief that catfish fins and whiskers actually 'sting', though they cannot and do not).

While admiring himself in a mirror after his transformation, Leopold himself comments *in the film* on how little like a Walking Catfish he appears ("Nothing at all like the catfish—but it's *beautiful!*"). While the ad art lent an almost Mandrill (*Mandrillus sphinx*)-like appearance to the monster's visage, the Zaat Leopold most closely resembles the 'Planet M-113 salt vampire' of *Star Trek*'s debut episode "Man Trap" (September 8th, 1966) with a haircut. Zaat Leopold in many ways seems more *leech-like* than catfish-like, with his triangular head (sans elongated catfish barbels, a.k.a. 'whiskers') terminating in that red-lipped circular mouth ringed with tiny teeth. In this regard, Zaat Leopold anticipates the hideous parasitic Flukeman of *The X-Files* episode "The Host" (September 23rd, 1994).

Among those who've registered their incredulity at the Zaat Leopold monster outfit, online Blu-ray critic Jeffrey Kaufman most memorably cited "the unbelievable monster costume, whose frilly boa neck trim must be seen to be believed."[15] Silly as that "'frilly boa neck" looks—actually 'green and red carpet' patches plugged here and there amid the crudely-sculpted skin texture, which with disrepair come to resemble a dingy green scarf in later shots—its especially absurdist when the Leopold monster is seen shambling about in his lab or in broad daylight above water. However, when Leopold is underwater, the patchwork 'carpet pieces' do look and flow like algae blooms.

Furthermore, contrary to many cheapjack monster and cryptid movies of the 1970s, we get to see a *lot* of the Zaat-mutated Leopold onscreen: he is *constantly* active and visible, and I for one love **ZAAT** for this. The fearlessness of this approach is admirable in and of itself, and makes **ZAAT** that rare 1970s monster movie to offer ample opportunity to savor (or sneer and snicker at!) what Kivett and his team created. Given the limitations of the costume and the grueling conditions (and temperatures) Wade Popwell worked within, Popwell's physical performance is adequate, but the constant narration maintains this monster registering as a *character*, whereas most 1970s cryptid movie monsters were mere elusive-at-best ciphers. Unlike any of **ZAAT**'s backwater cryptid kith and kin, Leopold is an artist, too: midway through the film, Leopold draws a little pencil portrait of the woman of his dreams (this idyll is interrupted by a flash-forward close-up of his first kidnap victim in the body basket, scratched but alive, about to be submerged into the Zaat mutagenic liquid tank). Leopold lovingly posts the little drawing over his scaly "Zaat Woman" sketch on his circular wall-chart (in the March/Pisces slice of the pie chart) and wistfully gives the human portrait's hair a few extra graphite strokes. Clearly, this monster has an active inner life. Maybe it's true love after all?

Hey, I take my entertainments as, and when, I can find 'em!

---

15 Jeffrey Kaufman, "ZAAT Blu-ray Review: Creature from the Black Buffoon," *Blu-ray.com*, February 26, 2012, archived online at http://www.blu-ray.com/movies/Zaat-Blu-ray/35923/#Review

"Nothing at all like the catfish—but it's *beautiful!*"

Pucker-Up! We're suckers for monsters like Dr. Leopold in **ZAAT**, his ancestors (the 'Planet M-113 salt vampire' of *Star Trek* ["Man Trap," Sept. 8th, 1966]) and descendants (Flukeman, *The X-Files* ["The Host", Sept. 23rd, 1994]).

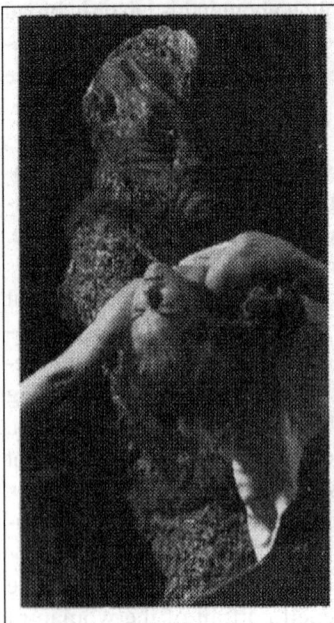

PRESS RELEASE #2

When underwater filming was being done at Marineland, Florida, for the monster movie ZAAT, customers were allowed to file through the Amazon porpoise exhibit as usual. Much to their amazement, what they saw was far-removed from a placid porpoise setting.

Action varied, from a giant, slimy green sea monster thrashing wildly, to a beautiful bikini-clad blonde strapped to a basket being lowered to the depths.

Commented one elderly gentleman, "I've seen porpoises before, but these Amazons are absolutely delightful."

Bucking 1970s trends in the big-screen Bigfoot bonanza and all but the *daikaiju-eiga* 'man in suit' monster movies, **ZAAT** gave Wade Popwell's catfish-man plenty of screen time and prominent placement in almost all advertising, as evidenced here.

III. The Selling and Re-Selling of ZAAT, 1972-80

The selling of a movie like **ZAAT** was as much an uphill battle in the 1970s as it ever would have been. With weak splashes of gore, lacking any nudity or sexploitation component, **ZAAT** was a PG-rated movie in an era of hard "R" horror and monster movies, and the further its playdates got from the brief tabloid frenzy of 1970 over the emergence of the Walking Catfish as a new invasive species in Florida, the less of a novelty 'hook' that timely reality tie-in was. Never mind that **ZAAT** looked not at all like a Walking Catfish, much less a bipedal Walking Catfish.

ZAAT premiered in Jacksonville, Florida in January 1971; per usual with regional horror films, the cast, crew, and investors turned out along with curiosity seekers. One can only wonder what they all made if it. Reportedly, **ZAAT**'s initial Florida playdates were better-attended than the popular maritime disaster favorite **THE POSEIDON ADVENTURE** (1972, USA), although there's nothing extant to substantiate such extravagant claims... but it *is* possible.

Don Barton himself tags Clark Film Releasing a.k.a. Clark Distribution as handling **ZAAT**'s initial distribution.[16] Clark handled the theatrical run of the steamy plantation-set race exploitation feature **QUADROON** (subtitled **THE BLACK MANDINGO**) that same year for the Southeast markets (Jacksonville, FL, Atlanta, GA, and up into Charlotte, NC), and reportedly handled dubbed-and-cut editions of Jean Rollin's **THE SHIVER OF THE VAMPIRES** (*Le frisson des vampires*, 1971/72) and **THE DEMONIACS** (*Les démoniaques*, 1977), Pierre Unia's **SEX AND THE FRENCH SCHOOL GIRL** (*Les maitresses de vacances*, 1974/75, all France), and Lui Gin's **CHINESE GODFATHER** (大蛟龍 / *Da jiao long*, 1974). It seems that **ZAAT** enjoyed wider national distribution (such as it was) via Horizon Films; it's Horizon Films that's tagged in the pressbook and one-sheet poster in my collection. **ZAAT** was an unusual fit for the firm. Reliable information is sketchy at best, but Horizon subsequently released the Miami, Florida-lensed sexploitation horror curio from Joseph P. Mawra (the auteur of the notorious 1960s *Olga* B&D+S/M features, credited here as "Joseph G. Prieto"), **MISS LESLIE'S DOLLS** (1973). Horizon seemed to specialize in fairly esoteric import fare like Manuel Caño's mummy/zombie shocker **VOODOO BLACK EXORCIST** (*Vudú sangriento*, 1974, Spain), Jerzy Kawalerowicz's art-house Ancient Egyptian historical epic **PHAROAH** (*Faraon*, 1966/77, Poland), Roger Fritz's romantic drama **RABBIT IN THE PIT** (*Häschen in der Grube*, a.k.a. **RUN, RABBIT, RUN**, 1975, West Germany), Rolf Thiele's comedy **SLAP IN THE FACE** (*Ohrfeigen*, 1970/75, West Germany), Lucio Fulci's *commedia erotico* nunsploitationer **THE EROTICIST** (*Nonostante le apparenze... e purchè la nazione non lo sappia... all'onorevole piacciono le donne*, a.k.a. **THE SENATOR LIKES WOMEN**, 1972/75, Italy/France) and Marco Ferreri's **LOVE TO ETERNITY** (*Liza*, 1972/76, Italy/France), among others.

ZAAT's initial release on the Southern US hardtop and drive-in circuits was accompanied by public appearances from Wade Popwell in Ron Kivett's Zaat Leopold monster suit, on city streets and country roads as well as theaters. While in many ways Popwell was following in the footsteps of fellow Floridian Ricou Browning (who played the underwater Gillman in **CREATURE FROM THE BLACK LAGOON** and **REVENGE OF THE CREATURE** back in 1953 and 1955), Popwell went further than Browning and far, far more than the extra mile to promote *his* monster role. This rather ill-timed

---

[16] Barton mentions Clark Distributon by name—"...we first launched the movie, through the Clark Distribution company, which we were very, very grateful; they did a really awesome job of putting this movie in theaters all over the south..."—on the Blu-ray commentary track, 32m 37s–52s.

(see the final sentence) article, from Anniston, Alabama in 1973 shows Popwell still on the road *two years* after **ZAAT**'s Jacksonville premiere:

"I talked with a green monster last week. He seemed like a fairly nice fellow except for that funny green hair on his chest. But he had a nice voice. Zaat is his name and he was appearing at a local drive-in movie. That day he was wearing a 75-pound solid rubber suit, no tie, and was spattered with a tinge of blood. Not exactly the neatest monster around but cordial.

"He was hanging around the corner of 10th and Noble Streets [in Anniston], calmly enduring jeering screams from passersby and a few laughs from sidewalk critics. He was drawing a lot of attention, though, in that get-up.

"Zaat in real life is Wade Popwell of Jacksonville, Fla., an actor who plays the role of a half man, half fish in his first movie. He is touring the Southeast promoting it.

"Popwell said it was interesting being a monster, but it sure was hot in that suit. In one scene of the movie he wore the rubber suit, plus 45 pounds of lead weights while he walked on the bottom of the ocean. He enjoyed his first film experience, but hopes to move into other types of movies.

"Popwell was cast as the monster because he fits the six-foot-five suit and is an experienced swimmer and scuba diver. He answered a newspaper ad listed 'Monster Wanted.' Zaat ended Saturday at the Bama Drive-In."[17]

Like its later regional low-budget companions **THE MILPITAS MONSTER** (1975), **SLITHIS** (a.k.a. **SPAWN OF THE SLITHIS**, 1978, both USA), or the previously-discussed Louisiana bayou curio **NUTRIAMAN** a.k.a. **TERROR IN THE SWAMP** (1985), the Florida-spawned **ZAAT** was swimming upstream in a national distribution environment that was decidedly rigged against such films gaining *any* traction, whatever their virtues or exploitable elements—and let's face it, Bunky, **ZAAT** wasn't a particularly 'good' or easily-exploit-

---

[17] Patricia Greene (Star Staff Writer), "'Green Monster' seen on Noble", *The Daily Star* (Anniston, Alabama), March 11th, 1973; clipping provided by David Szulkin. Deepest thanks, David!

This rare **ZAAT** photo clearly shows the venomous 'spur' protruding from the creature's elbow, based on the embedded defensive *Clarias batrachus* 'sting'

able movie, by any mainstream standards of what's good or exploitable—a hard-sell to even the least-discerning audience tastes.

One immediate regional successor to **ZAAT** bucked the trend—Charles B. Pierce's Arkansas-lensed **LEGEND OF BOGGY CREEK** (1972)—but Bigfoot had far more visibility and exploitation traction than the Walking Catfish (much less the *faux*-Walking-Catfish-man). Pierce was able to build a fairly successful regional filmmaking career on the bedrock of **LEGEND OF BOGGY CREEK**, something which **ZAAT**'s producer/director Don Barton couldn't even dream about in the wake of **ZAAT**'s consignment to the fringes, despite his best efforts to get his film seen.

According to ED (that's how he spells it) Tucker's fond recollections in **ZAAT** co-writer Ron Kivett's article "Boy Meets Monster: A 30 Year Journey" at the official Zaat website,[18]

"...In the summer of 1971, the movie opened in the southeast. It did well, even against such blockbuster films as THE POSEIDON ADVENTURE, and the unforgettable KANSAS CITY BOMBER, starring Raquel Welch. When the caged Monster made a live appearance at any local theater, the film would always play to a packed house. That was thirty years ago and since then ZAAT has played in movie houses and drive-ins all over the world. Not long ago, a friend told me that the film was playing somewhere in the Far East and still drawing crowds."[19]

Well, OK, maybe. I don't doubt the local draw for the film in the south, given the regional empires now-forgotten mini-moguls like North Carolina's Earl Owensby built on exploitation films made almost exclusively for the southern state circuits.

But **ZAAT**'s distribution history is a little more complicated than that. For how long it may have still secured playdates under the title "**ZAAT**", who can say? But according to the published record, for those paying attention, it was less than four years.

As the 1970s wore on, and the once-novel Walking Catfish became an ever-more-distant memory for all but Floridians who grew increasingly accustomed to the critters, Bigfoot's attraction and allure only grew: note his guest appearance on *The Six Million Dollar Man* and *The Bionic Woman*, the phenomenal box-office success Sunn Classic Pictures had with the theatrical pickup of an already-successful network TV special, Robert Guenette's **THE MYSTERIOUS MONSTERS**, in 1976. **ZAAT** debuted just as "four-walling"—indie distributors' practice of renting theaters outright (hence, all "four walls") for the run of a picture, thus guaranteeing profits to the theater-owner while maximizing the distributor's take of the actual box-office—was ramping-up as a distribution strategy for independents. Sunn Classic specialized in using the four-wall booking strategies to propel the likes of **THE LIFE AND TIMES OF GRIZZLY ADAMS** (1974, USA) into solid hits, emulating the success Tom Laughlin had reaped with his reacquired-from-Warner-Bros. rerelease of **BILLY JACK** (1971, USA). Four-walling proved lucrative enough to launch films like Joe Camp's family hit **BENJI** (1974, USA) into an indie franchise for the 1970s, and prompted Bing Crosby Productions and Cinerama Releasing Corp. to emulate Laughlin's **BILLY JACK** strategies to elevate the initial performance of Phil Karlson's shot-in-Tennessee Buford Pusser violent vigilante biopic **WALKING TALL** (1973) into a $23-million phenomenal grosser, using "audiences cheered" ads and extended four-walling runs to build word-of-mouth into a 1970s mega-hit. Various market forces soon closed similar windows of opportunity, but until the four-walling trend had run its course by the end of the decade, four-wallers raked-in at-times *stratospheric* box-office earnings.

This strategy was beyond Don Barton's means or schemes, or that of Clark Distribution and Horizon Films, the nominal theatrical distributor of **ZAAT**, either. He (and they) made do with all he/they had, though. As in many initial openings in the southern drive-in circuit, "Wade Popwell, the six-foot, eight-inch star of **ZAAT**... donned his monster costume and greeted patrons at various drive-ins in the New Orleans, La., area."[20]

A record of **ZAAT**'s actual earnings is tough to find, even in old issues/annuals of *Boxoffice* and *Variety* in my archives, but maybe I just haven't dug deep enough. I've long thought that **ZAAT** was initially just so far beneath the radar that it's no surprise I've never seen, nor can't find, any hard figures recorded in the trades. Then again, Don Barton admits to **ZAAT** having suffered the fate of many a regional genre film, including classics like George Romero and John Russo's **NIGHT OF THE LIVING DEAD** (1968, USA); at some point, small distributors glommed-onto **ZAAT** as being up for grabs, and Barton found himself dealing with all manner of opportunist hucksters:

"...there's a lot that's happened to this movie that's not of my knowledge... I talked to a distributor in Texas who was distributing this movie without our permission, and I said that, 'I want you to cease from distributing this movie.' He said, 'Mr. Barton... I was in Spain last year, and your movie is being shown and sold there.' We lost control of it, and unfortunately didn't have the wherewithal to bring people to account for their theft."[21]

In the May 11th, 1977 issue of *Variety* (one of their massive film annuals, which I collected and held on to), International Cine-Film Corp. of New York ran a full-page ad for their acquisitions then available for theatrical booking. Along with recycled exploitation docs like Richard Winer's **THE DEVIL'S TRI-**

---

18 See *http://zaatmovie.com/index.php*

19 See *http://zaatmovie.com/Feature.htm*

20 "*Boxoffice* Showmandiser", *Boxoffice (Western Edition)*, March 26th, 1973, p.43; excavated from the SpiderBaby Archives, with special thanks to Mike Accomando.

21 Don Barton, Blu-ray commentary track, 88m 23s–59s. That Texan distributor was most likely Starline Pictures Co. of Dallas, Texas; the **ZAAT** pressbook in my collection sports a hand-stamping of their name and contact information on the back cover!

FILMED IN FLORIDA!

ZAAT

PRODUCED AND DIRECTED BY DON BARTON

AN ALL FLORIDA PRODUCTION WITH AN ALL FLORIDA CAST AND CREW

The State of Florida coordinated the use of State Parks with the Department of Natural Resources.

Marineland of Florida offered their facilities for filming "abandoned sea laboratory" scenes.

Green Cove Springs provided the perfect setting for a small backwoods town—and over 500 extras for the evacuation scene.

Rainbow Springs was ideal for underwater photography of "the creature."

Switzerland, Florida offered some of the most beautiful southern country settings to be found anywhere.

Processing of 35mm negative and dailies—and all editing—was done in Florida by Floridians.

Florida is the ideal setting for your next motion picture production. It has great weather. Excellent facilities. And almost every type of location imaginable.

For further information contact:

Florida Department of Commerce
301 Almeria Avenue
Coral Gables
Florida 33134
305/446-8106

FLORIDA
THE STATE OF EXCITEMENT

ANGLE (1974), boasting narration by Vincent Price and music by King Crimson (!), and the Rod Serling-narrated curio DEADLY FATHOMS (1973), ersatz family fare like Steve (BLOOD FREAK [1971]) Hawkes' STEVIE, SAMSON, AND DELILAH ([1975] "...a boy, a lion and a tiger—alone against a hostile world..."), and decidedly non-family-friendly gory exploitation like Perry Tong's Texan psychothriller STEPSISTERS (1974), Paul Leder's cheapjack Vietnam-vet-atrocity MY FRIENDS NEED KILLING (1976), Robert Hensley and Tom Anthony's SCREAM EVELYN SCREAM (1970, all USA), and THE SEXORCISTS ([*"The Devil Made Them Do It... And They LOVED It!"*] an altered/reedited version of the sexploitation item BEAUTIFUL PEOPLE [1971, USA]), we find ZAAT back in circulation under a new title: THE BLOOD WATERS OF DR. Z.[22]

Thus, International CineFilm was handling the Capital Productions rerelease of ZAAT under its now-better-known title (thanks to *MST3K*; more on that shortly) BLOOD WATERS OF DR. Z, which landed new reviews of ZAAT under that title and theatrical run in various late 1970s/early 1980s photocopied genre fanzines like Bill Landis's *Sleazoid Express* and others. It didn't get much love under any title, let me tell you. Though *imdb.com* lists BLOOD WATERS OF DR. Z's rerelease date as June 25th, 1982, it was playing under that same retitle in some markets even prior to '82 (at least as far back as 1974, as the copyright notice on some US posters/ads bearing the BLOOD WATERS title confirms).

So, BLOOD WATERS OF DR. Z is likely the title under which, as ZAAT devotee ED Tucker noted, the film "played in movie houses and drive-ins all over the world… *[and is still]* playing somewhere in the Far East and still drawing crowds."

But that's *not* the title which ZAAT found a new, if-only-fleeting lease on life under during the home video revolution of the early 1980s…

IV. Zis After ZAAT; Or: The Afterlife of ZAAT

Monsters never die. Not really. Even neglected, unloved, unwanted, long-forgotten monsters live on in some form.

Like the Walking Catfish ZAAT was ostensibly derivative of, once the water dried-up in one pond, ZAAT made its way over inhospitable turf to a fresh pool.

ZAAT found new life in the 1980s. Under both titles, it popped-up on late-night TV movie broadcasts; that's where a friend of mine first saw it, and told me about it, as one of those after-midnight bleary-eyed wonders one isn't really sure they didn't, in fact, dream. I ached to see it after his account of this bizarre movie I'd never heard of before, and I soon got my chance. In those days, tracking down such regional fare was a challenge: besides, there were other titles one might stumble upon ZAAT under, including HYDRA (Canada and the UK), DR. Z, or the highly 'cryptid'-sounding LEGEND OF THE ZAAT MONSTER.

Top: Larry Buchanan's impoverished made-in-Texas TV movie CURSE OF THE SWAMP CREATURE (1966) was easily confused for the Elvira "ThrillerVideo" retitling of ZAAT as ATTACK OF THE SWAMP CREATURE, packaged with new cover art (by an unidentified artist) completely unrelated to either film.

---

22 *Variety*, May 11th, 1977, p.205. Note that also cited in the ad were THE FEARMAKER, which is Anthony Carras' Mexican thriller RANCHO DEL MIEDO (1971), and Robert J. Emery's shot-in-Florida oddity MY BROTHER HAS BAD DREAMS (a.k.a. SCREAM BLOODY MURDER, 1972).

I first caught **ZAAT** on video as **ATTACK OF THE SWAMP CREATURE**, where it joined the Cassandra Peterson/Elvira-franchised "Elvira Thriller Video" big-box video lineup. For those of you who weren't around then, the first few years of videocassette rentals were as intoxicatingly heady a fusion of the banal and the beatific as any I've ever experienced. Before there were actual video shops, videos were rented from the oddest places, primarily TV repair and hardware stores in our neck of the woods. Before we owned a video player of our own, we'd be invited over to our friends' for weekend marathons, working through stacks of mad rental binges of movies we'd seen, movies we'd only heard of, and (often the most memorable, for reasons good and bad) movies we never even dreamed existed. By the time we purchased our first player, the best selections of weird new videos were in two nearby TV repair shops: a huge one in Greenfield, MA, and a smaller but much closer one in Brattleboro, VT.

I grew up watching a clutch of the 1960s AIP-TV (American-International Pictures Television) super-low-budget Azalea Pictures remakes of vintage AIP drive-in hits that were churned-out of Texas by a film professor and filmmaker named Larry Buchanan. Though atrocious by any measure, Buchanan's films had their own uncanny, dreamy rhythms, palpable air of desperation, and grubby images I was quite fond of, and none were more uncanny than his non-remakes like **MARS NEED WOMEN** (1967) and **IT'S ALIVE!** (1968, both USA) with down-on-his-luck former Disney superstar Tommy Kirk (note: that latter film bears *no relation whatsoever* to the same-named 1974 Larry Cohen sleeper, and only the scantest resemblance to the 1950 Richard Matheson short story "Born of Man and Woman" which many dubiously attribute its 'inspiration' to). Among Buchanan's originals is a bottom-of-the-barrel John Agar mad scientist opus set beside a swimming pool, entitled **CURSE OF THE SWAMP CREATURE** (1966, USA), which I mentioned earlier. The latter ended with the revelation of Agar's creation, which even by Buchanan standards was a miracle of making a nominal 'monster' despite impoverished means: a beefy man with green greasepaint and the slightest of monster facial makeup, comprising fangs, outsized fake eyes with slit pupils, exaggerated reptilian putty brow, and pointed ears.[23]

It was during one of the weekend video binges at our own home, with our new player, that a new big-box atrocity captured my eye at the local TV repair joint's bulging video wall display. **ATTACK OF THE SWAMP CREATURE!** Could it be that Larry Buchanan movie I saw on Channel 22 in 1969?[24]

There seemed to be no end (but there was) to the opportunistic retitling of feature films by successions of exploitation distributors; thus, **ZAAT** was retitled **THE BLOOD WATER OF DR. Z**, and **BEAUTIFUL PEOPLE** (1971) became **THE SEXORCISTS** six years later.

"Maybe they just changed the first word of the title", I thought, trying to divine that which cannot be divined from the elaborate painted box art featuring a multi-tentacled monster with

---

23 Buchanan's **CURSE OF THE SWAMP CREATURE** has since become an easy-to-find DVD public domain title, one edition of which (double-billing Buchanan's film with the 1977 made-for-TV pseudo-Yeti thriller **SNOWBEAST**) sports an original painting of Swamp Thing himself on the cover. Note that this Larry Buchanan monster has enough cult cultural cache these days that a full over-the-head rubber mask of the creature is currently available from Paper Magic Men; see https://www.amazon.com/Paper-Magic-Curse-Swamp-Creature/dp/B0052CCM7K/ref=sr_1_9?ie=UTF8&qid=1502395813&sr=8-9&keywords=Curse+of+the+Swamp+Creature

24 I was relieved upon my initial *Myrant* blog posting of this portion of the original serialized essay that I wasn't alone in my love for Larry Buchanan comingled with **ZAAT**. David Jones a.k.a. "Johnny Bacardi" commented, "**ZAAT** aired on Turner Classic Movies a few months ago, one of its *TCM Underground* series—though I'd heard of the film (mostly under its **BLOOD WATERS OF DR. Z** title) for years, I had never seen it. I was glad I finally got the chance. I've also had a fascination for Larry Buchanan flicks since seeing **IT'S ALIVE!** and **MARS NEEDS WOMEN** on Nashville Channel 5's *Big Show* back in the '70s, and reading about some of his other efforts in *The Monster Times*' "Worst" issue. One of Buchanan's company of players settled in my small town here in south central Kentucky—Agar running buddy (by many accounts) Warren Hammack, who appeared in **MARS NEEDS WOMEN** (as Tommy Kirk's right-hand man/Martian) as well as **THE EYE CREATURES**, and established a repertory theatre that continues here to this day. I tried my best to get him to share some stories about Agar and Buchanan and making those movies, but he declined, mostly shrugging it off as 'just doing a job'. He was dubious and skeptical that anyone could be 'really' interested in those films he made, despite my best efforts to convince him otherwise. *Oh well!* He was always nice to me and mine, and really helped my kids out when they were employed there for several years"(comment posted to *Myrant*, December 17th, 2011, 11:30 p.m., archived at http://srbissette.com/z-z-z-zaats-all-folks/)

a reptilian bat-like visage, taloned claws on what appeared to be wings or elongated fins, and a red-bikinied buxom blonde beauty wrapped in its grip. It looked like it referenced every low-budget faux-cephalopod movie's "I wish my monster looked like *this*" ballyhoo, with the credit "Starring Frank Cromwell" (*who?!*) being the only clue to the film's true identity.

I *had* to know.

Prepared to make my apologies to my viewing companions when they realized what a shot of Novocain to the brain I'd *deliberately* rented, I eagerly brought the lurid color box to the counter; at least there would be Elvira on hand to argue my case for the rental, since she hosted this stellar presentation.

As was so often the case, the title and box art had almost nothing to do with the movie on the cassette. **ATTACK OF THE SWAMP CREATURE** was nothing more or less than the first official video release of **ZAAT**!—and it was love at first sight for me.

I was *mesmerized* by the movie. In its murky pan-and-scan video incarnation, this had to be among the most miserable swamp monster movies I'd ever seen… and that was a formidable record to top.

I adored every mind-numbing, cortex-searing second of it. I rented it a couple more times, and when the shop was selling off their copy, the owner suggested I buy it. "You're the only one who ever rented it, and not only didn't complain, but came back to see it again", he said, shaking his head at the faded cover in his hand. It was mine for a measly five-spot. Like most video shops in the 1980s, this rental outlet had most of the Elvira Thriller Video titles from that era, or damned near all of them—mighty fine company for **ZAAT**, if you ask me![25]

So, that was the beginning of my love affair with **ZAAT**. But it's important to note that the film had already begun to have an unexpected influence on some sensitive viewers, like Atlanta, Georgia artist R. Land, who has long "incorporated Zaat into a lot of things. When I do three-dimensional Florida maps with little pieces stuck to them, I always put a little Zaat in the upper-right-hand corner".[26] Now, *that's* **ZAAT** love, baby, and there ain't nuthin' wrong with love!

Equally creative are some of the online essays engaging with the uncanny **ZAAT** moral universe, primary among those stands Jeffrey Sconce's "**ZAAT** and the Poetics of Despondent Indifference", which moves me to tears whenever I even *try* to read it, or at least prompts me to blow my nose. Twice.[27]

More typical, especially given **ZAAT**'s popularity as an *MST3K* artifact, are online reviews like the one which con-

---

[25] For an online cover art gallery of all the Elvira Thriller Video titles, go to http://www.critcononline.com/thrillervideo_vhs_covers.htm

[26] Curt Holman, "Plaza series puts artistic inspiration in deep focus: R. Land's gone fishin' with **ZAAT**-themed work for Art Opening and Movie's current installment", *Creative Loafing*, July 6th, 2009, archived online (@ http://www.creativeloafing.com/culture/article/13030061/plaza-series-puts-artistic-inspiration-in-deep-focus)

[27] See http://ludicdespair.blogspot.com/2010/05/zaat-and-poetics-of-despondent.html

A ZAAT by Any Other Name…: **ZAAT** begat **BLOOD WATERS OF DR. Z** as a retitling as early as 1974, and foreign releases (theatrically and, come the 1980s, via home video) spawned more variant titles like **HYDRA**.

cludes, "For reasons I can't explain, I felt filthy after watching this movie and required a hot shower".[28]

There are exceptions, like CaveDogRob's review which tracks his first experience back to a 42nd Street viewing of **THE BLOOD WATERS OF DR. Z** release,[29] or the exquisite meditation on **ZAAT** at The House of Self Indulgence, celebrating the fact that

"...like a European art film, ZAAT poses many questions. Of course, I missed most of them, but I did hear a lot of the answers. I also learned that nature is a volatile morass, one that is full of unseen danger; Miss Ringhaver looks her best while sitting with her legs crossed in short shorts; and if you have an underwater camera, don't be afraid to use it".[30]

What more do you need to know?

Everything changed, irrevocably, possibly forever for **ZAAT** in 1999, casting a long, dark, funny shadow we cannot ignore.

I have to take all post-1998 references or discussions of **ZAAT** with a grain of salt, knowing they've likely been tainted by *MST3K*'s dance with the film (Episode #1005, first broadcast on May 2nd, 1999),[31] which has pretty much ensured:

(A) a 21st Century following for **ZAAT** that it never would have had otherwise, and
(B) the inevitability that **ZAAT** will never again be screened on its own terms, as it was originally meant to be.

Oh, what a world! *What a world!!*

But most important of all is the fact that the creators of **ZAAT** are *still* at it!

Possibly mistaking the loving but nevertheless corrosive devotions of *MST3K* and its audience for a long-delayed commercial opportunity, the original filmmakers have resurrected their Walking Catfish man/monster.

For over six years now, the official ZAAT® *The Classic Movie* website/blog has been active and growing.[32] The blog also features essays on the making of **ZAAT** which I highly recommend to any and all who are curious to learn more about this marvelous mongrel monster movie.[33] In 2011, the site promoted 40th Anniversary theatrical showings of **ZAAT** and Jacksonville, Florida's own Don Barton announcing his plans for a sequel to his chestnut monster movie. One year lat-

er, Barton and his team successfully packaged and released the definitive home video transfer to date, working with its surviving 35mm elements for a unique high-definition Blu-ray/DVD Combo pack from Cultra/HD Cinema Classics. This **ZAAT** edition boasts the kind of bonus features that should have rendered essays like this one forever obsolete: the original 35mm trailer, TV spots and outtake footage, a photo gallery, a radio interview with Wade Popwell and author/film historian ED Tucker, and an exhaustive-but-entertaining audio commentary with **ZAAT** creator Don Barton, Zaat monster costume creator Ron Kivett, and "Sheriff Lou Krantz" himself Paul Galloway, moderated by ED Tucker.

Blu-ray.com critic Jeffrey Kaufman by-and-large complimented the image quality of this release,

"...courtesy of Film Chest and Cultra with an AVC encoded 1080p transfer in 1.78:1. This has evidently been sourced from a 35mm print that was in acceptable condition, but which had faded considerably and showed signs of damage. The restoration featurette included on the Blu-ray demonstrates quite good color correction, as well as some digital sharpening and (bugaboo alert) some digital noise reduction. Even DNR doesn't affect the stock footage here in any great degree, and it still looks rather grainy and fuzzy. Colors pop quite well on this release, though reds especially tend to bloom slightly from time to time. The entire film has a sort of garish look that was probably inherent in the original theatrical exhibition. Fine detail isn't superb here, but it suffices most of the time... Considering the shape of the elements used to make this high definition presentation, things look really rather surprisingly good, but those who are expecting state of the art HD imagery had best keep looking".[34]

Where they might look is anyone's guess; even in this era of even the most esoteric of genre fare getting high-grade restorations and releases, it's unlikely that **ZAAT** will ever receive this devotional a showcase again in our lifetimes.

Given the excellent restoration at last available, adventurous—or suitably sadomasochistic—viewers should consider concocting a home video triple-bill of **THE INCREDIBLE MR. LIMPET, STING OF DEATH**, and **ZAAT**, which offers the optimum thematic thru-line of the very peculiar subgenre which **ZAAT** inhabits.

V. Zaat's ZAAT; Or: How ZAAT Transduced the Swamp Thing Merchandizing of the 1990s

I once tried to smuggle Zaat himself into a *Swamp Thing* comicbook cover, along with a batch of other swamp monsters (the cover to *Swamp Thing* #47). Fearless and ever-eagle-eyed editor Karen Berger was on to my game, though, and the cover looked a bit crowded—it was, after all, the Parliament of

---

28 See *http://shane-movies.blogspot.com/2009/11/zaat.html*
29 See *http://moviemeltdown.blogspot.com/2010/01/z-marks-spot.html*
30 See *http://houseofselfindulgence.blogspot.com/2010/02/zaat-don-barton-1975.html*
31 See *http://www.mst3kinfo.com/aceg/10/1005/ep1005.html*
32 See *http://zaatmovie.com*
33 See *http://zaatmovie.com/index.php* and *http://zaatmovie.com/Feature.htm*

34 Jeffrey Kaufman, *Ibid.*

ZAAT as conceptual art artifact: 21st century creators like Atlanta, Georgia artist R. Land have appropriated **ZAAT** and the monstrous form of Dr. Leopold as a cultural icon, populating all manner of merchandising, online, and gallery artifacts.

Trees, not the Senate of Sappy Swamp-Creatures. "I think you went overboard with this one, Steve," Karen cooed, and I immediately agreed. Zaat and the other swamp critters I'd crammed-in were, some of 'em, "meat things", after all. So, I cheerfully stuck to the chlorophyll creatures, offered a *saner* rough for the cover, which was approved, and I then jumped into the pencils for John Totleben's inks.

The only ones that made the final cut, from the original rough, were the actual plant monsters with comicbook instead of movie associations, but I must confess, I played on Karen's relative ignorance of comics esoterica. John, though, knew the monster menagerie I was drawing from (including, I'm happy to note, Man-Thing, the Heap, *Morlock 2001*, and one really forgotten Pre-Code horror comic swamp monster). But Zaat from **ZAAT** was scratched.

I wish he'd made the grade, it would have seemed... well, *prescient*, given what happened just five years later.

But what, pray tell, does all this have to do with Swamp Thing? I have a final connection to make:

Consider Zaat's—Dr. Z's—laboratory, and his purpose: changing humans into... *things*.

Then consider what the brains behind the ill-fated *Swamp Thing* toy line cooked up in 1990-91 for the toy and DIC cartoon version of *Swamp Thing*—or, to me more specific, what they cooked up for Swamp Thing's nominal nemesis, their radical revamp of the villain formally known as "Arcane".

The Kenner "Arcane" was a human action figure with a finger-puppet 'mask' that could go over his little plastic-action-figure-man head; once that was in place, he was the transformed monstrous Arcane. See, evil ol' Arcane transmutes human beings into his monstrous "Un-Men"... a rather pathetic distillation of the Len Wein/Berni Wrightson Anton Arcane and Un-Men into one of the silliest toy concepts of the 1990s. I always thought Kenner used generic rubber finger puppet monsters, purchased in vast quantities, as the bonus heads packaged with the action figures to 'transmute' badly-sculpted, crudely-articulated action figure villains into absurd, ersatz 'un-men', but I was wrong. My South Carolina-born, Atlanta, Georgia-dwelling online pal Devlin Thompson corrected me back in 2011, writing,

"Minor factual correction: while the Un-Men's 'masks' resemble generic finger puppets, and fit poorly enough that you'd imagine that they're being badly repurposed, they were entirely new crappy sculpts. On the other hand, the Elvira pinball machine from that time period does use off-the-shelf puppets on its playfield; your students who produce Drop Target Zine can probably back me up on that".[35]

Given all this, I've never commented on the 'concept' behind the whole Swamp Thing toy line shebang (see Sidebar).

Consider, if you will, the Transducer (which sounds a bit cooler in French, don't you know; the way the Cajuns would say eet...)...

The 1990-1991 Kenner Swamp Thing action figure for the franchise's nominal villain Anton Arcane, shown here without and with the easily-fit-over-the-head "Spidery BioMask."

---

35 Devlin Thompson, comment on *Myrant*, December 17, 2011, 5:19 pm, archived at http://srbissette.com/whats-zaat-part-4/ . The creators/writers/artists of the excellent pinball fanzine *Drop Target* weren't my students, BTW: they were former Center for Cartoon Studies Fellows and CCS fellow faculty members Alec Longstreth and Jon Chad, and *Drop Target* can still be found at http://droptargetzine.blogspot.com and is most highly recommended. Also see the review at https://creditdotpinball.com/2014/08/27/people-drop-targets-jon-chad-alec-longstreth/ and check for availability of back issues at https://www.radiatorcomics.com/product-category/zines/page/2/ and at https://microcosmpublishing.com/catalog/zines/3380/

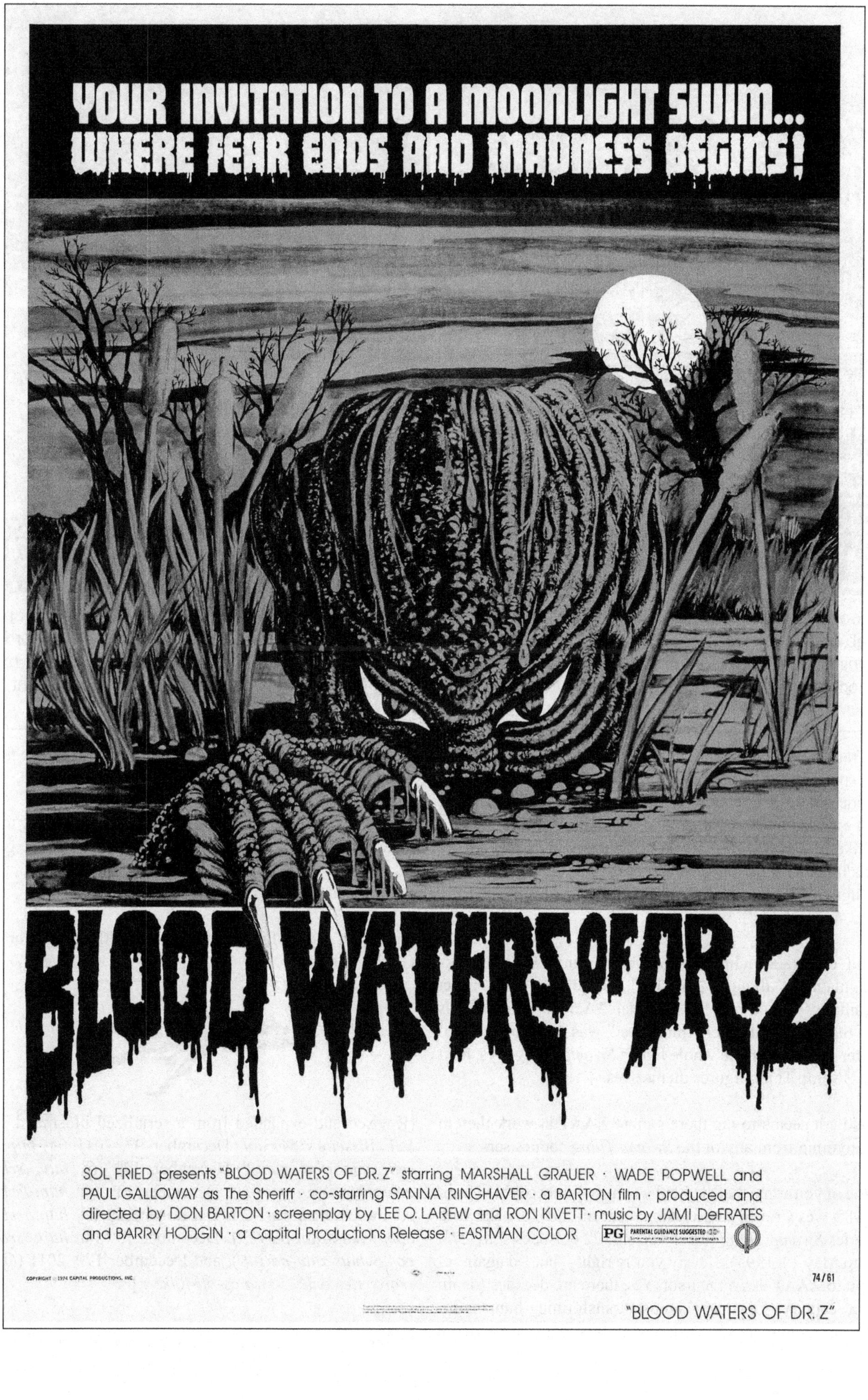
YOUR INVITATION TO A MOONLIGHT SWIM...
WHERE FEAR ENDS AND MADNESS BEGINS!
BLOOD WATERS OF DR. Z
SOL FRIED presents "BLOOD WATERS OF DR. Z" starring MARSHALL GRAUER · WADE POPWELL and PAUL GALLOWAY as The Sheriff · co-starring SANNA RINGHAVER · a BARTON film · produced and directed by DON BARTON · screenplay by LEE O. LAREW and RON KIVETT · music by JAMI DeFRATES and BARRY HODGIN · a Capital Productions Release · EASTMAN COLOR
PG PARENTAL GUIDANCE SUGGESTED
COPYRIGHT © 1974 CAPITAL PRODUCTIONS, INC.
74/61
"BLOOD WATERS OF DR. Z"

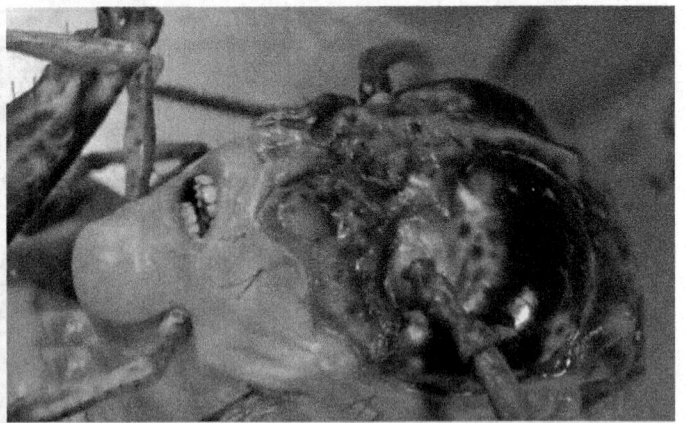

Echoes of **ZAAT**: Kenner's "Swamp Thing Transducer Playset" and its "Bio-Mutator Changes Men Into Monsters" lab equipment was based upon the invertebrate/human Un-Men created by Dr. Anton Arcane (Louis Jordan, returning from the 1981 Wes Craven **SWAMP THING**) in **THE RETURN OF THE SWAMP THING** (1989), makeup effects by the Todd Masters Company team and Dean Gates, Steve Neill, Michael R. Jones, Cora Knight, and David Minkowski.

The Transducer was actually a fairly clever little gizmo: there was a spinning table at its center, with a human figure strapped into one side of the table; close the roll-top, turn the crank, which appears to infuse the green-colored transducing formula (*just* like in **ZAAT**!) into the hapless victim, and—*voilà!* The mantis/humanoid strapped to the other side of the identically-designed tabletop was now visible when you opened the device. *Formidable!*

Instead of "transducing" human beings into Walking-Catfish-humanoids, though, "Arcane" turned 'em into insect thingamajigs, including a "Mantis Man." Actually, the "Mantis Man" that came with the "Transducer" was the coolest bit of monster modeling in the whole line of *Swamp Thing* toys, next to the Swamp Thing figures themselves.

Honestly, it seems to me there's more **ZAAT** at work therein than anything from any of the *Swamp Thing* comics series.

If some of you argue that element was most likely cobbled from the 1982 Wes Craven film version, or from the USA Network TV series *Swamp Thing* (three seasons, 72 episodes, July 27th, 1990 to May 1st, 1993), I'd say you're right—but I'd again refer you to **ZAAT** as a precursor. Yes, there are decades (damn near a century) of mad-scientists-transforming-humans-into-monstrous-humanoids predating all this, but... well, damn

it, **ZAAT** is what came immediately to my mind the first time I laid eyes on the Transducer toy.

If you'd care to see more of the Kenner Swamp Thing toys, pop on over to the Virtual Toy Chest and enjoy the online gallery.[36]

For me, though, it's back to **ZAAT**...

Hmmmm, should I watch it this time with eggnog, or Cuervo Gold?

[Revised and expanded from a serialized illustrated essay at *S.R. Bissette's Myrant*, December 9th, 2011 (@ *http://srbissette.com/whats-zaat/*), December 12th (@ *http://srbissette.com/whats-zaat-part-1/*), December 13th (@ *http://srbissette.com/whats-zaat-part-2/*), December 14th (@ *http://srbissette.com/whats-zaat-part-3/*), December 15th (@ *http://srbissette.com/whats-zaat-part-4/*), and December 17th, 2011 (@ *http://srbissette.com/z-z-z-zaats-all-folks/*).]

---

36 See *http://www.virtualtoychest.com/swampthing/swampthing.html*

ZAAT

SYNOPSIS

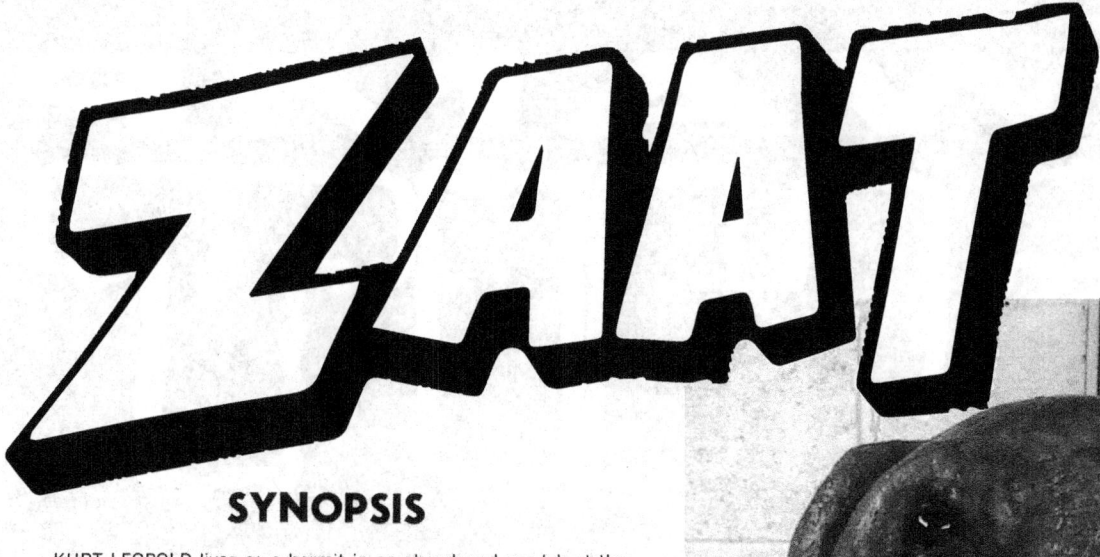

KURT LEOPOLD lives as a hermit in an abandoned sea lab at the edge of the Atlantic Ocean in Florida. He has experimented for 25 years, trying to prove his theory that a human can be changed biologically and live underwater as a fish. He realizes his lifelong dream by transforming himself into an underwater creature with the aid of a new chemical solution he discovered, ZaAt. Encouraged by this success, LEOPOLD begins his plan of revenge on the society that has rejected his idea as "lunacy." He pollutes the rivers and streams in the area with his radio-active ZaAt solution. Fish grow oversize and mutate onto the lawns, farms, highways! Burly SHERIFF LOU KRANTZ is desperate to solve this problem even to the extent of working with a black marine biologist, REX, from state headquarters.

LEOPOLD, the monster fish, kills off, in succession, two former supervisors in the lab. He deliberately drowns the son of one and stings the man's wife into a state of suspended animation.

The SHERIFF and REX's request for help is answered in the form of a team from INPIT, (Inter-Nations Phenomena Investigation Team), which arrives in a rolling laboratory. WALKER STEVENS and MARTHA WALSH are experienced in solving unusual phenomena, particularly in the field of ecology and marine life.

After examining the evidence, WALKER detects a pattern to the creature's movements and sets a trap. The monster, curious about the net, starts to tear it and the trap is sprung. He is able to break out and he goes after WALKER. Both are injured in the fight.

There is great fear now among the townspeople. Since WALKER doesn't yet know the nature, nor number, of the enemy, he tells SHERIFF KRANTZ to evacuate the town.

The monster must now accelerate his plan which is to climax with pollution of the Atlantic Ocean. But he needs drugs to treat his injury. The next night he sneaks into town and breaks into a pharmacy, downs a drug and proceeds to tear up the store. Now berserk, he attacks a teenage couple on a porch, clawing the boy to death and then sucking his blood.

With help from a detector, WALKER picks up the radio-active trail of the monster who, in the meantime, has gone to INPIT quarters and kidnapped MARTHA to transform her into his mate, a feat he has failed at with two other women.

At the lab, the SHERIFF and REX discover the fantastic activity of LEOPOLD, and as SHERIFF KRANTZ rushes from the lab to radio WALKER, the monster attacks and chokes him to death.

The monster, not knowing that REX is still in the building, straps MARTHA to the body basket and starts to lower her into the ZaAt polluted tank. REX, alterted by MARTHA's screams, intercedes and a bloody fight ensues. The monster grabs the ZaAt cannisters and heads toward the ocean, leaving REX to die. As the basket with MARTHA in it inches down toward the solution, REX, in a last gasping effort, is able to pull MARTHA over to the side of the tank. He dies. MARTHA starts to climb from the basket.

Outside on the beach, the monster moves quickly toward the ocean. Several shots ring out from WALKER's gun, and the monster is stunned. WALKER, exhausted, stumbles toward the wounded monster in hopes of capturing him. The monster struggles to retain possession of the canisters and dives into the ocean as WALKER collapses into the sand. MARTHA walks, dazed, toward a motionless WALKER. He raises his head and calls to her as she walks slowly past him and disappears into the ocean.

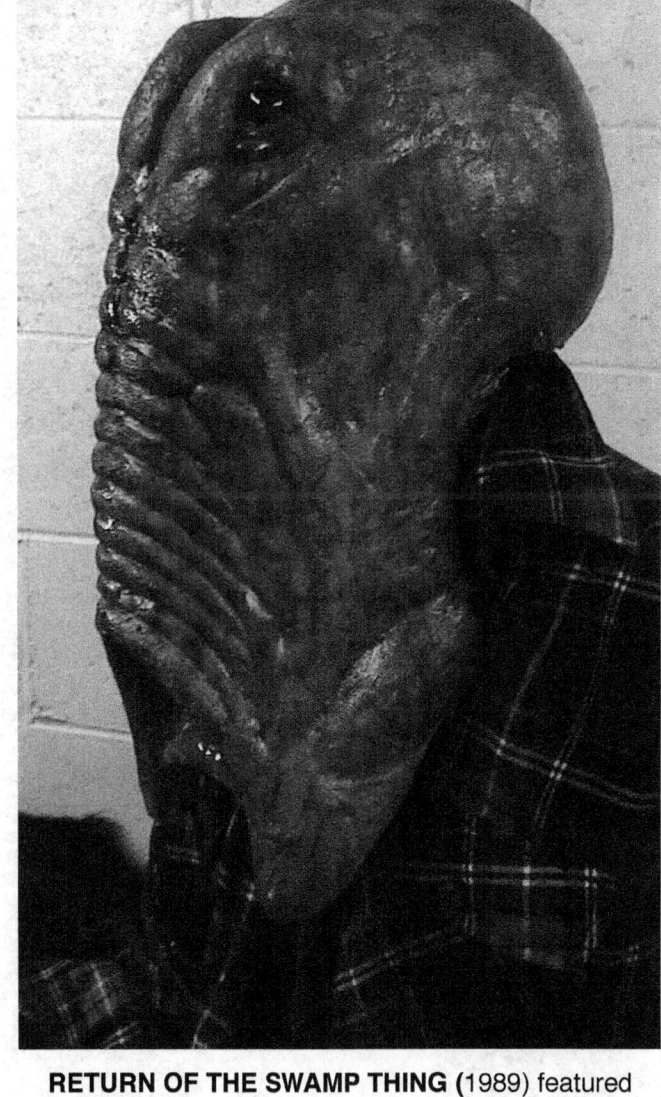

RETURN OF THE SWAMP THING (1989) featured a terrific "Leechman" (Christopher Doyle). Backstory: when our fellow Joe Kubert School of Cartoon and Graphic Art Inc. classmate (and 1980s makeup effects creator) John Bisson applied for the special effects makeup gig for this film, John Totleben and I (having drawn Swamp Thing for DC Comics at the time) forwarded John Bisson some monster designs, per his request—and John Totleben included a great 'leech man' design in that artwork. John Bisson didn't get the job, but Totleben's 'leech man' showed up in the film. Coincidence? We think not.

SIDEBAR:

SWAMP SHIT

Inspired by the online blog *Mike Sterling's Progressive Ruin*,[1] specifically Mike's postings on the worst of all the early 1990s Swamp Thing merchandizing crap, I am prompted to commit to print my own impressions of these artifacts of what might be the true nadir of the Swamp Thing character's legacy.

I have all this mind-boggling drizzle in my own collection—now, and forever, housed for all to see at the Stephen R. Bissette Collection at HUIE Library and Henderson State University in Arkadelphia, Arkansas. Special Collections librarian and amazing HUIE Goddess Lea Ann Alexander (now retired) in fact had the HUIE Library glass display cases brimming with this insane Swamp Thing pop debris back in November of 2005, when Marge and I made our pilgrimage to Arkadelphia for the opening of the Collection.

I'll give you my personal choice of the lamest Swamp Thing merchandise ever (using photos from *Mike Sterling's Progressive Ruin*, which I urge you to visit if you want to see more!), with special thanks to comics scholar/fan/historian Bob Heer for navigating me there, and to Mike Sterling (who has granted permission for me to quote his writings here) for harboring such loopy delights online.

Now, Bob maintains that the admittedly crap "Swamp Thing Chalk" (!!!) is the single most absurd of all the Swamp Thing merchandizing to date, and he's got a point. It is singularly bizarre; here's what Mike Sterling had to say about his eBay acquisition:

"This piece of merchandise boldly tells you, the consumer, just what exactly you're getting. 'I'M CHALK!' exclaims the package, and by God, chalk is exactly what you get. Chalk carved in the general likeness of Swamp Thing and colored green, perhaps, but that, my friends, is Washable, Dustless chalk in its purest form. According to the back of the package, some of the suggested uses for Swamp Thing chalk are 'Do Your Homework,' 'Play Games,' and 'Draw Funny Pictures'—yes, Swamp Thing chalk can cover the full spectrum of life. Also, according to the package, the Swamp Thing chalk 'works great on chalk boards' which must come as great relief to someone.

Okay, seriously, I'm sure the 'I'M CHALK!' legend on the front is some kind of warning that this item isn't candy, just in case having 'CHALK' in orange letters on the front, and having pictures of kids drawing things with chalk on the back, weren't clue enough."[2]

---

1 *http://www.progressiveruin.com/2004/09/20/yes-i-really-own-all-these-things/*, all quotes herein permission of Mike Sterling.

2 Quoted from Mike Sterling's Progressive Ruin, Monday, September 20, 2004 post; scroll down to read the post, archived online at *http://www.progressiveruin.com/2004/09/20/yes-i-really-own-all-these-things/*

In the same September 20th, 2004 posting, Mike also unveiled the likewise silly-ass Swamp Thing Bop Bag[3]—also high on the "What the fuck?" list of Swampy merchandise, though I can tell you there were late nights penciling issues of the comic book where I wanted to punch *something*—but at least one can cite 1960s movie monster bop bags as precursors, thus reducing the absurdity component of the Swampy bop bag to near nil.

As the attentive comics and Swamp Thing fans likely can make out from Mike's posted photo, here, the artist of note on these merchandizing miracles was none other than Alfredo Alcala—or, I should say, those are definitely Alfredo's *inks*, perhaps working over some uncredited penciller. You may recall that it was John Totleben who first suggested Alfredo as the best fill-in inker on *Saga of the Swamp Thing* (during the tag-team collaborative effort editor Karen Berger orchestrated on the title around the buildup to Alan Moore's ambitious *Swamp Thing Annual* #2 script, "Down Amongst the Dead Men," which necessitated some fancy footwork on *SOTST* #30 and #31 to buy me time to pencil the *Annual* without a break: it was double-page-count, natch, and we were starting behind the deadline eightball—where we'd been, like, forever). Anyhoot, it was John T who suggested Alfredo as the best alternative to his own inks, an astute call given John's and Alfredo's shared roots in Franklin Booth's pen-and-ink aesthetic. This was so that Rick Veitch and John could collaborate on #30 while I pencilled (the tightest pencils of my career) for Alfredo to ink on #31, allowing John and I to collaborate on the *Annual* (with a couple of pages of pencil assist from Rick Veitch). So that's how Alfredo was brought into the fold—leading, ultimately, to his becoming the regular inker on Rick Veitch's subsequent mind-blowing *Swamp Thing* run (as penciller with Alan scripting, and later with Rick writing and pencilling), culminating in these ST merchandizing monstrosities.

A long road to China, indeed.

Well, OK, so now you know Bob Heer's choice of most absurd Swamp Thing merchandizing item ever. Though Mike Sterling doesn't indulge such nominations, he does bring special personal history to this gem, which also rank pretty high in my personal choice for most absurd Swamp Thing merchandizing ever—the Swamp Thing Pencil Sharpeners!

I have 'em all—again, now in the HUIE Library Bissette Collection archives (thank God, I didn't have to move them again!)—and there are indeed three different designs, as shown on the back of the packaging. Mike's original post reads:

> "This is one of the very first things I'd ever bought on eBay, over six years ago now. In fact, I think this may be the very item that inspired me to get an eBay account in the first place. Let me distract you from that highly embarrassing and very sad bit of personal information and draw your attention to the ballyhooing of 'ACTION! Movable arms' blurbed on the pack-

This is one of those perverse merchandizing items that not only must be seen to be believed, but must be held and actually used—sharpening a pencil jammed into a plastic Swamp Thing's abdomen—to be fully appreciated. Photo ©2004 Mike Sterling, used with permission.

> age. While, yes, the arms do appear to move, I would have had a hard time attributing any kind of exciting 'action' to that. Maybe you could pretend to move his arms around as if he were writhing in pain as you jab a pencil into his hip...."[4]

Now, I have no such history. I bought these damnable things at local toy stores (in Keene, NH and down in Massachusetts) as they surfaced in the blow-out sale bins. I've harbored these in my archives for thirteen years before donating them to the HUIE Library Special Collection. Thankfully, I didn't have to suffer the public humiliation of bidding for them on eBay! That might have prompted a Heidi MacDonald column or something: Good Lord, Bissette bidding on *Swamp Thing* shit

---

3 http://www.progressiveruin.com/2004/09/20/yes-i-really-own-all-these-things/

4 http://www.progressiveruin.com/2004/09/20/yes-i-really-own-all-these-things/

on eBay. No, I just put up with my kids saying, "Dad, why are you buying that? It's not for me, is it?", with relief beaming from their wet little eyes (brown for Maia, baby blue for Danny, like his Poppa) when I told them it was for (choke) me.

"Oh, good," they said, with heart-shattering relief.

My misguided affection for these pencil sharpeners, though, lies in the fact that you're using a tiny Swamp Thing idol to further carve/maim a wood product already mechanically sculpted from ravaged trees—a pencil, natch—thus using a replica of DC's protector of the trees, the Plant Elemental incarnate, to, like, sharpen pencils. Among tree-huggers, this isn't only misapplication of a false idol, it's ideologically abhorrent in the extreme on so many levels, one can't comprehend them all. And that, I love.

But for me, the nadir of the Plant Elemental's false idols, the ultimate absurdity of all the 1992 Swamp Thing merchandizing, the most perverse and brain-wrenching of all these misbegotten horrors, that-which-should-never-have-been-made, much less worn and adorned, are—

—*AAAAAGGGGH!*

SWAMP THING SLIPPERS!

Beastie booties for wee feet! Yep, the worst of all the Swamp Thing merchandizing were bright green fuzzy kid's slippers with the dumbest little bright green hollow plastic Swampy heads imaginable perched (well, actually, glued) atop the iskyli'l toes of the tots who tottered around in 'em.

Of course, licensed merchandizing isn't licensed merchandizing until you've slapped the official registered trademark logo on the damned things, so there 'tis, Swamp Thing, on the sides of the slippers, adding elegance and grace to these hideous mass-production nightmares.

That's it, the point at which I concede that those who once held all rights, save comics rights, to Swamp Thing did their utmost to exploit every conceivable niche market abomination the human mind could concoct.

"The slippers, the slippers"—Marge catches me some nights, muttering that in my sleep as I lay, slavering and glistening with cold sweat, in the grip of some dreadful recollection of what once lurked in my own home.

"The slippers! IT WAS THE DAMNED SLIPPERS!"[5]

And that, my friends, is all I can stomach of that.

Again, all this—and more!—is forever sheltered and selectively showcased in the Bissette Collection at HUIE Library/Henderson State University.

Thankfully, this is only a tiny fraction of the collection, which houses much more interesting and invaluable things, including Alan Moore scripts, Bissette art, and all manner of matter from my 30+ years in comics.

But oh, baby, those slippers! Now, about that merchandizing artwork…

---

5   See, if you dare, Mike Sterling's Progressive Ruin, Saturday, January 13, 2007 post, archived online at *http://www.progressiveruin.com/2007/01/13/i-had-no-idea-such-a-thing-even-existed/* and also see: *http://www.progressiveruin.com/2009/02/08/the-terrifying-beauty-of-ephemera/*

First, a little arcane (pun intended) Swamp Thing history...

Back in the late 1980s, a man named Bruce L. Stein became the president of the toy manufacturing corporation Kenner. Stein instituted a more aggressive licensing of media properties and the expansion of certain properties with replacement figures before waiting to see how Kenner's current lines had performed in retail venues. This meant expanding lines that hadn't proven themselves in the marketplace, a risky policy that scored some real hits (*The Real Ghostbusters* toy line prominent among those), some OK sellers (*Beetlejuice, RoboCop*) and a string of pricey losers (*Police Academy* in 1989, Rat Fink in 1990, etc.).

Going into 1991, Stein and Kenner's self-dubbed 'starting Lineup' had The Batman Dark Knight Collection about to launch—which retailers were clamoring for—and three new lines about to debut: Robin Hood Prince of Thieves, Bill and Ted's Excellent Adventure, and Swamp Thing.

Kenner also had Princess Vanessa and Her Royal Family about to launch, but the less said about that clunker clan, the better.

So, Swamp Thing.

Ya, uh, Swamp Thing.

Kenner's Swamp Thing toyline was fabricated around the DIC animated series which had no real airplay—instead of emerging from a popular TV program, Kenner sold the animated *Swamp Thing* pilot episode "The Un-Men Unleashed" as a self-standing 23-minute videocassette sold in toystores, which retailers purchased in a 24-video counter dump (industry term for 'display carton').

The cartoon show was a disappointing mash of the live-action TV series, elements of the two movies, and what still appears to me to be a ploy to spin an action-figure line around pre-existing monster finger puppets, and pretty lame-ass monster finger-puppets at that.

There were ten figures in the Swamp Thing line, only two of which bore any relation to the DC Comics title—Swamp Thing himself and a monstrous Anton Arcane that in no way resembled any incarnation of Arcane in any Swamp Thing comicbook ever published.

Four of the ten figures were Swamp Thing variants: Bio-Glow Swamp Thing, Snap Up Swamp Thing, Snare Arm Swamp Thing and the never-did-it-really-work-as-intended Camouflage Swamp Thing, each with their own plastic prop to enhance play value (the log bazooka was the singular hoot). There were two more Swamp Things released in the ill-fated second series—Capture Swamp Thing ("With Organic Net and Cypress Club") and Climbing Swamp Thing ("With Bayou Staff and Shield of Reeds"), which barely surfaced on the market given the dire fate of the first series.

The rest—well, like I said, there was a crappy Anton Arcane rendered more 'monstrous' when a ridiculous fanged spider-monster finger puppet (oh, excuse me, I meant the "Spidery BioMask") was fixed onto his pointy purple head.

It looked and (despite Devlin Thompson's correction) still looks to me like Kenner's toy designers glommed on to grosses of existing cheapjack made-in-China fingerpuppets and concocted the villains of the series—Kenner's version of the Un-Men—around those plastic embarrassments: Dr. Deemo came with a fanged-snake-spider fingerpuppet ("Serpent BioMask"), the zombie-like Skinman with a bat ("Fangbat BioMask"), and, uh, Weed Killer, a hazmat-wearing specialist in herbicides, Agent Orange and defoliants, I reckon. His finger puppet Un-Man head was an arachnid with two glowing eyes and a gaping red maw. Go figure.

There were also two human characters, Bayou Jack ("With Swamp Water Blaster") and Tomahawk ("With Swift Shot

The 1990 *Swamp Thing* animated TV series pilot was released direct-to-video by Kenner ("A Division of Tonka Corporation") to launch their Swamp Thing toy line. It's possibly the only videocassette ever to boast on its cover art that it was "Safety Tested."

Three of the ten Kenner Swamp Thing plastic action figures, revealing variable body sculpts and "play value"; photo © 2004 Mike Sterling, used with permission.

Crossbow"), who arguably had certain affiliations with DC's venerable Tomahawk comicbook, but not really.

There was also a small fleet of outsized vehicles and gadgets: the Bayou Blaster, Marsh Buggy, Bog Rover, Swamp Trap "With Vine Snare and Giant Venus Fly Trap") and my personal favorite, the Transducer, if only because it came with an Un-Man that actually was kind of cool. The "Mutated Insect Figure" was a neat little Mantis-Man; if only the entire Un-Men line had been similar!

Still, the line stiffed.

Big time.

It should be noted that the other spin-off merchandizing—the puzzles, games, box-bop inflatable, fuzzy slippers, and so on—sported better packaging art than the Kenner line… because DC Comics saw to it themselves.

So, looking at the non-Kenner packaging art, in 2009 Italian fan and collector Salvo Bombara emailed me scans of an original art collection Salvo just acquired—with the hope that I or someone might be able to identify, for certain, who the pencil artist might have been.

Again, the inks are most definitely Alfredo Alcala's—but who penciled the merchandizing art?

All the merchandizing art was generated by DC itself—note the DC paper, its corporate imprint visible in the scans Salvo sent—and at the time they arrived I guessed from the exaggerated action poses and a couple of uninked pencil drawings that José Luis García-López might be our man, but—well, then again, maybe not.

In the fall of 2009, we discovered the truth, and I am sharing it here, in print, for the first time. What follows is a slightly edited (for smoother reading, and to eliminate the extraneous off-topic comments) transcript of the comments thread that led us to the revelation of who penciled the DC Swamp Thing merchandizing artwork:

Mark Masztal (September 9, 2009, 10:06 am):
I've sent Kevin Nowlan, who consistently works with JLG-L a message to take a look at your blog and see if he has any insight on the penciller.

James Robert Smith (September 9, 2009, 12:21 pm):
Interesting stuff. I do recall from my collectible toy business days that there was a Swampy line, but I don't ever remember anyone asking me to look out for anything from it. Is there much demand in the collectibles market for that stuff now? I do know that the stuff that tanked is what's always attractive to the later collectors. Yeah, García-López would be my guess too. Whoever it was did a pretty good job of the old "dynamic" poses that editors and packagers like to see.

Bob Heer (September 9, 2009, 10:06 pm):
Mark beat me to suggesting Nowlan to weigh in on it being JLGL. If you go to Nowlan's blog[6] you can see a lot of exam-

6 See http://kevinnowlan.blogspot.com and Kevin's posts showing José Luis García-López's pencil art can be found via http://kevin-

149

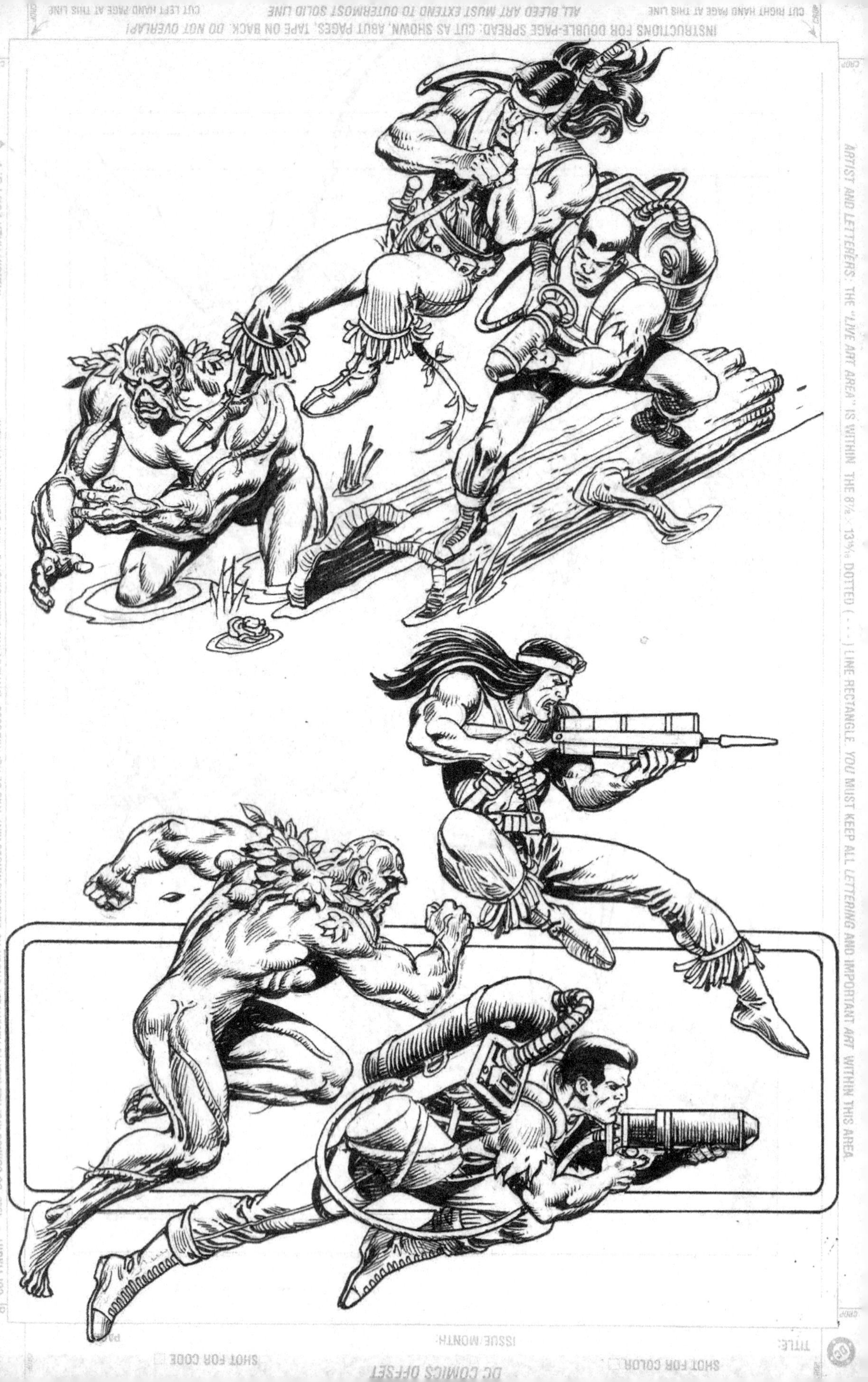

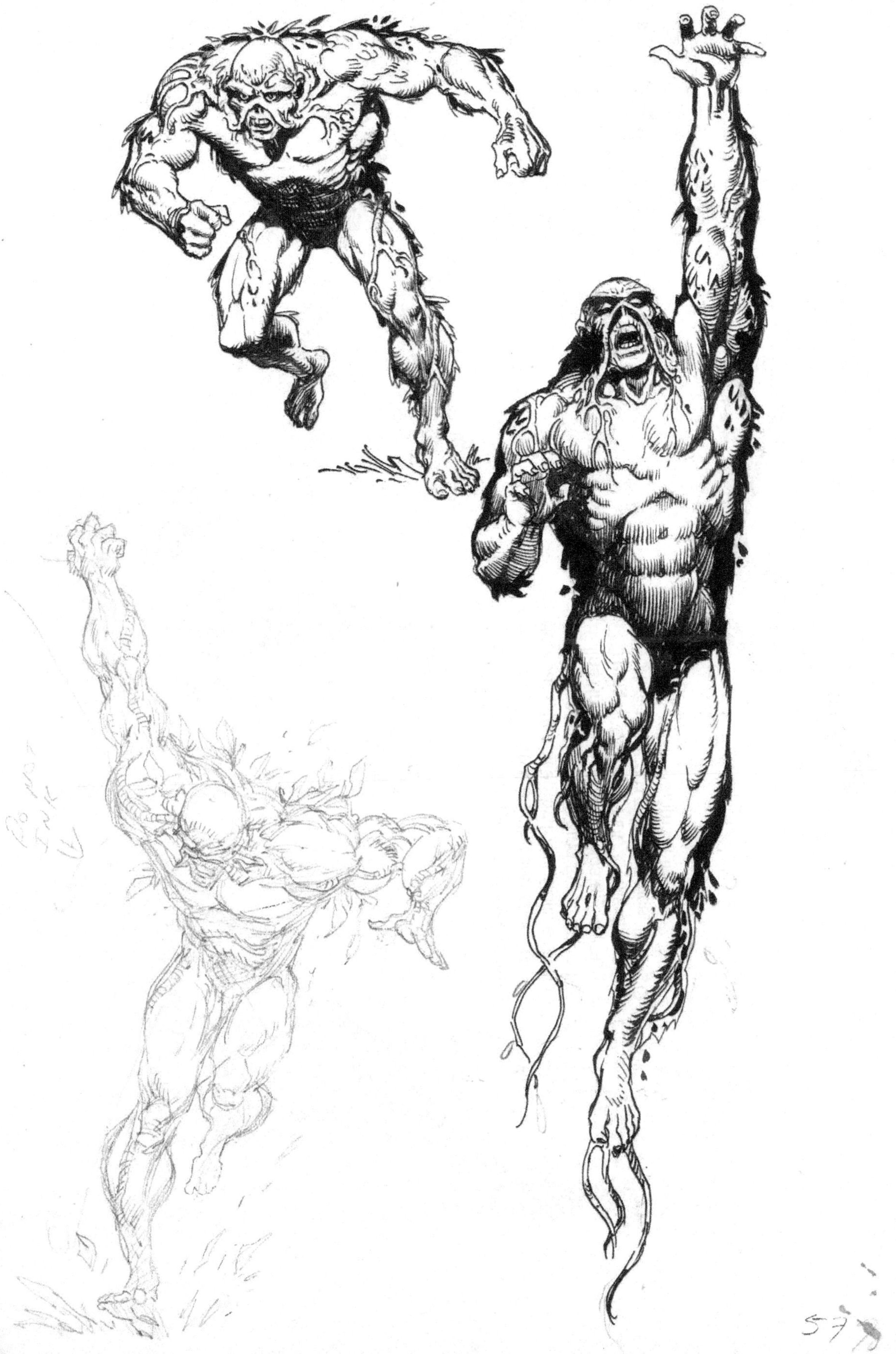
57

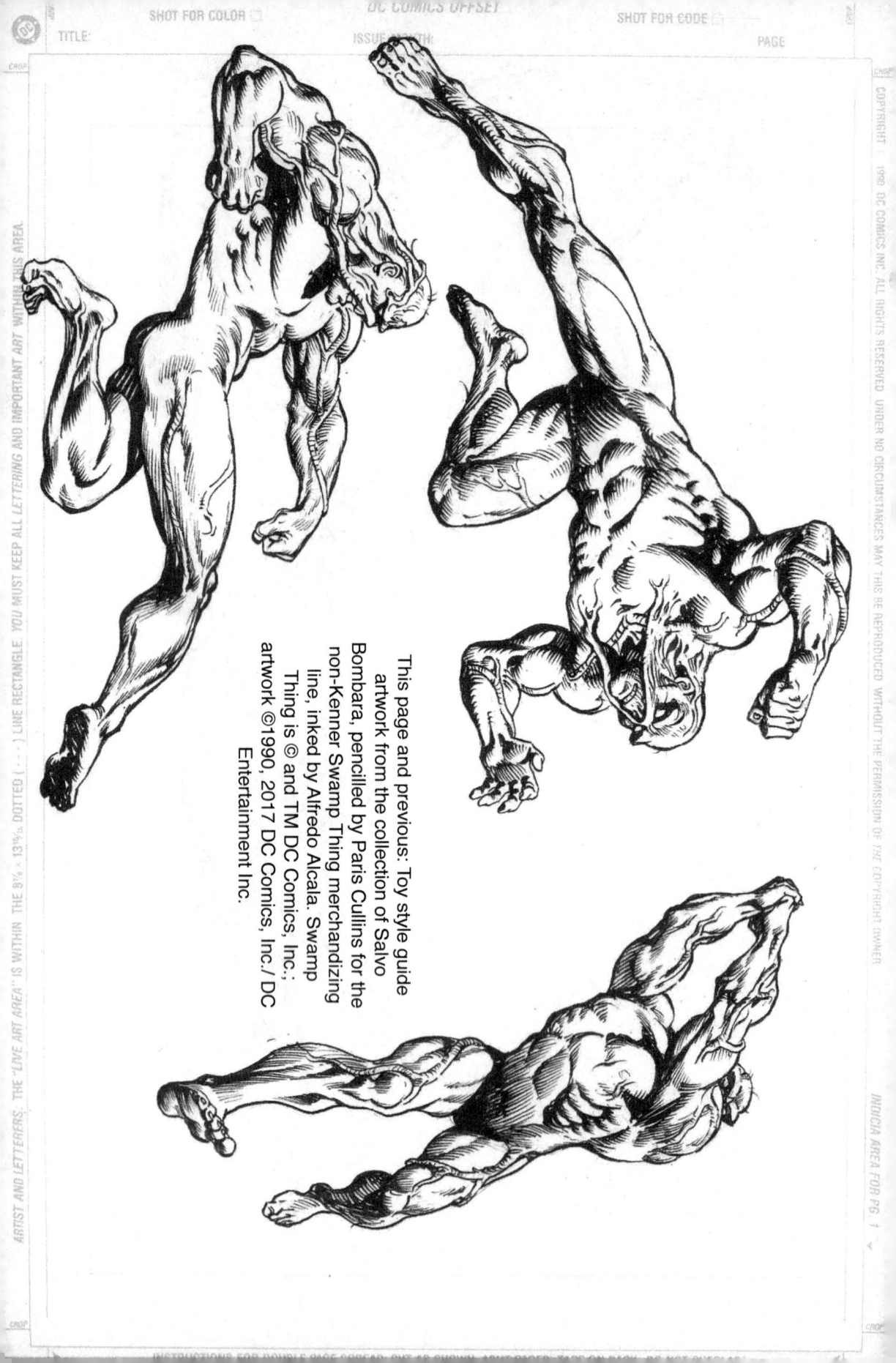

This page and previous: Toy style guide artwork from the collection of Salvo Bombara, pencilled by Paris Cullins for the non-Kenner Swamp Thing merchandizing line, inked by Alfredo Alcala. Swamp Thing is © and TM DC Comics, Inc.; artwork ©1990, 2017 DC Comics, Inc./DC Entertainment Inc.

ples of JLGL's pencils. The look is very similar to the cover of DCCP #8 by JLGL.[7]

Mark Masztal (September 10, 2009, 5:57 am):
Hi Steve, I heard back from Kevin Nowlan: Maybe this helps? Cheers

> "Hi, Mark, Here's José's take on it: 'About Swamp Thing I've never did anything with the character and the drawings in Steve's blog are new for me. A have a wild guess…Paris Cullins may be the penciler, the time period coincides and I remember inking some Supermans he did for the guides and he also did the pencils for a back up feature in Atari Force so I was in someway familiar with his style…but, who knows!'…"

Stephen R. Bissette (September 10, 2009):
Paris Cullins pencilled the excellent (sadly short-lived) *Blue Devil* for DC while I was still working on *Saga of the Swamp Thing*, and I always enjoyed Paris's work. So—for sure it's not Jose on the Swamp Thing merchandizing art pencils, and Kevin suggests maybe Paris Cullins did 'em. Thanks, Mark—thanks, Kevin!—thanks, José! Let's see where this takes us now…

Salvo Bombara (September 11, 2009, 3:25 am):
Following your precious infos, I did a small research on the web and I've found a pics of a ST merchandizing drawing done by Paris Cullins. It's not for a game/toy but most probably for a campaign against enviromental pollution. Even if the art looks a little bit different from the drawings I own (maybe different inker), It gives more chance at the guess he is the penciller.

Vinnie Bartilucci (September 11, 2009, 6:52 am):
Just dropped Paris a note on his Facebook page – let's see if he offers any onsight.

Dave Elliott (September 11, 2009, 8:49 am):
Definitely Paris. Know his pencils anywhere and he was doing a lot of DC style guide work at the time.

Stephen R. Bissette (September 11, 2009, 10:13 am):
Thanks, Dave, Rich, Vinnie—this is terrific. If you can stomach my politics, I've posted confirmation of Paris having pencilled at least some of the Swamp Thing art (though to my eye, it all looks like his work now) on today's 9/11 post. It's a piece of art Salvo found online from the collection of Tim Easterday, posted (I believe) at CAF. Breakthrough! Vinnie, I would love to know if Paris replies — it would be great to confirm his place in the rogue's gallery of ST artists.

Dave Elliott (September 11, 2009, 11:15 am):
Steve, I actually have some of his pencils still and the comparison is dead-on. I left a message for Paris, you can find him on FB now.

Dave Elliott (September 11, 2009, 10:11 pm):
Hey, Steve Paris just confirmed that it was indeed himself behind the pencils. Best, Dave

Paris Cullins (September 12, 2009, 12:00 am):
I worked on many toy style guides for lots of companies and enjoyed every moment of it, especially working with master inkers like Tony Dezungia, Frank Giacoia, Alfredo Alcala, Tom Sutton, García-López, Bob Layton , Bob Smith—these are just a few but wow what a rush.

—

And there you have it, Ladies and Gentlemen: Paris Cullins penciled the non-Kenner Swamp Thing merchandizing artwork, inked by Alfredo Alcala…

…and that, my friends, is how we used to find out things on the internet, from the sources.

———

[Revised and expanded from *Myrant*, "Swamp Thing Shit," January 15, 2007, archived online at *http://srbissette.blogspot.com/2007_01_15_archive.html*, and S. R. Bissette's Myrant, "Who Pencilled the Swamp Thing Merchandizing Art?," September 9, 2009, archived online at *http://srbissette.com/who-pencilled-the-swamp-thing-merchandizing-art/* ; all the comments cited were from the latter *Myrant* post, with original dates of each commented cited above. Swamp Thing is © and TM DC Comics, Inc.; artwork ©1990, 2017 DC Comics, Inc./ DC Entertainment Inc.; toy photographs (including the photo below) ©2004, 2017 Mike Sterling, used with permission; original merchandizing art scans appear here compliments of Salvo Bombara from his collection, used with his kind permission.]

---

[7] Bob is referring to *DC Comics Presents* #8 (April 1979), archived online at see https://www.comics.org/issue/33256/

Let's get to the point...

A film by Matthew Smith

The Glasshead

A freak of Science.
An immortal hunger.
One black night of terror.

VERMONT INDEPENDENT FILM!

CRACKING THE GLASSHEAD

Or: How I Tracked Down a Forgotten-Before-It-Was-Known Regional Horror Opus and Its Maker from a Chance Discovery of a Found Object in a Dank Corner of a Failed Enterprise

---

This article is dedicated to the memories of Pat Salois, and to my own teenage-years monster-movie partner in 8mm and Super 8 filmmaking, William Hunter.

R.I.P., once-dear friends and fellow travelers; you are not forgotten.

Here! Here is the damned thing!

Do you see it? Can you see it? *Dare* you see it?

You see it here before you, just as my eyes found it—or, as best as a mere reflection of the artifact can lay it before your own—an *object*.

No, less than an object: objectless, abject and abandoned, evidence of an object that might never have been, or if it once was, was no more.

It is not the object: it is its shell, empty, hollow, free of its sluglike inhabitant, dropped, spilled, split, crushed, slithered away or abandoned by its host, shed like an eggshell, a snail's spiral, a mollusk's armor. Gone, that which gave it name and title and illusion of substance, the promise of motion, emotion, story, flesh, blood, or whatever simulacrum of those vows: when first I saw it, it was as vacant as a cardboard box pretending to provide shelter, left by some vagrant wanderer.

Understand, you must, that this gutted orphan only made that which was lost, gone, unseen and unseeable all the more tantalizing, all the more beckoning.

This madness that seizes my being from time to time tenders me prey to such loveless allure, as if that which has been truly discarded can only have once harbored one fairer, one more fulfilling, than any vain and colorful maiden or master that promises me more. Promise me nothing, and I am yours!

Facing page: The original VHS release box art just as it appeared to the author, from his collection. The photo pixelation is not an artifact of our reproduction here—that is how the photo appears on the original box art. **Above:** The fetish objects themselves! The two subsequent videocassette releases of **THE GLASSHEAD**: the 1998 Salt City Home Video cassette *[top]* and the 2000 Sub Rosa Studios cassette

---

And surely this husk promised nothing: free of any color save a laminated pallid gray-blue, like that of a dead roadkill's eye; so impoverished of means or clarity as to be from its origins murky, muddied, muddled, and vaguely distasteful, such covering as it ever boasted woven threadbare and dull from birth. Indeed, as unpromising to the eye as ever it was, it was even more unpleasant to the touch, at the same time slippery and yet sticky—like a used condom—tarnished though it seemed to have never been worn, held, much less caressed or adored. Who or what could love this?

Yet I was fixated by it at first glance. It held me and my interest as surely as would a found coin, a lost 20-dollar bill uncovered, a rare jewel gleaming from a mud puddle. Its curious announcement of its conception—"Vermont Independent Film!"—was scrawled in ballpoint pen on a dime-store sticker, ivory as a broken tooth, in its lowermost right-hand extremity.

More tantalizing still was the almost indecipherable image, a crudely photocopied or otherwise cheaply-reproduced photograph: a young man rearing up from a textured (straw-covered?) flooring, the hollows of his eyes and mouth agape but expressionless, a partially-shadowed flat of barnboards behind his head, the silhouette of pitchfork tines poised above (but, like the whole of this atrocity, obscured and initially confusing to the eye, the projections of the spines alone just visible enough to hint at penetration, punctures, the spilling of fluids and of life itself).

The first word of the text within this gray fog was likewise lost: "get to the point…" became, upon closer study, "Let's get to the point…"

And so we shall.

But first, do, *do* look upon that which I beheld that day, glimpsed only partially jutting akimbo amid a bent, crimped heap of sheaths in a milk crate in a forgotten corner, just another lost treasure or trash item. Here, here is the damned thing, though you can neither touch nor smell nor taste it on sight, as I did that day, though part of me dreaded to even touch it, much less know any more of its sensory despair: touch it not, and certainly never, ever put it near one's nostrils, one's mouth, nor any vulnerable organ or opening. Nothing good could come of that, ever, though it called to me as surely as anything ever has.

Here, here it is, a shadow of that shadow of its self, birthed a shadow, lost from its first unleashing, damned though unseen it was and unknown it was and unknowable it remains…

Here! Here is the damned thing! And as I have been, so to, now, ye be damned!

Behold:

THE GLASSHEAD!

"Let's get to the point…"

It was the year 2000, and I was doing what we seemed to be doing a lot of at that time: sorting through the debris of a video store back room, cherry-picking whatever backstock might still be of some value in what was left of the video rental market.

I was also at the time knee-deep in a personal quest for regional films and videos with any link to my home state of Vermont. That years-long research obsession eventually yielded a video-illustrated lecture I delivered in a number of local libraries between 1998 and 2005, and a single book—*Green Mountain Cinema Volume 1* (Black Coat Press, 2000)—that I self-distributed in-state, in person, and that can still be ordered online, for those with any interest whatsoever in such a venture.[1]

It seemed at times I alone had any such interest. Though I ended up selling almost a thousand copies of my book, it was a long, slow slog, researching my home state's rich cinematic legacy (no joke: it *is* rich and long, dating from before 1900 and stretching into the present, punctuated with masterpieces by the likes of D.W. Griffith, Alfred Hitchcock, Walt Disney, and Tim Burton, and less-than-masterful creations I found and still find even more appealing and revealing).[2] But enough on that:

My search, my obsession, informed every waking moment of my day-to-day work in the video retail industry, where I labored in obscurity from 1991 until I left the trade in the spring of 2005. I've many stories, but for now, only one matters:

A video store in the Northeast Kingdom had gone belly-up. I drove almost three hours north with a blank check and instructions to bring back anything of value to our own still-thriving business, First Run Video (Brattleboro, VT, the area's first "super store," which lasted from 1991 until it closed its doors early in 2014; a healthy run by any standards). This included fodder for our annual blowout VHS sales, so almost anything that was still in a box

Late, great local VT hero Fred Tuttle, **MAN WITH A PLAN** (1996), was the cover "star" of the one and only volume of *Green Mountain Cinema* published to date (available @ http://www.blackcoatpress.com/non-fiction-green-mountain-cinema.html) [photo © 2000, 2015 Jack Rowell]

---

[1] You can still order your copy of this one and only volume of *Green Mountain Cinema* (224 pages, fully illustrated) from http://www.blackcoatpress.com/greenmountaincinema1.htm

[2] I eventually shared an abridged chapter concerning the many horror films made and/or set in Vermont with long-time friend, associate, and fellow genre scholar Michael H. Price. Michael and co-author John Wooley included most of that material as a "bonus" chapter in their recent *Forgotten Horrors to the Nth Degree: Dispatches from a Collapsing Genre* (Cremo Studios, 2013); available at http://www.amazon.com/Forgotten-Horrors-Nth-Degree-Dispatches/dp/1481986171/ref=sr_1_6?ie=UTF8&qid=1432091072&sr=8-6&keywords=Forgotten+Horrors+Michael+H.+Price

The Glasshead

**Paul Guiles   Chad Sweet
Shawn Rouillard**

Screenplay by Pat Salois and Jeff Hurd
Produced and Directed by Matthew Smith

Three young actors head a cast of unknowns to join with emerging director Matthew Smith in telling the tale of a murderous, implacable menace that may be *more* than just a campfire story. In the 1860s, humble farmer Jebediah Decker (Guiles) becomes the subject of a horrible experiment, which grants him an eternity of madness and sparks a legend of horror that continues to the present day. Matthew Swan (Sweet) tracks the now-bloodthirsty Decker, and Nikki (Rouillard) unsuspectingly leads his college-friends, out for a camping trip, straight into the path of the monster.

1998, Black & White, Horror, Not Rated.

Suggested for Mature Viewers.
Contains graphic violence and adult language.
Running time: 52 minutes

©1998 Trakk Productions. All rights reserved.

Let's get to the point…

A film by Matthew Smith

The Glasshead

A freak of Science.
An immortal hunger.
One black night of terror.

VERMONT INDEPENDENT FILM!

Here is the unfolded box art for the first VHS edition of **THE GLASSHEAD,** self-distributed by the filmmakers (Trakk Productions, 1998). It's most likely that the film's star, Paul Guiles, or someone in his circle had sold or gifted this VHS original to the northern VT video shop where the author later found the box, sans cassette, among other discarded VHS boxes. This is not a fabrication, this is the real McCoy, from the SpiderBaby Archives

---

clean enough to display and/or any VHS tape that still appeared playable was fair game. DVD was a still a very new format, and laserdiscs were long gone from our rental and sale stock; VHS' days were numbered, but it was still profitably racked and sold.

Canvassing and assessing the readily visible stock on the racks in the main room of this out-of-business Mom and Pop store was easily done. I was down to the crud, the boxes and milk-crates in the back room, dominated by beaten and sun-faded big-box videocassettes from the early 1980s, a few boxes of grotty adult XXX porn, and, against one filthy sheetrock wall, a cobwebbed stack of plastic milk-crates labeled "Dump."

Having accomplished my primary task—cherry-picking the cream of the rental stock—I was now knee-deep in the *shit*. To me, this was where the gold usually lay, the titles of absolutely no interest to my friend and boss Alan Goldstein or my co-manager April Stage, or of much use to the store either; but this was where I usually found something rare and delectable, and sometimes even a movie I'd never heard of.

There was only one this trip.

It was malingering in one of the last crates labeled "Dump", which seemed to be filled with empty video art sleeves: the remnants of movies that had been damaged beyond repair, stolen, or lost. Almost all these sleeves, even those drained of their original color by exposure to sunlight in the front windows of the shop, were still competing for grabbing my eye with their flamboyant color schemes.

Only one grabbed my eye by having almost no color, none whatsoever.

Curious, I reached down and stopped:

What the fuck was this?

The box was dingy, ugly by design. There was a barely readable photo—or, rather, a blurred photocopy of a photo or framegrab—and no less than three or four type-fonts on the cover, the largest reading "The Glasshead."

"A freak of science.

THE GLASSHEAD

An immortal hunger.

One black night of terror."

Cooler still, a plain white sticker below that vague ballyhoo read, in hand-written ballpoint pen, *"Vermont Independent Film!"*

Love. Love at first sight!

But the tape was gone, and my questions fell on deaf ears. "Oh, that stupid thing," the woman I was dealing with replied, "I think that tape was lost a while ago." My asking a second question prompted an odd look, wondering why anyone cared anyway, much less a savvy super-store manager from way down southern Vermont.

"You want that box, take the whole crate. Take 'em all for free, maybe you can use them to replace boxes you've lost."

So I did—and so the search for **THE GLASSHEAD** began…

What was odd was the back of the box read "©1998 Trakk Productions"—the movie was only two years old, but the box looked like it had been in that back room for at least five or more years, and it was sandwiched between discarded videocassette boxes and shells that dated back to 1980.

This only deepened my interest, and made this forbidding apparently "pre-aged" artifact all the more curious.

I'll spare you the search. Suffice to say, I'm a pretty savvy pop culture detective, and this new-fangled thing called "the Internet" and "email" brought the world into sharper focus faster at times.

And so it was that after much legwork and many questions to fellow video professionals who didn't give a flayed rat's ass about why I was interested in this movie of all movies, and considered me and it kind of peculiar that there even was an unknown movie entitled **THE GLASSHEAD**, I was directed to the folks at Sub Rosa Studios (from whom First Run Video had purchased many an odd independent super-low-budget gore and horror title). That lead led to an exchange with Ron Bonk at Sub Rosa in late 2002; at that time, Sub Rosa was based in Liverpool, New York. A mere $15 plus $5 shipping and handling would land a copy of **THE GLASSHEAD** videocassette into my player.

Sub Rosa's website described **THE GLASSHEAD** ("Item Number: SR18437") as a "black and white 50 min film… centers around three young campers who fall prey to a murderous, implacable menace when a campfire tale turns out to be all too real! In the 1860's, humble farmer Jebediah *[sic]* Decker lived a simple life with his sick bride. But his peaceful world was shattered when three intoxicated hillbillies brutally raped and murdered her, then attacked Jebediah, smashing his head in and leaving him for dead! Through a horrible experiment, he is brought back from the edge—yet with his newfound life comes an eternity of murderous madness that goes well beyond revenge—sparking a legend of horror that continues to the present day!"

THE GLASSHEAD director Matthew S. Smith continues to work in the genre as a cinematographer and in other capacities. He recently handled the photography for Brett Piper's Lovecraftian feature **THE DARK SLEEP** (2012), a contemporary spin on Lovecraft's "Dreams in the Witch House."

When I pressed to know more about the movie itself, Ron replied, "Don't know much of the history of the movie. We licensed it direct from the filmmaker and have been selling it for a few years, but haven't moved many copies (mainly due to it being a short), so yes, very hard to find. It is in stock, BTW…"

A little over a month later, I awoke one fine February morning (the 18th, to be precise) in 2003 to find an email in my inbox that read:

"Hello,

My name is Matthew Smith and I was the producer of the 'no budget' film **THE GLASSHEAD**.

I received a series of emails between you and Sub Rosa Studios regarding this film.

If you have any questions please feel free to contact me. Email seems to be the quickest way to get a hold of me because I'm away a lot.

Thank you."

Here, then, faithful and oh-so-constant reader, is the secret of **THE GLASSHEAD**, poured out before you in all its shuddery, shimmering glory…

THE GLASSHEAD unreels in less than an hour—52 minutes, to be precise—and it's a curious concoction by any definition.

Shot and presented in black-and-white—an unusual move for any narrative film shot and released commercially in the 1990s— **THE GLASSHEAD** opens during the 1860s, during the War Between the States, a.k.a. The Civil War. We see uniformed soldiers, weary and worn, in close-up and medium shots, in a forest and a grassy plain. This atmospheric prologue and opening credits imagery undulates, like a waving flag or fan-blown movie screen.[3]

Deadpan black humor informs the final credits edit, from the 1860s battlefield footage of a cannon being pulled along by Union soldiers (actually, it's the 4th New York Independent Light Artillery, whose flag

---

[3] During our March 2, 2003 interview exchange via email, **THE GLASSHEAD** star Paul Guiles explained how this was achieved: "An interesting tidbit about that opening sequence is how Matt achieved the wavy effect which ran under the battle footage and opening credits. He did it, not using any fancy-pants computer program, but by projecting the images on a bedsheet, as his wife put ripples in the sheet. I think it came out marvelously, and when one knows the secret, it is all the more remarkable."

Matthew Smith was the cinematographer on Jon McBride, John Polonia, Mark Polonia, and John Oak Dalton's WW2 soldiers-vs.-the-occult tale **BLACK MASS** (2005)...

...and did the same (with Brett Piper) for the Polonia Brothers' living-scarecrow-ravages-a-college-party bloodbath **HALLOWEENIGHT** (2011).

Nikki (Shawn Rouillard) and Josh (Tyrone E.S. Marsh), beer cans in hand, watch two mysterious strangers from the safety of the woods. Rouillard and Marsh were college students when they co-starred in **THE GLASSHEAD** in 1995-96; when Rouillard returned in fall of 1996, he'd cut his hair, prompting the creation of the film's coda in place of the planned ending

we briefly see in this final shot of this sequence), to Matthew Smith's director/cinematographer credit, to the first crisp shot of the film's contemporary setting. We see sneakered feet walking along an overgrown grassy path; a beer cooler is being carried between them. What we carry can kill us…

We meet the quartet carrying the cooler and camping gear. Close friends, two couples: Nikki (Shawn Rouillard) and K.C. (Elisa Silverglade), who refer to their young son Zack being safe with K.C.'s mother for the duration of the outing, and Josh (Tyrone E.S. Marsh) and Deanne (Maria Cirielli), whose relationship comes across as warmer than that between Nikki and K.C.

Brash and more intent upon his drinking than anything else, Nikki's first line—the first dialogue of the movie—is "Are we there yet?" It's Nikki's brash impatience, strut, and boisterous arrogance that gets them all into harm's way when Nikki and Josh go for a walk and meet two strangers, Tim (Gary Breinlinger) and the silent, hulking wood-carrier "Peter" (Paul Guiles). The two men seem odd; by this point, we've already seen a stranger—Tim, we later ascertain—light a match, his cigarette, and climb into a car, leaving what appears to be a body by the side of a remote stretch of road. Soon after Nikki (stupidly) tells the ominous pair where the foursome are camping and invites them over for a beer later, we're also privy to the bloody death of a woman (Leah Hudson) out walking her dog, her severed head left as adornment atop a ragged straw scarecrow along another desolate field.

159

As Captain Beefheart used to say, "Bad fuggums."

The urban legend aspect of **THE GLASSHEAD** is brought to the fore as the film cuts to K.C.'s face partially lit by a campfire burning in the dark of night, as she tells a familiar scary story[4] ("I'm coming to eat you, Chucky, and I'm on the third step…!"). Ah, but I'm getting ahead of our story; we'll get into more of these urban legend connections in a page or two.

If Nikki's interruption of K.C.'s telling of the campfire tale (blowing her punchline completely) seems rude, ruder still is the arrival of Tim and Peter with Tim's deadpan exclamation, "I can do better."

Thus begins the lengthy visual flashback—it comprises 26 minutes of the film's running time; fully *half* of the movie—at the black heart of **THE GLASSHEAD**, which we're to take as being Tim's tale, told to the two couples. Narrated by Tim (Gary Breinlinger, who also served as one of three production assistants on the film), this is "the monster movie" portion of **THE GLASSHEAD**.

Tim's story: In 1863, during the Civil War, a poor and somewhat "slow" dirt farmer named Gebadiah Decker a.k.a. Geb[5] (Paul Guiles) lived in "the

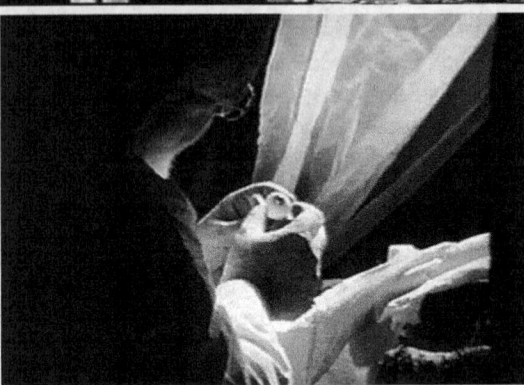

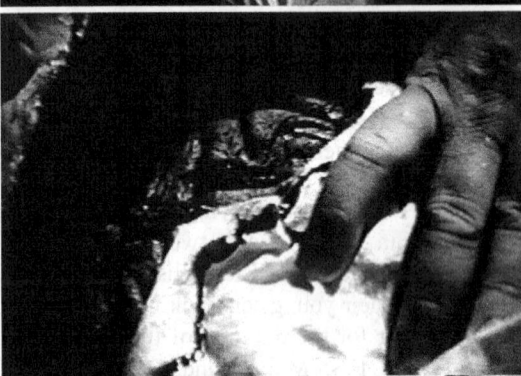

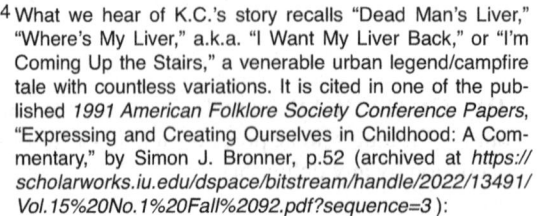

Never-before-seen images from **THE GLASSHEAD** *[top to bottom]*: Civil War POW prison camp surgeon Dr. Swan (Jeff Whitaker) ponders his brutal experiments; Swan at work; in one of the film's few makeup special-effects shots, Swan performs crude brain surgery on the mortally wounded Gebadiah (Paul Guiles); the resurrected Geb a.k.a. "The Glasshead" pays a visit to Dr. Swan's nursery to feed on one of the good doctor's year-old infant sons

---

[4] What we hear of K.C.'s story recalls "Dead Man's Liver," "Where's My Liver," a.k.a. "I Want My Liver Back," or "I'm Coming Up the Stairs," a venerable urban legend/campfire tale with countless variations. It is cited in one of the published *1991 American Folklore Society Conference Papers*, "Expressing and Creating Ourselves in Childhood: A Commentary," by Simon J. Bronner, p.52 (archived at *https://scholarworks.iu.edu/dspace/bitstream/handle/2022/13491/Vol.15%20No.1%20Fall%2092.pdf?sequence=3*):
"One such story is sometimes identified as a subunit under the heading 'Johnny, I Want My Liver' (a subtype, as it has been categorized by folklorists, of Aarne- Thompson Tale-Type 366), although the narrative technique repeats in many stories used by children.
"This lady gave this boy named Johnny a dollar to go to the store to get some liver. But he spent it on something else before he got the liver, and he had to bring this lady her liver. So he saw this graveyard right next to the store. So he unburied a guy, and he got the guy's liver and brought it to the lady. The lady said, 'This is a real good liver.' But that night they heard, 'I want my liver back, I want my liver back, I want my liver back.' Then they hear, 'I'm on your first step, I want my liver back, I want my liver back, I want my liver back.' Then 'I'm on your porch, I want my liver back, I want my liver back. I'm in your living room, I want my liver back, I want my liver back. I'm in the bedroom, I want my liver back, I want my liver back' (teller grabs listener in abdomen) [Bronner, *American Children's Folklore* 158 [Simon J. Bronner, *American Children's Folklore*. Little Rock: August House, 1988, p.158]; see also Opie and Opie 36; Virtanen 76; Tucker 370-73,495-96]."
Also see *http://americanfolklore.net/folklore/2011/01/wheres_my_liver.html* and *https://www.youtube.com/watch?v=932OGZakXNE* and *http://urbanlegends.about.com/u/ua/horrors/your_favorite_scary_urban_legends.05.htm*

[5] This is the filmmaker's own spelling of the name, per the final credits. All spellings in this article of either characters in, or the creative team of, **THE GLASSHEAD** are correct, and

---

Matthew Smith was a key grip on the set for Anthony Palma's and Zachary Shourds' Pennsylvania-filmed high school reunion revenge thriller **KNIGHTMARE** (2011).

THE GLASSHEAD: At the turn of the 20th century, Gebadiah Decker a.k.a. Geb a.k.a. "the Glasshead" (Paul Guiles) enters the barn of Matthew Swan—the twin he did not kill—seeking revenge

Finger Lakes region of New York State" with his wife Sarah (Marlene Perry). When Sarah became ill while four months pregnant with their child, Geb risked the five-mile trek through the snow from their remote cabin to get medicine. While Geb was gone, three drunken locals—Price (Dan Hoskins), Willie (Andy Moulton), and Dick (Greg Morrell)—broke in and assaulted Sarah, who succumbed to injuries from the brutal gang-rape. Returning just as the men emerged from the cabin, Geb was mocked and savagely beaten and left for dead with a crushed skull.

At this point a drunken Nikki interrupts Tim to stumble off into the woods to take a piss. Tim ignores Nikki (who we see collapse, unconscious, in the darkness) and continues his story:

Enter nearby prison surgeon Dr. Swan (Jeff Whitaker), who lifted Geb's body from the bloodied snow and took him back to his lab to further the doctor's ongoing experiments with the reanimation of dead tissue. Swan restored and reanimated Geb as a blood-addicted creature, the so-called "Glasshead", wracked with agony until

and unless his appetite was slaked. Geb killed Swan and entered the nursery of Swan's year-old twin sons, killing the infant Mark to drink its blood. Interrupted by the nanny (Andrea Ajemian), who rescued the baby Matthew, Geb fled for his home, where he found the decomposing body of his beloved Sarah and their unborn child. Overwhelmed with grief and the craving for revenge against her killers, Geb burnt Willie and Dick alive in their home, confronting Price alone in the woods before crushing his head with a rock.

The flashback continues as Tim tells of Geb/the Glasshead's reign of terror. "Gebadiah the Glasshead continued his blood quest throughout the decades. The killings crept into the 20th Century, and the scope of destruction increased over and over. No one knew when or where the Glasshead would strike next..." By the time Dr. Swan's surviving son Matthew (Chad L. Sweet) had grown to adulthood, the young man had studied his father's papers and uncovered the truth about the Glasshead. Intent on destroying Gebadiah once and for all time, Matthew led a torch-bearing mob to scour the countryside, but Geb eluded them, doubling back to confront Matthew in his barn and kill him with a pitchfork.[6]

---

should not be considered incorrect, whatever scant online "information" states otherwise. Note that Paul Guiles' name is misspelled in the opening credits, but correctly spelled in the closing credits.

[6] Despite the occasional black-and-white gore—including

161

Tim says, "...and to this very day the Glasshead remains at large, victimizing anyone who happens to be in the way when Gebadiah feels the pangs of his blood thirst." Tim suddenly holds aloft a severed head, which K.C. and Deanne dismiss as "a toy head," while Josh, alarmed, asks for a closer look. "In good time," Tim cryptically replies. K.C. and Deanne make their excuses and leave the fireside, K.C. to find Nikki, Deanne to take a piss; only Josh remains with Tim and "Peter."

"Peter" is, of course, Geb/the Glasshead, and he murders Josh, tossing his body into the fire. Separated and apparently unable to hear Josh's screams, Deanne is decapitated by a car hood and K.C. is strung up from a tree limb like a slain animal as Nikki, still intoxicated, stumbles back to the campsite and vomits at the sight (and, presumably, smell) of Josh's burning remains. Nikki flees.

The film cuts to a coda, years later: Nikki is in hiding, blamed for the murders, embittered and fearful. After completing an audiocassette message to mail to his son Zack, we finally see Nikki's last name: the envelope is addressed to "Zack Swan" (c/o State Foster Home, Jackson, NY). It appears Nikki and his son Zack are Dr. Swan and Matthew's last living descendents.

Nikki sets out to hunt down the Glasshead—followed by an unseen stalker as the film ends.

If the whole of **THE GLASSHEAD** evokes any specific—and specifically New York State—urban legend, it is that of the so-called Cropsey Maniac, a.k.a. The Cropsy Legend, a.k.a. The Cropsy Horror (note the variant spellings of "Cropsy/Cropsey"), a late-20th Century "scary story" of an escaped mental patient who malingered in an old abandoned asylum and preyed by night on local children. This pervasive New York-based 1960s and 1970s urban legend's basis in fact—grounded in an unsolved series of Staten Island, NY, disappearances and murders—was explored in Joshua Zeman and Barbara Brancaccio's intriguing feature-length documentary **CROPSEY** (2009).[7] As veteran and/or attentive *Cryptid* readers already well know, the "legend" had already been openly exploited for Tony Maylam's, Bob Weinstein's and Peter Lawrence's **THE BURNING** (1981, USA/Canada), which played up the associative link in its promotion and advertising (*"A legend of terror is no campfire story anymore!"*).

But **THE GLASSHEAD** isn't a cryptid, is he? No, but he is a backwoods bogeyman.

This is why you need to know that **THE GLASSHEAD** is as much a regional American *Frankenstein* variant as anything.

Actually, it's closer still to H.P. Lovecraft's story "Herbert West – Reanimator" ([1921-22] first serialized in *Home Brew* #1-6, February-July, 1922), which was eventually adapted into Stuart Gordon's, William J. Norris' and Dennis Paoli's celebrated **RE-ANIMATOR** (1985, USA). The military prison setting specifically recalled Lovecraft's fifth Herbert West tale, "The Horror From the Shadows" (in which West, serving as a medic in Flanders in WW1, harvested what he needs from wounded and dead soldiers) and anticipated the prison setting of Brian Yuzna's, Miguel Tejada-Flores' and José Manuel Gómez's sequel **BEYOND RE-ANIMATOR** (2003, Spain).

And if those connections seem like a bit of reach, allow me to remind you I began on this torturous path because of a sticker that read, "Vermont Independent Film!"

It turned out the Vermont connection was tenuous, at best. As Matthew noted in our first email exchange (February19, 2003), "this film was made in Elmira, New York and not in Vermont."

How I found the empty crude video box art for **THE GLASSHEAD** in northern Vermont would become clear shortly.

The making of **THE GLASSHEAD** was something Matthew was happy to share. "It's a long story but I'll try to condense it," he wrote.

"**THE GLASSHEAD** was my first venture into 'movie' film production. I like to think of it as my student film. It's where I made my mistakes and learned the most. It was penned by a friend of mine. He used to make short 8mm films in high school for fun. At times I would help and that was the catalyst that brought us together 20 years later to make **THE GLASSHEAD**. Also we were both avid horror and Sci-fi fans. Part way through filming, my friend was diagnosed with cancer and died before the editing started. The continuity and direction of the film was lost for a while and when I took up the task of

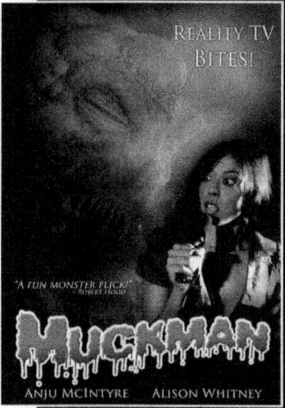

---

a vivid surgical close-up of the top of Geb's skull being sawed open and apart to expose his injured brain—Smith cuts away from Geb's pitchfork thrust to a close-up of a fork stirring an open can of stew as Josh digs in by the campfire while listening to the end of Tim's tale.

7 For more on the legend(s), see *http://cropseylegend.com/urban-legends* and visit the official film website at *http://cropseylegend.com/* (where the movie can be streamed), and/or on Netflix and other online venues. Recommended!

MUCKMAN (2009, no relation to the Teenage Mutant Ninja Turtles character) features a regional cryptid, a cable-access reality TV show in need of ratings, an investigative reporter, and another lively collaboration between writer/director Brett Piper, producer/actor Mark Polonia, and cinematographer Matthew Smith.

Youthful Mike Patton as he appeared in the music video which **THE GLASSHEAD**'s director Matthew Smith worked on (he "painted sets and filled sand bags"), Faith No More's "A Small Victory" (band: Mike Bordin, Roddy Bottum, Billy Gould, Mike Patton; single released September-October 1992). The WW1-set video was directed by Marcus Nispel, who went on to helm feature film remakes, including **THE TEXAS CHAINSAW MASSACRE** (2003) and **FRIDAY THE 13th** (2009). The video can be screened at www.youtube.com/watch?v=i9_hCjcFNO0

The Polonia Brothers Mark and John (or is it the other way around? Here with Mark's son Anthony, center) offered a haven and creative outlet for filmmakers like Matthew Smith when traditional "gates" were shut.

editing, I found that there was a lack of coverage that I could not recreate. The finished project is the result of that. I have been criticized and praised for this film. Yet, to me, it was a project that took on a life of its own and it was more important to me to follow through with the process of completing the project than the story itself."

I pressed Matt for more information on his filmmaking roots; I wanted that "long story," not just the condensed version. Thankfully, Matt was forthcoming. Wouldn't you know it? Matt was a "Monster Kid."

SRB: What led you and your friend into making movies?

Matthew Smith: The first time I held a film camera I was eight years old. My father had a 16mm Kodak camera that he would shoot hunting films *[with]*. My first experience on an organized movie was an idea that my older brothers had of a stop motion film featuring a small clay man that suffered trials and tribulations at the hands of some 1960's Aurora famous monster models. Sort of an early *SNL* "Mr. Bill."

Then in high school, I was involved in a couple of short films with some friends that had a 8mm film camera and a knack for creating bizarre films. Ironically, I would work with these same people again on my first real film, **THE GLASSHEAD**.

It wasn't until the birth of my daughter in 1987 that my interest in the moving image took on a new momentum. I purchased a new 8mm video camera and started video taping everything. (Much to the dismay of my family).

Soon, I found myself wanting more and I started to shoot and edit shorts for myself. One such project earned me a National first place award and a check for $1500.

I was hooked. I took my amateur skills and started to apply them to a semi commercial market, Public Service Commercials and industrials for non-profit organizations. These organizations were very pleased to have someone write, direct, shoot and edit programs for them at almost no cost. It turned into a way to work on filmmaking skills by doing actual projects.

SRB: That's what leads some to attend film school, but there you were, in upper New York State—

MS: Since my college days have passed and the chances of going to a film school were nil, I would read all I could about filmmaking to gain knowledge and insight to the art of filmmaking. My best learning experience came when a local film production company, Blind Faith Films, decided to shoot a feature in Elmira. Fourteen-hour days, endless lugging of heavy equipment and not a shred

THE GLASSHEAD: Somewhere in rural upper New York State, an unsuspecting woman (Leah Hudson) out walking her dog passes a ragged straw scarecrow along a grassy field, not knowing the Glasshead is watching—and waiting, needing human blood!

of recognition from the director was what I put up with. I didn't care. I was on an actual film shoot. I asked enough questions and listened to enough responses to earn a little respect and by the end of the shoot I was assisting with the camera activities.

After that experience I looked for any opportunity to further my knowledge of filmmaking. I was fortunate to have a brother that was an artist in heart but made his living doing special effects for film and commercials and eventually becoming an art director. On occasions, this offered me chances to work on professional union shoots. I washed windows and helped create a false office set for a commercial for CBS news with Connie Chung. I painted sets and filled sand bags for a World War 1 foxhole set on a Faith No More music video. I even had a full body cast mold made of myself to create a cadaver in a morgue scene for a feature film.[8] All of these events supported my goal in creating my own movies.

───

Despite its short running time, **THE GLASSHEAD** took two years to complete. "The film was started, I believe in 1995," Matthew told me. "Final filming wasn't completed until 1996. What was interesting was the fact that we lost some of our key college student actors due to the fact that summer vacations came around. When they returned to college in the fall, they looked drastically different. So different that we had to re-write the ending.

"Editing took place throughout 1997 and at times I was convinced it was a lost cause. At this point I was the only one left working on the project.

And in spring of 1998, the final Beta SP Master was dubbed. (it was never released on a film print)…"

That was the short version. As I said, I wanted the *long* version:

───

SRB: So, how *did* **THE GLASSHEAD** actually come together, and who was the friend you mentioned you began the project with?

MS: In 1995, after talking about it for two years, I was ready to start my first feature, **THE GLASSHEAD**. This project turned out to be my formal education. Any mistake that can be made was made. Three months after starting the project, Pat Salois was diagnosed with cancer. He would pass away in the next year. This left the film with a lack of motivation and direction. It took all the commitment that I could muster to continue the project. The film was finally completed in 1998 and was signed with a distributor for worldwide promotion. It was not the same film that I started. It went through a complete metamorphosis. It became

---

8 Matthew later used this cadaver in **THE GLASSHEAD** as a "stand-in" for Josh when Josh's body is thrown on the campfire to burn.

164

what it is and not what I wanted it to be. That was a lesson that every filmmaker should learn.

SRB: Could you tell me more about Pat—and who was Jeff Hurd? He has more than one credit on the film.[9]

MS: Jeff Hurd and Pat Salois were the writers of the story. Their backgrounds were that they enjoyed writing stories and never feared the chance to produce their ideas into something tangible. Actually **THE GLASSHEAD** was written on note paper, probably back in 1983. It sat in a box with other story ideas that Pat and Jeff came up with. In the early 1990s I joined forces with the two of them to produce a couple of local cable comedy shows called *SSHHH*.[10] They were fun and successful and that led to us discussing doing an actual film.

We were all fans of the horror genre so Pat suggested his "Freddy" spoof[11]—**THE GLASSHEAD**. The original story had quite a few gags in it. Mainly the creature traveling in present day with a trunk load of Windex that he would use to shine his fabricated glass dome. We went around with the plot line and agreed that the Civil War angle was the best. It was based upon some truths. There actually was a POW camp here in Elmira, and there was a doctor who was discharged from the military camp due to his questionable operations on the prisoners. I tried to chisel a serious approach to the story but often wonder if a more comical style would not have worked.

I appreciate your consideration for Pat Salois.[12] Knowing that the film continues to spark some interest is probably the best tribute that can be made.

SRB: The opening prologue and credits looks like you worked with a local Civil War/War Between the States reenactment group.

MS: The war footage was shot on Newtown battlefield outside of Elmira NY. This is a civil war reenactment that is performed every year. I knew that we were going for the civil war angle so I showed up in the morning and spent the day wandering around. No one asked any questions as to what I was doing. The group's name escapes me but they are listed on the credits.[13] We knew that we needed the civil war footage in B&W, and we planned on shooting the rest in color.

SRB: I was surprised **THE GLASSHEAD** is in black-and-white, given the video marketplace today—but I love the look of it.

MS: Honestly, it was a matter of funds that we stayed with the black and white film and I am happy that that choice was made.

SRB: There's a peculiar structure to **THE GLASSHEAD**, dominated by the extended flashback to the killer's origins, related by a male narrator as the quartet of college students sit around the campfire.

MS: The narration was *[performed/recorded]* by Tim *[Gary Breinlinger]*. That whole night sequence around the campfire was lost from what it was supposed to be. I think the biggest problem was that we started shooting that sequence after a full 10 hours of shooting during the day. That was my fault. As director I should have sent everyone home and rescheduled the night shoot. Chalk that one up to inexperience. I didn't realize the full impact of how that night went until I started editing. It was towards the end of that year's shooting and by that time the project was left up to me to finish. I'm not making excuses just looking back at it objectively.

Like so many independent horror films—particularly student genre fare—the premiere was a humble event, but met with an enthusiastic debut audience. "In mid 1998, I had a premiere showing of the film in a lecture hall at Elmira College," Matthew recalled, "the same college that the actors

---

[13] The 4th New York Independent Light Artillery.

Another decapitated victim (Leah Hudson) of **THE GLASSHEAD**, her severed head left to adorn a scarecrow...

---

[9] "Conceived and written by Pat Salois and Jeff Hurd," and Hurd is also credited as Production Manager and "assistant camera," along with M. Kelly Smith and Polly Blackwell.

[10] Note that **THE GLASSHEAD**'s opening credits presents itself as "A SSHHH Film."

[11] "Freddy" as in Freddy Krueger, of Wes Craven's classic **A NIGHTMARE ON ELM STREET** (1984, USA), natch! The reference to "Chucky" in K.C.'s campfire story excerpt we hear is perhaps a nod to Tom Holland's **CHILD'S PLAY** (1988, USA).

[12] Pat appears briefly in the film during the lengthy flashback, as one of the torch-carrying "Angry Townsfolk" that Matthew (Chad L. Sweet) rallies to search for the Glasshead.

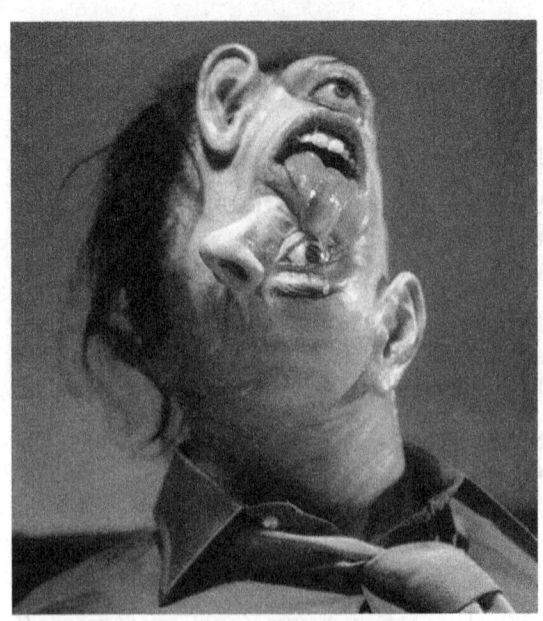

Makeup artist Ed French's fleetingly seen–and, in the film, badly photographed–victim's head for Nick Zedd's **GEEK MAGGOT BINGO** (1983). While working on the same Zedd "Cinema of Transgression" curio, Tyler Smith created a severed head cast from Fangoria founder/editor Robert "Uncle Bob" Martin's features; that head also appeared in (not *as*!) **THE GLASSHEAD** (see pp. 170–171 to see that particular makeup effects prop)

had attended. The turnout was wonderful. It was great to see these people after a year or so hiatus."

In many cases, that would have been that, particularly for a feature running less than an hour that didn't even exist except on videocassette. When I pressed Matthew about **THE GLASSHEAD**'s distribution history (short though it may have been, after only five years), his reply provided the link to Sub Rosa Studios:

"Through a few contacts, I was put in touch with Ron Bonk from Sub Rosa studios, who had seen the film and was interested in distributing it. He wanted to re-shoot the film on video and add scenes that he thought would be interesting. I told him to keep it as it is and see what happens."

Sub Rosa's box art was more eye-catching than that I'd found buried in a milk-crate in northern Vermont. Alas, there was precious little to work with as far as images to promote **THE GLASSHEAD** goes. When I asked Matt if any still photos from the film or the making of the movie existed, he replied, "No, I was wearing a lot of hats during the production but still photographer was not of them." Nor was anyone else.

Though the grotesque profile on Sub Rosa's box art seemed somewhat familiar, it was obviously a frame grab—the pixels were evident, once again lending a crude "home-made" look to the graphic—one taken, it turned out, from footage of a spinning severed head under **THE GLASSHEAD**'s final credits.

But why did it look more eerily recognizable than that? "You might notice that the head on **THE GLASSHEAD** might look a little familiar," Matt informed me. "It was a prop off the film **GEEK MAGGOT BINGO** (1983) and it is a cast from Bob Martin's head (Ex-*Fangoria* editor). A little goes a long way in bad horror movies."

And that's how Bob Martin ended up "cast" in **THE GLASSHEAD**. He didn't know it then, but he *does* know it now—because I *told* him!

When I asked Matt how in the hell they ended up with the severed head prop—which has been historically and incorrectly credited to makeup artist Ed French, created for Nick Zedd's **GEEK MAGGOT BINGO**[14]—Matt replied, "I have a brother, Tyler *[Smith]*, who is an Art Director. He was also the Formaldehyde Man in **GEEK MAGGOT BINGO**. All of the masks and costumes used on that film were created by Tyler. I believe it was a matter of ego stroking with Ed French that he was credited with the makeup. That is something that Tyler would know better."

Point of contention and correction: actually, Tyler Smith *was* correctly credited for his work for **GEEK MAGGOT BINGO** in the first newsstand article ever published about the film—which was written and edited by Bob Martin! About the head, and the confusion over who did what, Bob Martin told me, "...the head *[Bob's severed head]* is the work of Tyler Smith, there's not much to add.

---

14 Nick Zedd's **GEEK MAGGOT BINGO** a.k.a. **GEEK MAGGOT BINGO, OR, THE FREAK FROM SUCKWEASEL MOUNTAIN** (1983, USA) is one of a number of genre and borderline genre films to emerge from the so-called Cinema of Transgression Movement, of which Nick Zedd was a primary mover, shaker, filmmaker and shameless self-promoter. Zedd a.k.a. Nickodemus Zedd a.k.a. Nick Z. and Donna Death were the creators of **GEEK MAGGOT BINGO**, and Matthew's brother Tyler Smith was indeed credited as special makeup effects artist (with Ed French and Tom Lauten), illustrator, and creator of props. Costume design was credited to Zedd and Donna Death. The film was briefly released legally on DVD (Eclectic DVD Distribution, October 2002), and *Monster!* readers may wish to track it down, if only for Zacherle's appearance in the film (*see* http://www.amazon.com/Geek-Maggot-Bingo-Robert-Andrews/dp/B00006JDS3/ref=sr_1_1?ie=UTF8&qid=1432079833&sr=8-1&keywords=Geek+Maggot+Bingo —at the time of this writing, new and used copies are still available, starting at about $21 US). Bob Martin dedicated some print to **GEEK MAGGOT BINGO** in *Fangoria*, including #25 (January 1983), and *Fangoria* did run photos of both Tyler Smith's severed Bob Martin head, and (later, in an article about French's makeup effects work) of Ed French's very cool "skewed features" head.

Matthew's first collaboration with the Polonia Brothers was as producer and cinematographer for John and Mark Polonia's haunted house shocker **THE HOUSE THAT SCREAMED** (2000), not to be confused with the American-International Pictures 1970 retitling of Narciso Ibáñez Serrador's **LA RESIDENCIA** (1969).

Nick Zedd's **GEEK MAGGOT BINGO** (1983) a.k.a. **THE FREAK FROM SUCKWEASEL MOUNTAIN**, narrated by the Cool Ghoul, John Zacherley himself.

There was a *[different]* misshapen head—a well-formed head with features that are placed askew on the head that in the film *[GEEK MAGGOT BINGO]* represented the fate of someone who got all twisted up, seen briefly and shot poorly, but was done much more artfully than Tyler's crudely-cast mold of my head, and this is what Ed French was credited for, not my severed head. Tyler's work on my head was documented in *Fango*, no credit to Ed French."[15]

Again, as Bob clarified: Ed French created the anatomically-jumbled **GEEK MAGGOT BINGO** head. That wasn't the Bob Martin severed head—the Bob Martin head was the creation of Tyler Smith, and Bob Martin let the world know about Tyler's work in Fangoria the very year **GEEK MAGGOT BINGO** was completed and (ahem) "released" (for the most part, it was self-exhibited and distributed by Zedd).

---

15 So said Robert "Uncle Bob" Martin, quoted (with permission) from a Facebook private message conversation I had with Bob on May 19-20, 2015. Actually, it took some time to explain what **THE GLASSHEAD** even *was* to Bob. When I asked if he knew he was "in" it, or at least that a casting of his head was, Bob replied, "No, I didn't know. I still don't. What is **GLASSHEAD**—a zine?" If it isn't now, I may make it one! *DIBS!* As to the point of how poorly-shot Ed French's and Tyler Smith's makeup effects and effects props were in **GEEK MAGGOT BINGO**, Bob also said, "One thing I might add; a friend of mine once asked Nick Zedd why he didn't bring in talent to handle camera, which wasn't a strong point for him. He *[Zedd]* said that it wouldn't be his vision. My friend pointed out Zedd's camera handling shortcomings—Zedd said, 'My vision is impaired.'..."

Two different heads, one of which was only seen in **GEEK MAGGOT BINGO**, the other (by Tyler, of Bob Martin) was seen in both **GEEK MAGGOT BINGO** and in **THE GLASSHEAD**.

So, there we go, cleaning up another bit of monster movie history!

You're welcome.

Sub Rosa's Liverpool, NY headquarters was just shy of 100 miles from Elmira, where **THE GLASSHEAD** was produced and first exhibited. But there's many a mile twixt the lip and the cup, and there's more to **THE GLASSHEAD**'s distribution history than Matthew shared with me.

The fact is, **THE GLASSHEAD** is a "lost film" twice over: "lost" from video distribution (which it barely had), and "lost" in the already-forgotten history of online movie distribution via streaming.

In terms of digital filmmaking history, **THE GLASSHEAD** is not quite up there with Stefan Avalos and Lance Weiler's influential Jersey Devil horror mockumentary **THE LAST BROADCAST** (also 1998, USA), but I was surprised to find that **THE GLASSHEAD** did play a role in a means of distributing and watching movies that millions upon millions now take for granted. Odder still, **THE GLASSHEAD** played its part almost immediately after its college venue debut, even as **THE LAST BROADCAST** was making digital filmmaking and exhibition history (thunder subsequently stolen, respectively but not respectfully, by Daniel Myrick's and Eduardo Sánchez's **THE BLAIR WITCH PROJECT** and George Lucas' **STAR WARS: THE PHANTOM MENACE**—another story, for another time[16]).

According to *Business Wire*, the online magazine, on October 29, 1998:

"LAUREL, Md.--(ENTERTAINMENT WIRE)-- Oct. 29, 1998--The Sync, the global leader in the production and presentation of original Internet video programs, has established another entertainment milestone. The Sync and Salt City Home Video of Syracuse, NY, have teamed up to present the first simultaneous premiere of a feature film in both the webcast and home video channels. The historic presentation is Matthew Smith's 1998 thriller **THE GLASSHEAD**, which is now having its Internet debut at The Sync web site (http://www.thesync.com) while, at the same time, is also being released in the home video market courtesy of Salt City Home Video.

---

[16] See pp. 77–81 in this book.

"'The presentation of **THE GLASSHEAD** opens a new door for home video distributors who wish to preview their releases to a global market,' says Thomas Edwards, founder and president of The Sync. 'Net surfers can see this film on our site and, if they enjoy the production, they can obtain the video version from its distributor, Salt City Home Video. Since **THE GLASSHEAD** is being presented in RealVideo, there is no risk of pirating since the film is viewed in real-time and cannot be downloaded.'

"A stylish black-and-white drama running only 50 minutes, **THE GLASSHEAD** follows four playful college students who travel to their favorite camping grounds for a brief vacation. During the trip, they encounter a dubious duo who join them around a campfire with an eerie local legend concerning a 19th century farmer who was brutally attacked and left for dead. According to the legend, the farmer was brought back to life with a vengeance in a bizarre medical experiment. The campers soon learn that tales of the past have a strange way of resonating today.

"The Internet debut of **THE GLASSHEAD** is the latest breakthrough for The Sync, a major creative force in producing and presenting original high-quality entertainment to an Internet audience. The company is best known for its exclusive made-for-Internet programs including The Jenni Show starring the controversial Jennifer Ringley of JenniCAM fame; the daily comedy program Snack Boy starring funnyman Terry Crummit; and CyberLove, a lively panel discussion of love and relationships which recently celebrated its first anniversary online. ...The Sync made history earlier this year with its presentation of Erica Jordan's **WALLS OF SAND**, the first contemporary feature film webcast to a global Internet audience. ...

"**THE GLASSHEAD** is being released on home video for a suggested retail price of $19.95 from Salt City Home Video, an independent producer and distributor. The company also operates the popular B-Movie Theater web site and the new B-Movie Hall of Fame."[17]

This is pretty phenomenal, and places **THE GLASSHEAD** within a key juncture of digital filmmaking and distribution history. Thus, **THE GLASSHEAD** followed **WALLS OF SAND**[18] as

---

[17] "The Synch Presents the Internet Debut of Matthew Smith's '**THE GLASSHEAD**'; First Film to Have Simultaneous Home Video and Webcast Release", uncredited, *Business Wire*, October 29, 1998, archived online at http://www.thefreelibrary.com/The+Sync+Presents+the+Internet+Debut+of+Matthew+Smith's+%22The...-a053144770

[18] **WALLS OF SAND** was an $80,000, black-and-white 16mm 115-minute feature film by San Francisco State University students Erica Jordan and Shirin Etessam, funded in part by credit cards, and in part by the nonprof-

Were these in fact the first horror feature films ever webcast? According to The Sync's history, they were! Max Schreck as **NOSFERATU** (1922); **THE GLASSHEAD** (Paul Guiles) takes out a victim (Chad L. Sweet) in the 1998 first-original-horror-feature ever webcast; Werner Krauss, Conrad Veidt, and Lil Dagover in **THE CABINET OF DR. CALIGARI** (1920)

The Internet was never the same after the arrival of David Blair's **WAX, OR THE DISCOVERY OF TELEVISION AMONG THE BEES** (1991)

the *second* contemporary feature film to be webcast on the Internet—making **THE GLASSHEAD** *the first new horror movie ever webcast*. Period.[19] The Sync had previously offered short films and two public domain silent horror films, Robert Wiene's, Hans Janowitz's and Carl Mayer's **THE CABINET OF DR. CALIGARI** (*Das Cabinet des Dr. Caligari*, 1920) and F.W. Murnau's and Henrik Galeen's **NOSFERATU** (*Nosferatu, eine Symphonie des Grauens*, 1922, both Germany)

it organization Women Make Movies. It debuted in 1995 at the Independent Feature Film Market in NYC and the Film Arts Festival in San Francisco, and never landed a theatrical distributor; Sub Rosa gave it a fleeting US VHS release in 2000 (never on DVD). It's a drama concerning a female Iranian immigrant (Shirin Etessam) stranded in the US when she breaks up with her boyfriend. She ends up rooming with a single mother (Jan Carty Marsh) whose abusive ex tricks the Iranian woman into playing a part in the pending custody battle over the single mother's child.

19 For those who wish to split hairs, and oh don't we all: David Blair's enigmatic and wonderful cyberpunk oddity **WAX, OR THE DISCOVERY OF TELEVISION AMONG THE BEES** (1991, USA/Germany), the first independent feature edited on a digital non-linear setup, was webcast in 1993—but not as an open webcast. WAX was an invitation-only, one-time only, non-webcast hypertext transmission to only a select group of computer laboratories. See "Cult Film is a First On Internet" by John Markoff, *The New York Times*, May 24, 1993, archived at *http://www.nytimes.com/1993/05/24/business/cult-film-is-a-first-on-internet.html*

as part of their webcast content, but **THE GLASSHEAD** made horror history as the new "kid" on the block. In hindsight, there was method to this madness: the gritty black-and-white textural terror of **THE GLASSHEAD** indeed echoed that of **CALIGARI** and **NOSFERATU**, however crude its methods or meager its means.

The Sync is an already forgotten keystone in this history; founded in Laurel, Maryland in 1997 by Tom Edwards and Carla Cole, The Sync was an independently owned and operated webcasting outfit. By contemporary accounts, The Sync was a pioneer in the webcast of original and exclusive content online; along with the programming cited in the article above, The Sync also showcased indie short film festivals in which surfers/viewers voted on the winning titles in their monthly competitions. Alas, it all went down in flames in 2002, evaporating offline in the dust of the dot-com industry implosion.

It's the Salt City Home Video edition of **THE GLASSHEAD** that Sub Rosa distributed under their own label—meaning **THE GLASSHEAD**, along with its historic role in The Sync's launch, enjoyed three videocassette releases: the homemade "first edition" I found in that northern Vermont video store's back room, the Salt City Home Video edition, and Sub Rosa's pickup of the latter, using color photocopies of the Salt City box art insert, without even bothering to supplant Salt City's logo with their own. Only the new videocassette labels reflected the new distribution arrangement.

By 2003—one year after The Sync went offline—Sub Rosa was barely pushing **THE GLASSHEAD**, save passive promotion in their online catalog only.

Had I never found that "Vermont Independent Film!" discarded box art, I never would have known **THE GLASSHEAD** existed.

This Page and Facing Page: *Fangoria* founder and pioneer editor Robert "Uncle Bob" Martin's severed head (originally designed and constructed by Tyler Smith for Nick Zedd's **GEEK MAGGOT BINGO** [1983]), as it appeared 15 years later (!) in Matthew Smith's **THE GLASSHEAD** (1998). The prop rotated behind the final credits [above] and a pixel-punctuated frame-grab was used for the striking cover art for the second and third official VHS editions of **THE GLASSHEAD** *[facing page]* from Salt City Home Video (1998) and Sub Rosa Studios (2000)

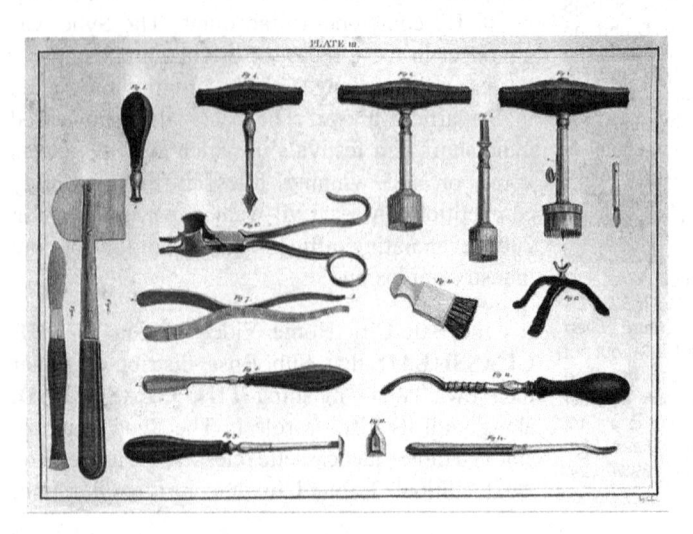

Late 18th-century trepanning instruments. Engraving by J. H. Savigny. Image courtesy of the Wellcome Library, London.

✝HE
GLASSHEAD

THE GLASSHEAD's resident "Dr. Frankenstein", Hellmira prison surgeon Dr. Swan (played by the late Jeff Whitaker, beloved 1990s DJ for WELM, 1410 kHz, serving Elmira-Coring, NY), based in part on real-life 19th Century Army physician William Beaumont and his own experiments

Set in "the Finger Lakes region of New York State" (per Tim's narration), shot in and around Elmira, NY—why, then, did a northern Vermont video store once promote **THE GLASSHEAD** as a "Vermont Independent Film!"?

"The Vermont Tie", as **THE GLASSHEAD** producer/director Matthew S. Smith explained it to me, was via his lead performer in the film. "We cast theater students from a local college to act in the film. The lead role was cast to Paul Guiles," who at the time of our exchange had moved on to Sherman Oaks, California. "Paul is a native of Waterville, Vermont, and he was instrumental in putting that sleeve you found in the state of Vermont."

Matthew urged me to contact Paul directly. "…Paul is a very articulate, dedicated individual with a passion for films that is unrivaled by more successful people in Hollywood. It's because of that passion that we are collaborating on a new film to be shot this summer in Elmira. **IN THE HANDS OF AN ANGRY GOD** is the name of the film and Paul was the screenwriter."

Paul responded to my initial email on February 19, 2003. "Thanks for your interest in **THE GLASSHEAD**, and my other film work," he wrote. "It would be my privilege to discuss these things with you, at great length and filled with circuitous shaggy-dog stories. It is not every day that someone appears out of the mists with inquiries about **THE GLASSHEAD**, and to commemorate the occasion, I can load you up with all sorts of anecdotes, miscellany, and otherwise long-dead lore."

As I noted earlier, almost everyone I had approached to interview in connection with my re-searching Vermont films and filmmakers found the concept itself bemusing—and Paul was no exception. "Without doubt, I should congratulate you for convincing an editor some place that there is enough of a body of work from Vermont filmmakers to fill a whole darn book. Whatever I can do to help pad that out and give it some heft will be a pleasure."

Well, there was no editor—I was editor and publisher of *Green Mountain Cinema*, as it turned out—but I made the most of this opportunity to find out more about **THE GLASSHEAD**, and Paul more than lived up to his word.

It turned out, too, that Paul had worked on Russ Dexter's seminal mockumentary **DADETOWN** (1995, USA), which belongs in the pantheon of truly great feature films in that most curious (and now most pervasive) of genres.[2]

Paul Guiles as Gebadiah, tormented by the transplanted agonies of the prisoners-of-war whose very bones were ground into **THE GLASSHEAD**; the actor was born in Ontario, Canada, and raised in Waterville, Vermont

SRB: When and where were you born?

Paul Guiles: June 30, 1975, in Mississauga, Ontario, Canada. I stayed long enough to form a handful

---

[2] What, you've never heard of **DADETOWN**? Though it's never enjoyed a legal home video release on any format, **DADETOWN** was and remains an essential and really quite brilliant feature film for anyone interested in the now-all-pervasive mockumentary genre. It's a landmark American film, and it's tragic that it's dropped out of circulation and become so overlooked in such a short period of time. See "The Faking of DADETOWN: Hammondsport, NY plays a neat trick on audiences" by "EW Staff" (from *Entertainment Weekly*, uncredited 1996 issue, posted online on January 17, 2015), archived at http://www.ew.com/article/1996/10/11/faking-dadetown

Full cover art for the second VHS release of **THE GLASSHEAD**, from Salt City Home Video; note that the same cover art (or rather, a color photocopy of this cover art) was also used for the subsequent wider VHS release via Sub Rosa Studios. The original TRAKK Productions VHS front cover art appears on p. 157—despite three (!) VHS releases in less than three years, **THE GLASSHEAD** never found an audience

---

of early memories, then my family pulled up stakes and came to the States.

SRB: *What in your upbringing led you into film production?*

PG: Growing up surrounded by mountains in Waterville, my family's tee-vee reception was lousy. We got two local channels, and when the weather was good we pulled in channel 2 from Québec. While I'd like to say watching Francophone television taught me about how to tell a story visually, it was probably my father's frustration that brought in a satellite receiver, thus giving me more exposure to movies and tee-vee than any growing child needs. I am glad to report that even the wonders of two hundred channels dulls after a while, and I was often faced with entertaining myself outside, among the mountains and rivers of my tiny town. My imagination fueled with what I had suckled from the glass teat, and absorbed from stacks of comics, I used to spin elaborate adventure stories for myself in the field behind my parents' house.

In high school, this (and the pretty girl playing Emily in *Our Town*) led me into drama, which ultimately brought me all over Vermont, from running lights for *Hamlet* in a barn in Montgomery to acting in *The Grapes of Wrath* for a statewide tour. Spurred on by this excitement, I went to Elmira College in upstate New York for a degree in Theatre. Near the end of my freshman year, someone posted a bill outside my dormitory, searching out crewmembers for an independent film shooting in Hammondsport. I called the number, and spent the next six weeks as Boom Operator (and bit player) on **DADETOWN**, which showed at Sundance in 1996. From that point, I've been hooked on film—not just as something to while away the hours watching, like when I was a kid, but as a way to tell exciting stories, and a creative process that I find intensely fulfilling.

SRB: *When did you leave Vermont—and, if I may be so forward, why?*

PG: I left twice, the first time right after college to seek my fortunes in the theatre world of New York City. After spending some months as a starving waiter, (though I could always pinch some banana bread after Sunday brunch shifts...) I returned to "Verd-Mont" to put together what little bankroll I could, working nights at IBM and then days at

DADETOWN, a film so rare that this blurry image is the only available one in all the worldwide web!

Morristown Elementary School (by far the better job of the two)—nine months later I left again, this time heading west for Hollywood.

As for the why of it, I reckoned that if I wanted to make movies, I should go where movies are made.[3]

SRB: Prior to **THE GLASSHEAD**, *what were you up to, creatively?*

PG: **THE GLASSHEAD** got its wheels in motion at the start of my sophomore year in college, and was the second film on which I had worked. Up until that time, I had been clawing around in all the college theater shows I could find, writing one-act plays, doing articles for the school paper, and after being bitten by the filmmaking bug with **DADETOWN**, making dreadful home-video movies with my high school buddies back home.

As we got better at shooting our own videos, my friends and I stepped up to Super-VHS and Betacam, making a short subject with a friend for his class at St. Michael's College in Colchester [VT]. We shot a wordless eight-minute action picture and called it **ONSLAUGHT**. This not only got my friend his "A" in the class, thus keeping him eligible to play baseball, but it also was accepted into a festival at VideoSpace in Boston in 1996. They called it the "Festival of Copyright Infringement", and we qualified because we had stolen a multitude of sound effects and music from our favorite action pictures to use in **ONSLAUGHT**. It was quite ticklish to think that attendees at the festival paid seven bucks each, at least in part, to watch something we had made.

SRB: OK, now, that's cool. This is long before the Creative Commons organization or movement existed.[4] I've got to know more—

PG: Writing, shooting, acting in, and editing your own movies is quite an educational process, and as godawful as some of our material was, there were always valuable lessons to be learned. On our first effort, a not-quite-masterpiece on VHS, we went into the editing room at my college only to find that scene after scene from the footage was unusable, mostly because my writing was so overwrought and pompous. (My acting was bad, too.)

We began to cut judiciously. This improved things dramatically, but we found ourselves with one critical scene that was probably the stinkiest of them all. It had to go. But how, then, to have our main characters say their farewell, and do it without my sucky dialogue? My collaborator, the genius Adam Kropelin, and I took silent bits and pieces from several other sucky scenes we had already cut, assembling them in an order that showed our characters entering together, and then one leaving. Underneath the silence we placed stolen music from Duke Ellington's "Single Petal of a Rose". I tell you, that finished as the best damned scene in the whole stinking picture. Artsy as all get out. And it came from a desperate salvage operation, as we scrambled to find any footage even barely usable, to hold our flimsy plot together. If there was a lesson to be had in making that picture (besides

---

[3] I've pulled an exchange from the interview here, since it has nothing to do with **THE GLASSHEAD**, but since this is no doubt the only time or place this article will ever see light of day, I'm compelled to footnote this part of Paul's and my conversation for the sake of completion:
SRB: Where did you move to, and where do you live now [circa February 2003]?

PG: All my worldly possessions packed into my rusty 1989 Ford Escort, I drove westward, taking my time and camping out along the way. Two weeks later, I landed in North Hollywood, surrounded quite neatly by several Used Tire stores. (When you drive an old Escort, your budget is such that used tires will come in handy quite often.) Four years later, I headed to another spot in the famous San Fernando Valley, Sherman Oaks. (Though to be honest, neither Sherman nor his oaks are anywhere to be seen in this vast parking lot...)

[4] The Creative Commons (CC) 501 (c)(3) non-profit organization was founded in 2001; Hal Plotkin's first public announcement of the organization via an article stating their intentions was published in February 2002, followed by CC's rollout of their copyright licenses in December of that year. To find out more, see *http://creativecommons.org/* and *http://en.wikipedia.org/wiki/Creative_Commons*

Adam Kropelin

simply to get more coverage and cutaways), it was that sometimes true art (whatever that is) appears in unlikely places, arising from even the most practical needs.

SRB: Um, Adam Kropelin—so, was Adam the friend you created **ONSLAUGHT** *with?*

PG: Adam, formerly of Cambridge, and these days living in Rochester, NY, was the cinematographer on that mini-masterwork, and he braved some hairy set-ups to get the right shots. Courageous man.

Matthew Baker, a schoolchum of mine from Waterville, was the co-writer and other principal actor in the picture. It was for his class that we designed the project, and on St. Mike's equipment that we shot it. He and his sisters did all the editing.

SRB: You also refer to "our first effort, a not-quite-masterpiece on VHS..." What was the title, and with whom was that video created?

PG: That was called **TRAVELS WINDWARD**, and aside from the handful of us who made the picture, nary a copy has been released into the world. We have our reputations to protect, you know. (All kidding aside, we are proud of the achievement, and all agree there was a wealth of education gleaned from planning, shooting, editing, and mixing that little beauty. It was never ready for worldwide consumption, and that's all right.)[5]

---

[5] Paul notes, on **TRAVELS WINDWARD**, the following: "The principals, aside from yours truly, on that particular flick were: Adam Kropelin, co-writer, co-director, co-editor, co-music-stealer, primary cinematographer, and supporting actor.
Dan Parker, lead actor.
Brian Adams, supporting actor, location manager, equipment support, and co-cinematographer.
Ben Hinkley, supporting actor and sound-man Tom Sheuerman, supporting actor
Amanda Tilton, supporting actress
Tom Olsen, supporting actor
Eric Parker, supporting actor

We used locations all over Waterville, Smuggler's Notch, Stowe, Jeffersonville, Morrisville, Bakersfield—we got around Lamoille County all right." Again, my primary interest at the time was Vermont films and filmmakers; for more, see my book Green Mountain Cinema Vol. 1 (2000, Black Coat Press), available from http://www.blackcoatpress.com/greenmountaincinema1.htm. For the sake of completion, allow me to include the next Q&A exchange, edited from the meat of this interview since it has nothing to do with **THE GLASSHEAD**, but will likely never see print in any form otherwise: In a subsequent March 26, 2003 email exchange, I asked Paul, "Do you know who I might contact at St. Michael's to discuss their film and video studies? (One of the real hurdles of the book has been the lack of any archiving of student films, or even titles of same, at the college level... and as professors come, go, or pass on, any possibility of reconstructing such information is lost.)"

Paul replied, "I wish I could help you. I asked my friend Brian Adams, who graduated from SMC in '99, but he has no contacts in that department, and I have lost track of my other friends who went there. If you need contact information for any of my principal collaborators on past movie projects,

Paul Guiles as the vengeful **GLASSHEAD**: the lack of budget meant that "the Glasshead" appeared sans any makeup—or, indeed, without any evidence of having undergone any cranial surgery whatsoever

---

The time has come, before we continue, to relate what, precisely, **THE GLASSHEAD** was and is—not only because Paul played the lead role, the titular monster, but because this is, after all, a *monster* magazine.

So, we return to the core question, still unanswered:

What in hell was—*is*—**THE GLASSHEAD**?

I was coy about that in Part 1's synopsis of the film itself. It's more than a little arcane, and though its explanation takes only a couple minutes of screen time, it's an odd idea—and it isn't really *visible* onscreen.

Paul never wore any real makeup for his role as the titular menace—aside from what appears in a few shots as a birthmark-like staining of his face, his character survived the Frankensteinian surgery with his curly hair and forehead unscarred and intact, though the buildup remains evocative. That wasn't the original plan, as Paul will soon explain.

About 22 minutes into the movie, Tim's grim narration details the operation and the reason for the title as he details Dr. Swan's bizarre surgical experiments:

---

such as Adam Kropelin, Brian Adams, or Dan Parker, please let me know and I can put you in touch with them."

I subsequently had an email and snail-mail exchange with Dan Parker, who not only provided me answers to my questions, but also gifted me with a VHS dub of **TRAVELS WINDWARD**. Dan wrote on February 11th, 2004, "Movie making wasn't something I took seriously—it was fun to dream big, but when it came time to grind it out and get something done it became clear I didn't have a real passion for it."

"...With the body of Gebadiah, *[Dr. Swan]* could experiment as he pleased—oh, and he pleased. ... Based on a theory he had, he decided to construct an organic plate to replace the side of Gebadiah's skull. He used the ground-up bones of the tortured POWs from the camp—figuring that the bones being human originally, they'd adhere to the skull better than something non-organic. He was able to construct this glass head by substituting finely-ground bone in place of sand..."

At this point, director Matthew Smith gave **THE GLASSHEAD** its Frankenstein money-shot: a vivid close-up of Swan running a bone-saw over Gebadiah's forehead, right below the hair line. Geb's skull is sawed open and the cranial top (noisily) lifted up and back, exposing Geb's damaged brain within.

Tim's narration continues:

"...With the aid of a local glassblower, they were able to blow a glass dome the way a glass craftsman might make a crystal ball."

Cue shot of the glass dome in all its clean perfection, lifted aloft by Dr. Swan.

Barracks #3 of Camp Rathbun a.k.a. Camp Chemung was dubbed "Hellmira" by those incarcerated at this the infamous Union Army prisoner-of-war camp for Confederate military and civilian personnel, in Elmira, New York between July 1864 to July 1865.

"The operation did have a strange side effect on Gebadiah. Unknown to him, the ground-up bones used to create his glass head would only remain reanimated by him devouring the blood of human beings. Without blood, the pain in his skull would become unbearable."

Dr. Swan's voice (Jeff Whitaker) picks up the narrative thread:

"Some believers in the occult think that by using the bones of the tortured and dissected POWs, the angry souls of the dead prisoners have bonded together in the matrix of the subject's skull to cause him unbearable mental and physical torture..."

Thus was born the conceit of the monstrous Glasshead: a fusion of Mary Shelley's *Frankenstein* and what the pop culture had made of Shelley's 1818 novel, with elements of vampires and vampirism—including the linkage of blood-drinking and apparent immortality—*and* of an actual 19th Century surgical experiment conducted by a military surgeon...

———

Prison doctors, doing whatever they wish to with prisoners-of-war (POWs), using the bodies, limbs, flesh and bones of the imprisoned as fodder for scientific experimentation: where did *that* notion arise from? **THE GLASSHEAD** presumes military prison doctors were capable of *anything*, really, and could get away with their atrocities without punishment or penalty.

First of all, as noted by both Matthew and Paul, there really *was* a Union prison camp for Confederate *and* Union prisoners held in Elmira, NY, from July 6, 1864 through July 11, 1865.

"Hellmira," as it came to be known, earned its short, brutish legacy; 12,121 Confederate soldiers were incarcerated there, and within their ranks the Union prisoners were considered fair game. Starvation, food shortages, lack of adequate shelter, disease outbreaks (dysentery, smallpox, pneumonia, typhoid), shoddy to nonexistent medical facilities, and even flooding claimed over 25 percent of the prison population. The area's own newspaper, the *Star Gazette*, marked the Elmira prison camp's 150th anniversary in July of 2014 with a grim article peppered with ample real-life horrors. "When rats became a problem at the prison camp, a medium-sized black dog was used to catch them," reporter Ray Finger wrote.[6]

---

[6] Ray Finger, "20 Facts about Elmira's Civil War prison camp," *Star Gazette*, July 26, 2014, archived at http://www.stargazette.com/story/news/local/2014/07/26/elmira-civil-war-prison-camp/13191117/ ; also see Diane Janowski, *In Their Honor: Soldiers of the Confederacy, the Elmira Prison Camp*

Behold, Dr. Swan unveils the titular **GLASSHEAD**—or all the film ever reveals of it—constructed "by substituting finely-ground bone in place of sand...With the aid of a local glassblower, they were able to blow a glass dome the way a glass craftsman might make a crystal ball"

View of the officers' quarters on what was then Water Street, including the observation platform from which visitors could look down upon the suffering and dying Confederate prisoners of "Hellmira" for ten cents apiece, circa 1864–1865.

"Rat meat was sold to prisoners for 5 cents, but few could afford it. Eventually, two Rebel soldiers from North Carolina were sent to the guardhouse for 30 days after they captured and cooked the dog…" The horrors became a spectator attraction: "…An observation platform with chairs and binoculars was built outside the prison camp across Water Street west of Hoffman Street. Visitors were charged 10 cents apiece to look at the prisoners. Refreshments were sold to spectators while the Confederate soldiers starved." Hellmira more than lived up to its nickname.

But another piece of regional lore arguably fueled the speculative surgical madness of **THE GLASSHEAD**…

On June 6th, 1822, 18-year-old (some accounts say he was 19 years of age) Alexis St. Martin was shot in the stomach at an American Fur Company trading depot when a fellow fur trapper's musket accidentally discharged in the lad's proximity. Army physician William Beaumont, stationed in Fort Mackinac at Mackinac Island, Michigan, tended to the boy's wound, which was presumed terminal. However, Beaumont's surgical care rescued St. Martin, who responded well to a procession of surgical procedures (despite their being performed sans anesthesia or antiseptics) over a period of months. In the end, St. Martin recovered, albeit with a fistula—an unhealed and apparently unhealable opening—through the young man's abdomen into his stomach.

Beaumont hired-on St. Martin, all the while tending to the daily ordeal of keeping St. Martin's fistula clean—and allowing Beaumont to observe and study, for the first time in medical history, the process of digestion at work *in a living subject*. Beaumont was later revered as a "Father of Gastric Physiology." Beaumont's rigorous observational studies and notes revolutionized medical understanding of the gastronomical system, digestion, and related diseases; it also ushered in later 19th and 20th Century experimentation with creating fistulas and "windows" in living subjects (usually animals, including canines and bovines) to further study living anatomies at work.

For his troubles, St. Martin survived long enough to eventually leave the tender ministrations of Dr. Beaumont, eventually returning to fur trapping and becoming a farmer before he died at age 83.[7]

(New York History Review Press, 2010)

[7] For more on the case history of Alexis St. Martin, see *Life and Letters of Dr. William Beaumont*, edited by Jesse S. Myer (1912, C.V. Mosby Company); *Great Scientific Ex-*

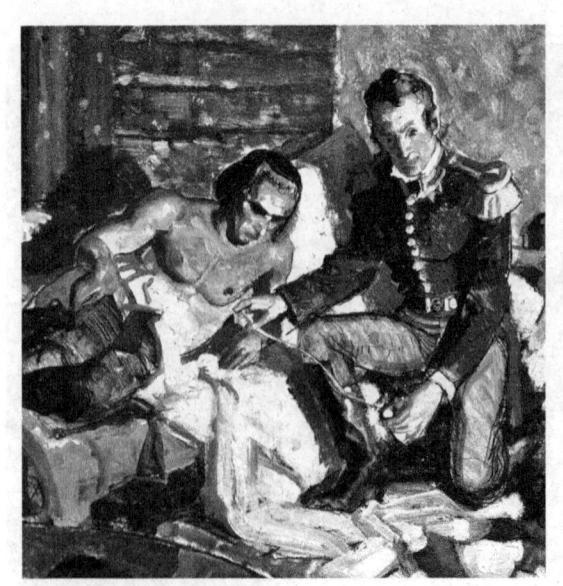

Detail from an oil study for the painting "Beaumont and St. Martin" by "The Dean of Illustrators" Dean Cornwell (March 5, 1892-December 4, 1960); the final painting was completed in 1938, and prints are still available (see http://www.amazon.com/Photo-William-Beaumont-Alexis-Martin/dp/B007WUTXRW)

*How could the creators of **THE GLASSHEAD** have possibly heard this tale?*

After all, Mackinac Island is located in Lake Huron in Michigan; Fort Mackanic was built by the British during the Revolutionary War, and later became the site of two War of 1812 skirmishes.

Dr. Beaumont, a native of Lebanon, Connecticut, was stationed at Fort Mackinac sometime after he rejoined the U.S. Army in 1819—having trained to be a physician eight years earlier apprenticing under Dr. Truman Powell in St. Albans, Vermont, and then serving in the Army as a surgeon's mate from 1812 to 1815. After the war, Beaumont launched a private practice in Upper New York State—Plattsburgh, NY, on the shores of Lake Champlain—where he returned briefly on leave in 1821 to marry Deborah Green Platt before returning to Fort Mackinac.

With his wife and their handyman, Alexis St. Martin, Dr. Beaumont relocated in August of 1825 to Fort Niagara—at the *other* end of upper New York State. It was there that Dr. Beaumont began his serious observations of St. Martin's digestive processes; by September, St. Martin moved away from Beaumont's employ to live and work in Canada. Years later, St. Martin returned to Beaumont's employ—while Beaumont was stationed at Fort Crawford in Prairie de Chien, Wisconsin—and the good doctor resumed his digestive experiments with St. Martin and his remarkable fistula.

Beaumont's *Experiments and Observations on the Gastric Juice, and the Physiology of Digestion* was published in 1833. St. John again departed, returning to Québec, while Beaumont and his wife moved to St. Louis, Missouri, never again to meet, despite Beaumont's constant overtures to St. Martin to return to the doctor's care.

Beaumont took a nasty fall on icy steps in 1853 and died as a result of his injuries. St. Martin died at St-Thomas de Joliette in Québec in 1880. Ever wary of doctors and "medical men," St. Martin's family refused to inter St. Martin's body until decomposition had begun, preventing the promised/threatened autopsy, much to the chagrin of many. Thus, anatomists and bodysnatchers alike were foiled, and Alexis was at last at peace when he was laid to rest forever at Saint Thomas Cemetery, Joliette, Québec.

It turns out a *lot* of folks in upper New York State and nearby Québec and northern Vermont grew up knowing about Dr. Beaumont's unusual relationship and experiments with St. Martin. In fact, *I'd* heard of it while growing up in northern Vermont, and it was my Vermont folklorist friend Joseph A. Citro[8] who reminded me of the relevance of Dr. Beaumont and Alexis St. Martin's story to the matter at hand, here.

It might be considered the stuff of urban legends, were it not so well-documented—and *so true*.

No wonder "Hellmira" and the extraordinary tale of Dr. Beaumont and his experiments with a living

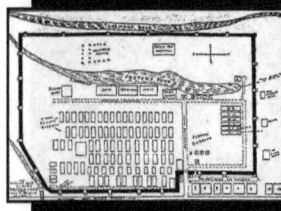

30 Acres of Hell... surrounded by a twelve-foot wall; a hand-drawn map of "Hellmira," circa 1864.

---

periments by Horace Romano (aka Rom) Harré (1981, Phaidon/Oxford, pp. 39-47); also see "Holey Cow," *Radiolab*, April 2nd, 2012, archived at http://www.radiolab.org/story/197149-holey-cow/ , "Inquisitive Doctor, Reluctant Patient: The Story of Alexis St. Martin's Gastric Fistula & America's First Physiologist, Dr. William Beaumont," by Jay B. Dean, archived at http://www.the-aps.org/fm/125th-aps-anniversary/beaumont.pdf , and "Man With Hole in Stomach Revolutionized Science" by Tia Ghose, *Live Science*, April 24, 2013, archived at http://www.livescience.com/28996-hole-in-stomach-revealed-digestion.html

[8] My pal Joe Citro knows his stuff, having written the Vermont-based horror novels *Shadow Child* (1987), *Guardian Angels* (1988), *The Gore* a.k.a. *The Unseen* (1990), *Lake Monsters* a.k.a. *Dark Twilight* (1991), and *Deus-X* (1994), as well as multiple short stories (collected in *Not Yet Dead* [2012]) and his collections of New England "stories that might not be fiction," starting with *Green Mountain Ghosts, Ghouls and Unsolved Mysteries* (1994) to the present. I've illustrated three of Joe's books: the original hardcover limited edition of *Deus-X* (1994), and the mass-market *The Vermont Ghost Guide* (2000) and *The Vermont Monster Guide* (2009), and we did the illustrated map "Vermont's Haunts" together. My thanks for his pointing this associative link out to me, which indeed prompted on my part a much deeper reading of **THE GLASSHEAD**'s roots in its geographic history.

Finger Lakes Frankenstein: Dr. Swan (Jeff Whitaker) tends to his bandage-swathed creation, **THE GLASSHEAD** (Paul Guiles)

"Camp of Rebel Prisoners at Elmira, New York", from *Harper's Weekly* (April 15th, 1865, p.236).

human "host" were linked, festered, and took root as they did in the imaginations of **THE GLASSHEAD** screenwriters Pat Salois and Jeff Hurd.

As for the grinding of bone to make glass—well, that's based in fact, also.[9]

"Bone China" was long the treasured material of which the finest tea cups were made, invented in the late 18th Century in Stoke-on-Trent in Staffordshire, England, by a potter named Josiah Spode. The high demand for imported porcelain from China prompted Spode's innovation, matching the non-porous durability and treasured translucence of imported Chinese porcelain ware (made from a clay mixture kiln-fired at extreme temperatures to render it glass-like). Spode's formula mixed reduced oxen bone (burned and ground to the finest powder) with clay. Bone China "contains up to 50 percent animal ash" and the bone component lend it "strength and excellent whiteness."[10]

As to Dr. Swan's occult interpretations of Gebadiah's unnatural state following his resurrection, and the means by which the "glasshead" surgical transformation lent apparent immortality to Geb—well, that is either invention or purely speculative. It's a loopy, atavistic premise ripe with vintage 1920s pulp *Weird Tales* craziness, the stuff of fairy tales and urban legends.

Of course any glass made with the ground-up bones of tortured and butchered prisoners-of-war would be haunted, possessed, and instill immortality and damnation! *Of course!*

Back to Dr. Swan, that prison surgical laboratory, the damned glass, and the resurrected Gebadiah:

Dr. Swan is shown, in this extended flashback, feeding the bandaged Geb bottled blood from the camp POWs, which only prompts the Glasshead/Geb to writhe in agony, experiencing the agonies of those whose blood he's supped.

No surprise, then, when Geb/the Glasshead breaks his bonds and tears into the not-so-good doctor, killing him. It is surprising, though, when we see (in shadow and silhouette only) the Glasshead lift Swan's infant son Mark from his crib and bite into the baby's throat before holding the exsanguinated body aloft (by its head) before throwing its body to the floor.

So, remember this: Swan's twin sons. *Mark* is killed. *Matthew* survives…

---

[9] **THE GLASSHEAD** composer Daniel Zongrone pointed out in a May 26th, 2015 email to the author, "Corning, NY—'glass capital of the world'—is near the filming locations." See how all this fits together?

[10] According to Shona Patel, "Making no bones about bone china," at *Tea Buddy: Shona Patel's thoughts on Tea, Writing & Life*, April 20, 2012, archived at *https://teabuddy.wordpress.com/2012/04/20/making-no-bones-about-bone-china/*

We're then shown Geb's return to his own abode (a cabin that never in the movie looks like anything but a 1970s cabin in design and construction) to find Sarah's smoldering body and lift her severed head as narrator Tim describes the wretched Glasshead "cradling her decomposed head to his bosom…"

The Glasshead's murder of Willie and Dick is described by Tim—we never see the men, drunk in their beds, as Geb reportedly tied them and torched their rooms—but we do see a ramshackle two-story house in the woods (looking more like a 19th Century farmhouse than did Geb's and Sarah's dwelling) from a variety of angles, and we do watch as smoke spreads from the upper floor windows, and flames lick and spread, gradually consuming the entire structure. Like the burning of Babs Johnson (Divine/Harris Glenn Milstead)'s trailer in John Waters' **PINK FLAMINGOS** (1972, USA), this, too, was/is a real "money shot" in such a low-budget movie.

We then do see the Glasshead's murder of Price—gripping him by his throat and lifting him off the ground, with the then-already-cliché shot of Price's feet being lifted off the ground—and the crushing of Price's skull with a rock, with Price's point-of-view shot of Geb standing over his victim. This is followed by the brief arc of Dr. Swan's surviving son Matthew in his adult year (Chad L. Sweet), Matthew's rousing a torch-wielding band of villagers against the Glasshead, and Matthew Swan's eventual death-by-pitchfork in a barn.

One image from this sequence—40 minutes into the film, of young Swan cringing from the pitchfork tines in the foreground—is the murky photocopied frame-grab I first saw on that damned empty VHS box I found in northern Vermont.

That, as it turned out, was most likely the first-ever released-to-the-public TRAKK Productions VHS edition of **THE GLASSHEAD**, no doubt *sold to the video store I found it in by the Glasshead himself*, Paul Guiles!

But—**THE GLASSHEAD**? He—Paul—*never* looked like a "glasshead" in the film.

Alas, **THE GLASSHEAD** sported no glass dome with partially-exposed brain sloshing within—that, after all, was beyond the filmmaker's means. Such an elaborate makeup effect had already informed Monte Hellman/Carlos Laszlo's bizarre direct-to-video sequel **SILENT NIGHT, DEADLY NIGHT III: BETTER WATCH OUT!** (1989, USA)—in which Santa Claus Killer Richard "Ricky" Caldwell (Bill Moseley) awakened from a six-year coma with a homicidal rage burning and his brain throbbing within a transparent dome atop his head, cutting-edge surgery repairing his damaged skull. Moseley seemingly specialized in such roles at the time, having made an indelible mark as

THE GLASSHEAD (Paul Guiles) emerges from the nursery after feeding on the blood of Swan's infant son

the similarly-chromed-domed "Chop Top" in Tobe Hooper's and my (late) pal L.M. Kit Carson's **THE TEXAS CHAINSAW MASSACRE 2** (1986, USA), but Paul Guiles had no such legacy, nor did Matthew Smith have access to makeup effects even *remotely* as elaborate as those provided by Nina Kraft (makeup creator for **SNDN3**) or Tom Savini (**TCSM2**).

As already detailed, **THE GLASSHEAD** had far, far humbler origins.

It's time, then, to turn this over to the Glasshead himself, and let *him* tell the story. Here, then, is the truth about **THE GLASSHEAD**—the makeup that was and wasn't, the money shots, the spectacular footage of the torched house, those who lived and died during the making of the movie, and oh so much more. Though we've now heard producer/director Matthew Smith's memories about the film, as Matt suggested they might be, Paul's were even richer and more detailed.

SRB: Paul, what led you to **THE GLASSHEAD** *project?*

PG: Matthew Smith, director of **THE GLASSHEAD**, and his co-conspirators had made the de-

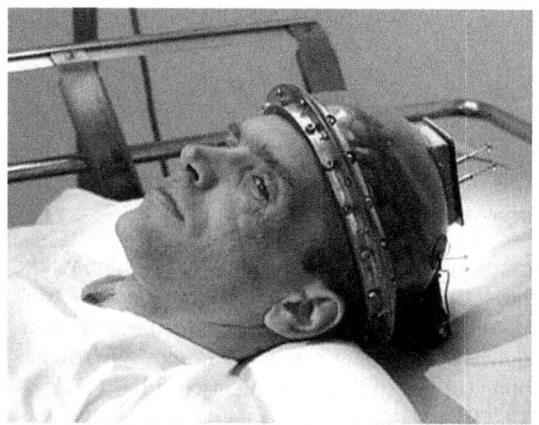

SILENT NIGHT, DEADLY NIGHT III: BETTER WATCH OUT! (1989, USA): Santa Claus Killer Richard "Ricky" Caldwell (Bill Moseley) awakened from a coma as the first "Glasshead" (makeup FX by Nina Kraft)

cision that their casting needs might be well served by utilizing students from the local college. This school has a very small Theater Department, with only three full-time professors and a few dozen students in all. So word travels fast. A bill was posted outside the Theater House, and of course an independent horror movie searching for actors was an exciting prospect to all of us. Come that Saturday morning in late September, we dragged ourselves

Price (Dan Hoskins) pays the ultimate price for his transgressions once Gebadiah (Paul Guiles) gets his hands on his tormentor; these "lifting victim by the throat" sequences (complete with shot of Price's feet lifted from the forest floor) were a staple of post-**STAR WARS** (1977) American movies for decades

181

out of bed and showed up for the audition in whatever force we could muster.

SRB: What is Jeff Hurd's background?

PG: While, as you now know, it was Pat Salois who died of cancer during post-production, I can offer you a bit on both Jeff and him.

Pat, for his part, was good-humored throughout the shoot, and a very companionable fellow. He took some measure of scientific interest in on-set tasks, such as determining which would show up better as blood (of which there was plenty in **THE GLASSHEAD**) on the black-and-white film stock—colored corn syrup or chocolate sauce. He settled on the latter, much to my delight, as it was less sticky and much better-tasting. And Pat had an eye for detail, even on little things, like how to manage the dressing for my character's head-wound. Pat was always fun to see on-set, and even discussed his cancer with an upbeat, accepting tone. I enjoyed getting to know him.

Jeff described himself as the set's official Beer Wrangler. He was never far from camera, wearing his Rumpel Minze ballcap and a gaudy Hawaiian shirt, making jokes to keep crew spirits high.

(Incidentally, Pat's passage was not the only permanent change which came about during the filmmaking process. The actor who played the mad scientist, a local radio disk jockey *[Jeff Whitaker]*, also died before we premiered in 1998.[11] The stately monastery used for establishing shots of the mad scientist's lab was demolished, and a house belonging to Matt's parents was burned to the ground,

as you watched in all its black-and-white glory.[12] Working on this film taught me something about the impermanent nature of things, and how fortunate we were to capture even a bit of these people and places, while they were here.)

SRB: How did Jeff Hurd and Pat Salois' story concept mature into a script?

PG: Matt Smith would be too humble to say so, but in my opinion, it was his input that provided any thematic and conceptual maturity to the final script. There were numerous changes from that first draft we read in the Theater House on the Saturday morning of the audition, and they were mostly, if not all, the product of Matt's filmmaking sensibility. While he has spoken of the original script's humorous flavor, and lamented at the loss of that early vision as the production wore on, I always thought the more dramatic elements added later were the film's primary interest.

SRB: What material do you recall that was scripted, but could not be shot (or make the final cut)?

PG: This provides an excellent illustration for the preceding question. Even Matt's later draft had a very different ending from what we shot. In the script, the Glasshead monster has his glass-domed skull smashed by a large rock from the protagonist, Nikki (who was described in the script as an "Emilio Estevez-type"). As Nikki walks away from the now-dead-again Glasshead, he lights up a joint and wisecracks, "People who live in glass heads shouldn't get stoned." I did not look forward to shooting this ending, because I didn't know if I could restrain myself off-camera from groaning at that line.

But before we could shoot the finale ultimo as written, the production's steam ran out, and we broke for summer vacation. Both the actor playing Nikki and I came back with substantially altered haircuts. Matt found himself in a trap—it was now the blaze of autumn, and not the green of springtime, so location shooting wouldn't match, and both of his leads looked very different. Thus, he came up with the "Time Passes" ending as it was shot that autumn, with Nikki on the run from the cops, and tracking the Glasshead to wreak his vengeance. It features a darkly ambiguous final shot, showing the monster following Nikki into a parking garage, then panning up to a cityscape as this story is over but life goes on for the city, and…fade out. I thought this ending was leaps and bounds ahead of the earlier one, in execution and concept. It legitimized much of what had gone before, and

---

11 Jeff Whitaker broadcast on WELM, on 1410 kHz (the station began broadcasting in 1947, the third radio station of the Elmira-Coring, NY market). In fact, Jeff and Pat Salois are cited on the Wikipedia entry for the station, which sheds further light on Salois' extraordinary character, his regional celebrity, and utterly pitch-black sense of humor, and will be of interest to *Monster!* and **THE GLASSHEAD** devotees: "Jeff Whitaker and Pat Salois were popular personalities on the station, voicing several original characters on Salois' evening show in the early 1980s and later hosting the morning drive and afternoon drive shows. One of their characters—the Lake Welmer Swamp Monster—developed a following throughout the community. The mythic creature allegedly lived in 'Lake Welmer,' their nickname (which has stuck) for a swampy area between Lake Street and Grand Central Avenue near the station's three towers. They referred to the creature often in bits, and sometimes produced 'news reports' in which an intrepid reporter would try to interview the monster. The responses typically were clips of lyrics from popular songs (clearly influenced by [Bill] Buchanan and [Dickie] Goodman's "Flying Saucer" [1956 novelty hit]). Whitaker and Salois later hosted the morning show until late 1995, when they were released and the station format was changed to sports. Both were in poor health at the time—about which they often joked on the air—and died within a few years. At Whitaker's viewing, Salois came in—oxygen tank in tow—and said, 'I win,' in reference to a bet over who would die first." (quoted from http://en.wikipedia.org/wiki/WELM)

12 **THE GLASSHEAD** composer Daniel Zongrone also noted in a May 26th, 2015 email to the author, "I never did learn how Matthew got that house fire on film without the fire department interfering!!"

The Other 'Glasshead': VHS cover and video packaging spine art for Monte Hellman's **SILENT NIGHT DEADLY NIGHT III: YOU BETTER WATCH OUT!** from IVE/International Video Entertainment, Inc. (1989)

THE GLASSHEAD director Matthew Smith worked on the set of the Faith No More music video "A Small Victory" (1992), and a body-cast of Smith used as a prop in the video—perhaps in this very shot?—later appeared in **THE GLASSHEAD**. The WW1-set video was directed by future horror feature film director Marcus Nispel

used some very interesting camera effects in Nikki's shabby hotel room.

The new ending had some real class, and while Matt may have had to dream it up on the fly, it was one of the film's most interesting, and technically-polished parts.

Other bits which were altered in the final cut included the scene in which the largely-unseen Glasshead monster kills a dog and then its owner *[Leah Hudson]*, stringing her up like a scarecrow. Matt shot this footage without me, and I thought it came out very nicely. Originally, there had been a sequence of Glasshead killings, one of which involved breaking a dog's neck at the end of a leash. When I read the script on that one, I was excited to see how we would accomplish something as tricky as killing a dog onscreen, without of course actually harming the animal. Though that scene never came to fruition, the material he did shoot builds tension neatly, and was a far sight more feasible for Matt's effects budget.

Speaking of effects, one which goes totally obscured in the underexposed campfire sequence was the most memorable of the whole production. The idea was to show that Tim was a zombie, with the unspoken implication that the Glasshead was feeding off him over the course of several years. The "reveal" for this was Tim being pushed backwards off a log, and as he hits the ground, his guts fall out and terrify the campers. To shoot that bit, Matt had his friend Jeb—who did the narration throughout the story—fall off the log in one shot. Then he outfitted Jeb with a garbage bag covering his chest, and on top of that we placed a genuine, sure-enough cow digestive tract, which was kept nearby in a ten-gallon bucket. Matt and the rest of the crew were very particular in the way they handled the cow-guts, always referring to this mess as The Product, and saying things like, "It's time for the Product shot," "Somebody get the Product," and, "The Product, flying in!" It was terribly funny, to see how everyone dissociated himself from the true nature of our special effect. But no matter how clinical the description, nobody could dissoci-

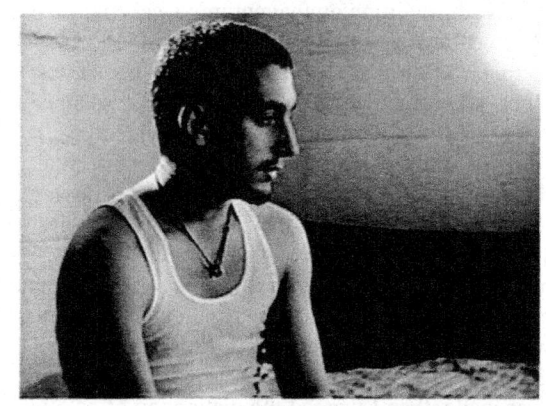

Nominal hero Nikki (Shawn Rouillard) in the coda to **THE GLASSHEAD**: When college actor Rouillard returned from summer break with a haircut, director Matthew Smith was forced to rethink the originally-scripted finale into one star Paul Guiles considered "leaps and bounds ahead of the earlier one, in execution and concept"

183

Bruce Dern (at right, with Berry Kroeger), *not* eating a baby as wealthy mad scientist Dr. Roger Girard in **THE INCREDIBLE 2 HEADED TRANSPLANT** (1971)

ate himself from the hideous reeking odor of The Product. The memory lives in my nostrils still, nine years later.

SRB: *Paul, you landed the lead role. I mean, you are* the Glasshead! *How did that happen?*

PG: At the audition on that autumn weekend, each of the college actors was brought into the Department Head's office, where Matt and his closest allies asked him or her a few questions, snapped some Polaroids, and put everyone on videotape. It was my first film audition, and to be honest, in all the hundreds of auditions I have done since moving to Hollywood, **THE GLASSHEAD** was as professionally managed as any of them. For my part, I had looked over an early draft of the script, and its cheesiness was evident from page one. I decided, without telling any of my friends, that if I was going to be involved in possibly the cheesiest movie ever made, then I wanted the distinction of having the cheesiest role of them all, which was obviously the monster. Inside the audition room, I made special mention to Matt and the others that I was interested in playing the lead. And to be honest, I think that is the reason I got it. Because I asked, and nobody else did.

SRB: *Any other memories of the shoot? You've shared a great deal already, but I wonder—you've talked about some of the ordeals, but was it fun?*

PG: Shooting the film was tremendous fun, especially given all the hideous and strange things my character got to do, like eating a baby and beheading a girl with the trunk of a car. (In fact, I have actually been recognized in Los Angeles by someone who saw parts of **THE GLASSHEAD** on cable tee-vee. A stranger turned and asked me, "Are you the guy I saw on public access at midnight, eating a baby?" I kid you not.)

SRB: *Bruce Dern used to claim in interviews that he'd "eaten a baby" in* **THE INCREDIBLE 2 HEADED TRANSPLANT** *(1971, USA), though he hadn't, and was banking on the ignorance of the interviewer.[13] But you DID!*

---

13 Well, we don't actually *see* Guiles/the Glasshead *eat* the baby: seen only as shadows on the wall, we see Geb pick up a wriggling infant (clearly a doll), bend down to "bite" it, make it writhe, hold it aloft by its head, and then viciously throw it to the floor; he then stumbles out of the shadows, his head still bandaged, with blood on his mouth and chest. But as to Bruce Dern's claim: To the best of my knowledge (and by my experience, reading interviews with Dern at the time he made the claim), Dern originally made this outrageous, unfounded, but always entertaining and head-turning claim during the promotion of Mark

184

PG: The production abounded with interesting on-set moments, such as when the three hillbillies raped and murdered my character's wife. The three men got so involved in the intimidation, and were so threatening and brutal to this tiny young woman playing the role, that I thought she would certainly be shaken by the experience. I went over to her after camera stopped rolling to ask how she was, and she smiled, saying she was having fun. In that scene, Andrew Moulton played one of the hillbilly rapists with such improvisational flair that he grabbed some deer antlers off a nearby dresser and began to menace Marlene with them on the bed. Andrew's inventiveness always impressed me.

It was an exciting time. I brought my college reading assignments to Matt's house for the shooting of the first sequence. In between doing takes as a murderous movie-monster, I was having my mind blown by every page of Aldous Huxley's *Brave New World*. What a way to spend a Saturday afternoon!

And it was great fun to see how the picture was fitting together. Matt invited us up to his house to watch some rough-cut footage, and for the first time, I was able to see how my roommate Chad's scenes had come out.

Boy, that guy acted the guts out of his torch-wielding mob incitement scene! And to see the way Matt assembled the shots from our day in a barn in Golden Glow, NY—that was my favorite sequence, visually, as the Glasshead overpowers the doctor's son and murders him. Matt used framing and slow-motion very effectively (especially if you ignore Chad's too-modern sneakers in the 19th-century setting). That particular killing was done with a pitchfork, and the fatal stabbing transitioned brilliantly to a camper plunging a plastic fork into his baked beans. Bits like that one showed real technical polish, and some true storytelling skill. Rough as the finished product is, and compromised as the original vision may have become due to a variety of human factors, nevertheless I look at **THE GLASSHEAD** as one of the best experiences of my college years. I am proud of my association with that film, and especially with director Matt Smith, whose commitment to filmmaking has inspired me throughout my own difficult times in Hollywood. Regarding one of Matt's comments to you in an earlier message, he mentioned the "full body cast mold" which he made of himself for another feature *[in fact the Faith No More music video for "A Small Victory," 1992]*. He wasn't kidding—the body cast was full, indeed—anatomically correct, that is. And we burned it up real good during **THE GLASSHEAD**—that's the body I toss on the fire and stomp into the coals near the end.

*SRB: Paul, my deepest thanks for sharing your **GLASSHEAD** memories with me.*

———

There is one more aspect of **THE GLASSHEAD** that bears mention and makes it unique: its musical soundtrack, its score, credited to former Earthstar member and composer Daniel Zongrone. This soundtrack broke Zongrone's decade-long retirement from public performance and composition.

This doesn't place **THE GLASSHEAD** in the company of, say, low-budget wonders like Timothy Carey's **THE WORLD'S GREATEST SINNER** (1962, USA) and the western **RUN HOME SLOW** (1965, USA, D: Ted Brenner)—an inversion of Zongrone's career orientation to **THE GLASSHEAD**, as both of those 1960s films were scored by Frank Zappa in his formative years, *before* forming the Mothers of Invention in 1965—but it does add further to the musky mystique of this most mysterious of regional monster movies.

Earthstar had enjoyed its heyday in the late 1970s and early 1980s. While I'd tuned in to some of the German "Kosmische Musik" electronic scene in the early 1980s, I'd completely missed Earthstar. By 1988, Zongrone had abandoned that scene to live his life away from the hubbub and start a family.

Backing up, we once again find that Upper New York State provided the geographic connective tissues between Zongrone and **THE GLASSHEAD**—specifically, Utica, NY in the case of Earthstar. Craig Wuest was founder and leader of Earthstar; according to the biography of Zongrone at the online resource Discogs:

"Zongrone grew up in Utica, New York, where he met Dennis Rea and Norm Peach during the early '70s. In 1977 all three musicians joined together with Craig Wuest and other area musicians to form Earthstar, with Zongrone serving as percussionist. They were signed by Nashville-based Moontower records which released their debut album, Salter-

---

Rydell's John Wayne western **THE COWBOYS** (1972, USA), wherein Dern played the lead villain who shot John Wayne to death onscreen—in the back. I recall laughing when he made the claim in an interview in the Canadian magazine *Take One* and in an article in the Sunday *The New York Times* Entertainment section at this time. I'd of course seen **THE INCREDIBLE 2 HEADED TRANSPLANT**, and knew no such thing happened in the movie! I couldn't even figure out where such a scene *might have ever existed*, had it been cut. It's a claim still being made as Dern promoted his starring role in 2013 in Alexander Payne and Bob Nelson's **NEBRASKA**: See *NJ.com*, "Finally, for indie vet Bruce Dern, a big-studio leading role," by Stephen Whitty (November 10, 2013, archived at http://www.nj.com/entertainment/movies/index.ssf/2013/11/bruce_dern_a_big-studio_leading_role.html): Dern on **THE INCREDIBLE 2 HEADED TRANSPLANT**: "I ate a baby in that movie," he said in wonderment years later. "Ate a baby!" Can't you just *hear* Dern saying that? Clearly, Dern loves the story and claim, bogus though it's been for almost half-a-century!

The online *New Gibraltar Encyclopedia of Progressive Rock* describes Earthstar's second album—which Zongrone wasn't part of, apparently—and their third, *Atomkraft? Nein, Danke!* by crediting leader "…[Craig] Wuest's vision" as their fuel: "…his desire apparently is to create music that doesn't necessarily suggest a particular instrument, rather creates a new texture. Therefore, though there are credits for flute, guitar, bass, violin, viola, French horn, sitar and vocals, it's pretty hard to distinguish any of these…" However, according to band member Dennis Rea, the bulk of the Earthstar material was recorded in Utica, NY.[15]

I'll leave it to others to divine the associative links between Zongrone's Earthstar collaborative work with his solo composition of **THE GLASSHEAD** score. On its own terms, Zongrone's score for **THE GLASSHEAD** was and remains striking. The only standard-bearer is heard over the opening credits, which flow over a traditional military drum theme attuned to the War Between the States/Civil War imagery. In fact, Matthew Smith composed this portion of the score; Matthew is credited onscreen with composing the "**GLASSHEAD** theme."[16]

As fortune would have it, we needn't speculate on such matters. Thanks to the help of Peter Comley and Earthstar's own Dennis Rea, we were able to interview Daniel about his scoring of **THE GLASSHEAD** (note that all ellipses are Daniel's):[17]

SRB: *Daniel, what led you into and onto the musical path, and how did you eventually come to meet your Earthstar compadres?*

Daniel Zongrone: My mother was a singer (think Ella *[Fitzgerald]*). She recorded a few tunes on 78's, locally circa 1945. I was raised around her singing—always!! My dad was a jazz bebop trumpet player, mostly big band stuff. He played piano nightly as well.

Earthstar was written in the stars! We were all raised in upstate New York (Utica) and collaborated all through high school and beyond. My brother married Earthstar founder Craig Wuest's sister!

Top: Daniel Zongrone, **THE GLASSHEAD**'s soundtrack composer. **Bottom:** Earthstar's third album, *Atomkraft? Nein, Danke!* ([1981] translation: "Nuclear power? No, thanks!"—a common anti-nuke slogan in Germany)

Sleeve art for the Earthstar LP *French Skyline* (1979, Sky Records [SKY 031]).

barty Tales, *the following year. Earthstar was then encouraged by electronic music artist, composer, and producer Klaus Schulze to relocate to Germany where they were signed by Sky Records. Zongrone made the move in time to join the recording sessions for the band's third album,* Atomkraft? Nein, Danke! *(1981), playing piano and vibraphone.*

"After Earthstar dissolved Zongrone again collaborated with Dennis Rea, composing music for an exhibition of painter and former Earthstar violinist Daryl Trivieri's work at the Semaphore East Gallery in New York City in 1985. The following year Zongrone received a "Meet the Composer" grant for NYC dance composition. He also recorded his solo album Absolute Zero *in 1987."*[14]

---

14 http://www.discogs.com/artist/1047661-Dan-Zongrone

15 Uncredited entry, followed by clarifications by Dennis Rea ("a former member of Earthstar") detailing the Utica NY sessions, "Earthstar," updated 9/5/07, at http://www.gepr.net/ea.html

16 In a May 26th, 2015 addendum email after we'd completed the interview, Daniel Zongrone confirmed, "Yes the marching drums and orchestral string section used at *[the]* opening was arranged by Matthew. Elmira NY area has a civil war battle reenactment annually."

17 Interview with Daniel Zongrone, conducted via email/iPhone on Monday, May 25th, 2015; published with permission.

SRB: *What, in your assessment, was your primary contribution to Earthstar, and any fondest memories to share about that?*

DZ: I filled the rhythm and percussive element. Also composed and arranged a few tunes. I played drums, vibes, keyboards and electronics.

It was my second tour of Europe, but with Earthstar we all lived together in the countryside. It was a wonderful time because we began working with Tangerine Dream founding member Klaus Schulze who was on the cutting edge of music technology.

We were also meeting celebrities including Arthur Brown & Michael Shrieve. We ended sharing the same record company with Brian Eno. It was a great learning experience.

We had access to state of the art audio & visual equipment. We all shared some really magical times together living in the countryside of Germany. When I first arrived I lived alone for the first few weeks because the house was empty. I did quite a few electronic experiments on my own.

SRB: *From what I've read, you stepped away from Earthstar at a certain point in the 1980s. What prompted this creative and life change for you (as best I can find, you moved back to upper New York State to start a family)?*

DZ: The '80s were quite exciting.

Earthstar returned from Europe and staged a benefit concert at a turn of the century landmark theater in Utica (Stanley Theater), a full production of the music including string section. We all relocated, separately, to the East Village of NYC. We each began to establish ourselves as solo artists. I continued to collaborate with Dennis Rea—my brother from another mother....

I fell in love with a beautiful Puerto Rican woman and decided to start a family. I continued to commute to NYC and received a grant from NEA to compose a modern dance performance. I continued to work on my own while raising four wonderful children.

Upon relocating to Elmira NY, I met film artist Matthew Smith and he incorporated my soundtrack music into **THE GLASSHEAD**.

SRB: *How did he coax you into working on* **THE GLASSHEAD**?

DZ: Matthew put a short advertisement in the local newspaper…I answered the ad…with a sample of my soundtrack…he liked it…simple as that

SRB: *Was this your first feature film soundtrack score?*

DZ: The soundtrack work I had completed in the past were produced for live theater and galleries

Photograph of the rare original poster for the April 25th, 1998 world premiere of **THE GLASSHEAD** at Elmira College, NY; compliments of Daniel Zongrone

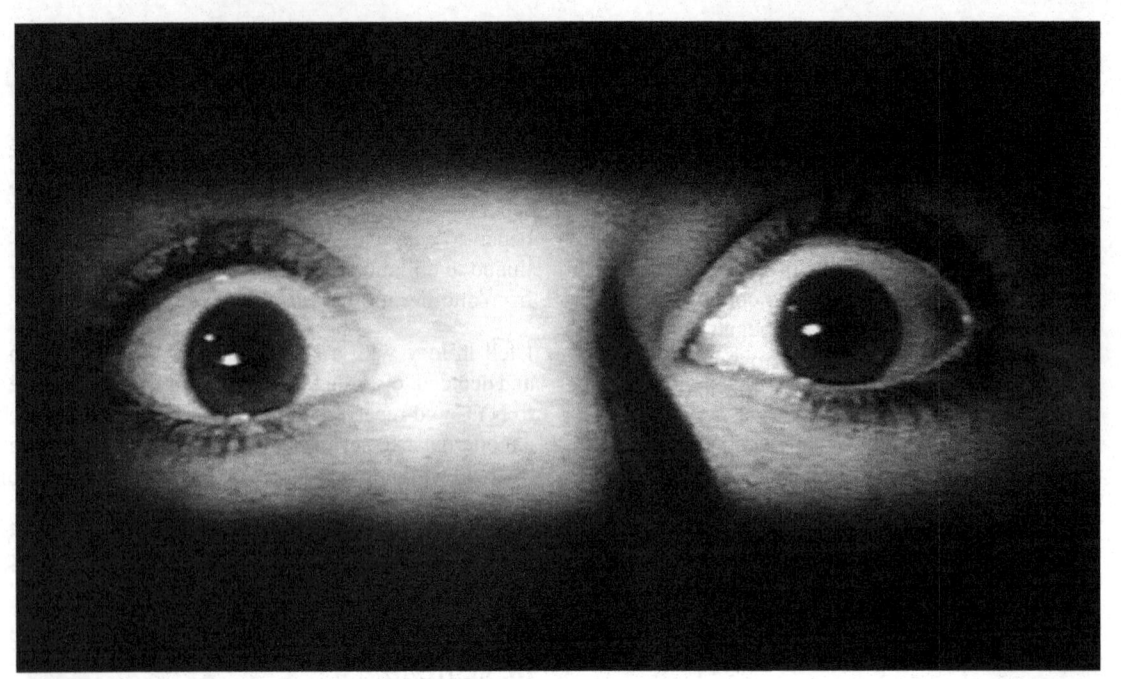

The Nanny (Andrea Ajemian) of Dr. Swan's twins reacts in horror to what she sees after **THE GLASSHEAD** has "dined" in the nursery...

and short film experiments. **THE GLASSHEAD** was the first film production I worked on that was completed in a professional environment.

SRB: How did you approach work on the film?

DZ: I presented Matthew my soundtrack and he chose certain parts along with other soundtrack audio he compiled. I did not choose where to place the audio in the film.

This was the first and only time I collaborated with Matthew. We only collaborated long distance. I was not involved in production or post-production.

SRB: There's a wonderfully eerie musical/tonal composition that accompanies the appearances of "Tim," the campfire storyteller and the mysterious killings—it seems to layer chanting, vocals, and dissonant tones, and is very haunting. What was your process?

DZ: I'll have to watch it again but, if what you're describing is part of my soundtrack it most likely was analog audio tape manipulation along with some environmental enhancement, i.e. spatial placement of instrumentation and microphone.

SRB: What have you been up to since **THE GLASSHEAD***?*

DZ: Shortly thereafter, I moved south to South Carolina. I then completed a self-serving CD titled *Absolute Zero*. Following that I dedicated most of my time to family responsibilities and activities.

The kids have now launched and I'm twice divorced! For the past 7 years I have been composing and performing film soundtrack as well as jazz standards at local venues.

SRB: Thanks for making time to talk to me!

DZ: Thank you for your support.

Having since caught up on some of the classic Earthstar collaborations, I can recognize Zongrone's sound more readily in the film. I particularly like the dissonant "zombie theme" associated with Tim's early appearances in the film. This music is discomforting —a distressed, distressing fusion of spectral voices and non-melodic tones, just as I described it to Daniel in one of my interview questions—and is sparingly used to eerie effect, arguably echoing Hahn Rowe's score for Lodge Kerrigan's **CLEAN, SHAVEN** (1993, USA). This musical passage proffers an audio echo of whatever it is driving Tim and "Pete"/Gebadiah (whatever *they* are)—the soundtrack tuning its (and our) own internal "radio" to their respective frequencies of malevolence and madness.

As Daniel clarified in the interview, these choices were Matthew Smith's alone, working with Zongrone's tracks during post-production: thus, Zongrone wasn't sculpting the audio to fit the film, but Smith clearly *was*.

Smith's application of Zongrone's most memorable musical contribution enhances the flashbacks involving Dr. Swan, particularly Gebadiah's attack

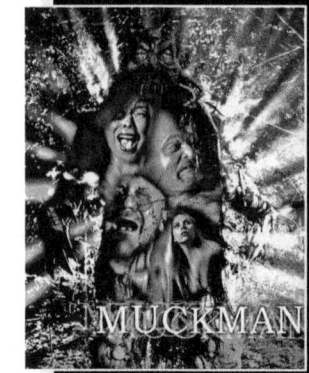

Ad art for Brett Piper's 'swamp creature' cryptid gem **MUCKMAN** (2009); a promotional shot of A. J. Khan and the titular Muckman (monster designed and executed by Brett Piper).

188

on the nursery and murder of the infant Mark.[18] At other points in the film, Smith's application of Zongrone's score dials it back to a singular sound—a drawn-out scratching (of a pick or fingernail?) across a single guitar string—and the whole for the most part works with the film, as it stands.

Since **THE GLASSHEAD**'s fleeting release—as Dennis Rea noted (in an email)—"Dan is more active musically than ever."[19] Fleshing-out what Daniel mentioned in the interview above, *Discogs* notes that "currently Zongrone plays drums and vibraphone in the South Carolina based blues and jazz trio Tipping Point with guitarist Terry Jones and bassist Andy Nagel."[20]

Long may he rock!

THE GLASSHEAD's final onscreen text, save for the copyright notice, read:

"Pat, we finally did it."

Thus, Matthew Smith completed the personal circle that culminated in **THE GLASSHEAD** with this loving farewell to his late friend and the creative catalyst for the film, Pat Salois.

We too easily forget that many of these mere "monster movies" are indeed labors of love, evidence of lives lived—and lost.

My final email exchange with **THE GLASSHEAD** director Matthew Smith during this period came in May, 2003. Our last exchange ended on the best of terms, with Matt writing about his then-current work with Mark and John Polonia, whose names and work are most certainly familiar (and perhaps infamous) to many readers:

"It has been a while since **THE GLASSHEAD** *came up in a discussion and it was quite enjoyable to relive the story and events. And please, keep me informed of the progress of your writings; it truly sounds like a wonderful project.*

"Oddly enough, I do not own any copies of my work. I'm not sure the reasoning or the motives behind this, but it seems that once I finish shooting and if I'm not involved with the editing, I'm on to the next project.

"The film **THE HOUSE THAT SCREAMED** *(no, not the Italian [sic] film[21]) was finished and released, I think, in 1999. I saw it at the premiere and last fall when I went to do an audio track for the DVD release this spring. It was produced and directed by the Polonia brothers, Mark and John, from Pennsylvania. I'm expecting a copy of the DVD to come my way and I would be happy to send it along to you. I'm not sure if you've heard of them or seen any of their work, but either you love them or hate them. They cut their teeth on making movies shot on video and continue to do so today. I was their initiation into the world of film and I am quite pleased the way the images look.*

"Well, I've rambled enough. Thank you again for your interest in my work. The new film with Paul has been put on hold for a year until we can secure the proper locations. We're looking for a college campus with an old world look, architecturally. The ones we found were not interested in a film crew on campus. A hard nut to crack.... if you know of any willing financial investors looking to invest in an upcoming film, don't hesitate to drop my name. I won't be mad.

"Thanks again."

Soon after, I had to change my email account, and I lost track of Matthew and Peter through no fault save my own. I have since tried to reach them both and reestablish contact; at the time of this writing, I've not been successful. Maybe the long-overdue publication of this article will change that for the better.

To the best of my knowledge, Paul got out of film altogether. His sole post-**GLASSHEAD** movie appearances—essentially offscreen (a stand-in) in Darn Ferriola's **SOULKEEPER** (2001, USA), and as a reporter briefly visible in Sam Selick's and Dam Hamm's **MONKEYBONE** (2001, USA), their most curious adaptation of Kaja Blackley's and Vanessa Chong's graphic novel *Dark Town* (1995, Mad Monkey Press)—seemed to be it. Where *are* you, Paul?

Henry Selick's and Sam Hamm's **MONKEYBONE** (2001) features what may well be Paul Guiles' final film appearance to date.

---

18 In two May 26th, 2015 follow-up emails to the author, prompted by Daniel's impulse decision to pull his own video copy of **THE GLASSHEAD** off the shelf and watch it after so many years, Zongrone specifically cited these sequences as his favorites in the film, sending along video clips of the nursery sequence and the Nanny's slow walk down the stairs and discovery of the dead twin brother. Of the latter he wrote, "I think this is one of the best scenes! Notice how her head floats off the bottom of the screen!"

19 Dennis Rea, email to Peter Comley, Monday, May 25th, 2015, quoted with permission.

20 Cited at May 23, 2015, at *http://www.discogs.com/artist/1047661-Dan-Zongrone*

21 Matthew is referring to the *Spanish* classic **LA RESIDENCIA** (1969), which was successfully released in the US by American-International Pictures as **THE HOUSE THAT SCREAMED**. It was the debut feature helmed by the great Narciso Ibáñez Serrador (director of **WHO CAN KILL A CHILD?** [¿*Quién puede matar a un niño?*, a.k.a. **ISLAND OF THE DAMNED** [1976, Spain]), who was born in Uruguay to Argentinan actress Pepita Serrador and father/filmmaker/theatrical director Narciso Ibáñez Menta (whose Edgar Allan Poe portmanteau feature **OBRAS MAESTRAS DEL TERROR** [1960], was cut and dubbed and released stateside by Jack H. Harris as **MASTER OF TERROR**). Serrador made his major mark in Spanish television, including the genre series *Historias Para no Dormir* (1966-82).

feature film *imdb.com* associates with TRAKK Productions, with Matthew credited as producer and cinematographer. Matthew's own IMDb synopsis is lean: "A terrible secret haunts a small-town preacher, threatening to destroy his marriage. The one man who shares this secret is a criminal on the run, who has just roared into town on a black motorcycle. Suddenly three lives hang in the balance." A longer synopsis for this "noir thriller" graces the TRAKK website: "Something terrible happens between two friends on the night of their high school graduation, and they vow to go their separate ways forever—each shaped by this horrible event. Ten years later, one has become a career criminal, while the other, still wracked by guilt, enters the ministry. He serves in the small country church of Waycross, a town on the edge of dying out. The criminal—on the run & needing a place to hide—breaks the decade-long promise and roars back into his old friend's life. He brings with him their secret, which threatens to destroy the preacher, his fragile marriage, and anyone else it touches."[23]

In fact, Matthew's work since **THE GLASSHEAD** has been entirely as a genre direct-to-video producer and/or cinematographer. The other titles on the TRAKK Productions site (those that seemed to have actually been completed and/or distributed in some format) are Polonia Brothers creations: The Polonia Brothers' **THE HOUSE THAT SCREAMED** (2000, USA) credited Matthew as associate producer and cinematographer, and it was released on DVD by Sub Rosa, as was the Polonia Brothers sequel **HELLGATE: THE HOUSE THAT SCREAMED 2** (2001, USA), along with many of the twin brothers' genre concoctions. These include films directed by Brett Piper, another regional indie genre filmmaker (formerly of New Hampshire, and director of two genre gems shot in Vermont: **PSYCLOPS** [2002] and **ARACHNIA** [2003]) whose work is a favorite of mine. With Pennsylvania-based Mark Polonia, Piper has completed **MUCKMAN** (2009), **THE DARK SLEEP** (a.k.a. **H.P. LOVECRAFT'S THE DARK SLEEP** [2013]—Lovecraft, it's *not*!)—both of which Matthew handled photography for—and **QUEEN CRAB** (as yet unreleased). In fact, it's Piper and Mark Polonia's **MUCKMAN** that's most prominently spot-lit on the TRAKK Productions website to this day—as "Coming soon!"—though it's been available on DVD (from Chemical Burn) since September 2011.

The other titles and promotional art on the TRAKK site—**ARMY OF WOLVES, WEREWOLF EROTICA**, and **HALLOWEENIGHT**—are al-

Top: The Gorgo-like Cabin Lake monster featured in the late John Polonia's final feature, **MONSTER MOVIE** (2008, USA); completed by surviving Polonia brother Mark after John's untimely death (it was produced by J.R. Bookwalter). **THE GLASSHEAD**'s director Matthew Smith appears in the DVD bonus featurette "Tribute to John Polonia" accompanying the film, having photographed numerous Polonia productions, including Brett Piper and Mark Polonia's **MUCKMAN** (2009, USA [pictured above])

Matthew indeed remained busy in film production. The TRAKK Productions website is still online, but no longer active or interactive.[22] As of 2011, Matthew and TRAKK were still based in Elmira, New York. Paul Russell Laverack's three-actor drama **WAYCROSS** (2005, USA; TRAKK copyrights their online promo 2010) is the only other

Matthew Smith's most recent collaboration with fiercely independent writer-director-special effects master Brett Piper was as cinematographer for Piper's lively monster movie **TRICLOPS** (2016).

---

22 Though it was last updated in 2011, you can still visit Matthew's and TRAKK Productions' site online; go to *http://www.trakkpro.com/index.html*

23 At the time of this writing, **WAYCROSS'** promotional materials are still online at *http://www.trakkpro.com/page3/page3.html* with distribution attributed to White Night Studios at *http://www.whitenightstudios.com/*

luring, and the cover art for **THE GLASSHEAD** remains; none are live links any longer. The Polonia Brothers' **HALLOWEENIGHT** (2009, USA) saw light of day, with Matthew's cinematography credit; **ARMY OF WOLVES** (2010, USA) was previewed online, though I've never seen or found it available anywhere.[24] **WEREWOLF EROTICA** must have gone through a major title change, or never reached completion.

Working with the Polonia Brothers has no doubt been a whirlwind decade for Matthew; the boys have been prolific, to say the least (over *forty* titles in all to date, with more to come; Sub Rosa, Tempe Entertainment, and Sterling have handled most of the DVD releases to date). Matthew's collaborative work with the Polonia twins shouldn't be overlooked or underestimated: as he wrote to me in May of 2003, "I was their initiation into the world of film and I am quite pleased the way the images look."

Alas, John Polonia died unexpectedly (reportedly in his home, due to an aneurysm) on February 25th, 2008, at age 39.[25] Mark has soldiered on—as has Matthew S. Smith.

So, I asked you to remember this about **THE GLASSHEAD**: Remember Dr. Swan's twin sons? *Mark* died. *Matthew* survived…

Not to be perverse (forgive me, Mark and Matthew, please), but there's curious resonance in the reality that it is *Mark* of the Polonia Brothers who survives, to work with *Matthew*.

As ever, life mirrors art, and vice-versa, even when that art might be low-budget horror movies.

Of Matthew's IMDb cinematographer credits, there's also Jon McBride (**CANNIBAL CAMPOUT** [1988]; **WOODCHIPPER MASSACRE** [1988]; **FEEDERS** [1996, all USA]) and the Polonia Bros' **BLACK MASS** (2005) and **WILDCAT** (2007, both USA), with the two Brett Piper titles already cited and his Key Grip credit for Anthony Palma's and Zachary Shourds' **KNIGHTMARE** (2014, USA)—cinematography and editing by Mark Polonia, special effects by Brett Piper—being the most recent.

Matthew, clearly, has remained active and plenty busy, making movies.

And to think, it all began with **THE GLASSHEAD**: a labor of love.

---

24 See *http://www.dreadcentral.com/news/15213/get-ready-for-an-army-of-wolves/*

25 See *https://cinemaslave.wordpress.com/2008/03/02/a-tribute-to-john-polonia/* and *http://d2dvd.blogspot.com/2008/02/john-polonia.html*

And for me, it all began with an empty video box, in a closed-up video store in the Northeast Kingdom of Vermont, laboring thereafter to find that which was abandoned, unloved, *the lost…*

Here! Here, *here* is the damned thing!

Do you see it? Can you see it? Dare you see it?

I see it here before me, just as my eyes found it—or, as best as a mere reflection of the artifact can lay it before your own—an object.

No, less than an object: objectless, abject and abandoned, evidence of an object that might never have been, or if it once was, was no more.

I have since gone digging for that which gave it name and title and illusion of substance; and lo, I found the lost object from within—the videocassette—and found it more than fulfilled that empty cardboard box's promise of motion, emotion, story, flesh, blood, a peculiar simulacrum of those vows.

It had a name—**THE GLASSHEAD**—and what I beheld once I found that-which-had-been-lost, that-which-had-been-out-of-reach, was much more than what was promised.

That husk I'd found that gray day promised nothing: free of any color save a laminated pallid gray-blue, like that of a dead roadkill's eye; so impoverished of means or clarity as to be from its origins murky, muddied, muddled, and vaguely distasteful, such covering as it ever boasted woven threadbare and dull from birth. Indeed, as unpromising to the eye as it was, it was even more unpleasant to the touch. Who or what could love this?

I could. I did. I do…

Here! Here is the damned thing! And as I have been, so to, now, ye be damned!

Behold:

THE GLASSHEAD!

TRICLOPS writer/director/special effects artist Brett Piper

THE GLASSHEAD

(1998, USA, TRAKK Productions, "a SSHHH Film")

Director: Matthew S. Smith. "Conceived and written by" Pat Salois and Jeff Hurd. Cinematography: Matthew S. Smith. Music: Dan Zongrone; "Glasshead Theme by" Matthew S. Smith. Production Manager: Jeff Hurd. Production Assistants: Matt Cook, Gary Breinlinger, Kevin McCann. Location Audio: Ken Cook. Assistant Camera: M. Kelly Smith, Jeff Hurd, Polly Blackwell. "Extreme Thanks to" Tyler Smith, The Elmira Eagles Club, Steve Ramsdell, Padua, Fred Goodson, Elmira College Department of Theatre, Greg Morrell, Paul McLane, The 4th New York Independent Light Artillary.

CAST: Paul Guiles (as Gebadiah Decker/"Peter"), Shawn Rouillard (Nikki), Tyrone E.S. Marsh (Josh), Elisa Silverglade (K.C.), Gary Breinlinger (Tim), Maria Cirielli (Deanne), Jeff Whitaker (Dr. Swan), Chad L. Sweet (Matthew Swan), Dan Hoskins (Price), Andy Moulton (Willie), Greg Morrell (Dick), Marlene Perry (Sarah), Andrea Ajemian (the Nanny), Leah Hudson (girl with dog), Delos Blackwell, Greg Clark, Jay Lagonegro, Pat Salois, Steve Ramsdell, Greg Morell ("Angry Townsfolk").

These credits are accurate, including the spellings of character names, and should be considered as such despite what any online resources may state otherwise.

©2015 Stephen R. Bissette, all rights reserved. This chapter would not have been possible without the kind assistance of Peter Comley, Dennis Rea, Rob Bonk at Sub Rosa Studios, Joseph A. Citro, and above all special thanks to Matthew S. Smith, Paul Guiles, and Daniel Zongrone for graciously agreeing to be interviewed. As noted, the interviews for this article were conducted between February 18th, 2003 and May 29th, 2003, with follow-up in February 2004, and the interview with Daniel Zongrone was conducted on May 25, 2015. The 2003-2004 digital files were recovered and restored in May, 2015, though I've irretrievably lost the two jpegs which Matthew sent me of the original 1998 **THE GLASSHEAD** premiere exhibition posters; thankfully, Daniel Zongrone provided the invaluable image of the original 1998 college premiere invitation; thank you, Daniel! All VHS box art graphics were preserved in the SpiderBaby Archives, and are exclusive to this article and publication.

"Why Don't You Ask Him If He Is Going To Stay?"
Taking **TUSK** On Its Own Terms

Kevin Smith's **TUSK** *(2014) was worth the four-hour-round-trip to catch it in its fleeting theatrical release at the closest multiplex showing this whacked gem; woe to those who missed it.*

This review is precisely what I'd avoided reading beforehand.

I went in knowing nothing *about it—I don't listen to Kevin's podcasts—and kept it that way, and just went for the ride. So, my recommendation is to avoid reading this review until after you've seen* **TUSK** *yourself.*

I can't put it any simpler than this: this is what going to the movies should *be like!*

Fleetwood Mac's LP *Tusk* (released on October 12th, 1979); album cover design by Vigon Nahas Vigon.

SPOILER ALERT: it's impossible to discuss **TUSK** without spoiling something, honestly, but I'll do my best for this first page.

Once you turn the page, we'll be tipping some ashtrays, spilling some beans, and showing some hands, even though I'm trying my best not to. It's a certainty that in illustrating this analysis, my editors will reveal too much. If there were a way to contrive to bind the pages together, forcing you to cut them apart to read this, I would find a way to do that—but that's not viable.

Look, just take my word for it: If you love outrageous horror movies, stop reading right now, and just see **TUSK** first by whatever means necessary or possible (and there, I've already said too much).

Then again, if you love Kevin Smith movies, that means you've most likely heard the fateful *SModcast* podcast and/or participated fully in the twitter decision and crowd funding campaigns (#Walrusyes from @ThatKevinSmith) and already know what **TUSK** is and from whence it sprang.

In that case, you're already in—and in on—the movie.

TUSK is Smith's latest opus, and oh what an opus it is. Not wanting to give away the game(s) but wanting to write a proper assessment creates quite a quandary. I'll be coy, but it's an ungainly and impossible task.

Smith and his creative team and cast pool their considerable resources and pull off a savvy, relatively low-budget (by 2014 standards), punch-drunk, and frankly astonishing genre effort that works beautifully—as an exercise in absurdist surgical horror, as a cautionary satire for Podcasters everywhere, and as a ruthless parody of this past decade's cinematic genre abuses.

If you don't dig it, well, what can I say? This was my cup of tea (oops, spoiler #1)…

Let's see: if we're going to play the name game, we can dance around spoilers a wee bit. Smith knows his shit: this is **FREAKS** (1932) by way of **CALVAIRE** (2004), and resonates as richly with Smith's wicked sense of play and humor pitched to the fore. **TUSK** would have been an ideal 1970s drive-in opus—and it is that, in spades, joining **CREATURE** (2011) as my favorite recent American monster movie that knows exactly what the hell it wants to be, puts all its resources up on the screen, and doesn't let up or back off.

In 1973 drive-in movie terms, Smith spins on **THE STRANGE VENGEANCE OF ROSALIE** (Jack Starrett/Anthony Greville-Bell and John Kohn's adaptation of Miles Tripp's novel *The Chicken*) by way of Bernard L. Kowalski/Hal Dresner/Daniel C. Striepeke's **SSSSSSS!**, with Robert Kurtzman and his **TUSK** team's makeup FX (supplant pinniped obsession for the reptilian obsession) playing as key a role as John Chambers (and Striepeke) did for the latter. In more Millennial movie terms, for those with shorter memories, it's **MISERY** (1990) loves company of **THE HUMAN CENTIPEDE (FIRST SEQUENCE)** (2009)…oh but don't let that put you off. Don't avoid **TUSK** fearing more of the brand of **THE PASSION**/Bush/Cheney-era "extraordinary rendition" nastiness the *Saw* series reveled in, because believe you me, Smith's got your number, too, as well as theirs.

—

Michael Parks makes **TUSK** essential viewing. For my generation (I turn 60 in 2015), Parks is forever Bus Riley (**BUS RILEY'S BACK IN TOWN**, [1965]) and above all the motorcycling hero of the TV series *Then Came Bronson* (1969-70), his TV-theme-song Top-40 hit (which also scored 41st for country that year) "Long Lonesome Highway" launching a short-lived recording career with MGM before his stint as Philip Colby on TV's *Dynasty* spawned *The Colbys* (1986-87). For most of my peers, Parks seemed to disappear other than that, but for me, he was omnipresent in the unlikeliest places: playing Robert F. Kennedy for Larry Cohen's **THE PRIVATE FILES OF J. EDGAR HOOVER** (1977), directing and starring in (the title role Clint Eastwood defined) **THE RETURN OF JOSEY WALES** (1986), as the Irish crime lord up against the real Bronson (Charles) in Michael Winner's **DEATH WISH V: THE FACE OF DEATH** (1994), and beautifully playing one of my all-time-favorite authors, Ambrose Bierce, in the sorely underrated **FROM DUSK TILL DAWN 3: THE HANGMAN'S DAUGHTER** (2000). But for most readers, Parks popped the radar playing the insidious French-Canadian criminal Jean Renault in *Twin Peaks* and Texas Ranger Earl McGraw for Robert Rodriguez and Quentin Tarantino in **FROM DUSK TILL DAWN** (1996), **KILL BILL: VOL. 1** (2003; Parks

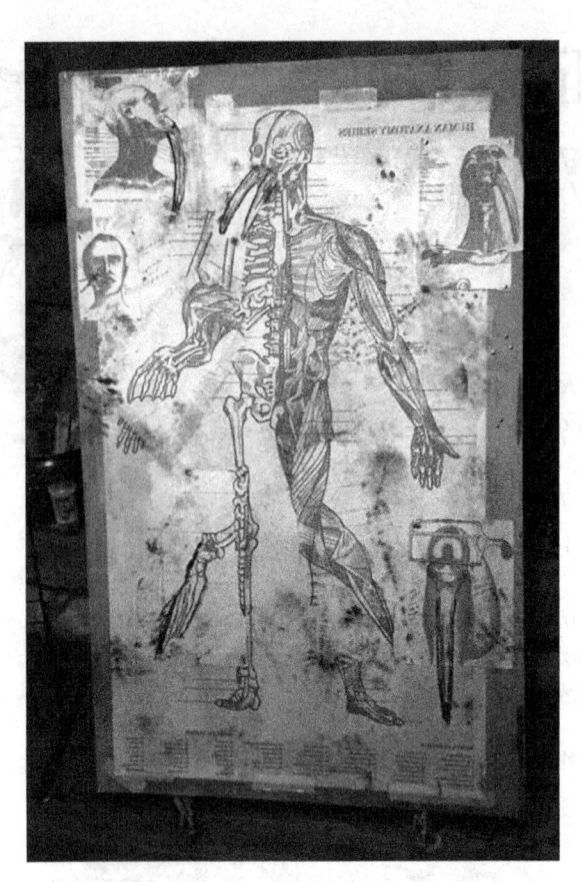

Smith cooked this up effortlessly (truly: the script was improvised on-air as a *SModcast* riff on a Gumtree prank sex ad/post—a prank, it turned out, by Brighton poet Chris Parkinson, who earned an associate producer credit here—hence the dubious "based on a true story" title announcement/warning) plundering a century of "mad doctor" rural horror pulp, comics, and movies clichés. Pirating those clichés while unflinchingly sticking to its comedic guns, **TUSK** is essentially a pinnipedal revamp of everything from Gaston Leroux's novel *Balaoo* (1911) to movies from Sam Newfield's **THE MAD MONSTER** (1942) to **SSSSSSS!** (1973), with Michael Parks in the George Zucco/Strother Martin role.

Michael Parks—who was, let us not forget, John Huston's Adam in **THE BIBLE: IN THE BEGINNING** (1966)—makes the most of the role, as had Zucco and dear old Strother, too. In one way, Parks is riffing on every one of moviedom's isolated, predatory rural mad doctors since Lon Chaney established the archetype in **THE MONSTER** (1925)—and seriously, **THE MONSTER** is *the* template for **TUSK**, absolutely. In another way, he is spinning off his memorable TV turn as the vengeful Canadian silent partner on One-Eyed Jacks in David Lynch and Mark Frost's *Twin Peaks* TV series (1990-91), and if that alone doesn't get your ass into a theater or home theater seat, nothing will.

Left: TUSK's mad doctor (Michael Parks) is a man with a plan, with an illustrated chart on his laboratory wall to prove it. **Below:** the Russian theatrical release poster for **TUSK** spelled the film's premise out a bit more clearly.

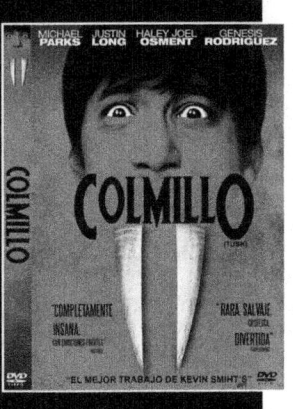

TUSK's South American DVD release packaging

played Estaban Vihaio in **KILL BILL: VOL. 2**, 2004, all referenced in **TUSK** via the central narrative function of the Kill Bill Kid, played by Douglas Banks), and **GRINDHOUSE** (2007, both features—and note that his real-life son, James Parks, played McGraw's son in **KILL BILL, FROM DUSK TILL DAWN 2: TEXAS BLOOD MONEY**, and **GRINDHOUSE**). I'll forever rue the day his role as the late, great comics creator Jack Kirby was trimmed from **ARGO** (2012), but that's hardly Parks' fault, is it?

Parks has quietly blistered the screen in numerous genre outings since 2000, but his most recent turns for Smith as fanatical Pastor Abin Cooper for **RED STATE** (2011) and as Howard Howe in **TUSK** elevate him even further into the stellar pantheon of cinema crazies (add to this Parks' role as Doc Barrows in Jim Mickle and Nick Damici's **WE ARE WHAT WE ARE**, the 2013 remake of Jorge Michel Grau's harrowing **SOMOS LO QUE HAY** [2010]). Parks is in top form in **TUSK**. It's almost impossible, given the utterly absurd premise of **TUSK** and specifically Parks' role, to claim he is underplaying the part, but damned if he isn't. By turns sly, sinister, and hilarious as the most attentive but loopiest host imaginable, Parks coaxes both the unwary hero and the audience into the web with considerable guile, and keeps toying with his and our affections to the bitter end. Though few have seen fit to notice or (if they have) comment upon it, but we're seeing a renaissance of 1930s-1940s poverty-row mad doctors of late, amped to the max—and I'd place Parks' Howard Howe up there as the contemporary George Zucco to, say, Dieter Laser's Peter Lorre of Tom Six's **THE HUMAN CENTIPEDE (FIRST SEQUENCE)**. The latter is indeed the closest associative companion to **TUSK** in many ways, including the twisted "master and his pet" obsessions/relationships central to both films, but there's a world of difference between the how far both filmmakers dare to go, to what ends, and which edges they drive us over. Like director Kevin Smith (compared to Tom Six), Parks plays the gentleman in **TUSK**, even as he tips his hand about his fixations, his madness, and his true colors, and that's the performance that really makes Smith's insane little potboiler simmer and roil.

Keeping pace with Michael Parks doing the ultimate 21st century George Zucco resurrection, Smith assembled a terrifically game cast, with Justin Long, Haley Joel Osment, and Genesis Rodriguez (Génesis Rodríguez Pérez) as the gender-inversion-of-**PSYCHO** (1960) leads (this time, it's a guy's fate-worse-than-death disappeared that brings out an unlikely couple and investigator in search of the truth). They each bring their own baggage to their roles, as is right and proper in every Kevin Smith movie.

Génesis Rodríguez Pérez is the loving girlfriend who has had quite enough of her beau's insensitive shit, but can't help but fret over his disappearance and propel the investigation that drives the second and third acts; for those who only know her from her feature film roles (debuting in **MAN ON A LEDGE** [2012], followed by **WHAT TO EXPECT WHEN YOU'RE EXPECTING** the same year and **THE LAST STAND, IDENTITY THIEF**, and **HOURS** in 2013), Génesis is the Traci Lords of Telemundo infamy. English-speaking

The Doctor Is In: That's *not* needlepoint Howard Howe (Michael Parks) is threading in Kevin Smith's TUSK—and, no, we're *not* going to show you what he's up to!

195

Old Wine, New Bottle: **TUSK**'s Howard Howe takes his cues from Lon Chaney/Dr. Gustave Ziska's bedside manner in Roland West, Willard Mack and Albert Kenyon's adaptation of Crane Wilbur's **THE MONSTER** (1925)

American soap opera viewers first saw Rodríguez Pérez in *The Days Of Our Lives* (2005-2006), but she had actually debuted in the Telemundo network's telenovelas *Prisionera* (2004) at age 16 and was involved in a scandalous love affair with her telenovela co-star Mauricio Islas (then aged 30 and married), resulting in an out-of-court settlement that kept Islas out of prison and earned Génesis millions (including a major windfall from Telemundo). Génesis openly riffed on that notoriety with her role in **CASA DE MI PADRE** (2012), and she brings kittenish candor to her role in **TUSK** that lends some emotional resonance to the whole giddy concoction (her character here is also not above using her sexuality to coax a confession at one point out of her boyfriend).

Haley Joel Osment's genre credentials are indelibly, almost genetically coded into anyone who grew up with **BOGUS** (1996), **THE SIXTH SENSE** (1999), **A.I.** (a.k.a. **A.I. ARTIFICIAL INTELLIGENCE**, [2001]), and direct-to-video Disney fare like **BEAUTY AND THE BEAST: THE ENCHANTED CHRISTMAS** (1997), **THE HUNCHBACK OF NOTRE DAME II**, **THE COUNTRY BEAR** (both 2002), and **THE JUNGLE BOOK 2** (2003). Osment survived his share of post-child-star tabloid scandal (his 2006 auto accident, suffering minor injuries while drunk and carrying, pleading no contest for DUI and drug possession and the usual probation/rehab/fine/AA penalties), and his current career reboot is enhanced by his role here and in Smith's forthcoming **YOGA HOSERS**, the second in a proposed trilogy set in Canada (with Osment reportedly playing Smith's fictionalized surrogate for infamous anti-Semitic fascist journalist and self-proclaimed Canadian *Führer* Adrien Arcand, putting him in league with Michael Parks previous role for Smith in **RED STATE**).

Always affable Justin Long earned his genre stripes early in his career with the one-two punch of **GALAXY QUEST** (1999) and **JEEPERS CREEPERS** (2001, with a cameo in its 2003 sequel), followed by roles in **THE SASQUATCH GANG** (2006, a.k.a. **THE SASQUATCH DUMPLING GANG**), **IDIOCRACY** (2006), **DRAG ME TO HELL** (2009) and more. Long's only tabloid turns have been tied to his relationships—with Drew Barrymore and of late with Amanda Seyfried—having completely skirted taint-by-association with **JEEPERS CREEPERS** director Victor Salva, but his squeaky-clean rep justifiably stands, and that lends his adventurous onscreen role here rich resonance: Long and Smith play off and against Long's persona.

Long suffers the brunt of **TUSK**'s torments, on and offscreen (consider, if you will, the makeup sessions he must have endured), playing podcaster Wallace Bryton as the insensitive-but-likable asshole who pays beyond the ultimate price for his narcissistic hubris.
And oh, does he pay.

It's a fearless performance and a lot of fun, especially once Long's most recognizable boyish attributes are buried. Like Christopher Lee's Kharis in Terence Fisher's **THE MUMMY** (1959), by the final acts all Long is left to work with onscreen are his eyes—the very eyes the Creeper (Jonathan Breck) lusted after in **JEEPERS CREEPERS**—and he delivers to the last shot.

As I noted earlier, the roles here are a gender inversion of those in Robert Bloch's and Alfred Hitchcock/Joseph Stefano's **PSYCHO** (the novel and the film). Closer to the roots, what Smith and his cronies have concocted here is an extreme spin on Roland West's venerable chestnut **THE MONSTER**, West's adaptation of Crane Wilbur's play (co-scripted with Willard Mack and Albert Kenyon). That essentially-forgotten silent vehicle for Lon Chaney cast Chaney as Gustave Ziska, a backwoods renegade surgeon whose capture of a young woman (Gertrude Olmstead)—the latest in a procession of mysterious disappearances and kidnappings—prompts her lover (Johnny Arthur), his co-worker (Hallam Cooley), and a local constable (Charles Sellon) to trace her disappearance and hopefully rescue her from Ziska's mad experiments in an "abandoned" asylum.

Like **TUSK**, **THE MONSTER** was first and foremost a comedy, too. You see, the setup and template was just that familiar in the 1920s, already!

Crane Wilbur's play's pulp scenario has fueled countless horror films and horror film parodies since, from James Whale's **THE OLD DARK HOUSE** (1932) to Georges Franju/Jean Redon/Pierre Boileau/Thomas Narcejac/Claude Sautet's **LES YEUX SANS VISAGE** (a.k.a. **EYES WITHOUT A FACE**, a.k.a. **THE HORROR CHAMBER OF DR. FAUSTUS**, 1960/1962) and all the spin-offs of and riffs on those classics. It's

Kevin Smith essentially self-distributed his first horror feature via SModcast Pictures; **RED STATE** (2011) played one-week-only in June 2011 at the New Beverly Cinema, roadshow for one night only in select theaters on September 23, 2011, released to video-on-demand via Lionsgate that same month, and on home video October 18, 2011.

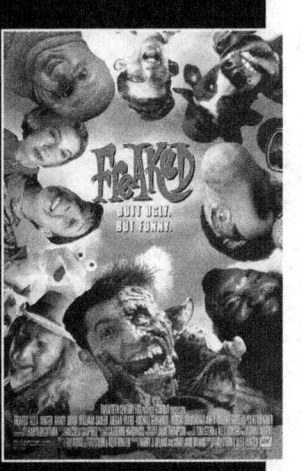

I'd have paid good money to sit-in on the 20th Century Fox executives' first screening of Alex Winter's and Tom Stern's **FREAKED** (1993)!

telling both of the nature of genre, and of Kevin Smith's affection for and knowledge of the genre, that Smith could just spit out this comedic claptrap so gleefully with Scott Mosier in one sitting of his *SModcast* (give it a listen: *http://smodcast.com/episodes/the-walrus-and-the-carpenter/*). Yes, we *all* know this story—but you've never heard or experienced this version, even after you've tuned into the *SModcast*. There's many a mile twixt the lip and the cup (or, in this case, **TUSK**), and the fun is in the telling.

The most volatile career baggage of anyone onscreen is something I can't go into without the ultimate spoiler alert. Suffice to note **TUSK**'s key role of Guy LaPointe, the ex-police investigator, boasts the funniest casting coup since Ortiz the Dog Boy in Alex Winter and Tom Stern's **FREAKED** (1993, oddly enough the movie I most wanted to revisit after **TUSK**). The cat's been out of the bag since the movie opened, but I won't give that game away, either, save to say it added enormously to the perverse fun.

For all the cozy familiarity duly noted with the narrative template, this is one crazy-ass movie, the kind we rarely see in a theater these chicken-shit days with theatrical distribution as locked-down into studio monopolies as ever it was before the U.S. v. Paramount Pictures Supreme Court ruling. The ferocity of both the horror and the humor is delightful, punctuated by what is almost the most perverse use of a Fleetwood Mac tune in film history (I say "almost" because given the implications of where the movie might have been heading, given the revelation of one of the souvenirs Howard keeps in his living room, I must emphasize again that Kevin Smith chose to be a gentleman as a storyteller here—he could have and threatens to go much, much further than he does, and in that context the thrust of the titular 1979 Fleetwood Mac tune would have been a much raunchier feat). In fact, a close listening to Mac's "Tusk" lyrics provides yet another elegantly simple template for the narrative: "Why don't you ask him/if he's going to stay?/Why don't you ask him/if he's going away?/Why don't you tell me/what's going on?/Why don't you tell me/who's on the phone?" etc. to "Just tell me that you want me!"

I know, I know. I do go on.

Basically, it's all silly shit. This started and ended as another rude Kevin Smith joke, right?

I know I'm in a minority, but I was riveted and chilled by Smith's **RED STATE** (2011) and regretted not making the pilgrimage out to see it during its fleeting self-distributed theatrical run. Not making that mistake twice, I can only add that **TUSK**'s fond fearless fusion of horror and hilarity worked in spades for me. Structurally, there are certain similarities between the two films—the setup, the "dare", the trespass, the transgression, and Michael Parks' pivotal role—but these are superficial at best, save for the moral thrust (don't go where angels fear to tread, kids, for the consequences will be dire). **TUSK** is Kevin Smith's best film, in many ways. **TUSK** and **RED STATE** unexpectedly places Kevin Smith at the top of my short list of favorite contemporary genre filmmakers—even though it tanked, by mainstream barometers.

Many of my favorite creature features did, you know.

Like **FREAKED** and 2011's **CREATURE** (no, I'm not damning with faint praise: I championed **CREATURE** in 2011 and continue to, which may lose me any shred of credibility I may have for many), **TUSK** was declared an instant box-office bomb (earning in its first month $1.6 million, up against its reported $3.5 million budget). It was despised by many (Erik Lundegaard in The Seattle Times declared it "the most disgusting and pointless movie I've seen...I spent half the movie sick to my stomach," in his September 18th, 2014 review).

To which I say, again:

Fuck 'em if they can't take a joke.

Special thanks for the initial heads up from Sean Morgan and for the road trip with Ian Richardson; I'm glad Sean and Ian alerted me to this in time! *Thanks*, guys!

Spoiler Alert! Sidebar:

I AM THE WALRUS
Making a Walrus of Wallace in TUSK

"...the movies I grew up watching, man, were like FROM BEYOND, RE-ANIMATOR; rubber movies. When I was a kid, when I was about thirteen we started getting cable in our neck of the woods. And suddenly you were seeing all these movies that you didn't even have access to because the video store didn't exist yet at this point. So, in the early '80s, man, I was—it sounds weird to say it—but I was a rubber freak, man! Like, I loved prosthetics, I loved effects. Before I ever wanted to be a filmmaker, I wanted to be a makeup artist."

—Kevin Smith[1]

"The time has come," the Walrus said, "To talk of many things…" Justin Long, sans moustache, indicating what's in store for his character Wallace before the first hour of Kevin Smith's **TUSK** is over. It ain't pretty; look to the next two pages at your own risk! (Justin Long at TUSK's L.A. premiere on September 16th, 2014. *[Photo by Richard Shotwell/Invision/AP.]*)

Time to spill the beans I so rigorously avoid spilling in my review of the film itself: **TUSK** is Kevin Smith's first 'rubber movie,' and KNB EFX Group, Inc.'s founding partner Robert Kurtzman created **TUSK**'s walrus-man makeup effects. Now, there's precious few 'giant walrus' or walrus-monsters to be found in the cinema: outside of animated cartoons and Lewis Carroll *Alice in Wonderland* adaptations, Eiji Tsuburaya created one (Maguma [マグマ] a.k.a. Magma) for Ishirō Honda's Toho SF spectacular **GORATH** (妖星ゴラス / *Yosei Gorasu*, 1962), which was cut from the American release, and stop-motion animation monster-maker Ray Harryhausen had one pop up out of the ice in **SINBAD AND THE EYE OF THE TIGER** (1977). On television, Eiji Tsuburaya's Maguma a.k.a. Magma returned to play the giant walrus monster Todora (トドラ) in *Ultra Q* (ウルトラQ / *Urutora Kyū* [Episode #27: "The Disappearance of Flight 206," July 3rd, 1966]), and a creepy stop-motion-animated 'stalker' walrus (!) figures in the Swiss kids' TV series *Pingu* ("Pingu's Dream," May 12th 1990).

But *walrus-men*? There *ain't* no such cryptid.

Until now…

For **TUSK**, Justin Long (**GALAXY QUEST, DODGEBALL, JEEPERS CREEPERS, DRAG ME TO HELL, AFTER**

---

[1] Kevin Smith, interviewed by Germain Lussier, "Kevin Smith Interview Part 1: How the Making of 'TUSK' Was Inspirational"; slashfilm.com, Tuesday, December 30th, 2014 (@ http://www.slashfilm.com/kevin-smith-interview-tusk-part-1/2/)

LIFE, etc.)—playing unlikable, smug sexist podcaster Wallace Bryton—endured one of the most absurd makeups ever created… and that's sure saying something. According to Kevin Smith's DVD/Blu-ray commentary track, all of Long's make-up effects scenes were shot in one prescribed block of time to avoid prolonging the arduous makeup-effects work having to be endured over days; and these effects involved two-to-three hours for Kurtzman to apply Long's facial makeup appliances (including magnetic tusks affixed to the prosthetics). When it came time for filming, Long would be slid into the elaborate body suit, which involved interaction with a yoga ball-like device. Kurtzman's special effects makeup team comprised Krisz Drouillard, Tate McLellan-Boland, David Greathouse, and Alan Tuskes, with Joel Harlow seeing to Johnny Depp's makeup effects.

The grotesque transformation of man-into-walrus is visually cued in the film itself by Wallace's moustache (which no less than *The New York Times* included in their cautionary rating warning to readers, "*Dorm room language, operating room gore and distressing facial hair*"[2]). "I don't know if I should be proud to say," Justin Long told interviewer Tony Timpone, "but it was my idea.":

"*First of all, the guy's name is Wallace. There was some very obvious foreshadowing going on, and if we're gonna do it, why not go for it, why not go for as much of the walrus look as you can, before you are a walrus. Robert Kurtzman, who did the special effects, who was incredible especially considering how little time he had to do this, I thought he was going to incorporate the mustache into the prosthetics for the walrus. They at least tried to do it, but it came out looking too comical and not quite walrus enough. So the mustache felt like a must-fit for this douchey podcaster, like a Bruno Kirby character. He needed a mustache.*" [3]

Wallace-the-Walrus is onscreen a great deal in the film—and revealed early on, well before the first hour has unreeled. It is meant to be audaciously absurd and disturbing, and it is. "I know some people have been like, 'It doesn't look real,' which always made me laugh," Kevin Smith says. "Of course it don't fucking look real, man! Like, do you know a *real* human walrus somewhere in the world?!" The appalling surgical artifice and utterly ludicrousness of Wallace-the-Walrus is *the point*:

"*Usually you don't show something because some people are like 'That looks fake.' But this* is *fake. There is no antecedent in the real world which somebody can point to and be, like, 'That doesn't look like a human walrus. So I was, like, 'Let's show it as often as we can,' because as a horror movie fan or as a rubber movie fan, you hate when they cut away. You wanna sit there and stare at it, look at all the seams and see what they put in the design and whatnot. And usually it's quick cuts in movies like that. But here, we just hold on that motherfucker so you can see it. Warts and all. And, it's part of the effect…hanging that camera on the walrus and having him early in the movie just felt like the more honest thing to do.*" [4]

During his commentary track for the **TUSK** disc, Smith says, "We owe a great debt of gratitude to **HUMAN CENTIPEDE**," referring to Tom Six's horrific

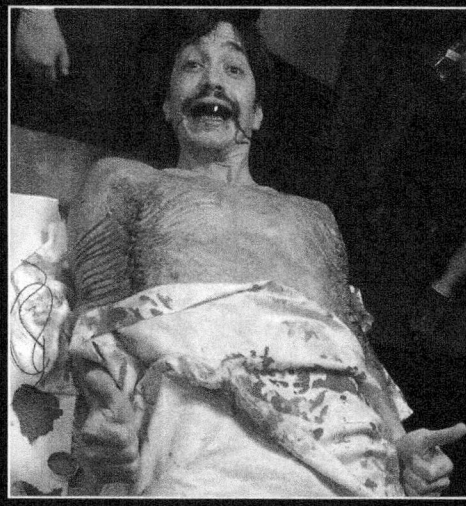

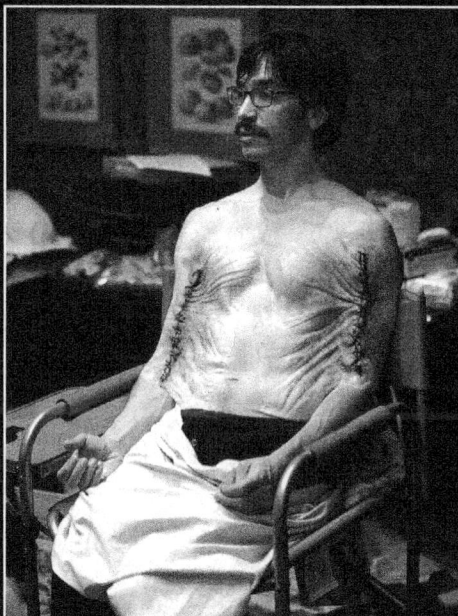

Enduring the fate of the kidnapped jogger in Peter Saxon's (nom de plume of Stephen D. Frances) novel *The Disorientated Man* (1966) and its film adaptation **SCREAM AND SCREAM** AGAIN (1970) is only the beginning for Wallace in **TUSK**. The next stage, shown here—for both Wallace and actor Justin Long—involves a surgical procedure never before shown in any horror or science-fiction 'mad doctor' movie. And then, of course, those upper teeth must go.

---

2 Jeannette Catsoulis, "Beware the Old Sailor Bearing Tea: Kevin Smith's 'TUSK,' Horror With a Loony Twist," *The New York Times*, September 18th, 2014, archived online (@ *https://www.nytimes.com/2014/09/19/movies/kevin-smiths-tusk-horror-with-a-loony-twist.html?mcubz=1*)

3 Justin Long, interviewed by Tony Timpone, "Q&A: Justin Long on Kevin Smith's 'TUSK'"; Fangoria.com, September 22nd, 2014 (@ *http://www.fangoria.com/new/qa-justin-long-on-kevin-smiths-tusk/*)

4 Smith, interviewed by Lussier, "Kevin Smith Interview Part 2: The Walrus Suit, 'Yoga Hosers' Production And His Only 'Tusk' Regret";*slashfilm.com*, Friday, January 2nd, 2015 (@ *http://www.slashfilm.com/kevin-smith-tusk-interview-part-2/*). In the same interview, Smith says his only regret is "I wish that we had put the fucking suit in the trailer… In retrospect, I was, like, 'Wow, how stupid of us to not show the fucking walrus!' But the whole philosophy was, if we show it, people might not go… we're making two more rubber movies. There's **YOGA HOSERS**, and there's rubber monsters in that. And then **MOOSE JAWS**, and there's a big rubber monster in that. You can guarantee in the trailer, man, you're gonna see *every piece* of the monster, 'cause that's the hook. Now there are a bunch of people online going 'Holy crap, that's just weird, I wish I'd known.' That was irresponsible. We should have put the walrus in the trailer. So I'll fucking do that from now on. Even if the walrus *isn't* in the movie I made, I will put the walrus in the trailer." Kevin Smith is *finally* channeling his inner Roger Corman!

THE HUMAN CENTIPEDE (FIRST SEQUENCE) (2009) and its sequels. **TUSK** star Justin Long offered this handy point of comparison between the films:

"This is a fun 'Would you rather?' Would you rather be human centipede or a walrus, and I would choose human centipede. At the end of the day, if someone were to find you, it would be much easier to be surgically altered back. But a human walrus, you're gonna have a hard time; at best, you can look like a messed up version of BOXING HELENA. At one point in TUSK, the danger becomes how he's going to survive as a walrus. But I like **HUMAN CENTIPEDE**; *it's less disturbing than* **TUSK**, *and I never thought I'd say that* [laughs]." [5]

Kevin Smith's nominal sequel to **TUSK**—**TUSK** being the first of his so-called 'True North Trilogy'—was **YOGA HOSERS** (2016), which rather than offer insights into how a walrus-man's gonna deal with life as a walrus-man chose to follow the misadventures of **TUSK**'s two Canuck 'Eh-2-Zed' convenience store clerks, Colleen Collette (Lily-Rose Melody Depp) and Colleen McKenzie (Harley Quinn Smith—yep, the daughters of Johnny Depp and Kevin Smith), en route to a high-school senior party. It sort of becomes a monster movie (really), since getting to the party involves run-ins with Satanists, a trigger-tempered yogi (Justin Long), Canadian fascists, "and an army of talking Nazi bratwursts with a thirst for blood" led by shoddy-CGI-enhanced Kevin Smith, in another Kurtzman makeup creation.[6] This time, it's Johnny Depp wearing the film's most extreme makeup job, returning as **TUSK**'s inspector. **MOOSE JAWS** is scheduled to follow at some point in time, but Smith's forthcoming **KILROY WAS HERE** is being spun as a spin-off as well. **KILROY WAS HERE** is a horror anthology film, co-scripted by Smith and executive producer Andrew McElfresh, with makeup effects by Robert Kurtzman; the film was shot on a college campus I co-taught (with James Sturm) week-long comics storytelling workshops at some years back, Sarasota, Florida's Ringling College of Art & Design.[7] (Here's a shout-out to Professor Joe Tiner and everyone there; you got rid of us to bring Kevin Smith on campus?! OK, I totally get that. Hugs & kisses!)

Note that Kevin Smith's View Askew Production produced a Canadian cryptid feature film: Malcolm Ingram's and Matt Gissing's black-and-white curio **DRAWING FLIES** (1996) in which a pack of slackers (Jason Lee, Jason Mewes, Renee Humphrey, Carmen Lee, Martin Brooks) are stranded in the woods en route to Jason Lee's uncle's cabin. Turns out Lee is actually searching for Bigfoot, and Sasquatch does show up before the final credits; the title of this deadbeat comedy references the Soundgarden song. "A Good Monster is a Terrible Thing to Waste" was the movie's film fest and (2002) VHS/DVD release tagline, and for most viewers, that pretty much summed-up the movie itself, though I quite liked it, and still like it. **TUSK**'s Justin Long also co-starred as a mullet-sporting redneck bully in Tom Skousen's cryptid comedy **THE SASQUATCH GANG** (a.k.a. **THE SASQUATCH DUMPLING GANG**, 2007) and Peter Gaulke and Fred Wolf's cryptid-centric **STRANGE WILDERNESS** (2008).

The look in Justin Long's eyes beneath the Wallace the Walrus-man makeup makes it look here as if makeup expert Robert Kurtzman (left) is up to no good—or putting the actor through something as grueling as what Long's character has already been subjected to! Kurtzman's ingenious design included the tusks being held into place with magnets.

A doctor's work is never done! After sexual-abuse-survivor, Duplessis orphan, and retired seaman Howard Howe (Michael Parks) completes his work on Wallace—stitching him into a 'walrus body' comprised of human skin, with tusks carved from Wallace's own severed leg tibia bones, and something to do with a pinniped baculum or oosik—Howe tells of his long-lost love Mr. Tusk, and how Wallace-the-Walrus is essential to rekindling the bond with his long lost savior…

---

5 Long, interviewed by Timpone, *Ibid.*

6 Bryan Bishop, "YOGA HOSERS and the tragedy of Kevin Smith's stoner era"; *The Verge*, January 26th, 2016 (@ https://www.theverge.com/2016/1/26/10834790/yoga-hosers-review-kevin-smith-sundance-film-festival-2016)

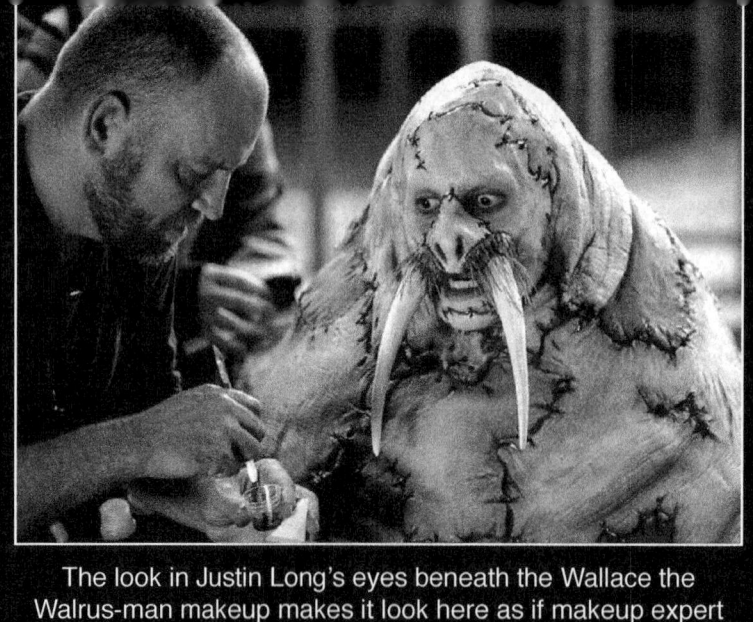

   Smith and his crew worked with the Ringling students back in June 2017; see local newspaper coverage of this: Jimmy Geurts, "Kevin Smith on filming "Killroy Was Here" in Sarasota with Ringling students"; *Herald-Tribune* [Sarasota, FL], June 16th, 2017, archived online (@ http://www.heraldtribune.com/news/20170616/kevin-smith-on-filming-killroy-was-here-in-sarasota-with-ringling-students)

THE *STRANGER THINGS* STUDY & VIEWING GUIDE

Millie Bobby Brown as "Eleven" aka "El" from *Stranger Things* (2016).

An Apple For The Reacher: Eleven (Millie Bobby Brown) asserts herself in the classroom in the summer of 2016 hit Netflix series *Stranger Things*

Were you among the many who were instantly enraptured by, and addicted to, binge-viewings of Netflix and Matt and Ross Duffer's 2016 original series Stranger Things?

What captured you first: the irresistible cast of child characters/performers; the small-town specificity disrupted by the covert government/paramilitary base's secret experiments; the androgynous telekinetic lass "Eleven" (a.k.a. "El" for short [Millie Bobby Brown]) with the shaved head and odd, intense manner; the plight of the alcoholic single mother whose youngest son mysteriously vanished, only to manifest within the walls of her and her older son's ramshackle home; or was it the whole bundle, wrapped-up in a 1980s-style synth score that recalled an era of SF/horror films which a generation grew up with as staples of cable TV and video-store catalogues?[1]

---

[1] Do I really have to cite fan postings and favorable reviews? They were everywhere this summer! Just go looking, and you'll find 'em in abundance.

"Now I Know My ABC's…": Distraught single mother Joyce (Winona Ryder), her eldest son Jonathan (Charlie Heaton) and his *not*-girlfriend Nancy (Natalia Dyer) sit tight under the Christmas lights while awaiting a message from Will-"Down-Under" (and we *don't* mean Australia!) in *Stranger Things*

Or were you among those befuddled by the phenomenon[2]—*put-off by, rather than engaged by and with, its cast of at-times cloying kid actors*[3]*, including the androgynous big-eyed orphan "Eleven", who is capable of moving things telekinetically*[4] *and making things happen with her mind; its reliance on the overt and ongoing physical, mental, and emotional abuse*

---

2 Tim Lucas (*Throat Sprockets*, *The Book of Renfield*, *Mario Bava: All the Colors of the Dark*, *Video Watchdog*, etc.) wrote in the Video Watchblog, "I keep thinking there must be some underlying sociological reason I'm missing—possibly its ties to Stephen King, whose novels are certainly referenced here (even the title seems to pinion off of King's *Needful Things*), and whose body of work never held the fascination for me that it has for the rest of the world. It can't just be 1980s nostalgia because *Stranger Things* borrows ideas and images from films as recent as **UNDER THE SKIN** and going as far back into the 1960s and '70s as **THESE ARE THE DAMNED** (with its government-sanctioned experiments on children) and **SHIVERS** (with its slug-like parasites vomited down bathroom drains). I could point to nearly every scene in the series and find not just a precedent for it but visual quotations in many. (My favorite was in the last episode, a wink at Joe Dante's **THE HOWLING**.) As I say, I thought it was alright but people had me all but running to my TV set to catch this before the spoilers caught up with me. That's what I don't understand. I can see people getting a kick out of a greatest hits album but not a greatest hits album of cover versions.… Possibly, the way this series has been so warmly embraced may have something to do with its familiar, comfort food values. Set in 1983 and allowed to roll out in a manner consistent with that era (which is to say, without the usual attention-deficit editing that has become the norm for Millennials), it's not really a product of its time, but a straightforward, unpretentious Young Adult novel for television that tells us what we all want to know: that government is not just bad but evil, that family (however screwed-up it may be) is good and always there for us, and that the victors in any situation will hail from the Island of Misfit Toys—like the pre-adolescent Dungeons and Dragons players who are the chief protagonists of this show…." See *Video Watchblog*, "Familiar *Things*," July 22nd, 2016, archived online (@ *http://videowatchdog.blogspot.com/2016/07/familiar-things.html*); quoted with permission.

3 On August 13th, 2016, UK screenwriter and author Stephen Volk (**GOTHIC**, *Ghostwatch*, *Afterlife*, *The Parts We Play*, etc.) wrote on Facebook, "Okay I *am* going to give *Stranger Things* more than one episode.... but as a general statement I'm finding American child actors really, really disconcerting... in this series, as well as M. Night [Shyamalan]'s **THE VISIT** *[2015, USA]*, as examples, I find them disturbingly over-mature, lacking in any semblance of innocence or inner life, way too knowing and false in their acting, as if 5,000 (adult) acting styles and movies have been downloaded into their heads and they are conscious of the camera in a way that is borderline showing off. I just find it so creepy, like totally self-absorbed grown-ups before their time, it makes me squirm. Please don't tell me that American children are all like this." Mind you, Stephen Volk isn't *per se* against kids or child actors; later on August 13th, in a comment on the same thread, Volk wrote, "Maybe if they don't over-characterize they don't feel they're doing their job. There's something in silence and listening that is much more compelling in a character sometimes than a whole avalanche of ticks and quirks!... Sit them all down and get them to watch **KES** *[1969, UK, D: Ken Loach]*. Then watch it again. And again," adding via personal message to me, "… the small children who perform in **THE VVITCH** *[2015, USA/UK/Canada/Brazil, D: Robert Eggers]* are quite extraordinary!" On August 23rd, 2016, Stephen posted to Facebook: "**MIDNIGHT SPECIAL** *[2016, USA/Greece, D: Jeff Nichols]* is one of the most enjoyable genre films I have seen in a long, long while. Perfectly realised by the writer-director and beautifully acted throughout. … I'll only say it is an old story told in a new way, that I found captivating. More so than say, *Stranger Things*, with which it does bear comparison." **MIDNIGHT SPECIAL** involved a "mutant child" capable of extreme acts of telekinesis and more, played by Jaeden Lieberher. (NB. Stephen Volk granted permission for the appearance here of his Facebook posts/comments.)

4 One of my closest friends, horror novelist and folklorist Joseph A. Citro (*Shadow Child*, *Guardian Angels*, *The Gore*, *The Unseen*, *Deus-X*, etc.), told me he gave up on watching the series as soon as the little orphan girl was eating in the back room of the diner, and moved the fan blades by concentrating. "I immediately shut it off," he said. (Quoted with permission.)

Top to Bottom: UK author/screenwriter Stephen Volk prefers child actors like David Bradley in **KES** (1969), Anya Taylor-Joy *[pictured]*, Harvey Scrimshaw, Ellie Granger, and Lucas Dawson in **THE VVITCH** (2015), or Jaeden Lieberher in **MIDNIGHT SPECIAL** (2016, also featured in **STEPHEN KING'S IT**, 2017).

The Monster Squad: The kids at the heart of *Stranger Things* —Lucas (Caleb McLaughlin), Dustin (Gaten Matarazzo), Mike (Finn Wolfhard) and the orphan Eleven (Millie Bobby Brown)

Artist/activist Annie Murphy on the character of single mother Joyce (Winona Ryder): "I'm overtired of seeing media in which the women's mental health is completely demolished before the men/boys actually believe."

of that child by a shadowy patriarch (Matthew Modine) that drives the narrative; its initially one-note caricature of a hard-drinking single mom as a showcase for a once-beloved screen actress (Winona Ryder) that rips on her own troubled adult reputation[5]; its painful synth-dominated soundtrack that reminds you of low-budget films you'd rather forget, mixed with top-40 "period" hits to cement its timeframe while manipulating your emotional responses with Pavlovian cynicism; its shamelessly derivative "K-Tel Greatest Hits"-style cannibalization of countless past horror/SF/fantasy riffs, prominent among them the self-evident rebrand of Stephen King motifs (which were, as evidenced by King's own plethora of interviews, his own revamps of venerable 1950s horror/SF literary and movie tropes)?[6]

Me? I was initially straddling both camps.[7] In the end, I wrote this article.
Make of that what you will.

---

5   Artist/activist Annie Murphy (*I Still Live, I Never Promised You A Rose Garden, Part One: My Own Private Idaho* and *Part Two: Ken Death is Dead, The Shirley Jackson Project*, etc.) posted on Facebook on August 2nd, 2016: "SPOILER ALERT: DEBBIE'S DOWNER [*Stranger Things* rant]: Please lord let that be the last time I bingewatch hours of men and boys telling women and girls that they are crazy. I'm overtired of seeing media in which the women's mental health is completely demolished before the men/boys actually believe. It's fiction for fuck's sake, why does that have to be the only element that survives from reality? It's bad modeling. It was brilliant in **THE HAUNTING**, but 50 years later it's just tired.... Don't get me wrong: I love horror, I love nostalgia, I covet the 80s, and I love cheese. I love feminist horror the best and honestly, it is not that hard to pull off—just ask Christopher Pike. But good lord this show could have been much, much better. And shorter. Without the misogynist plot delays or the heavy-handed 80's-product-placement (oh my god!! Remember *Trapper Keepers*??!) it would have been about 3 episodes. I'm gonna go watch **GHOSTBUSTERS** now dammit." Quoted with permission.

6   Kentucky-born artist/musician J.T. Dockery (*Despair* Volumes 1-3, *Hassle, Spud Crazy*, etc.) wrote, "...It had some fun moments, but it had a lot of problems, both gob-smacking plot holes and some disbelief I couldn't suspend and some of the stereotypes and stock footage, one dimensional characters/character development seemed pure corn starch to me. I will say there seemed to be maybe a solid two hour movie hiding in it, and I was hipped to the fact that it actually was a movie project that got turned into a tv show." Facebook comment, August 2nd, 2016, 3:00 p.m.; quoted with permission.

7   FYI, and whatever it's worth, I posted July 18th, 2016, 9:34 a.m. on Facebook, "Dove into *Stranger Things*; I'm enjoying it, but just that. The sub-Tangerine Dream/sub-*[John]* Carpenter synth score is obtrusive, as are the interruptive (and oh so typical) overlays of 'here's another song to tell you how you should feel now,' and the narrative is awfully derivative in a piecemeal way (*[Joseph]* Losey's **THE DAMNED/THESE ARE THE DAMNED** via **DEAD KIDS/STRANGE BEHAVIOR** by way of **SUPER 8** by way of **FIRESTARTER** with a shot of "Little Girl Lost" by way of Christopher Garetano's **MONTAUK CHRONICLES** via...). Still, I'm quite enjoying the characters and setup. Solid cast, slickly constructed, very nicely paced and shot, I'm on board for the duration. I'm not in love with this, though; give it time..."

Article continued on page 209 following this handy-dandy episode guide for *Stranger Things*!

ADRIFT IN THE UPSIDE DOWN

An Episode Guide to *Stranger Things*
(Netflix, July 15th, 2016)

ATTENTION: SPOILER ALERTS!! *If you have not yet seen the series, avoid reading the following. This synopsis serves only to remind those who have seen the series of key plot points. ~SRB*

Little Boy Lost: Will Byers (Noah Schnapp) bicycles to meet his fate in the opening episode of *Stranger Things*

Chapter 1: "The Vanishing of Will Byers"

1983, Hawkins, Indiana: A group of boys playing role-playing games—Will Byers (Noah Schnapp) and his friends Mike (Finn Wolfhard), Dustin (Gaten Matarazzo), and Lucas (Caleb McLaughlin)—break for the evening and Will, Dustin, and Lucas bicycle home despite the rain. Will is separated from his pals and gets spooked by *something* unseen that is following him—something that might be from the nearby off-limits Hawkins Laboratory—which stalks him to the shed behind his house…

Next morning, Will's single, alcoholic mother Joyce (Winona Ryder) and his older brother Jonathan (Charlie Heaton) can find no sign of him anywhere. Joyce reports Will as a missing person to local police chief Jim Hopper (David Harbour), but no one will believe her. Meanwhile, an androgynous young girl (Millie Bobby Brown) with a shaved head and garbed in a flimsy hospital gown shows up at the local Benny's Diner, unwilling or unable to speak. Benny feeds her and calls for social workers to rescue her; armed agents show up instead, killing Benny, and the girl—named Eleven—escapes, subsequently running into Will's pals while they are out searching for their missing friend. Waiting at her home for any news of her missing son, Joyce gets a mysterious phone call: through all the static on the line, she distinctly hears what is apparently Will's breathing…

Chapter 2: "The Weirdo on Maple Street"

The boys bring Eleven back to Mike's house and hide her there, coaxing her to eat Eggo waffles, which she takes an immediate liking to. Eleven—whom Mike informally dubs "El" for short—tells them that "bad people" are chasing her, and she demonstrates her telekinetic abilities by closing Mike's door without touching it. She recognizes a photo of the missing Will, and cryptically says he's hiding "from a monster". In concealment to avoid discovery by Will's mother, Eleven recalls being imprisoned in a cell out at Hawkins Laboratory. At the same time, Joyce gets another uncanny phone call from Will, corresponding with the lights in her home flashing on and off and the walls seeming to "warp".

Elsewhere in town, Mike's older teenage sister Nancy (Natalia Dyer) is invited by school stud Steven (Joe Keery) to a pool party at his house while his parents are *in absentia*, and Nancy asks her best friend Barb (Shannon Purser) to go with her. While the teens party by the pool, Will's brother Jonathan—searching the woods for his missing brother—watches from the treeline and snaps photos, envious of Steven's proximity to Jonathan's "crush", Nancy. Barb is abandoned at the poolside as the teen couples go upstairs to have sex; left alone, she is taken by the same unseen thing that stalked Will…

Chapter 3: "Holly, Jolly"

We glimpse Barb trapped in an altered version of the swimming pool: it is a dark, tendril-encrusted caricature of our world, from which Barb desperately flees something which is stalking her…

Unable to find her missing friend, Nancy breaks down and tells her mother about the party, and that Barb has gone missing. Downstairs, still hiding in the house, Eleven explores Mike's basement room; as she does, memories of her life in Hawkins Laboratory emerge, where the paternal Dr. Brenner (Matthew Modine) had tested her telekinetic powers. She also recalls using these abilities to kill the men who were guarding and abusing her. Meanwhile, Chief Hopper's investigation of Will's disappearance leads him to Hawkins Laboratory, where he is shown security footage as "proof" that Will was never there, but Hopper notices the lack of rain on the tape—it was raining on the night of Will's disappearance—and rightly suspects Brenner is hiding the truth.

At Joyce's house, she has established tentative contact with the invisible Will by stringing Christmas lights on the living room wall, corresponding to an improvised alphabetical grid she's scrawled onto it; the lights flash "Yes" when she asks Will if he's alive, and "No" when she asks if he's safe. The lights then flash wildly, as if expressing terror, and the very walls seem to stretch; Will is on the run, wherever he is. Outside—the boys, having asked her to lead them to Will—Eleven has led them to Joyce's and Will's home; they grow angry, and she tries to tell them he is there, in a place she calls "the Upside Down". Upon hearing sirens nearby, they rush to the source

Mike (Finn Wolfhard), the walkie-talkie, and Eleven (Millie Bobby Brown), with the tell-tale drop of blood trickling from her nostril...

Eleven, all-suited-up and ready to enter the Upside Down via the sensory-deprivation tank in Hawkins Laboratory

of the sound: a water-filled rock quarry, where the authorities are pulling Will's body out of the icy waters...

Chapter 4: "The Body"

Joyce refuses to believe the body on the slab at the coroner's office is really Will; it lacks an identifying birthmark, so she refuses to cooperate. Trusting Joyce's certainty, Hopper investigates further, finding irregularities in the reported autopsy; that night, he knocks out the guard and probes the boy's body with a knife, finding white stuffing material inside: the body is *fake*!

Meanwhile, Eleven uses the boys' walkie-talkies to locate the missing Will; making the connection, they hear Will softly singing The Clash's "Should I Stay or Should I Go", a song which his brother Jonathan had turned him on to. At the school parking lot, Steve is outraged to find out Jonathan surreptitiously took pictures of the pool party; he smashes Jonathan's camera and rips up the photos. After recovering the pieces, Nancy discovers Jonathan might have snapped a partial image of whatever abducted Barb. When she shares her suspicions with Jonathan, he realizes the same "thing" must have kidnapped his brother, too. The boys have also brought Eleven to school. When Mike is bullied, she uses her abilities to stop the bully and make him publicly piss his pants. However, flexing her powers thus leaves her weak, with a trickle of blood running from her nostril...

Chapter 5: "The Flea and the Acrobat"

Chief Hopper flouts security and makes his way deep into the bowels of Hawkins Laboratory, where he discovers the secret organic "doorway" to the "Upside Down"—only to be seized by Dr. Brenner's henchmen, drugged, then dumped back at his trailer. Upon awakening, he searches his trailer and finds a surveillance "bug", which he destroys. At the news that State Police found Barb's abandoned car at the village train station, Hopper realizes there is a high-level conspiracy going on to hide the fates of the local missing children. He lets Joyce know that her suspicions are correct, and they begin working together.

Eleven reluctantly agrees to lead the boys to Will in the Upside Down, but she deliberately misleads them in order to keep them safe from what lurks there. The boys are livid when they uncover her ruse, and Lucas turns on Mike for defending Eleven. When the conflict escalates, Eleven telekinetically hurls Lucas away from Mike with sufficient violence to knock the former out. Lucas recovers, but Eleven flees.

Nancy and Jonathan search the woods together at twilight, unsure of what they are seeking but hoping to find Barb; they instead find a wounded deer barely clinging to life. As Jonathan prepares to put it out of its misery, something unseen snatches it away. Panicking, the two teens separate, and Nancy shortly finds a slime-encrusted opening in a standing tree trunk. She tentatively looks inside, only to find herself in the Upside Down—with *something else* for company. Jonathan hears Nancy's screams, but he can't actually see her…

Chapter 6: "The Monster"

With the creature in the Upside Down stalking her, Nancy gropes her way back to the gap in the tree, where Jonathan pulls her free in the nick of time. Terrified, she asks him to sleep over at her house; he does so, sleeping on the floor of her room, but Steve shows up and is furious at Jonathan being there. The next day, the conflict between Steve and Jonathan escalates, culminating in a fistfight that results in Jonathan being arrested while Steve and his cronies get away.

Eleven wanders alone into the town of Hawkins, sparking calamity when her hunger drives her into a local supermarket, where she uses her powers to shatter windows as a distraction to escape with an armload of Eggo waffles, which she gobbles down "raw". Elsewhere, the boys are still dealing with the rift between Lucas and Mike; Lucas refuses to make up with Mike and Dustin, and he goes it alone to Hawkins Laboratory while Mike and Dustin search for Eleven. They instead are found by the two school bullies, who are still bearing a grudge. They chase the boys to the quarry, forcing Mike at knife-point to leap off the ledge down into the icy waters far below. However, Eleven intercedes on his behalf, rescuing Mike by telekinetically stopping his fall right in mid-air then lifting him back up to safety before hurling one bully into the air and breaking the other's arm prior to them taking to their heels. Mike and Dustin happily reunite with her, even as Lucas warns them via walkie-talkie to hide: staking-out the Hawkins Laboratory, Lucas watches as Dr. Brenner and his militia pile into their vans and head into town in search of Eleven and the boys.

Elsewhere, Joyce and Hopper have tracked down a woman who had sued Dr. Brenner following her participation in one of his past experiments. She is unable to speak, but her sister can: the woman didn't know she was pregnant at the time Brenner used her as a test subject; Brenner and the authorities claimed she subsequently suffered a miscarriage, but the woman insists that she actually had the baby, which manifested "special abilities" before Brenner abducted the child. Could that child have been Eleven…?

Chapter 7: "The Bathtub"

Dr. Brenner and his militia's vans arrive at Mike's house, but Eleven and the boys elude them. Back at the police station, the parents of the bully with the broken arm seek to file a complaint against Mike and the boys, raving about Eleven and her uncanny "powers". Hopper connects the dots and immediately rounds up Joyce, Jonathan and Nancy, only to find Brenner's agents searching Mike's and

Open Wi-i-i-i-ide! The ravenous Demogorgon monster (suit worn by Mark Steger) from the Upside Down plays cookie-lookie; monster design by Aaron Sims, sculpted by Mike Elizalde's Spectral Motion, animatronic engineered by Mark Setrakian

Nancy's home. Using a walkie-talkie, they contact the boys, who are hiding-out with Eleven at a local scrapyard, even as Brenner's agents arrive in search of them. Hopper, Nancy, and Jonathan rescue the boys, and they all join forces at last to search for Will and Barb.

While recalling Brenner's experiments, Eleven remembers him repeatedly immersing her in an isolation tank filled with water to focus and amplify her powers, enabling her to access the Upside Down. She convinces Hopper and the team that she might be able to locate Will and Barb if they can improvise some sort of sensory-deprivation water tank, which they manage to do in the school gym. She immerses herself while Hopper and Joyce head back to Hawkins Laboratory. They succeed in breaking-in, only to be then captured by Brenner's agents.

The sensory-deprivation pool succeeds, and Eleven enters the Upside Down, only to discover that Barb is dead—her body apparently having been inundated with the creature's slug-like offspring—and that Will is still alive and in hiding, but soon to succumb if he is not rescued. Jonathan and Nancy propose that if they can somehow lure the creature hiding within the Upside Down to enter the earthly realm via Joyce's house, they *might* be able to kill it…

Chapter 8: "The Upside Down"

Back at Hawkins Laboratory, Dr. Brenner has separated Joyce and Hopper. He tries to coerce Joyce into accepting his "help", even as his agents torture Hopper with a Taser. They eventually agree to keep silent about the secret experiments and tell him where the kids are hiding—*if* Brenner will allow them to enter the Upside Down via the lab's organic "doorway" to rescue Will. Once inside, Hopper and Joyce explore the dark Upside Down landscape, discovering clutches of eggs and eventually Will himself, alive but incapacitated and unconscious. Hopper removes a nasty tentacle-like obstruction from Will's throat and frantically administers CPR, resuscitating the boy.

Back at Joyce's house, Jonathan and Nancy have rigged an elaborate series of booby-traps, intent upon luring the creature out of the Upside Down into our world with blood, then destroying it with fire. When a repentant Steve unexpectedly shows up, he is forced to go along with the plan as the monster erupts onto the scene. In the melee that follows, the monster gets torched, but it apparently escapes nonetheless, as, upon extinguishing the flames, Jonathan, Nancy and Steve can find no evidence whatsoever of the creature's body.

Back at the school gym, Eleven and the boys witness the arrival of Brenner and his agents, intent upon recapturing Eleven. The boys are corralled and trapped, forcing a drained and weakened Eleven to overexert herself, lashing-out against the armed intruders, killing many in the process. Having severely depleted herself, she faints as Brenner seizes her and his agents capture the boys—but the blood spilled in the conflict attracts the creature from the Upside Down, which does indeed still live. The monster proceeds to savage Brenner and his agents, and the boys find themselves face-to-face with the ravenous creature. Eleven recovers, bidding Mike a fond farewell before mustering enough power to cause herself and the monster to evaporate from our reality.

Coda: Christmas time, one month later. Will is apparently his old self again, reunited with his friends in a role-playing game at Mike's house. Jonathan stops by to pick up Will, pausing to say hello to Nancy and Steve, who are now dating one another. At the police station, Hopper leaves the office Christmas party to drive alone into the woods and place Eggo waffles in a food chest—presumably for Eleven?

Meanwhile, Jonathan and Will join their mother Joyce for Christmas dinner in their partially-repaired home. Will excuses himself to go to the bathroom—where he looks at his wan reflection in the mirror over the sink before before coughing-up a living, slug-like parasite which slithers down the drain, as memories of the Upside Down return...

[End of Season One]

That Sinking Feeling: Will Byers (Noah Schnapp) faces his uncertain future in the mirror during *Stranger Things*' coda...

Continued from page 203

Still The Ultimate! *Stranger Things* wears its shaping (and shape-shifting) influences quite openly; right on its sleeve, in fact. Among the various one-sheet movie posters seen decorating characters' bedroom walls in the show is the now-iconic Drew Struzan poster—that he reportedly painted overnight in a single sitting!—for John Carpenter's **THE THING** (1982), which originally bombed hard theatrically, but is now rightly revered as a classic

Given *Stranger Things'* conscious evocation of Stephen King's novels, short stories, and the film adaptations, King's best-selling 1986 magnum opus *It* remains the most obvious inspirational wellspring (first edition cover art by Bob Giusti, lettering by Amy Hill)

****

Whatever side of the camp you found yourself stranded in—happily or unhappily—there's no denying that *Stranger Things* was the among the most unexpected hits of the summer TV season, at a time when Netflix sorely needed some good news.[8]

And whatever side of the camp you set up your site in—willingly or unwillingly—here, we have just the "Study Guide" for you!

It's important to note that The Duffer Brothers immediately acknowledged, with pride, their debt to the pop-cultural roots of *Stranger Things*. As writer Zack Smith noted in July for IndyWeek.com:

"Fans of the era's genre films will spot plenty of visual and narrative homages in *Stranger Things*, from the synthesizer-driven score and the Stephen King-style title card to the presence of eighties mainstays Winona Ryder and Matthew Modine in major roles. There are shout-outs to movies such as **POLTERGEIST**, **THE GOONIES**, **E.T. THE EXTRA-TERRESTRIAL**, and **LESS THAN ZERO**, and to pop-culture touchstones from X-Men comics to Dungeons & Dragons. 'What we responded to when we saw films like that as kids was that they didn't talk down to us, that the stakes were really high,' Ross says by phone from Los Angeles, the day after the last episode of *Stranger Things* is finalized. 'If you read something like *It* or watch that train coming at them in **STAND BY ME**, you're afraid they could die. The kids felt real, and reminded us of us and our friends.'..."[9]

If you loved the series, this will inform your second, third, and fourth *Stranger Things* marathon viewings, enrich and deepen the entire viewing experience in ways that might surprise you, and steer you to more to savor until the sequel series to *Stranger Things* hits the streaming venues.[10]

If you loathed the series, this will lend your arguments credence, rekindle your love affairs with the wellsprings you didn't see a need to crudely retread, and provide ammunition for those unavoidable encounters with the pie-eyed devotees of the series.

With the shallow memories of all things "pop" and 21st Century, the buzz surrounding *Stranger Things* only seemed capable of recalling Stephen King's work. Well, sure; part of the appeal of *Stranger Things* is that The Duffer Brothers grew up reading King, watching Joe Dante and Steven Spielberg movies (and there's more of Joe Dante here than Spielberg, to my eye/ear[11]), and were clearly

---

8 See "Cramer shocked that so many Netflix users bailing over a couple extra bucks," July 19th, 2016, archived online (@ http://finance.yahoo.com/news/cramer-shocked-many-netflix-users-151454300.html): "Netflix's price increases scared people away from the streaming service, and the volume of unsubscribes surprised Jim Cramer."

9 Zack Smith, "Two Brothers Funnel Their Nostalgia for Eighties-Era Durham [NC] Summers Into New Netflix Series *Stranger Things*," Indyweek.com (serving Raleigh, Cary, Durham, Chapel Hill, NC), July 20th, 2016, archived online (@ http://www.indyweek.com/indyweek/two-brothers-funnel-their-nostalgia-for-eighties-era-durham-summers-into-new-netflix-series-stranger-things/Content?oid=5051936); quoted with permission of Zack Smith.

10 See "Stranger Things Renewed For Season 2 By Netflix!," July 5th, 2016, archived online (@ http://renewcanceltv.com/stranger-things-renewed-season-2-netflix/)

11 Nice to see Tim Lucas fully agreed on this point; "...it's important to remember that Joe Dante *invented* 1980s Young Adult fantasy in cinema. If you want to see where smart kid protagonists began, the way they still are today (in movies like **TOMORROWLAND** and **GOOSEBUMPS**, for example), you have to go back to **GREMLINS** and **EXPLORERS** and *Eerie, Indiana*...." See Lucas, *Ibid.* (@ http://videowatchdog.blogspot.com/2016/07/famil-

steeped in 1980s genre fare. The Duffer Brothers happily spread their influences all over the kid character's bedroom walls, from Sam Raimi's **EVIL DEAD** to John Carpenter's **THE THING** posters as markers, to the synth score copping from Tangerine Dream and John Carpenter scores of yore. You don't need me to list the Stephen King novels or King-adapted/derived 1980s feature films and TV miniseries, either; those are legion, and readily known and accessed.

But you deserve a wish-list and reference points to enrich your experience post-*Stranger Things*:

Without further ado, as a *Cryptid Cinema* courtesy, we offer you:

The *Stranger Things* Study/Viewing Guide

1. Joseph Losey/Evan Jones' **THE DAMNED** ([1963, UK] released in the USA in cut form as **THESE ARE THE DAMNED** in 1965) is the original wellspring from which *Stranger Things* flows, where the whole conceit of a secret para-militarized laboratory experimenting on children comes from. **THE DAMNED** is one of the classics of Cold War British science-fiction, starring MacDonald Carey, Shirley Anne Field, Viveca Lindfors, Alexander Knox, and Oliver Reed. Be sure to screen the full-length 95-minute original UK edit of this dark gem, which was misunderstood and reviled by its parent studio, Hammer Films (and its US distributor, Columbia Pictures), severely cut and relegated to a cursory theatrical release two years after its completion. It's available in its excellent original Hammer Films UK version[12] in the US; it's *required* viewing, not to be missed. It is *absolutely essential* that you start with this film!

2. Well, actually, the *real* wellspring from which Jones adapted his **THE DAMNED** screenplay was H.L. Lawrence's novel *The Children of Light* (London: MacDonald and Co., 1960), which is pretty

dear on AbeBooks (*www.abebooks.com*) and elsewhere, *if* you can even find a copy at all. I bought my paperback copy for over $50 some years ago, so I can only imagine it's got to be up in the $75+ range these days. But H.L. Lawrence is the author who *really* laid the bedrock, particularly its being the result of cold, cruel secret government installations and scientific experimentation.[13] Lawrence arguably owed a debt to Theodore Sturgeon's "Baby is Three" (*Galaxy*, October 1952), which Sturgeon expanded to novel form to become the magnificent *More Than Human* (New York: Ballantine Books, 1953).

These two novels are where all telepath/telekinetic/ mutant children in our pop culture were born. And yes, Stephen King knows all about all of this: from

---

[13] There's precious little available about Lawrence's seminal novel; see Tim Lucas, "On Reading *The Children of Light*", *Video Watchblog*, September 12th, 2016 (@ http://videowatchdog.blogspot.com/2016/09/on-reading-children-of-light.html)

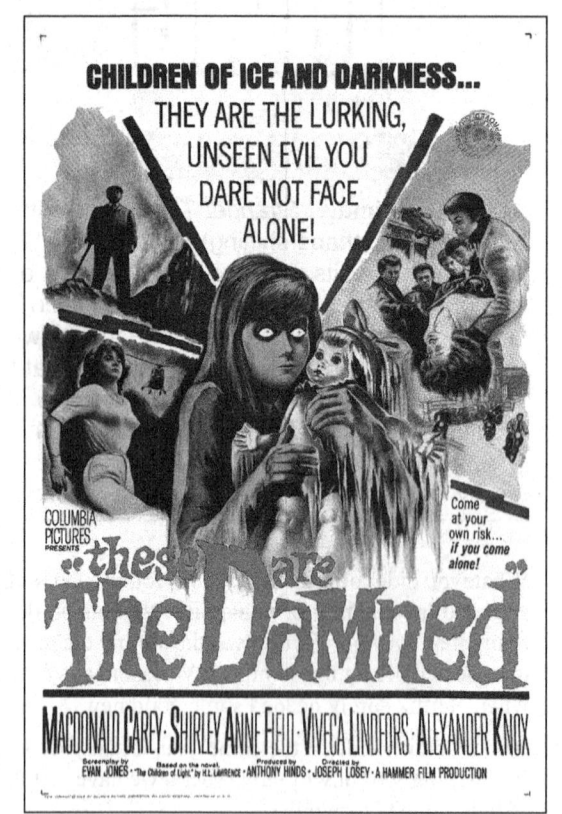

These *Aren't* The Damned! Well, *not* the alien-sired hybrid "damned" of the 1960 MGM hit **VILLAGE OF THE DAMNED**, which Columbia Pictures' publicity department tried like hell to convince potential audiences they were, anyway! (The misleading and lurid 1965 one-sheet poster for **THESE ARE THE DAMNED**, Columbia's abortive American release of the severely-edited Hammer Film **THE DAMNED**)

H. L. (Henry Lionel) Lawrence's novel *The Children of Light* (hardcover edition, London: 1960, MacDonald and Co.; paperback edition, 1962, Consul Books) offers the most caustic portrait of militarized British government of its time—one willing to maliciously use and manipulate its citizenry and its children to achieve its goals—and as such is definitely a landmark precursor of *Stranger Things*.

---

[12] As part of the 2010 Sony Pictures Home Entertainment DVD collection of the Columbia Pictures-distributed Hammer Films from the 1960s, *The Icons of Suspense Collection: Hammer Films*, featuring six of the studio's rarest titles, **STOP ME BEFORE I KILL!**, **CASH ON DEMAND**, **THE SNORKEL**, **MANIAC**, **NEVER TAKE CANDY FROM A STRANGER**, and **THESE ARE THE DAMNED**. Still available (from https://www.amazon.com/Icons-Suspense-Collection-Snorkel-Stranger/dp/B0034PWPHY/ref=sr_1_1?ie=UTF8&qid=1469012861&sr=8-1&keywords=The+Damned+Joseph+Losey) and other online venues.

Carrie to *Firestarter* and beyond, they're *all* offspring of Sturgeon's "Homo Gestalt".

3. There is another novel that *must* be cited as an essential source for *Stranger Things*: Robert Cormier's *I Am the Cheese* (1977, in both US and UK hardcover and paperback editions from Pantheon Books/Laurel-Leaf Library [US] and Victor Gollancz, Ltd./Fontana Lions [UK]). *I Am the Cheese* was and is a complex, compelling first-person novel in which its young protagonist, orphan Adam Farmer, struggles to make sense of his environment and circumstances while living in a decidedly *odd* facility, which might be a mental hospital (or worse); in doing so, he also juggles fragmentary memories of his former life with his parents and a repressed or buried tragic event. In time, Adam comes to discover the truth about where—and who and what—he is now.

To say anything more would spoil your reading of the novel, but rest assured that *Stranger Things* might not exist without Cormier's game-changing Y/A novel. It is as central to the *ST* narrative (and narrative structure) as *The Children of Light* and **THE DAMNED** are, if in a very different way. Though it starred young **E.T.** co-star Robert MacNaughton as Adam, Robert Jiras' and David Lange's feature film adaptation **I AM THE CHEESE** (1983, USA) never achieved the boxoffice, cable, or home video[14] success of *any* of the Stephen King movie adaptations, but Cormier's novel has remained in print since the late 1970s, also spawning many classroom and library study guide texts. *I Am the Cheese* was and remains one of the essential genre young adult novels; thus, it is a primary source for much that followed, including *Stranger Things*.

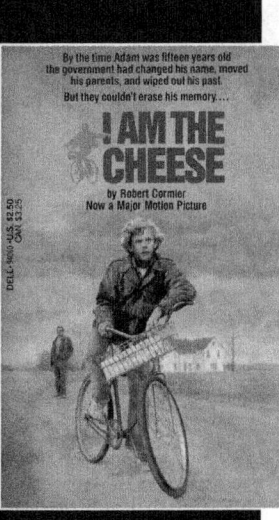

4. Somewhat of a precursor to *I Am the Cheese* is the eight-page comic story "The Loathsome" in EC's *Weird Science* #20 (July-August, 1953), story by Al Feldstein, art by Wally Wood. Though the narrative plays out in a very different manner than either of its successors, the setting and situation of the moving Feldstein/Wood story—an orphanage,

---

14 This might be the toughest of all films listed in this Study Guide to acquire a copy of, though I highly recommend it, and available copies are quite affordable at the time of this writing. **I AM THE CHEESE** was released briefly on VHS in 1984 from Vestron Video (and again in 1994 from Front Row Video; though these may have been bootleg editions), and on DVD in 2007 via First Run Features. Both are long-OOP; used copies may still be available via Amazon (see https://www.amazon.com/Am-Cheese-VHS-Robert-MacNaughton/dp/6303139663/ref=sr_1_1?s=movies-tv&ie=UTF8&qid=1474244426&sr=1-1&keywords=I+Am+the+Cheese+VHS and https://www.amazon.com/I-Am-Cheese-Robert-MacNaughton/dp/B0007YMW32/ref=sr_1_1?s=movies-tv&ie=UTF8&qid=1474244277&sr=1-1&keywords=I+Am+the+Cheese).

E.T.'s co-star (as Elliott's older brother) Robert MacNaughton landed his one starring role in a feature film playing Adam, troubled protagonist of the sadly forgotten movie adaptation of Robert Cormier's Y/A classic *I Am the Cheese* (1983); tie-in paperback cover art by G. Watson.

No Cheese Here! Before Y/A heroes like Eleven and her friends ever graced the screen, pioneer "young adult" writers like Robert Cormier blazed the trail for such characters in then-cutting-edge and controversial novels like *I Am The Cheese* ([1977] adapted into a shot-in-Vermont feature film in 1983). *ST*'s Eleven owes a clear debt to Adam, this novel's orphaned male protagonist

Bad Girls: Another precursor to *Stranger Things*' Eleven was the unseen-until-the-penultimate-page orphan mutant-girl drawn by Wally Wood for the classic EC Comics SF tale "The Loathsome", in *Weird Science* #20 (July-August, 1953)

Before *Stranger Things*, There Was... Bill Condon and Michael Laughlin's delicious set-in-Illinois-but-shot-in-New-Zealand sleeper **DEAD KIDS** (a.k.a. **STRANGE BEHAVIOR**, 1981). All visible on this one-sheet poster are Michael Murphy as the suspicious small-town cop, Dan Shor as the son taking it in the eye for science, Fiona Lewis as the needling nurse, and Louise Fletcher as worried stepmother

an orphan girl with a secret, and the adults' mounting anxiety about her secret and possible escape—certainly suggests key elements of both Cormier's novel and *Stranger Things*:

A doctor sends a deformed mutant child that was the product of her father's exposure to atomic radiation to be brought up in an orphanage. The women of the orphanage dislike her because she displays poor behavior. One day the younger nurse comments to the older one that the girl is behaving herself recently and the older nurse recalls that all children receive a birthday party at ten years old and the girl must figure she is going to get one. The young woman asks if she is going to give the child one and the older woman states that it wouldn't be right to expect the other children to attend, so they'll just skip it in the mutant girl's case. They discover that the girl was spying on them and when she returns to her room she smashes the mirror. She's punished, and that evening the younger nurse sees the girl on the grounds stuffing notes into tree hollows. She assumes that she must be up to no good and informs the older woman. The following evening they confront the child demanding the note and the girl flees from them. She climbs up a tree branch overhanging the orphanage's spiked wall and loses her grip. As the note slips from the hand of the dying impaled child, the older woman picks it up. It says "To whoever finds this note—I love you."[...][15]

5. Man oh man, has Bill Condon (script) and Michael Laughlin (director)'s made-in-New Zealand, set-in-America SF/horror gem **DEAD KIDS** (a.k.a. **STRANGE BEHAVIOR**, 1981) cast a longer shadow than anyone could have thought remotely possible when that odd, offbeat little jewel of a film popped up in fleeting theatrical release. Most of us (myself included) first caught it on late-night cable broadcasts; however you first experience **STRANGE BEHAVIOR**, I envy you your initial exposure!

It's as if the planned Condon/Laughlin "*Strange*" trilogy was completed by The Duffer Brothers...*seriously!* Condon and Laughlin did get **STRANGE INVADERS** (1983, USA) out, but couldn't mount the funding for the third feature in their planned trilogy. The Duffer Brothers got their title reference spot-on, didn't they?

I mean, seriously, watch **STRANGE BEHAVIOR**—a marvelous Tangerine Dream score enhances the film, the story involves the disappearance/murder of Illinois teen boys, a local cop (Michael Murphy) investigates to discover all the victims are sons of men who investigated the dicey lab/experiments of a long-dead scientist (Arthur Dingham), whose experiments continue on in a secret government lab and the cop's own son (Dan Shor) is the latest lab rat/research subject—look, just *trust* me on this!

Just see—*experience*—**STRANGE BEHAVIOR**![16]

---

15 Synopsis quoted from the Grand Comics Database, *Weird Science* #20, "The Loathsome!", archived online (@ http://www.comics.org/issue/10707/), which also lists all available reprint editions of the story, and which is highly recommended.

16 Currently available in the US from Severin Films as a 2014 Blu-ray/DVD combo under its original title, **DEAD KIDS** (see https://www.amazon.com/Dead-Kids-Blu-ray-DVD-Combo/dp/B00I9N56YK/ref=sr_1_1?ie=UTF8&qid=1475496519&sr=8-1&keywords=Dead+Kids+Blu-ray), or via either the Synapse Films 2008 Special Edition DVD (still at https://www.amazon.com/Strange-Behavior-Special-Michael-Murphy/dp/B001D5C1N0/ref=sr_1_1?s=movies-tv&ie=UTF8&qid=1474205050&sr=1-1&keywords=strange+behavior), or as one of the trio of features (the other two are **PATRICK** and **THIRST**) in the 2003 Elite DVD package set *The Aussie Horror Collection: Terror From Down*

Could Bill Condon and Michael Laughlin's **STRANGE BEHAVIOR** (1981) and **STRANGE INVADERS** (1983) be the first two parts of a 'strange' trilogy completed by *Stranger Things*?

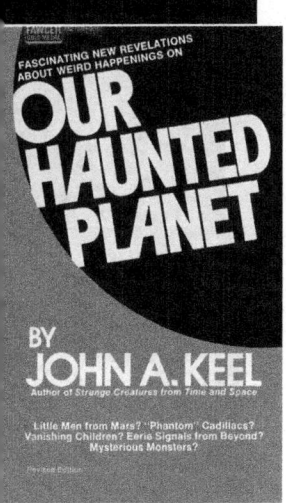

Are all cryptid sightings the result of barely-glimpsed dwellers from other dimensions 'peeking' through, as in *Stranger Things*? John Keel was the man who popularized that theory in the 1960s and 1970s. Expanding upon his unifying theories concerning inexplicable phenomenon and cryptid sightings in particular, John Keel's *Our Haunted Planet* (1971, Fawcett) collected various articles Keel had written for Saga and Male magazines in the 1960s, along with lectures Keel presented in 1970.

PS: The 1998 **DISTURBING BEHAVIOR** knowingly referenced Condon/Laughlin's film, as did that film's director, *The X-Files*' David Nutter; it's also a film well worth seeing in this context, despite what parent studio MGM did to it.[17]

6. Tough to say much without spoilers, but let's face it: *Stranger Things* emulates more than Stephen King. It's like a prequel to *The Mist*, in't it? Or a much better redraft/remake of *Firestarter*.

But where *Stranger Things* goes owes a debt to H.P. Lovecraft's short story "From Beyond" (1920, but first published in 1934)—read the story, it's all there in principal, and yes, Stephen King knows it well— and all other parallel worlds up to and including the Black Lodge and the Red Room (see: *Twin Peaks,* the complete series, and **TWIN PEAKS: FIRE WALK WITH ME**). According to *Twin Peaks* co-creator Mark Frost, that dimensional element central to the series was cribbed/extrapolated from Dion Fortune's 1935 non-fiction book *Psychic Self-Defense*, which is online[18] if you can't find or afford a hard copy.[19] There are countless examples of "secret experiments" (sometimes government/military experiments, sometimes isolated renegade scientists) in the Pre-Code horror comics of the 1950s (including EC Comics stories), but I won't get into those particulars, which would swell this Study Guide to unwieldy proportions. Suffice to note: like most sf-horror movies, EC Comics and and their Pre-Code competitors relied upon covert scientific labs to spawn most of their horrors.

In terms of how these dimensional elements unfold in *Stranger Things*, I'd also steer the curious viewer/reader to John A. Keel's books, particularly *Strange Creatures From Time and Space* (Gold Medal Books/Fawcett Books, 1970), which was revised and ex-

---

Under (still available at https://www.amazon.com/Aussie-Collection-Patrick-Strange-Behavior/dp/B0000TAYPC/ref=sr_1_2?s=movies-tv&ie=UTF8&qid=1474205050&sr=1-2&keywords=strange+behavior).

17 **DISTURBING BEHAVIOR**—and what it originally was *meant* to be (recoverable at last thanks to the bonus features)—is still available on DVD and Bluray; see https://www.amazon.com/Disturbing-Behavior-Blu-ray-James-Marsden/dp/B018WQBNEA/ref=sr_1_2?s=movies-tv&ie=UTF8&qid=1474205323&sr=1-2&keywords=Disturbing+behavior for the Blu-ray edition, but the DVD edition may take some searching (be sure to pick up the edition with the extra features to fully appreciate the film with its deleted scenes and alternate ending). Avoid streaming the film, as the theatrical version was severely truncated and tampered with.

18 http://jacquesricher.com/occult/psychic.pdf

19 https://www.amazon.com/s/ref=nb_sb_ss_c_2_19?url=-search-alias%3Dstripbooks&field-keywords=dion+fortune+psychic+self+defense&sprefix=Dion+Fortune+Psychi%2Caps%2C190

Before *Stranger Things*, There Was... The now-highly-collectible first edition of John A. Keel's seminal volume *Strange Creatures from Time and Space* (1970), which introduced Keel's theories of reported monster sightings as perhaps being attributable to visitors from a parallel dimension; its magnificent cover art was by Frank Frazetta

panded into *The Complete Guide to Mysterious Beings* (Doubleday Books, 1994). Keel expanded upon his views on paranormal events, UFOs, monster sightings, and what he called "ultraterrestrials" in a series of books: *UFOs: Operation Trojan Horse: An Exhaustive Study of Unidentified Flying Objects, Revealing Their Source and the Forces That Control Them* a.k.a. *Why UFOs: Operation Trojan Horse* (G.P. Putnam's Sons and Manor Books, both 1970), *The Mothman Prophecies: An Investigation into the Mysterious American Visits of the Infamous Feathery Garuda* (E.P. Dutton/Saturday Review Press, 1975; Signet Books/New American Library, 1976), and *The Eighth Tower: The Cosmic Forces Behind All Religious, Occult, and UFO Phenomenon* a.k.a. *The Eighth Tower: On Ultraterrestrials and the Superspectrum* (E.P. Dutton/Saturday Review Press, 1975; Signet Books/New American Library, 1977).[20]

---

20 There are now print-on-demand editions of all these Keel books; they are easily found and purchased in affordable new editions from multiple venues.

And that's *it*. I can't say more without spoiling key elements of *Stranger Things* for folks who haven't yet seen the series.

7. Beyond the John A. Keel speculation that opened this dimensional doorway, I've got to bring your attention to what followed in Keel's footsteps. Along with the so-called Philadelphia Experiment case history—which was a movie John Carpenter wanted to make, but Stewart Raffill [!!!] got to instead[21]—you want to dig into the Montauk case history, specifically the 1992 book *The Montauk Project: Experiments in Time*, by Preston B. Nichols and Peter Moon,[22] and Christopher Garetano's **MONTAUK CHRONICLES** (2015, USA).[23]

In fact, The Duffer Brothers owe a considerable debt to Christopher's film. The series was originally announced in April 2015 under the title *Montauk*; that is indisputably a fact.[24] The Duffer Brothers' pitch reel, it seems, reportedly incorporated/appropriated, *sans* permission, footage *lifted verbatim from* Garetano's **MONTAUK CHRONICLES**—but I'll leave *that* for Christopher to sort out. On July 23rd, 2016, Christopher posted the following open letter on Facebook (and for this, I have retained Christopher's use of capital letters, as in his original post):

---

21 Still on DVD, available from *https://www.amazon.com/Philadelphia-Experiment-Michael-Pare/dp/B005FQ2H8W/ref=sr_1_1?s=movies-tv&ie=UTF8&qid=1474206687&sr=1-1&keywords=philadelphia+experiment* —and the SyFy Channel's 2012 remake (on DVD and Blu-ray) is available (@ *https://www.amazon.com/Philadelphia-Experiment-Blu-ray-Nicholas-Lea/dp/B00BWHAP4Q/ref=sr_1_5?s=movies-tv&ie=UTF8&qid=1474206687&sr=1-5&keywords=philadelphia+experiment*). There's also DVD editions of documentaries on the subject: approach at your own risk! See, or *don't see*, the Al Bielek lecture-based documentaries **THE TRUTH ABOUT THE PHILADELPHIA EXPERIMENT: INVISIBILITY, TIME TRAVEL AND MIND CONTROL** (2010, available @ *https://www.amazon.com/Truth-About-Philadelphia-Experiment-Invisibility/dp/B002VRNIJA/ref=sr_1_10?s=movies-tv&ie=UTF8&qid=1474206687&sr=1-10&keywords=philadelphia+experiment*), which is included in the 3-DVD set **THE PHILADELPHIA EXPERIMENT REVEALED: FINAL COUNTDOWN TO DISCLOSURE** (2011, available @ *https://www.amazon.com/Philadelphia-Experiment-Revealed-Countdown-Disclosure/dp/B007I1TGQI/ref=sr_1_11?s=movies-tv&ie=UTF8&qid=1474206687&sr=1-11&keywords=philadelphia+experiment*). Beilek claims to be the sole survivor of the so-called Philadelphia Experiment; Beilek and author/fellow lecturer Preston Nichols link The Philadelphia Experiment with the subsequent Phoenix and Montauk Projects, hence its relevance here.

22 Peter Moon, Preston B. Nichols, and Nina Helms subsequently wrote three more books on the subject: *Montauk Revisited: Adventures in Synchronicity* (1994), *Pyramids of Montauk: Explorations in Consciousness* (1995), and *The Black Sun: Montauk's Nazi-Tibetan Connection* (1997). All are still available via amazon and various online sources.

23 *https://www.amazon.com/Montauk-Chronicles/dp/B00ISGZ65W/ref=sr_1_1?s=movies-tv&ie=UTF8&qid=1469011564&sr=1-1&keywords=montauk+chronicles*

24 See Dana Rose Falcone, "Netflix announces new series *Montauk* arriving in 2016," April 2, 2015, archived online (@ *http://www.ew.com/netflix-orders-montauk-for-2016*)

I recently read an article, this morning, stating that STRANGER THINGS was only based on MK ULTRA. The article never mentioned that the show was originally called MONTAUK.

This is very strange as the author is well aware of the Montauk Project.

The show was pitched and sold as MONTAUK, not MK ULTRA.

There are blatantly obvious reasons for all of this.

Bottom Line:

The show is good fun. I have no issues with it or ANYONE who is enjoying it. I'm not losing my mind over this at all. I'm fine and inspired as ever.

I'm busy working on my new movie.[25] I've only made a few posts about this on FACEBOOK that took me only a few moments to achieve.

I have my own (network) show that's in production, right now.

I'm not suing anyone. I was in full-support of STRANGER THINGS until I learned of the pitch process that allows VERY-RICH albeit lazy, in the pitch process, people to take the work of others (including independent artists) and use it as part of a proposal to sell a mega-show to a network. It's wrong but it's legal.

The sizzle-reel of my own show also contained scenes from my movie that were combined with work from my co-producers.

It was completely original.

So that's all folks. I think it should simply be illegal to do that.

These folks could afford to shoot a few things and THEN pitch a show.

STRANGER THINGS, was partially inspired by the work that I did with my picture, MONTAUK CHRONICLES. FULL STOP.

OK then, ONWARD and upward!!! Here's to originality, truth, and to the great movies, magazines, websites, and television shows of the near future.

---

25 Garetano's new movie will be of instant interest to *Monster!* readers: it's entitled **BIGFOOT** (slated for release later in 2016); the first trailer was posted earlier this year (@ *https://www.youtube.com/watch?v=7nxRmroZH3Q*)

The Montauk Connection: The original proposal title of *Stranger Things* was *Montauk*, referencing the case history covered in the book *The Montauk Project: Experiments in Time* (1992) by Preston B. Nichols and Peter Moon, along with Christopher Garetano's documentary **MONTAUK CHRONICLES** (2015).

Before *Stranger Things*, There Was... Christopher Garetano's doc **MONTAUK CHRONICLES** (2015, USA), from which the promo "pitch reel" for *Stranger Things* reportedly lifted imagery and sequences in order to sell the Duffer Brothers series. Tut-tut, Duffer Brothers—pay your dues!

The original authors of *The Montauk Project*, Preston B. Nichols and Peter Moon, extended their research into three more books co-authored with Nina Helms: *Montauk Revisited: Adventures in Synchronicity* (1994), *Pyramids of Montauk: Explorations in Consciousness* (1995), and *The Black Sun: Montauk's Nazi-Tibetan Connection* (1997)

Best Wishes,
Christopher Garetano.[26]

While *Stranger Things* takes a very different approach and narrative tack, and they're very different works, there's a major debt there. Maybe it's all worked out for Christopher after all; at the time of this writing, Garetano announced production underway[27] on a related TV series:

In only a few weeks we will begin principal-photography on our MONTAUK CHRONICLES network spin-off show. It's been a long and often an arduous journey making independent movies. The rewards are waiting for those who have the courage, drive, creativity, and conviction to stick to their vision. You must also have and develop a gargantuan sense of patience. Don't ever listen to those who tell you 'you can't.' ...I began shooting MONTAUK CHRONICLES in a suburban basement and now I'm working with a network on a show..."[28]

As to where Christopher was originally coming from, and the links to *Stranger Things*, the Supernatural Research and Analysis Institute's Mark Johnson wrote this past July,

*...most viewers who watch the show [*Stranger Things*] will have no idea that it is based on real events that took place in the United States from the early 1950's, all the way up to the 1970's...and may still be going on today. In 1953, the Central Intelligence Agency officially sanctioned a program known as MK Ultra[29]—an illegal mind control program that performed experiments on unwilling human subjects using mind-altering drugs (especially LSD), sleep deprivation, and torture.[30] President Gerald Ford commissioned an investigation into CIA activities within the United States, MK Ultra was shut down in 1973, and CIA Director Richard Helms ordered all documentation regarding the MK Ultra program destroyed. Yet there is eye-*

---

26 Quoted with permission. For more on Christopher's take on the associative links between THE MONTAUK CHRONICLES and *Stranger Things*, see the July 2016 interview with Christopher archived (@ http://sarinstitutecom.powweb.com/2016/07/19/stranger-things-mk-ultra-and-the-montauk-project/)

27 Garetano's own Montauk-based TV series proposal was, in Christopher's words, "in-development long before *Stranger Things* was even in production..."; quoted, with permission, from a personal message to the author, September 19, 2016. The series goes into production as of October 2016.

28 Christopher Garetano, Facebook post, September 15, 2016, 3:30 PM.; quoted with permission. On September 9, 2016, 9:58 PM, Christopher posted, "Our MONTAUK CHRONICLES network-show is now in pre-production and we're shooting by mid-October." Good luck, Christopher!

29 See https://en.wikipedia.org/wiki/Project_MKUltra; this link was "live" in the original online text.

30 Interjecting an SRB footnote here, not part of the original quoted text: The first book I ever found on this subject was John D. Marks' *The Search for the "Manchurian Candidate": The CIA and Mind Control* (Times Books, 1979; WW Norton, 1992), which is recommended; there are now others, too. Primary among the more recent texts are *Mind Wars: Brain Research and National Defense* a.k.a. the revised edition, *Mind Wars: Brain Science and the Military in the 21st Century*, by Jonathan D. Moreno (Dana Press, 2006; Bellevue Literary Press, 2012) and *Mind Wars: A History of Mind Control, Surveillance, and Social Engineering by the Government, Media, and Secret Societies*, by Marie D. Jones and Larry Flaxman (New Pages, 2015).

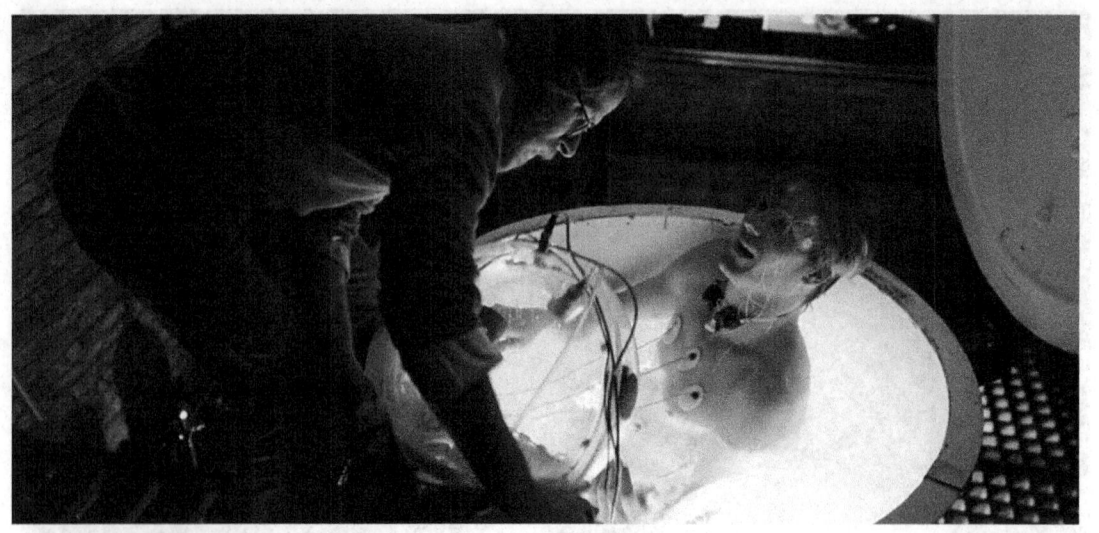

Before *Stranger Things*, There Was... Paddy Chayefsky's and Ken Russell's **ALTERED STATES** (1980, USA). Here, Arthur Rosenberg (Bob Balaban) helps Dr. Eddie Jessup (William Hurt) out of a standing isolation tank during their early experiments in the film

*witness testimony that these clandestine programs continued throughout the 1980's and longer. An excellent documentary on the subject, **THE MONTAUK CHRONICLES**, tells the story of the secret installation in Montauk on Long Island, NY.*[31]

8. Perhaps needless to say—but I'll say it anyway—the entire isolation tank angle was inspired by Dr. John C. Lilly's real-life sensory deprivation tank experiments in the 1950s and 1960s, which in turn inspired the 1963 James Kennaway/Basil Dearden film **THE MIND BENDERS** and, more famously, Paddy Chayefsky's and Ken Russell's mind-bending **ALTERED STATES** (1980), the ultimate "isolation tank" psychedelic film experience. *Essential viewing!*

9. The final text I must bring to your attention predates most of those inspirational sources previously mentioned (except for the Lovecraft short story). Richard Matheson's story "Little Girl Lost" was in many ways *Stranger Things*' Ground Zero of sorts: In a normal suburban home, a little girl disappears in her own bedroom, her voice audible from under her bed, but she isn't there; still, they can hear her, under the bed, behind or between the walls...

It was published in Matheson's second short story anthology *The Shores of Space* (1953), but most experienced it via the March 16th, 1962 *The Twilight Zone* dramatization (I remember it well: it broadcast just two days after my seventh birthday!).[32] It's

where the screenplay of **POLTERGEIST** (both versions, 1982 and 2015) was extrapolated from. Matheson pioneered this whole "parent(s)-lose-child-in-the-walls" template, including the need to scientifically parse-out a rescue from seemingly supernatural events. *Start there*, since everyone else has... whether they know it or not.

And, yes, again; Stephen King knows.

There's more, much more, but this gives you somewhere to go once you've savored—or despised— *Stranger Things*.

I'm on board for whatever The Duffer Brothers do hereafter.[33] May stranger things await us all!

---

[31] For a comprehensive overview, see everything the Supernatural Analysis and Research Institute has posted online (@ http://sarinstitutecom.powweb.com/2016/07/19/stranger-things-mk-ultra-and-the-montauk-project/)

[32] See Season 3 of *The Twilight Zone*, on DVD, still available via Amazon (@ https://www.amazon.com/Twilight-Zone-Season-Episodes-Collection/dp/B00C6F61S2/ref=sr_1_1?s=movies-tv&ie=UTF8&qid=1474214201&sr=1-1&keywords=Twilight+Zone+Season+3) or Blu-ray (@ https://www.amazon.com/Twilight-Zone-Season-Three-Blu-ray/dp/B01KOCLOJE/ref=sr_1_4?s=movies-tv&ie=UTF8&qid=1474214201&sr=1-4&keywords=Twilight+Zone+Season+3), or via streaming online.

[33] If you want to see what The Duffer Brothers (Matt & Ross) had done *before*, at the time of this writing their original short film *Eater* (2007, based on the short story by Pete Crowther) can still be viewed online (@ http://www.indiewire.com/2016/08/duffer-brothers-short-film-eater-stranger-things-directors-1201713815/); their first feature film, **HIDDEN** (2015, USA), is available via streaming online and at amazon, or via DVD (@ https://www.amazon.com/Hidden-Alexander-Skarsgård/dp/B014K5F1KO/ref=sr_1_2?s=movies-tv&ie=UTF8&qid=1474205798&sr=1-2&keywords=Hidden). They were also the writers/producers of the Fox series *Wayward Pines* (May 14, 2015-July 27, 2016).

Before Will Byers disappeared behind the wall, six-year-old Bettina Miller (Tracy Stratford) disappeared under her bed in the classic 1953 Richard Matheson short story and *Twilight Zone* adaptation "Little Girl Lost" (broadcast March 16, 1962). As host Rod Serling put it, "Present location? Let's say for the moment... in the Twilight Zone."

DRAWING SASQUATCH:

A Preview of *S. R. Bissette's How to Make a Monster: The Cryptid Zoo*, an instructional book on how to draw cryptids and folkloric monsters, coming your way from Stephen R. Bissette

Having envisioned a sasquatch caught in the act of drinking out of his hands by a pool of water at the edge of a pond or wide stream, working "inside-out" this time, I sketch the skeletal position of a hominid kneeling by the water.

This instantly affords me a more naturalistic pose.

I also rough out enough to know what he's kneeling on, in terms of the picture plane:

As you can see, I had already begun to visualize how the shadows would fall, with the heavy drop shadow under his chin and neck.

So, I go to that. This one's a wiry, muscular fellow, but I again choose not to give him long human-like hair or facial hair. Let's stick with more primate-like features for the time being.

Tightening up the drawing as I flesh out what goes over those bones, I pay some closer attention to his face and expression, looking up with a bit of surprise at "us" seeing him.

I also give just a bit more to the environment (what we'll need to see of it) and his interaction with the water: the water cupped in his hands, and dripping out; the dripping into the pool and ripples that creates; his reflection.

Lean as he is, I still think it necessary to add some bulk to his shoulders, upper back, and neck. This isn't a carry-over from my Swamp Thing days; it's something cited in eye-witness account after eye-witness account. I also don't want him to look to chimpanzee-like, too long, lean, and lanky (thought that's always big fun to draw!).

218

At the next stage, I clean up my pencils and focus on his exterior and contours, and the masses I'm going to delineate by leaving some in light, and plunging others into deep, black shadow.

My pencil lines are loose and flowing. Everything about this drawing should feel lively and natural to me. I let that carry me along as I work out the muscles of the bent legs, the way he's sitting on his heels, the way his toes bend, and his whole posture hunkered over to drink.

As my mentor Joe Kubert taught me back in 1977, eye contact—either with the viewer, or with some component of the composition—is absolutely vital in making a drawing live and breath. I'll intensify that once I get to the inking stage.

I ink with a brush, staying close to my pencils. Since he's by a pool of water, I'm pretty bold using reflected light in some areas, ignoring it in others. Where it feels right to use reflective light to render form, I do so; where it doesn't, I don't. Much of this is instinctual for me, based on decades of observational drawing. The chest and crotch are obliterated by deep shadow, as is the lower arm and hand furthermost from our view.

The arm closest to us is given more cylindrical form by leaving a thin white area open on the underside of the upper and lower arm. Notice how the brushstrokes serve multiple purposes: strokes that render deep shadows on the upper arm, forearm, and thigh (those furthest from us) convey a bit about musculature, a bit more about weight (how he leans on that upper arm for balance), the contours of the kneeling leg. The same goes for the leg nearest us; most of the thigh and the visible edge of the gastrocnemius (the lower muscle at the back of the leg) is catching the light.

But the face is the focus of this drawing: the brow, the eyes, the nose (a touch of underlighting to delineate the nose, more human than a primate's nose), the long upper lip, a suggestion of the teeth, a full lower lip. The ink strokes by the chest define the thin "beard" on his chin, two brush strokes suggests water or saliva dripping from his lower lip.

Also note the loose, liquid brush strokes that define both the surface of the water, and his reflection.

I continue to refine the inks. Still primarily using my brush, I work with and through the muscles, again solely by using the lay of his hair/fur to detail how the muscles are at work and at rest, depending on which part of the figure I'm working out and through.

Also using my brush, I detail the face, the shoulders, the hands, and that one visible foot.

That's also brushwork alone detailing the fine stones he's crouching on by the water.

I use minimal pen lines on his fur or figure, and a few loosely laid in to specify the ripples of water. Ripples move away from the source of agitation: the most closely-aligned ripples are at the points where the water dripping from his cupped hands are hitting the pool. Then there are the ripples from the knee closest to us, partially (just barely) submerged; as the ripples move away from those points, they grow wider, looser, and then become scribbles. It's a bit impressionistic as linework, but it works to my eye.

Also note I've laid a touch of dry-brush in on the water, too. This may seem counterintuitive—dry-brush usually connotes rough surface textures, and the surface of water is a clear and crystalline texture rather than rough—but I needed a suggestion of more color on that water surface, and those few strokes of barely-visible dry-brush did it for me.

Finally, using my pen nib, I add the flies. If you've ever spent time in the woods in the spring, summer, or fall, by a stream, or (just as relevant when drawing a sasquatch) in a farmer's field by livestock, you know all manner of flying and flitting things are about; with livestock, I can't help but associate the clouds of flies and horse flies with the smell of the animals.

So, for me, flies are as much an indication of smell as they are of busy nature in motion—and I always aim to make my drawings fully engage the viewer's senses.

Hence: the flies.

THE CRYPTID CINEMA POLL

The following informal three-question Cryptid Cinema *poll was conducted on the author's Facebook page on August 20th, 2017. A list of participants, with deepest thanks to all who took part, appears at the end; anyone quoted in "Comments" is cited by the initials noted in parenthesis after their full-name listing at the end of this section.*

Question #1: *What's your favorite Bigfoot/Sasquatch novel, short story, or movie?*

MOVIE:

Charles B. Pierce's **THE LEGEND OF BOGGY CREEK** (1972) swept the category, winning top spot with 8½ votes.
Comments: "I'm going to go with **LEGEND OF BOGGY CREEK** because it was the first Bigfoot movie I ever watched." (AN)

"**THE LEGEND OF BOGGY CREEK** started the love. (Thank you Joe Bob Briggs)." (JH)

"Oh, those *Boggy Creek* movies kill me, in both a good way and a bad way." (LM)

"I remember being young and going to see **THE LEGEND OF BOGGY CREEK** at our local dollar theater with my brother. I had just read a ton of books on everything from UFOs to the Loch Ness Monster and specifically, one on Bigfoot. I started out laughing at the flick (mostly because it unnerved me from the opening sequence—the eerie woods similar to ones I grew up by) but by the time the trailer attack was in progress, I was almost hyperventilating. I excused myself to 'go get a drink of water' in the lobby and stood shaking in the bathroom, wondering why I was so freaked-out. I missed a bit of the film, and it wasn't until I tracked down a bootleg video of it years later that I finished it. Strangely, while I played it alone at 2 am, I was still fascinated that I had the same laughing and disarming responses through it...and it *still* creeped me out." (LW)

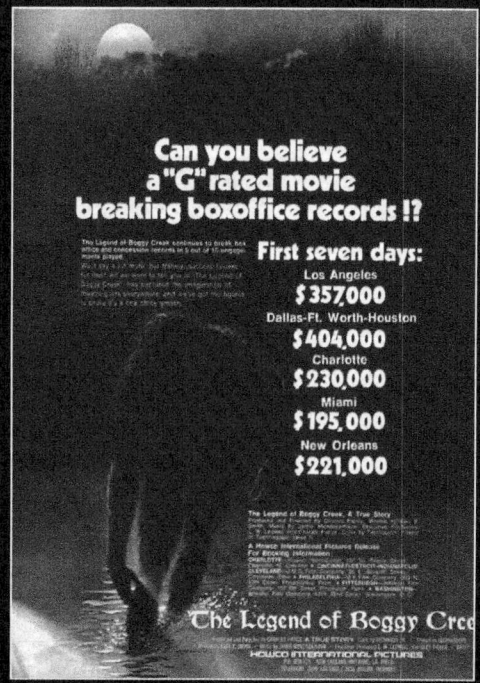

LEGEND OF BOGGY CREEK was the breakthrough "true life" cryptid movie—as a film-viewing experience for most who took part in the Cryptid Cinema Poll, and at the boxoffice in the early 1970s (as this trade publication ad boasted).

"LEGEND OF BOGGY CREEK. It made quite an impression on me as a child, along with the *In Search of...* episode on Bigfoot." (MG)

Runners-up:

THE ABOMINABLE SNOWMAN OF THE HIMALAYAS (1957) placed second (7 votes).
Comments: "A classic from Hammer Films that I found both scary and emotionally moving when I saw it at age seven. It was also my first real exposure to Yeti lore, sparking a lifelong interest. I still love rewatching it today. " (BD)

"Eerie and intelligent. Love it." (PF)

HARRY AND THE HENDERSONS (1987) (5 votes)
Comments: "As a kid this was as fun and heartbreaking as ET or any of those other 80s movies...and I dare anyone to say they didn't get a little teary when Harry is kicked back into the forest." (PH)

"Most movies in this genre are poorly done, and seem *[to]* be obscure *[or]* are SyFy fodder. But, I enjoyed both **HARRY AND THE HENDERSONS** and **SPLASH**. Sorry, most cryptid movies suck…" (AS)

SHRIEK OF THE MUTILATED (1974) (3 votes)

CREATURE FROM BLACK LAKE (1976) (3 votes)
Comments: "**CREATURE FROM BLACK LAKE**: They had a van full of gear, as I recall, that managed to make it up the deer trails into the deep woods. The first hour was *dull*, with the two guys bonding, talking about pretty much nothing, sitting about a campfire eating canned beans. Then the last half hour kicks in, and it was *great*, with a pretty well-executed Bigfoot creature terrorizing the guys. The impression I got was the Sasquatch was territorial, and truly *pissed* that two humans/other primates were in its 'house.' Ring a bell with anybody? I have to say the last half-hour of that flick was the best Bigfoot stuff I've seen in a movie.… I forgot about Jack Elam and Dub Taylor as old coots in the woods. One thing that always stayed with me was how great the cheap-ass Bigfoot costume was

---

THE ABOMINABLE SNOWMAN OF THE HIMALAYAS (1957) *[top left]* and **HARRY AND THE HENDERSONS** (1987; monster-maker Rick Baker 'touches-up' the hair on Kevin Peter Hall's Harry *[left]*) ranked high in the Cryptid Cinema Poll, but Michael Findley's and Ed Kelleher's **SHRIEK OF THE MUTILATED** (1974) *[center left]* placed in both 'Best' and 'Worst' categories! **Page 223, Top to Bottom:** Theater lobby exploitation suggestion in the **CREATURE FROM THE BLACK LAGOON** (1954) pressbook; father (Fuminori Ohashi) and son (Takashi Itô) from 獣人雪男 / **JŪJIN YUKI OTOKO / HALF HUMAN** (1955/1957); Ralph McQuarrie poster (and DVD cover) art for **CREATURE FROM BLACK LAKE** (1976); poster art for **THE MYSTERIOUS MONSTERS** (1975).

lit at all times, and now I just looked the movie up and Dean Cundey (!) shot it, which retroactively makes perfect sense. It used to be on UFH stations all the time in the '70s and '80s. I don't think I've ever seen it all the way through in one sitting, but I've seen it in chunks, having come in during the middle of it multiple times… The Bigfoot stuff at the climax was really gnarly." (MM)

"In 1976, the year I emigrated to Northern Ontario, Canada from the UK as a teenager with my parents, the memorable ads for **CFBL** were all over the local newspapers (as well as those in 'big city' [!] Sudbury, ON too), and it seemed to stick around in the regional drive-ins and hard-tops for ages. Unfortunately, I never got to see it first-run at either a drive-in or any other theatrical venue, but I did get a chance to catch it on a cheapo multibill (*'$3 for 4 Movies!'*) at a Toronto grindhouse (on the notorious Yonge Street strip) while an OCA(D) art student—and future flunk-out!—sometime around 1981-83 or so; although I can't recall whether it played at The Rio, The Biltmore or The Coronet, the three most-prominent downtown TO grindhouses (it most likely did the rounds at all of them at some time or other). As for the flick itself, despite its overlong build-up to the not-so-big payoff, it's still great fun in an endearingly down-home/folksy way. Adding to this aspect, the two male leads are like guys just about everybody's known at some point in their lives, and the double-barreled presence of the great Hollywood 'hick/hillbilly' character actors Jack Elam and Dub Taylor greatly adds to the production values. Once the monster action finally gets going, it's just fine (especially its attack on the heroes' van), but I mainly remember the film for its character development and local color more than anything else." (SF)

"That film scared the shit outta me as a kid! The dinner and flashback scenes work very well." (NC)

HALF HUMAN (獣人雪男 / *Jūjin yukiotoko*, 1955/1958) (2 votes)
Comments: "I have fond but distant memories of Toho's **JŪJIN YUKIOTOKO** ("Abominable Snowman"), known in its cutdown American version as **HALF HUMAN** (1955). Saw it on TV in the 50s/60s and was mesmerized by it. The film has since dropped off the face of the earth. The Monsterminions blog gives the original Japanese version a rave review: http://tinyurl.com/ybfzydsp." (PF)

"If Yeti movies count, I'm going to say 獣人雪男 / *Jūjin yukiotoko* [**HALF HUMAN**], because I'm sure someone else will say Hammer's **THE ABOMINABLE SNOWMAN**. Honorable mention for the Shaw Bros. **MIGHTY PEKING MAN**. However, if you specifically want a Bigfoot movie, then **LEGEND OF BOGGY CREEK** easily." (JM)

THE MYSTERIOUS MONSTERS (1975) a.k.a. **BIGFOOT: THE MYSTERIOUS MONSTERS** (2 votes)
Comments: "They say your first love is the one you never forget, or something mushy like that… After seeing this as a 6-year-old, I was hooked on the unusual." (WC)

WILLOW CREEK (2013) (2 votes)

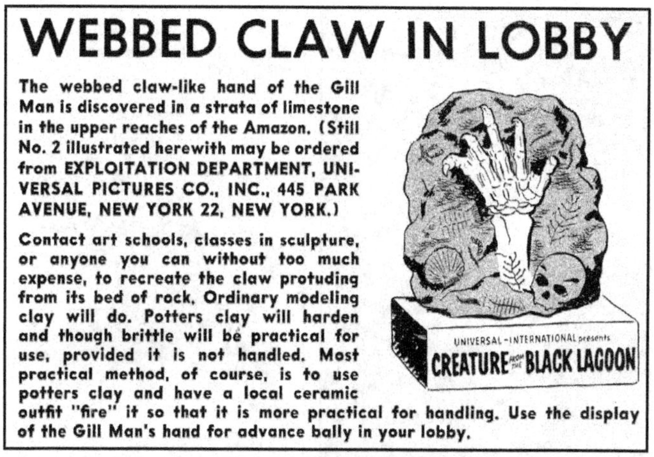

ABOMINABLE (2006) (1 vote)
Comments: "...nothing jumps out at me except this low-budget but superbly entertaining take on **REAR WINDOW**, but with Bigfoots..." (CLC)

AJOOBA KUDRAT KA (1991) (1 vote)
Comments: "...big dumb lumpy amblin' Yeti costume and features the classic (and regional Hindi hit) pop tune 'Yeti, I Love You!'..." (TP)

BIGFOOT (1970, "with John Carradine") (1 vote)

DEAR GOD NO! (2011) (1 vote)

EXISTS (2014) (1 vote)

NIGHT OF THE DEMON (1980) (1 vote)

NIGHT OF THE HOWLING BEAST (*La maldición de la bestia*, 1975) (1 vote)

SASQUATCH: THE LEGEND OF BIGFOOT (1977) (1 vote)
Comments: "...because I saw it in the theater and was properly terrified. My own bigfoot movie, **THERE'S SOMETHING OUT THERE** [2007], is on the list, though pretty far down, but I do have an unproduced screenplay tentatively (very tentatively) called 'BIGFOOT HOLOCAUST' which, if properly made, would zip right up to the top spot." (CV)

SASQUATCH MOUNTAIN (2006) (1 vote)

SNOWBEAST (1977) (1 vote)

SPLASH (1984) (1 vote)

STOMP! SHOUT! SCREAM! (2005) (1 vote)
Comments: "Assuming that a Skunk Ape counts as Bigfoot." (KE)

PRINT FICTION
(listed alphabetically by author):

Nights With Sasquatch, by John and Judith Frankle Cotter (1977) (1 vote)

The Mountain King, by Rick Hautala (1996) (1 vote)

Bigfoot, by B. Anne Slate and Alan Berry (1977) (1 vote)
Comments: "Best Bigfoot book...Some of the supernatural aspects in there were really creepy!" (AN)

Dweller, by Jeff Strand (2010) (1 vote)
Miracle Visitors, by Ian Watson (1978) (1 vote)
Comments: "Favorite Bigfoot/Sasquatch short story is easily 'Longtooth' by Edgar Pangborn. Well written and creepy. As Arnold Scheiman mentions, most of the films are pretty dreadful—where intended as a comedy or a horror tale. I can't really

From Top, Left to Right: The Ramsey Brothers' Hindi family opus **AJOOBA KUDRAT KA** (1991); original US poster art for **BIGFOOT** (1970) and **SASQUATCH: THE LEGEND OF BIGFOOT** (1977); mermaid-as-cryptid smash-hit **SPLASH** (1984); Adult Swim's and Jay Wade Edwards' made-in-Florida, Everglades-set Skunk Ape movie **STOMP! SHOUT! SCREAM!** (2005) a.k.a. **MONSTER BEACH PARTY A-GO-GO**; Drew Struzan poster art for Ryan Schifrin's **ABOMINABLE** (2006).

remember any Bigfoot novels, but there are a lot of decent comic book stories out there." (RA)

TELEVISION:

The Six Million Dollar Man Bigfoot episodes (February 1976; September 1976) handily scored highest (5 votes):
Comments: "*Six Million Dollar Man*: It presented Bigfoot as a warm, caring individual with a sci-fi twist. " (JJ)
"Never was a huge bigfoot fan, but yes, the *SMDM* episode was awesome!" (MS)

"Totally sentimental choice (and admittedly not a film but a TV series) but the first, two-part Bigfoot story from *The Six Million Dollar Man*. It was my introduction to the Bigfoot concept and I even got the toy—an oversized action figure complete with a chest that pops off to reveal robotics when Steve punches him in the stomach. Still have that one, actually." (GC)

"I still like **HARRY AND THE HENDERSONS**, because nothing compares with Rick Baker makeup and special effects. However, *The Six Million Dollar Man*: "The Secret of Bigfoot" (1976) is my secret favorite: That TV show *was* my childhood and that episode saw the forest behemoth personified by pro wrestler André the Giant." (JL)

"…'Return of Bigfoot,' *The Six Million Dollar Man/Bionic Woman* crossover. Ted Cassidy played Bigfoot. John Saxon was the villain and, of course, you had Stefanie Powers." (GH)

Runners-up:

"The *In Search of...* Bigfoot episode [April 28, 1977] with Leonard Nimoy" (2 votes)

Doctor Who, "The Web of Fear" (February 3–March 9, 1968) (1 vote)
Comments: "…robot Yetis in the London Underground…" (NG)

Kolchak: The Night Stalker episode "The Spanish Moss Murders" (2 votes)
Comments: "My favourite *Kolchak* episode …no wait, it ties with "Horror in the Heights" the one about the Indian *rakshasa* folk demon" (TP)

Southpark, "Volcano" (Legend of Scuzzlebutt) (Season 1, Episode 2, August 20, 1997) (1 vote)

Right, Top to Bottom: *Dweller* by Jeff Strand (2010); *The Mountain King*, by Rick Hautala (1996); *Doctor Who*, "The Web of Fear" (February 3–March 9, 1968); Ted Cassidy and Lindsay Wagner in a promotional photo publicizing the second incarnation of the *Six Million Dollar Man/The Bionic Woman* multichapter episodes, "The Return of Bigfoot" (*The Six Million Dollar Man*, September 19, 1976) and "The Return of Bigfoot (Part II)" (*The Bionic Woman*, September 22, 1976).

The Venture Bros: "Home Insecurity" (Season 1, Episode 3, August 21, 2004) (1 vote)

"Do those Beef Jerky ads count?" (VB)

OTHER MEDIA:

"Whiteman Meets Bigfoot" (*Home Grown Funnies* #1, 1971) by Robert Crumb (4 votes)

Runners-up:

Comments: "Corben's *Bigfoot* is one of his best graphic novels…" (DMA)

Abigail and the Snowman, by Roger Langridge (2016) (1 vote)
Comments: "…a charming all-ages title done in Langridge's inimical style…" (AF) (1 vote)

Josh Howard Presents: Sasquatch (2007) (1 vote)

Comments: "…from Viper Comics. An anthology by different writers and artists about Bigfoot…" (KH)

L'uomo delle nevi / The Snowman, by Milo Manara and Alfredo Castelli (1990) (1 vote)

Tintin au Tibet / Tintin in Tibet, by Hergé (1958–1959) (1 vote)

"…pretty much any *Weekly World News* Bigfoot article…" (TP)

Michael H. Price writes, "Favorite here is the unproduced screenplay for Terry Zwigoff's 'Sassy,' an elaboration upon Robert Crumb's 'Whiteman Meets Bigfoot.' Visualized in a set of exquisite conceptual drawings by Crumb His Ownself… Crumb and I have on various occasions discussed our mutual perception of **HARRY AND THE HENDERSONS** as an unattributed, sanitized knockoff."

And two shameless self-promotions, the first from Ray Raymos: "Favorite cryptid is the San Elizario Man-Dog… a cursed gunslinger from the old west who roams the streets of the little Texas town seeking redemption. He hunts and kills Bigfoot. He's the star of the comic I'm writing called the *Cryptidnals*." Good luck, Ray!

The second bit of shameless hucksterism comes from David J. Schow, who writes, "Modestly do I reserve opinion in favor of my yet-unmade masterwork … **CHUPACOBRA!** …It's my follow-up to **HAWKTOPUS VS. ANACONDOR**. The winner of the conflict will battle … **SWASTIQUATCH!**"

Cryptid Comics: *Tintin au Tibet / Tintin in Tibet* by Hergé (1958–1959); *Abigail and the Snowman* by Roger Langridge (2016); Steve Niles, Rob Zombie, and Richard Corben's *Bigfoot* (2005); original Robert Crumb sketch referencing Crumb's classic "Whiteman Meets Bigfoot" (*Home Grown Funnies* #1, 1971)

Kay Lawrence (Julie Adams) zealously defended by knife-wielding Zee (Bernie Gozier) from the Gillman (Ben Chapman); since the Gillman had earlier killed his brother Chico (Henry A. Escalante), Zee has it in for **THE CREATURE FROM THE BLACK LAGOON** (1954). In many ways, **ANACONDA** (1997) was essentially a remake.

Question #2: *What's your favorite cryptid novel, short story, or movie?*

MOVIE:

THE MOTHMAN PROPHECIES (2002) takes the top spot! (4 votes)

Comments: "…if one considers the Mothman a cryptid. To me, an eerie movie, especially in that you never *see* anything of the Mothman." (MR)

Runners-up:

ANACONDA (1997) (2 votes)
Comments: "My favorite cryptid movie is **ANACONDA** simple for the cheese factor, and Jon Voight intoning in that odd accent of his, 'The river can keel you inna tousand ways!' as well as being vomited up and re-eaten near the end. (A guilty pleasure, to be sure). However, I do award **THE PRIVATE LIFE OF SHERLOCK HOLMES** as a close runner-up film that 'solves' the mystery of the Loch Ness monster." (DF)

"…such over-the-top kitschy entertainment with an absurdly fun snake of legend, a scene-chewing Jon Voigt on steroids, an ultra-sexy Jennifer Lopez, the joy of seeing Owen Wilson crushed to death, and the awesome outcome of Ice Cube being a black guy that survives a horror film." (JL)

CREATURE FROM THE BLACK LAGOON (1954) (2 votes)

ALLIGATOR (1980) (1 vote)

THE CAT PEOPLE (1942) (1 vote)

GODZILLA, KING OF THE MONSTERS (ゴジラ / *Gojira*, 1954) (1 vote)
Comments: "The original Godzilla, absolutely. I caught it on PBS as a kid the same week they played the original **NIGHT OF THE LIVING DEAD** [1968] (which really got me), but Godzilla built a kind of cinematic tension and terror that gripped me all the way past the beast being eaten on a molecular level, sinking to the ocean's depths. It seemed totally serious and in the moment, not at all like campy or over the top horror or sci-fi of the era-just sweaty and breathless. Years

later, I caught **MOTHMAN** at a midnight showing, and it had a similar, but much slower building of tension that led to a few great cinematic moments for me." (LW)

INCIDENT AT LOCH NESS (2004) (1 vote)

KING KONG (1933) (1 vote)
Comments: "Not sure what counts as a cryptid movie, but **KING KONG** is always my favorite unknown creature movie." (AN)

MIMIC (1997) (1 vote)

SNOWBEAST (1977) (1 vote)
Comments: "Call me easy-to-please, but I've always been rather partial to this tabloid-trashy, trope-ridden Sasquatch/Yeti hybridization, which I think I may have seen on its original NBC TV airing, but can't say for sure (it's been a while!). I definitely do still remember the short-but-sweet tele-trailers for it though, which were real tantalizing back in the day, especially so because there was such a dire dearth of creature features to be had on the idiot box back then." (SF)

WENDIGO (2001) (1 vote)
Comments: "…a truly creepy, esoteric take on back woods creatures, where the horror of the monster is in the mind's eye, and features an early appearance of Erik Per Sullivan outside of *Malcolm in the Middle*!" (AF)

Note: Tim Paxton (who, like me, voted for **CREATURE FROM THE BLACK LAGOON**) adds, "…or maybe **BEAST FROM HAUNTED CAVE** *[1959]* or, geez, **X THE UNKNOWN** *[1956]* was a weird blob that appeared 'out of the depths.'…"

PRINT FICTION/NON-FICTION:

It's a tie!
Algernon Blackwood's short story "The Wendigo" (1910) (3 votes)
and:
The Mothman Prophecies, by John Keel (1975) (3 votes)

Runners-up:

The *Meg* series, by Steve Alten (1997-2018) (1 vote)

"The Foghorn" (originally published as "The Beast from 20,000 Fathoms") (1951) (1 vote)

Ancient Lake (2008) by David Coleman (1 vote)
Comments: "A very cool cryptid horror novel by one of my favorite Bigfoot mavens. I think it deserves much wider recognition among cryptozoology buffs." (BD)

The Lost World, by Sir Arthur Conan Doyle (1912) (1 vote)
Comments: "This has to be considered the very 1st cryptid

From Top: Joseph Stefano's and Herb Wallerstein's shot-in-Colorado TV feature **SNOWBEAST** (April 28th, 1977) made both our 'Best' and 'Worst' lists; evocative promo art for Bobcat Goldthwait's **WILLOW CREEK** (2013); Charles B. Griffith and Monte Hellman's filmed-in-South Dakota **BEAST FROM HAUNTED CAVE** (1959) was arguably an inspiration for elements of Stephen King's *It*; Matt Fox's double-page illustration for the pulp reprint in *Famous Fantastic Mysteries* (June 1944) of Algernon Blackwood's short story "The Wendigo" (1910).

story in the truest sense of the name. After hearing rumours of living dinosaurs a team of English scientists head into the wilds of South America to see if the rumours are true. Sounds like a cryptid story to me…" (PH)

Dwellers, by Roger Elwood (1990) (1 vote)
Comments: "Cool little novel with the premise that the Nephilim (offspring of men and angels copulating) have survived into modern day by hiding in caves and underground and are the source for many of our boogeyman and hairy man cryptids." (KH)

The Terror, by Dan Simmons (2007) (1 vote)

The Flock, by James Robert Smith (2006) (1 vote)

"I don't think I've ever read a Bigfoot/Yeti prose work. Really should. Favorite cryptid short-story would probably be Laurell K. Hamilton's 'A Scarcity of Lake Monsters.' Favorite novel would be Paul Zindel's *Loch* [1994], which is actually not about Nessie. Geoffrey Girard's *Tales of the Jersey Devil* [2004] is a good short story collection. I guess part of the question depends on what you mean by cryptid-fiction. I know Loren Coleman championed James Robert Smith's novel *The Flock*, but I wouldn't consider it cryptid-fiction, because as far as I know no cryptozoologists are looking for terror birds in the Florida Everglades. But again, haven't read as much crypto-fiction as I should have." (JM)

TELEVISION:

"The Discovery Channel cryptid specials of the past couple of years. They're all pretty well-made, so they all rank level with each other." (WC) (1 vote)

"The *In Search of...* episodes [1977-1982] that featured cryptids." (KE) (1 vote)

The Secret Saturdays (October 3rd, 2008 to January 30th, 2010) (1 vote)
Comment: "It's a show, but I figure it counts." (JJ)

The Six Million Dollar Man with Bigfoot [1976] (1 vote)

OTHER MEDIA:

B.P.R.D., Vol. 6: The Universal Machine (2006) and *B.P.R.D., Hell on Earth* (2011) by Mike Mignola, John Arcudi, and Guy Davis (1 vote)
Comments: "I recommend the nightmarish *[Daryl the]* Wendigo in Mike Mignola's *BPRD* comics. Introduced in *The Universal Machine* story arc. If you kill the Wendigo, you become the Wendigo, a supernatural man-eating creature. The tragic, heart-wrenching story follows a gentle man named Daryl Tynon who becomes the ferocious Wendigo and massacres his own wife and children. Unsettling, sad and horrifying. Terrific writing by Mike Mignola and John Arcudi, art by Guy Davis Artworks—Can't beat that combination." (PF)

TV Guide promo ad for the Ted Cassidy-as-Bigfoot episodes, "The Return of Bigfoot" (*The Six Million Dollar Man*, September 19, 1976) and "The Return of Bigfoot (Part II)" (*The Bionic Woman*, September 22, 1976); **comicbook cryptids:** "The Nightmare Maker" cover story for *Superman* #266 (August, 1973, cover by Nick Cardy), and Marvel Comics's Wendigo debuts in *The Incredible Hulk* #162 (April 1973, cover by Herb Trimpe and Sal Trapani).

L'uomo delle nevi / The Snowman, by Milo Manara and Alfredo Castelli (1990) (1 vote)

"Whiteman Meets Bigfoot" (*Home Grown Funnies* #1, 1971), by Robert Crumb (1 vote)

"…Stuff mentioned in my *Out of this World* book collection from the mid-'70s." (TP)

"Two favouite comics series from the 1970s (which aren't from Charlton) happened to feature an issues with hairy hominids. First up is *Superman* #266 where our hero must stop the Abominable Snowman from obliterating Earth by dreaming it away (if I recall the story correctly). Then there's *The Incredible Hulk* #162 where ol' greenskin is up in Canada and battles a Wendigo. Both comics are from 1973, released a year after the first **BOGGY CREEK** film." (TP)

Bigfoot (James Stellar) claims a potential mate (Joi Lansing) in the Cryptid Cinema Poll 'Worst Movie' contender, Robert F. Slatzer's **BIGFOOT** (1970); incredibly, actor/director Bruce Davison (**LAST SUMMER**, **WILLARD**, the *X-Men* franchise, etc.) remade the film for Asylum/Syfy under the same title (debuting on SyFy August 14, 2012) with Danny Bonaduce (*The Partridge Family*), Barry Williams (*The Brady Bunch*), Sherilyn Fenn (*Twin Peaks*), and Alice Cooper!

Question #3: *What's the worst Bigfoot/Sasquatch movie you ever made it all the way through watching (walkouts or turnoffs disqualified)?*

MOVIE:

"There are *bad* ones…?" (JT)

CRY WILDERNESS (1987) easily claimed the Worst Ever prize, no doubt due entirely to *Mystery Science Theater 3000* featuring it in their 2017 season. Would anyone have seen it, much less remembered it, otherwise? (7 votes)
Comments: "I was only able to watch this insipid Bigfoot movie all the way through because it was on *MST3K*. Does that count?" (BD)

"Wow, what a stinker. Thank goodness for *Mystery Science Theater 3000*!" (JW)

"It is so poorly done that it is not only amateurish but an insult to amateurs." (KH)

Runners-up:

BOGGY CREEK II: AND THE LEGEND CONTINUES (1984) (3 votes)
Comments: "Too many to count, but probably the second *Boggy Creek* film—just a shambling, poorly made disaster that hit big on all of the wrong notes. There's a lot of film out there on cryptoids and cryptids, and much of it blather and crap, relying on basic scare clichés and gore, which are the high marks of bad film-making and story-telling… For a long time, I always enjoyed a 'bad' flick almost as well as a good one, until I aged to a point to where I only want to devote time to a well-done film or book—no time for the wannabes." (LW)

HARRY AND THE HENDERSONS (1987) (3 votes)

RETURN TO BOGGY CREEK (1977) (3 votes)
Comments: "…undid everything that scared me as a kid/ moved me as an adult [in the first film]." (MattM)

"The *Boggy Creek* films. Wanted to love them, but found them unbearable even in the '70s. **SNOWBEAST** was a total wasted opportunity." (TP)

RUSSIAN YETI: THE KILLER LIVES (2014) (2 votes)

BIGFOOT (1970) (2 votes)
Comments: "Terrible film" (JS)

"...featuring John Carradine and a bunch of cross-eyed Bigfeets. It 'borrowed' elements from **KING KONG**, including Carl Denham's closing line. One of those so-bad-it's-*ALMOST*-good creature features." (MR)

THE SNOW CREATURE (1954) (2 votes)
Comments: "...that Yeti movie Billy Wilder's brother made. *Bleah!*" (CV)

"One of the most insipid, stilted, lethargic and ploddingly dull creature features—be it of the cryptid or 'regular' monster variety—ever made, and arguably the absolute *least* of W. Lee Wilder's sci-fi/horror-themed '50s low-budgeters. Give me the usually-execrable Jerry Warren's surprisingly enjoyable—at least for Warren—**MAN BEAST** (1956) any day!" (SF)

THE BEAUTIES AND THE BEAST a.k.a. **THE BEAST AND THE VIXENS** (1974) (1½ votes)
Comments: "For all its wretchedness in just about every department—pimply-bummed softcore grope sessions, ratty-assed, uh, 'gorilla' suit and hippy-dippy acoustic ballads included—this troglodytic cinematic coprolite at least has one (actually [*ahem*] two) things going for it... *Uschi! Digard!* Say no more." (SF)

THE GEEK (1971 or 1973) (1 vote)

IN SEARCH OF BIGFOOT (1976) (1 vote)

LITTLE BIGFOOT 2: THE JOURNEY HOME (1998) (1 vote)
Comments: **LITTLE BIGFOOT 2** gave Art Camacho the opportunity to star, write, and direct a feature film, and it was pure saccharine shit." (JL)

SEARCH FOR THE BEAST (1997) (1 vote)
Comments: "...the *worst*... Despite the fact David F. Friedman has a brief cameo in it, it's truly, ripely and even offensively bad. Direction... 'script'... editing... technical... acting... cryptid costume... all so terrible, it feels as if some meth-addicted, murderous hillbillies grabbed their latest victim's cell phone and made a feature, real-time and uncut, with it. To avoid fainting while watching it, keep repeating: 'It's *ONLY* not-quite a movie... It's *ONLY* not-quite a movie...'" (DC, who should know!)

SHRIEK OF THE MUTILATED (1974) (1 vote)

THE SIGHTING a.k.a. **BIGFOOT: THE SIGHTING** (2016) (1 vote)

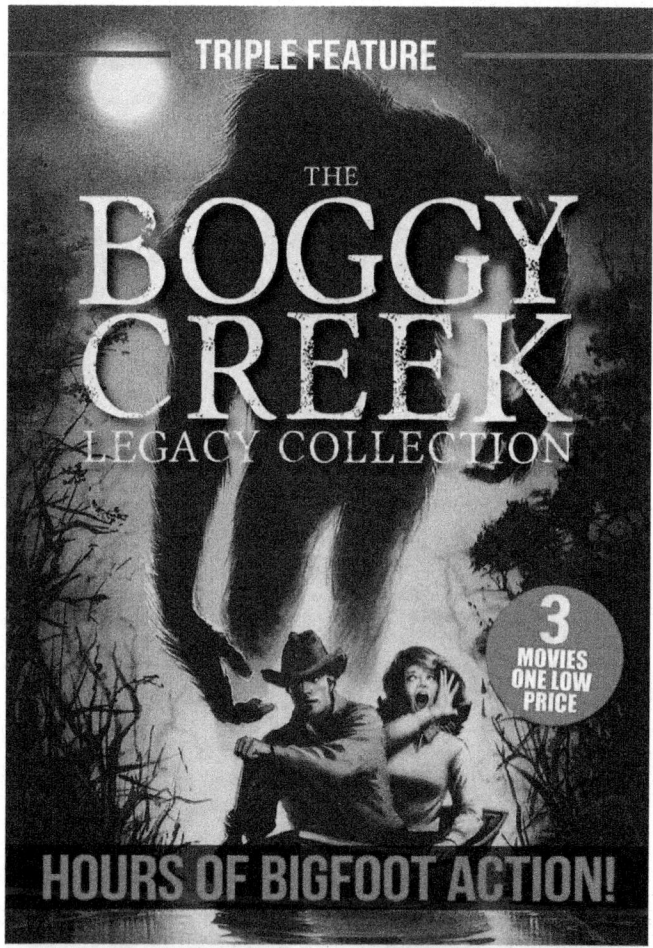

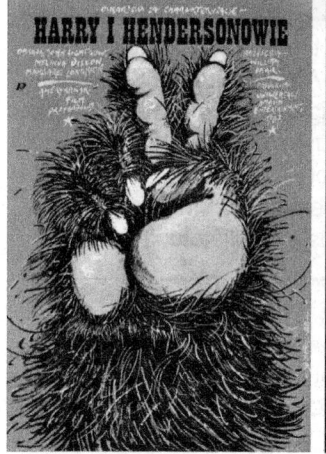

Top: This budget 2014 DVD set from Cinema First offers Robert Guenette's **THE MYSTERIOUS MONSTERS** (1975), **SASQUATCH: THE LEGEND OF BIGFOOT** (1976), and **SNOWBEAST** (1977). **Above:** Polish poster (art by Jakub Erol) for **HARRY AND THE HENDERSONS** (1987); a shot from **THE BEAUTIES AND THE BEAST** (1974) was featured on the cover of *Psychotronic Video #2* (Spring 1989).

Comments: "Starts out looking like a cross between the cheapest porn movie and **BLAIR WITCH**, and never really rises above that." (PH)

SNOWBEAST (1977) (1 vote)

231

Top: Is this shot from one of the unknown Bigfoot 1970s porn movies? Who knows?! **Above:** Joseph Butcher as Wildboy and Ray Young as Bigfoot in *Bigfoot and Wildboy* (September 10th, 1977 to August 18th, 1979); the co-creator of *Batman*, Bill Finger, co-scripted **TRACK OF THE MOON BEAST** (1976), in which a meteor fragment imbedded in Chase Cordell's skull creates a reptilian lunar monster.

TEENAGERS BATTLE THE THING / CURSE OF BIGFOOT (1959/1975) (1 vote)
Comments: "The *worst* Bigfoot movie I've ever sat through was, of course, **TEENAGERS BATTLE THE THING**, which was recut and expanded into the even *worse* **CURSE OF BIGFOOT**. For the record, I've sat through both versions, all the way." (MM)

TO CATCH A YETI (1995) (1 vote)
Comments: "Meat Loaf in a **HARRY AND THE HENDERSONS** homage…" (DB)

TRACK OF THE MOON BEAST (1976) (1 vote)
Comments: "As for my all-time worst, I would nominate **TRACK OF THE MOON BEAST**. True, the monster is transformed due to a meteor fragment, but he does become a Bigfoot-like monster, and the whole thing is a real chore to sit through, however it came about." (DF)

WILLOW CREEK (2014) (1 vote)
Comments: "… an insanely tedious carbon-copy of **BLAIR WITCH** that ends up not even being about Bigfoot, and not remotely scary or unsettling. One of the worst movies I've ever seen." (JS)

Unknown 1970s Bigfoot feature (1 vote)

"Worst Bigfoot movie I ever watched in the theater? I watched a crappy one in the '70s that was so bad I am sorry I paid good money for it. The whole movie was spent building up to the reveal, and the reveal was so fuzzy that I was sure it was some people in suits instead of a family." (AN)

Unknown Bigfoot porn (1 vote)

"…when we were researching Bigfoot movies while planning DGN, someone sent us a bigfoot porno that was terrible, but I made it all the way to the end (pun intended; bigfoot is into anal, of course)" (SM)

TELEVISION:

Bigfoot and Wildboy (September 10th, 1977 to August 18th, 1979) (1 vote)

Comments: "Worst Bigfoot I sat through: Complete 2 seasons of *Bigfoot and Wildboy*. Cheesy special effects, but decent plots. Really tried to make the show serious. One of Ruby/Spears' early projects." (GH)

The X-Files: "The Jersey Devil" (October 8th, 1993) (1 vote)

Participants: Leslie Sternbergh Alexander, Dana Marie Andra (DMA), Richard Arndt (RA), Scott Badger, Graham Garfield Barnard, Michael A. Baron, Vinnie Bartilucci (VB), Chris Bass, David Beckham (DB), Stephen R. Bissette, Irv Brock (IB), Greg Carpenter (GC), Chad Lee Carter (CLC), William Cash (WC) Nick Cato (NC), Dave Coleman (DC), Bob Deis (BD), Ken Eppstein (KE), Byron Fenris (as "Dlr MacKenzie"), Steve Fenton (SF), Dennis Fischer (DF), Alex Fitch (AF), Patrick Ford, Pierre Fournier (PF), Neil Gaiman (NG), Loren Gillespie III, Caldon Gyasi Glover-Wessel, Matt Griller (MG), Joshua Hand (JH), Gerry Hart (GH), Phil Hore (PH), Keith Howell (KH), Jamais Jochim (JJ), Dave Kiner, Andy Kolovos, John Lavitt (JL), Gregory LeVeque, Thad Linson, Tim Lucas, Michael Marano (MM), Mark Masztal, Matt Maxwell (MattM), Lisa May (LM) Ian McDowell, Lou Mougin, Shane Morton (SM), Justin Mullis (JM), Andy Nunez (AN), Tim Paxton (TP), John Platt, Michael H. Price, Mark Rainey (MR), Ray Raymos, Ian Richardson, Daniel W. Ring, Arnold Scheiman (AS), David J. Schow, Diana Schutz, Thomas Sciacca, Jeff Smith (JS), John Sowder, Michael Styborski (MS), Austin Swinburn, Jeff Trexler (JT), Caelum Vatnsdal (CV), Johnny Walker (JW), Lon Webb (LW), "Wretch Grizzly".

The Real Revenge of the Creature (Piranha Bait) For J.C.

CREATURE of the BLUE LAGOON

The Shape of Water

In this author's humble opinion, the *BEST* Cryptid movie ever (and that's a gross understatement!) is Guillermo del Toro's and Vanessa Taylor's **THE SHAPE OF WATER** (2017). Going back to this book's introduction, author/lecturer Justin Mullis asks, "I'm curious how exactly you're defining a 'Cryptid' here, Stephen," to which I reply: The Gillman is a cryptid in the **CREATURE FROM THE BLACK LAGOON** (1953). The Gillman is an entirely *fictional* cryptid, mind you, but it fits all the definitions of a cryptid within that film's constructed narrative. What began in real life with William Alland's having heard something about a possible cryptid down in South America, and in reel life with the discovery of a curious fossil of a skeletal hand in **CREATURE FROM THE BLACK LAGOON**, has blossomed into del Toro's and Taylor's **THE SHAPE OF WATER**—and a rare cinematic orchid it is, indeed.

1962, Baltimore: a mysterious "asset" from the Amazon (Doug Jones) is delivered to a government military research facility where a mute cleaning woman (Sally Hawkins) works. This "asset"—a heretofore-unknown/unclassified amphibious lifeform—has enough scientific value to the USA vs. USSR 'Space Race' (i.e., in determining how men might survive the rigors of space flight) that an undercover Soviet spy has infiltrated the installation; but it is what happens between the mute cleaning woman and the Amazonian "asset" that will determine its most-unexpected future...

A magnificent ensemble cast (Sally Hawkins, Michael Shannon, Octavia Spencer, Richard Jenkins, Lauren Lee Smith, and another uncanny Doug Jones performance as the humanoid creature from the Amazon) and creative collective collaborative between production design, cinematography, and every level of this production brings del Toro/Taylor's lovely adult fairy tale to life onscreen. **THE SHAPE OF WATER** works in ways that few genre films even approach, and (based upon its festival success this past fall) promises to appeal to mainstream audiences. The film unreels with deceptive ease, moving effortlessly—though of course, this all took an enormous amount of work to conjure-up—and with considerable wit and humor. **THE SHAPE OF WATER** teases, tantalizes, touches, and it ultimately seduced and gripped and moved me in ways precious few movies ever come close to doing.

It's also *the greatest* "**CREATURE FROM THE BLACK LAGOON**" movie ever made. *Period.* If you invert the implicit interspecies courtship of **CREATURE**—particularly when the Gillman (Ricou Browning), unseen by her beneath the water, sensually tracks Julie Adams' graceful swimming motions—you have some idea what emotional aquifers **THE SHAPE OF WATER** explores. Dave Coleman is correct when he writes that the film is "a poetic cross between *[THE]* **AMPHIBIAN MAN** *[Челов Ек-Амфибия / Chelovek-amfibiya, 1962, USSR; based on Alexander Belayev's 1928 novel]* and **REVENGE OF THE CREATURE** *[1955, USA]* in set-up," and that's true. But there's also much of films like Jean-Pierre Jeunet's and Guillaume Laurant's **AMÉLIE** (2001) at work here, too. In oh-so-many ways, it's both the movie that Universal Studios *would* and *will never* allow anyone to make with the Gillman—as well as the Swamp Thing movie that DC Entertainment will likely never permit to be made, either.

While we've enjoyed some solid storytellers among the filmmakers who've contributed to Cryptid Cinema over the decades, we've had precious few actual *artists* working in the genre. **THE SHAPE OF WATER** is the work of an artist, and a great one at that. – **SRB**

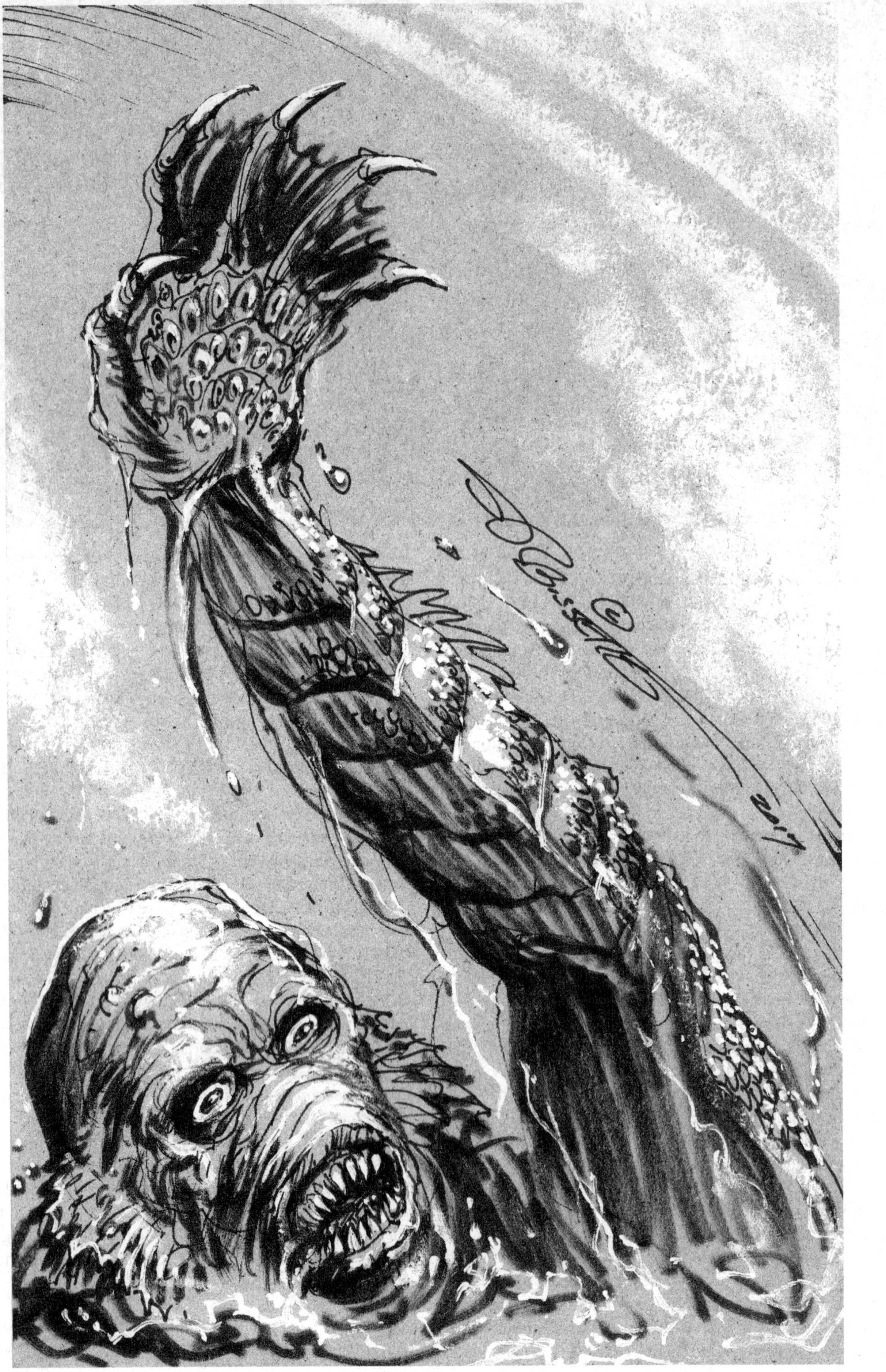

About the Contributing Authors, Artists & Designers

DAVID COLEMAN has written screenplays for Universal, Sony, and DEG, and Hollywood talent such as Michael Douglas, Phil Noyce, Dan Curtis, Dino De Laurentiis, Irv Kirschner, and many others. He has also previously worked for New World, London Films, The Samuel Goldwyn Company, and *The New Twilight Zone* TV series. As an early Internet enthusiast, Coleman created Bijou Cafe.com, one of the first independent videostreaming websites. Prior to the start of his professional career, Coleman attended the University of Southern California School of Cinematic Arts. Coleman's works as published author include *The Bipolar Express: Manic Depression and the Movies*, *The Bigfoot Filmography*, *Cryptozoology Anthology* (co-edited by Bob Deis and Wyatt Doyle) and *Ancient Lake*. His latest novel *Dismember the Alamo* arrives in Spring 2018.

KEVIN R. DANZEY was born in 1954 in the town where the classic '58 film **THE BLOB** was made, has written for fanzines including *Finders=Keepers*, *Cinemagic*, *Amazing Cinema*, *Cinemacabre*, and *Magick Theatre*, as well as painting covers for two issues of *The Missing Link*. He published several fanzines of his own, including *Xenomorph* in 1972. Kevin has been an independent experimental filmmaker since 1970, making nearly one hundred short sci-fi films, and is currently working on his first feature-length narrative film. He also worked as a special effects technician on **THE BRAIN** (1988) and **WICKED STEPMOTHER** (1989). Kevin lives in Arizona with his wife, Sharon, and their feline friend, Neko.

ROBERT HACK is a comic book artist and cover designer from Pennsylvania. He is the artist for *Chilling Adventures of Sabrina*, the hit horror series from Archie Comics. Robert has also been cover artist for a wide range of comic titles and publishers—*Doctor Who*, *Betty Boop*, *Dirk Gently's Holistic Detective Agency*, *Powerpuff Girls*, *Goosebumps*, *Jughead*, *James Bond*, etc. He is a life-long genre film fan and collector whose love of classic cinema pours directly into his art. You can follow Robert on Instagram @RobertHack or Twitter @Robert_Hack for more art and info.

LOU MOUGIN has been a comics fan since roughly 1958, having been corrupted by his Mom, who bought him an issue of *Mouse Musketeers* back then. Many years later, he wrote for fanzines such as *Amazing Heroes* and *The Comics Reader* and did interviews for *Comics Interview* and *The Comic Book Show*. Next he dabbled in writing comics scripts for Eclipse (*The Heap*), Marvel (*The Inhumans, The Swordsman*), Heroic (*Flare, Sparkplug, League of Champions, Icicle*), and Claypool (*Elvira*). Finally, circa 2013, he broke into New Pulp with Pro Se press (*Monster in the Mansions* and books featuring the League of Champions, Flare, and Liberty Girl). At about the same time he got into comics writing again at Charlton Neo (*Charlton Arrow*), Heroic (*Flare* and *Fletcher the Bowman*), Lucky (*Beetle Girl, Foxforce, Black Bat*), InDellible (*Neutro, Space Man, Enemy Ass*), AC (*Tara, Nyoka, Miss Masque*), Empire (*Dr. Seven*), *The Creeps*, and anyone else who will have him.

TOM WEAVER is Sleepy Hollow, New York's favorite son. Tom has been interviewing filmmakers since the early 1980s. *The New York Times* justifiably referred to Weaver as "one of the leading scholars in the horror field," *Sight & Sound* cited Tom as "one of our foremost fantasy film historians," and *USA Today* called him "the king of the monster hunters," and they are all absolutely correct to say so. A frequent Blu-ray audio commentator, he is the author of numerous acclaimed film books, including *Universal Horrors: The Studio's Classic Films, 1931–1946* (co-authored with Michael Brunas and John Brunas), *Poverty Row Horrors! Monogram, PRC, and Republic Horror Films of the Forties*, *The Creature Chronicles: Exploring the Black Lagoon Trilogy* (with David Schecter), *The Horror Hits of Richard Gordon*, and the recent *Universal Terrors, 1951–1955: Eight Classic Horror and Sci-Fi Films* (co-authored with David Schecter, Robert J. Kiss, and Steve Kronenberg).

Book Design/Editing Dept.:

TIM PAXTON is a tireless and dedicated supporter of small press publishing who has been involved in the field since the early 1970s when he and his brother Joel created and sold their own line of D.I.Y. "ditto" comics. In 1978 Tim moved into designing and publishing with his zine *Photo Fiends* (which scored one of the earliest-ever fan press print interviews with legendary '50s monster-maker Paul Blaisdell). Tim has since been involved with *Naked!Screaming!Terror!*, *Video Voice*, *European Trash Cinema* (a.k.a. *ETC*), *Monster! International*, and the glamor/cheesecake/sleaze glossy *Highball*. He took a self-imposed decade-long hiatus from the zine scene in the '90s before returning to the fold with *Weng's Chop* and the resurrection of his digest-size zine *Monster!* (resurrected from its initial influential run as a newsletter-style xeroxed fanzine in the late '80s / early '90s). In 2013, Tim partnered with Steve Fenton to produce *Monster!* for WK Books with publishers Brian Harris and Tony Strauss. Tim currently lives in a ramshackle hippie house in the wilds of Oberlin, OH, where he is often seen out on his front porch working feverishly at his laptop on some new publication.

STEVE FENTON used to operate under the pen-name Steve Fentone (note extra "e"!), the latter of which he stopped using after he dropped-out of the zine scene from the late 1990s until 2013, when a random cosmic/karmic act of fortuitous happenstance put him back in touch with his concurrent partner-in-crime Tim Paxton; this when Tim, much to Steve's delight, suggested that they should collaborate "for old times' sake" on resurrecting the long-dead-but-not-forgotten *Monster!* from the grave. Beginning in 1989 on into the mid/late '90s, Steve put out his own self-published, photocopied efforts *Killbaby* and the Mexploitation zine *¡Panicos!*, and also contributed to the likes of *Monster!*, *Monster! International*, *European Trash Cinema* (*ETC*), *Asian Trash Cinema* (*ATC*), *Sub-Terrenea*, *Asian Eye*, *She*, *Trashcompactor*, *Videooze*, *Giallo Pages*, *Splatting Image* and *Fatal Visions*, among others. His sole published book to date is *AntiCristo: The Bible of Nasty Nun Sinema & Culture* (FAB Press, 2000). Someone with a love for the publishing medium seemingly hard-coded into his very genes, Steve continues to collaborate incessantly on movie/pop culture-related printed projects, including doing editorial/design work and image restoration on various books. By comparison, his "real life" is totally fucking boring!

"Ahem..."

© 2014 SBissette
does "The Alligator People"

Bigfoot's Bibliography:
A Brief Stroll Through Hairy Hominids in Print

Charles Fort's 1931 *Lo!*—companion to Fort's seminal *The Book of the Damned* (1919), *New Lands* (1923) and *Wild Talents* (1932)—was a staple of paperback racks, compliments of Ace Books (in print via Ace from 1941 on); Ace's Frank Edwards titles (*Strange World*, *Stranger Than Science*, *Strangest of All*) further established Fortean weird-but-true books as an evergreen genre.

The hardcover publication of Ivan T. Sanderson's *Abominable Snowmen: Legend Come to Life* (1961, Chilton Books) dramatically marked Sanderson's shift from naturalist—author of a dozen mainstream zoology pop science texts and countless scientific articles—to the realm of cryptozoology. Sanderson revised his essential text in 1968 for the Pyramid Books paperback edition (cover art by John Schoenherr), ...later reprinted by Jove Books in a new edition (cover art uncredited) in September 1977.

THE LAKE WORTH MONSTER (1969)
There are a multitude of regional American self-published and 'vanity press' chapbooks and paperbacks on local cryptids, which are rarer than hen's teeth unless you stumble upon them in flea markets or antique shops or dig deep in the collector's market. Among the author's favorites is Sallie Ann Clarke's self-published *The Lake Worth Monster of Greer Island, Ft. Worth, Texas* (1969), amply peppered with photographs, newspaper clippings, and Clarke's interviews with eye-witnesses.

Ivan T. Sanderson's Pyramid paperbacks *Things* (1967) and *More Things* (1969) were essential Fortean texts for many; living up to their titles with a satisfying emphasis on cryptids, these collected Sanderson's scholarly essays from the pages of *Fate*, *The Saturday Evening Post*, and *Argosy*.

John Green authored and self-published a trio of books on Sasquatch, originally in softcover magazine-sized format: *The Sasquatch File* (1968), *Year of the Sasquatch* (1970), and *On the Track of the*

Sasquatch (1973), which he shortly thereafter repackaged for the mass market as *Bigfoot: On the Track of Sasquatch* (1973/1974, Ballantine Books/Random House). Green later compiled and revised all his work into the two-volume *On the Track of Sasquatch, Book One* and *Book Two* (1980, Cheam Publishing Ltd.; pictured here), and the whole was recently reprinted as *The Best of Sasquatch Bigfoot: The Latest Scientific Developments Plus All of On the Track of Sasquatch and Encounter with Bigfoot* (2004, Hancock House Publishing).

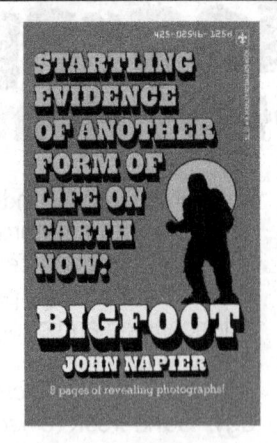

BIGFOOT by John Napier (1972)
The 1970s ushered in a plethora of Sasquatch and Bigfoot non-fiction (or, as folklorist Joseph A. Citro prefers to refer to his own true-weird-stories tomes, "stories that might not be fiction"), but precious few were in-depth, scholarly texts in the tradition of Sanderson's 1961 Abominable Snowmen— such as John Napier's *Bigfoot: The Yeti* and *Sasquatch in Myth and Reality* (1973, E.P. Dutton & Company/1974, Berkley Medallion).

Arkansas locals Charles Pierce had tapped to make his documentary— J. E. "Smokey" Crabtree— expressed his extreme displeasure with the shoddy treatment of he and his neighbors in the self-published *Smokey and The Fouke Monster* (1974, Day's Creek Production Corporation). Crabtree didn't know he was carrying on a tradition of sorts: two decades earlier, a totally-pissed-off Barry Storm tore into the filmmakers behind **LUST FOR GOLD (**1949) in his self-published chapbook *I Was Swindled by Red Movie Makers* (1954, Mollet Publishing Associates). **BOGGY CREEK** devotees, know that Crabtree continued the story of his life (and the fate of his first book) in *Too Close to the Mirror: The Continuing Story of the Life of Smokey Crabtree* (2001, Day's Creek) and T*he Man Behind the Legend* (2004, Day's Creek). How can you resist?

STRANGE ABOMINABLE SNOWMEN (1970)
Strange Abominable Snowmen by Warren Smith (1970) boasted one of the most eye-catching and spectacular of all 1960s or '70s cryptid paperback covers; this uncredited painting for the oddly-titled (aren't they all strange?) entry in Popular Library's *Fate*-spawned 'Strange' book wasn't ~~Bi~~gfooting around.

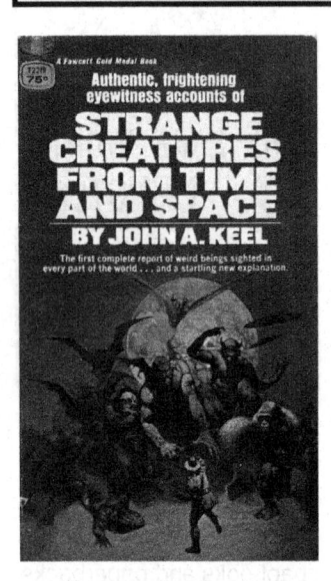

STRANGE CREATURES FROM TIME AND SPACE (1970)
Building upon the bedrock laid by Fort, Sanderson, Jacques Vallee, and others and his own articles for *Male* and *Saga*, John A. Keel (best-known today for *The Mothman Prophecies,* 1975) wrote this classic "complete report of weird beings sighted in every part of the world…and a startling new explanation," *Strange Creatures from Time and Space* (1970, Fawcett). The classic cover art was painted by Frank Frazetta; we'll be coming back to this book in the context of the TV series *Stranger Things* (see pg. 203).

SMOKEY AND THE FOUKE MONSTER (1974)
Even as **LEGEND OF BOGGY CREEK** was cleaning up at the box office, one of the key

THE MYSTERY OF MONSTER MOUNTAIN (1974)
Alfred Hitchcock meets Bigfoot! 1970s Bigfoot fever spilled into the

THE MYSTERIOUS MONSTERS (1975) Making the leap from top-rated TV special to revised and expanded theatrical feature film to the paperback racks, Robert and Frances Guenette's *The Mysterious Monsters* (December 1975, "A Sun Classics Pictures Book") is one of the primary media 'texts' of its generation, and was likely seen (and, in this form, read) by more people than any other single project/artifact of the era.

ever-popular young adult/"juveniles" mystery genre (Nancy Drew, The Hardy Boys, etc.) in M. V. (Mary Virginia) Carey's *The Mystery of Monster Mountain* (1974), an entry in the popular "Alfred Hitchcock and the Three Investigators" series created by Robert Arthur, Jr. for Random House; the boys (Jupiter Jones, Bob Andrews, and Peter Crenshaw) would indeed report to Alfred Hitchcock himself in the framing prologues and epilogues. The series spawned 43 novels (1964–1987), and this one was unusual for its Sasquatch turning out not to be a fake—but a real cryptid!

ON THE TRACK OF BIGFOOT (1974/78) Atypical of the anecdotal tomes rushed into print for various markets in the 1970s was Marian T. Place's *On the Track of Bigfoot* (1974, Dodd, Mead & Company; 1978, Archway/Pocket Books); living and writing in Oregon, Place specialized in 'young adult' fiction and non-fiction books (then referred to as 'juveniles'), detouring from her preferred genre (westerns) to write kid-friendly books on this subject, including *Nobody Meets Bigfoot* (1976), *Bigfoot All Over the Country* (1978), and *The Boy Who Saw Bigfoot* (1979).

BIGFOOT: AMERICA'S ABOMINABLE SNOWMAN (1975) Another of the books that made tracks on the racks in the mid-1970s was Elwood D. Baumann's *Bigfoot: America's Abominable Snowman* (1975, Franklin Watts, Inc.; 1976, Laurel Leaf/Dell)—no relation to the 1969 feature film documentary—which erroneously referred to **LEGEND OF BOGGY CREEK** as LEGEND OF FOGGY BOTTOM.

CREATURES OF THE OUTER EDGE (1978) Clearly stating their shared debts to predecessors Heuvelmans, Sanderson, Keel, Vallee, and others, Jerome Clark and Loren Coleman co-authored the companion originals *The Unidentified* (1975, "Notes Toward Solving the UFO Mystery") and *Creatures of the Outer Edge* (1978, cover art by Chick Bragg) for Warner Books. Anomalist Books put them back into print in 2006 as a single volume; Clark and Coleman subsequently coauthored the definitive encylopedia *Cryptozoology A to Z* (1999, Simon and Schuster), which is highly recommended.

SNOW MAN by Norman Bogner (1978) With a far less spectacular cover image than the British paperback edition (see pg. 42) of the same Norman Bogner novel, Dell's 1978 US edition of *Snow Man* enhanced its straightforward design with an embossed 'footprint.' Bogner's titular cryptid makes its way from the Himalayas to Siberia to Alaska to a mountain ski resort in California—a less direct route than W. Lee Wilder's movie **SNOW CREATURE** took a quarter-century earlier, but, hey, California Dreamin'!

241

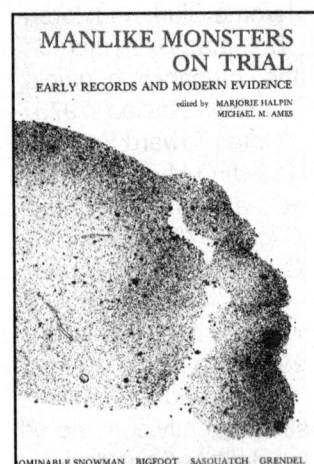

MANLIKE MONSTERS ON TRIAL (1980)
The granddaddy of all academic textbooks on cryptids is the seminal *Manlike Monsters on Trial: Early Records and Modern Evidence* (1980, The University of British Columbia Press), edited by Marjorie Halpin and Michael M. Ames and published in both hardcover and paperback editions. A staggering record of the first academic symposium on the subject—its publication funded in part by Social Science Federation of Canada and Intellectual Prospecting Fund grants—this illustrated compendium of the papers presented at the University of British Columbia's May 1978 "Sasquatch and Similar Phenomenon" conference is truly historic.

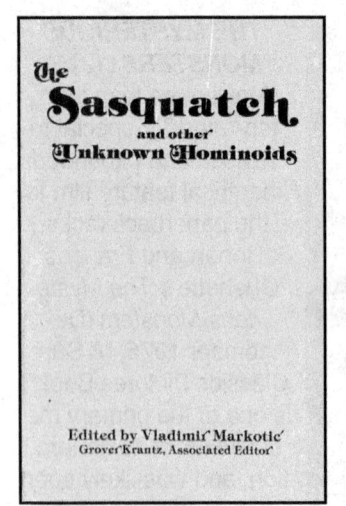

THE SASQUATCH AND OTHER UNKNOWN HOMINOIDS (1984)
The second academic text on the subject was *The Sasquatch and Other Unknown Hominoids* (1984, Western Publishers, who were based in Calgary, Alberta), which listed itself on its indicia page as *The Research on Unknown Hominoids, Vol. 1*. Edited by Vladimir Markotic and associate editor Grover Krantz, this collection includes Loren Coleman and Mark A. Hall's paper "From 'Atshen' to Giants in North America."

THE HISTORICAL BIGFOOT (2006)
Among the current print-on-demand explosion of regional publishers, Pennsylvania-based Coachwhip Publications specializes in cryptozoological volumes, including books like Chad Arment's invaluable *The Historical Bigfoot* (2006), a comprehensive state-by-state guide compiling (as its subtitle asserts) "Early Reports of Wild Men, Hairy Giants, and Wandering Gorillas of North America."

BIGFOOT! THE TRUE STORY OF APES IN AMERICA (2003)
Loren Coleman is still the go-to expert on the subject, and those seeking the best entry into Coleman's extensive body of work on Sasquatch are advised to start with *Bigfoot! The True Story of Apes in America* (2003, Paraview Pocket Books).

THE FIELD GUIDE TO BIGFOOT (1999)
An essential 'who's who' (or 'what's what') reference book we keep at our fingertips—fully illustrated by Harry Trumbore, with to-scale figure drawings of its cryptids—is Loren Coleman and Patrick Huyghe's *The Field Guide to Bigfoot, Yeti, and Other Mystery Primates Worldwide* (1999, Avon Books; reprinted as *The Field Guide to Bigfoot and Other Mystery Primates*, 2006, Anomalist Books, pictured below).

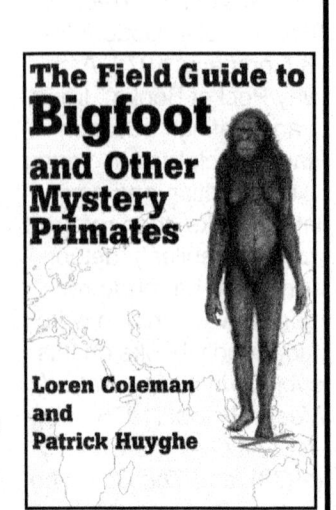

SASQUATCH: LEGEND MEETS SCIENCE (2006)
It's become harder to discern movie and TV tie-in tomes these days,

but they're still being published, and among the best of the recent bumper crops stands anthropologist Jeff Meldrum's *Sasquatch: Legend Meets Science* (2006, Forge/Tom Doherty Associates), the companion volume to producer/director Doug Haijcek, Whitewolf Entertainment, and the Discovery Channel's documentary of the same title that originally aired on January 9, 2003.

NEANDERTHAL (2011) and **THE MINNESOTA ICEMAN** (2016)
Were movies like **RETURN OF THE APE MAN** (1944) through **ICEMAN** (1984) based on actual events? What was it with the so-called "Minnesota Iceman"? In the late 1960s, magazines like *Argosy* (May 1969) began publishing startling photographs and articles by zoologists Bernard Heuvelmans and Ivan T. Sanderson of a frozen hominid, a sensation that seemed to disappear as quickly as it had surfaced. The stories about the 'iceman', its heist, and its replica(s) are fascinating, involving none other than famed Hollywood director Robert (**THE SOUND OF MUSIC**) Wise (!); a bogus 'iceman' later toured America (I saw it at the International Cryptozoology Museum in Portland, Maine in 2016), itself a curiosity as a fabrication. I recommend two books on the subject: Bernard Heuvelmans's *Neanderthal: The Strange Saga of the Minnesota Iceman* (2011, English translated edition 2016, Anomalist Books), and William Jevning's self-published *The Minnesota Iceman* (2016). More on this in a future *Cryptid Cinema* volume!

THE NIGHT WE SAW THE FOUKE MONSTER (2007)
Print-on-demand paperbacks have democratized the regional autobiographical, semi-autobiographical, and completely fictional regional cryptid book marketplace, yielding all sorts of curious volumes. *The Night We Saw the Foukes Monster* by Angelia M. Purvis (2007) is essentially a slim "juvenile" in the manner of Marion T. Place's Sasquatch juveniles, but it shares the unpretentious and rather ugly look (including three crude drawings by the author) and flavor of the genuine Skunk Ape testimonials.

BIGFOOT : THE LIFE AND TIMES OF A LEGEND (2009)
Academia has enjoyed a renaissance in cryptid tomes, prominent among the most recent *Bigfoot: The Life and Times of a Legend* (2009, The University of Chicago Press) by Joshua Blu Buhs, which (outside of the writings of Loren Coleman) provides an almost ideal one-stop historical overview of the hominid cryptid field and pop culture.

THE BEAST OF BOGGY CREEK (2012)
LEGEND OF BOGGY CREEK fans should seek out and read Lyle Blackburn's definitive *The Beast of Boggy Creek: The True Story of the Fouke Monster* (2012, Anomalist Books, cover art by Justin Osbourn), which carries years of field research and an exhaustive chronology of all sightings of (and pop culture associated with) the Fouke Monster into the 21st century.

ABOMINABLE SCIENCE (2013)
Authored by frequent contributors to Skeptic magazine and Skepticblog.org, this is the most handsome and most lavishly illustrated of contemporary academic cryptid texts: *Abominable Science* by Daniel Loxton and Donald R. Prothero, cover art by Daniel Loxton, design by Philip Pascuzzo (2013, Columbia University Press)

A *Heap* of Thanks…

As noted in the acknowledgements, some of the chapters in this book are revised and expanded from their original publication from my *Myrant* blogs (referenced, as applicable, at the end of relevant chapters) and from the pages of *Monster!* and *Weng's Chop*, with deepest thanks to the original editors: Tim Paxton, Steve Fenton, Tony Strauss, and Brian Harris.

About the Author:

Born in March of 1955, *Swamp Thing* artist and *Constantine* co-creator Stephen R. Bissette squandered much of his misspent youth and young adult years addicted to all things cryptid. He dreamt of living neodinosaurs in remote jungles or on faraway isles; he swam ponds, rivers, lakes, and fished in streams he hoped monsters swam and fished in, too; he hiked and explored the woods of his home state of Vermont looking for any signs of an East-coast Bigfoot; he scoured the skies for Thunderbirds, living pterosaurs, or UFOs. At home, he drew cryptids. Alas, the only cryptids he ever actually *saw* in 'real life' were on TV and at the movies, so whatever time he didn't piss away doing the above, he pissed away watching the kinds of movies and TV shows which this book is dedicated to—and he drew and wrote about those *all* the time!

At least the drawing led to a productive adult career as a cartoonist, writer, editor, and instructor. Entering the field with work published in *Sgt. Rock, Heavy Metal, Bizarre Adventures, Epic Illustrated, Weird Worlds, Dr. Wirtham's Comix & Stories*, and others, Bissette collaborated with Rick Veitch and Allan Asherman on the graphic novel *1941: The Illustrated Story* and worked with Alan Moore, Marty Pasko, John Totleben, Rick Veitch, and Tom Yeates as part of the creative team on *Swamp Thing* for DC Comics during the 1980s. He later had a hand in comics like *S.R. Bissette's Tyrant®*, the adult horror anthology *Taboo*, the Image Comics series *1963*, and many others, most recently contributing the occasional monster to *Spongebob Comics*. Bissette has authored, co-authored, and/or illustrated many books; those he co-authored include *The Monster Book: Buffy the Vampire Slayer* and *The Prince of Stories: The Many Worlds of Neil Gaiman*; he contributed short fiction to *Hellboy: Odd Jobs*, *Mr. October*, and *The New Dead*, and solo-authored both *Teen Angels & New Mutants* and Electric Dreamhouse/PS Publishing's forthcoming "Midnight Movie Monographs" series volume entitled *David Cronenberg's THE BROOD*. He has been a frequent contributor to magazines and zines, including *Deep Red, Ecco, ETC, Fangoria, GoreZone, Video Watchdog, Weng's Chop*, and *Monster!* Bissette's cover art and interior illustrations grace novels like Rick Hautala's Bigfoot tale *The Mountain King* and Joseph A. Citro's paranormal epic *Deus-X*, as well as the collaborative companion tomes authored by friend and folklorist Joe Citro, *The Vermont Ghost Guide* and *The Vermont Monster Guide*.

Bissette still lives and works in Vermont. A graduate of the pioneer Class of 1978 of the Joe Kubert School of Cartoon and Graphic Art, Inc., he has been teaching at the Center for Cartoon Studies in White River Junction, VT since 2005.